Lecture Notes in Computer Science 3219

Commenced Publication in 1973
Founding and Former Series Editors:
Gerhard Goos, Juris Hartmanis, and Jan van Leeuwen

T0223557

Maritta Heisel   Peter Liggesmeyer
Stefan Wittmann (Eds.)

Computer Safety, Reliability, and Security

23rd International Conference, SAFECOMP 2004
Potsdam, Germany, September 21-24, 2004
Proceedings

 Springer

Volume Editors

Maritta Heisel
Westfälische Wilhelms-Universität Münster
Institut für Informatik
Einsteinstr. 62, 48149 Münster, Germany
E-mail: heisel@uni-muenster.de

Peter Liggesmeyer
Fraunhofer Institut Experimentelles Software Engineering
Sauerwiesen 6, 67661 Kaiserslautern, Germany
E-mail: Peter.Liggesmeyer@t-online.de

Stefan Wittmann
Bundesamt für Sicherheit in der Informationstechnik
Godesberger Allee 185-189, 53175 Bonn, Germany
E-mail: stefan.wittmann@bsi.bund.de

Library of Congress Control Number: 2004112221

CR Subject Classification (1998): D.1-4, E.4, C.3, F.3, K.6.5

ISSN 0302-9743
ISBN 3-540-23176-5 Springer Berlin Heidelberg New York

Springer is a part of Springer Science+Business Media

springeronline.com

© Springer-Verlag Berlin Heidelberg 2004
Printed in Germany

Typesetting: Camera-ready by author, data conversion by PTP-Berlin, Protago-TeX-Production GmbH
Printed on acid-free paper   SPIN: 11317234   06/3142   5 4 3 2 1 0

Preface

The importance of safety and security is growing steadily. Safety is a quality characteristic that traditionally has been considered to be important in embedded systems, and security is usually an essential property in business applications. There is certainly a tendency to use software-based solutions in safety-critical applications domains, which increases the importance of safety engineering techniques. These include modelling and analysis techniques as well as appropriate processes and tools. And it is surely correct that the amount of confidential data that require protection from unauthorized access is growing. Therefore, security is very important. On the one hand, the traditional motivations for addressing safety and security still exist, and their relevance has improved. On the other hand, safety and security requirements occur increasingly in the same system. At present, many software-based systems interact with technical equipment and they communicate, e.g., with users and other systems. Future systems will more and more interact with many other entities (technical systems, people, the environment). In this situation, security problems may cause safety-related failures. It is thus necessary to address safety *and* security. It is furthermore required to take into account the interactions between these two properties.

Since their start in 1979 the SAFECOMP conferences have provided a platform for discussing topics related to dependable applications of computer systems. This requires us to deal with system aspects including hardware and software. Additionally, it is necessary to address a variety of properties, e.g., safety, security, reliability, and availability. The SAFECOMP conferences discuss research results, technical innovations, tools, processes, and organizational aspects. And they provide a forum for exchanging ideas between researchers and industry.

This year's program underlined system aspects. The majority of the contributions presented approaches that address complete systems including hardware, software, and the environment. The technical content covered a wide range from formal to informal methods. It seems that each approach is characterized by specific preconditions and has its own application domain.

We are convinced that the reader of this book will get valuable information on how to improve the safety and security of computer-based systems.

Authors from 17 countries all over the world responded to the call for papers. Out of 63 submitted papers, 24 were selected for the conference. We wish to thank the members of the International Programme Committee and the external reviewers for their excellent review work and fruitful discussions in setting up the programme of SAFECOMP 2004. They also helped a lot to disseminate all announcements.

We would like to express our special thanks to Massimo Felici. He maintained the tool CyberChair for us, and, being the organizer of the last two

SAFECOMPs, he was our oracle and early warning system of what could possibly go wrong.

Sincere thanks go to the invited speakers, Andreas Pfitzmann, Didier Essamé and Ralf G. Herrtwich, and the session chairpersons for their support.

Setting up the technical programme of the conference was one thing, to actually make SAFECOMP 2004 happen was another. Our organizing team Katrin Augustin, Hans-Peter Wagner, Carsten von Schwichow and Holger Schmidt did their best to make this event a success, and they did an outstanding job. Thank you.

Last but not least our special thanks go to the Hasso-Plattner-Institute in Potsdam for providing the premises, the conference infrastructure and the answers to all our questions.

Our best wishes go to the organizers of SAFECOMP 2005 in Norway, and we hope that SAFECOMP 2004 motivated many attendees to support next year's conference.

Potsdam, Germany   Peter Liggesmeyer
July 2004   Maritta Heisel
                                                          Stefan Wittmann

Organization

General Chair

Peter Liggesmeyer, Germany

EWICS TC7 Chair

Udo Voges, Germany

Programme Co-chairs

Maritta Heisel, Germany
Stefan Wittmann, Germany

Organizing Committee

Katrin Augustin, Germany
Hans-Peter Wagner, Germany

International Programme Committee

S. Anderson, UK
H. Bezecny, Germany
R. Bharadwaj, USA
R. Bloomfield, UK
S. Bologna, Italy
A. Bondavalli, Italy
B. Buth, Germany
P. Daniel, UK
M. Felici, UK
R. Genser, Austria
C. Goring, UK
J. Gorski, Poland
B.A. Gran, Norway
W. Grieskamp, Germany
E. Großpietsch, Germany
W. Halang, Germany
M. Heiner, Germany
M. Heisel, Germany
C. Heitmeyer, USA
C. Johnson, UK
M. Kaâniche, France
K. Kanoun, France
F. Koob, Germany
F. Koornneef, The Netherlands
B. Krämer, Germany
D. Kügler, Germany
P. Ladkin, Germany

P. Liggesmeyer, Germany
O. Mäckel, Germany
M. v.d. Meulen, UK
O. Nordland, Norway
A. Pasquini, Italy
G. Rabe, Germany
F. Redmill, UK
M. Rothfelder, Germany
J. Rushby, USA
F. Saglietti, Germany
T. Santen, Germany
E. Schoitsch, Austria
J. Souquières, France
W. Stephan, Germany
L. Strigini, UK
M. Sujan, UK
P. Traverso, Italy
J. Trienikens, The Netherlands
M. Ullmann, Germany
U. Voges, Germany
A. Weinert, Germany
M. Wilikens, Italy
R. Winther, Norway
S. Wittmann, Germany
E. Wong, USA
Z. Zurakowski, Poland

External Reviewers

C.P. van Beers

R. Carvajal-Schiaffino

I. Eusgeld

J. Jacky

H. Kelter

C. Kollmitzer

J. Krinke

J. Lei

R. Leszczyna

J. Li

P. Lollini

A. Nonnengart

S. Pozzi

G. Rock

M. Roveri

L. Save

H. Schwigon

D. Sona

N. Tillmann

A. Villafiorita

Table of Contents

Transportation

Software Development

Fault Tree Analysis

Invited Talk

Formal Methods and Systems

Security and Quality of Service

Hazard and Risk Analysis

Why Safety and Security Should and Will Merge

Andreas Pfitzmann

Fakultät Informatik
TU Dresden
D-01062 Dresden
pfitza@inf.tu-dresden.de

In the past, IT-systems at most were either safety-critical (i.e. no catastrophic consequences for the environment of the IT-system) or security-critical (i.e. even determined attackers cannot gain unauthorized access to information within and/or withhold resources of the IT-system). In future, more and more IT-systems will be both, safety- and security-critical. The reason for this is that IT-systems are embedded in ever more influential parts of our living- and working environment and that these embedded IT-systems are networked – be it to enhance their functionality now (or just as an option for future use), be it to ease maintenance.

Of course the safety community might (and should) issue warnings against this attitude of system design, because it undermines the classical way to engineer and validate safety. Of course the security community should frankly admit that using the present IT-infrastructures incorporating all kinds of unmanaged design complexity, security is mainly unachievable. But my experience of 20+ years in the area of security and privacy suggests that our warnings will not be heard or at least downplayed with arguments like:

- "These tiny embedded systems can't cause serious catastrophes, so safety is not an issue." (But if you network many systems and their failures might therefore occur at the same cause, the consequences might be much more serious.)
- "Is security really an issue? Who should have both a possibility and a motivation to attack?" (But if networking gets ever more pervasive and conflicts in our real world are not going to disappear, the answer will soon be: quite a few. But when this manifests itself on a larger scale – remember the warnings against viruses and worms issued more than 15 years from now – fixing the problem within a reasonable time span will be impossible.)

Therefore, the safety and security communities should combine and integrate efforts to designand build the networked embedded systems as secure and safe as possible given the constraints of legacy systems to be used and functionality deemed necessary for the end-users.

So far so easy to argue and understand. But do we have a chance to successfully combine and integrate? I hope so:

- Fail-safe and confidentiality as an essential security property have many structural similarities as do providing at least a gracefully degraded service and availability as another essential security property.

M. Heisel et al. (Eds.): SAFECOMP 2004, LNCS 3219, pp. 1–2, 2004.

- We have many mechanisms useful both for fault tolerance (security against unintentional "attacks") and security, where discerning between unintentional and intentional is mainly interesting for legal consequences, since stupid errors made in a complex IT-systems tend to behave quite intelligent in other parts of the systems or w.r.t. its output.

This suggests that unifying our approaches is both necessary and promising.

The Deconstruction of Safety Arguments Through Adversarial Counter-Argument

James M. Armstrong[1] and Stephen E. Paynter[2]

[1] Centre for Software Reliability, School of Computing Science,
University of Newcastle Upon Tyne, United Kingdom.
J.M.Armstrong@newcastle.ac.uk
[2] MBDA UK Ltd, Filton, Bristol, United Kingdom.
stephen.paynter@mbda.co.uk

Abstract. The project Deconstructive Evaluation of Risk In Dependability Arguments and Safety Cases (DERIDASC) has recently experimented with techniques borrowed from literary theory as safety case analysis techniques. This paper introduces our high-level method for "deconstructing" safety arguments. Our approach is quite general and should be applicable to different types of safety argumentation framework. As one example, we outline how the approach would work in the context of the Goal Structure Notation (GSN).

1   Deconstruction in a Safety Context

French philosopher Jacques Derrida's concept of *deconstruction* rests upon the idea that, ironically enough, the meaning of an argument is a function of observations that it excludes as irrelevant and the perspectives that it opposes either implicitly or explicitly. On the one hand, if we recognise an opposing argument explicitly, we might be tempted to misrepresent it as weaker than we really feel it to be; but if this misrepresentation is detected, or if our own arguments do not convince, we may succeed only in perpetuating the opposing view. On the other hand, if we try to suppress our acknowledgment of credible doubt, we leave the reader mystified as to why we feel the need to argue our conclusion. To 'deconstruct' an argument is to try to detect such failures of "closure". Such failures need not necessarily lead one to an opposed conclusion (Armstrong & Paynter 2003, Armstrong 2003).

A deconstruction of an argument tries to show how the argument undercuts itself with acknowledgements of plausible doubts about its conclusion and betrays a nervous desire for the truth of assumptions and conclusions rather than unshakeable confidence. This perspective recognizes that deductive argument is unequal to the tasks of resolving contradictions and unifying the different explanatory narratives that underlie our debates. The deconstruction of a deductive argument has two stages. The *reversal* stage develops a counter-argument from clues offered within the original argument; the *displacement* stage compares the two arguments. In the safety assessment context we view reversal as an opportunity for the reassessment of the existing safety acceptance criteria.

A safety argument is required to be inferentially valid in some sense and its empirical premises must be *justified* in such a way that they seem plausible. Empirical

M. Heisel et al. (Eds.): SAFECOMP 2004, LNCS 3219, pp. 3–16, 2004.
© Springer-Verlag Berlin Heidelberg 2004

claims can attain the status of knowledge only by means of supporting evidence of varying reliability. This is recognized in logics of justified belief that allow premises to be "warranted" to differing degrees; for example, Toulmin (1958). Starting with the *reversal* stage of safety argument deconstruction we ignore the warrantedness of the premises: instead, we try to produce a counter-argument that seems warrantable. Hence we provisionally assume that we could find sufficient evidence for justified belief in our counter-argument. In the *displacement* stage we deal with the relative strength of the warrants and backing evidence for both argument and counter-argument. Hopefully, after reversal we will be able to see that one argument (or both) is (are) unsatisfactory and act accordingly (either accept the system or require more risk reduction). However, there is a possibility that we get two opposing arguments that are "sufficiently" warranted. A deconstruction must explicitly recognize and analyze this particular failure of "closure". To question the "closure" of an argument is to try and find a possibility that has been excluded but which when re-introduced undermines faith in the argument by suggesting a plausible counter-argument. Thus the process of deconstruction is in the final analysis *adversarial*.

Section 2 of this paper presents a brief example of safety argument deconstruction using the Goal Structuring Notation (GSN). As yet we have no pragmatic justification (e.g. cost-benefit) for the use of safety argument deconstruction in safety processes. Therefore, in Section 3 we confine ourselves to a philosophical justification in terms of the lack of deductive closure in any non-absolute argument: we show that when safety decision makers act upon "sufficiently justified" beliefs – as they do when they accept or reject safety-critical systems – they are necessarily committing themselves to a variant of the 'lottery paradox'. We explain this using a *Warranted Deduction Schema* we have developed for the comparison of arguments and counter-arguments. Sections 4 examines political aspects of deconstruction in terms of the *Warranted Deduction Schema*. Section 5 outlines future issues in the pragmatic justification of safety argument deconstruction.

2   An Example: The Goal Structuring Notation

The example deconstruction in this section is done in the context of the Goal Structuring Notation (GSN) and is adapted from Kelly (1998). The example argues a sufficiency of protection against a risk of catastrophic failure. In the source text, the example is only part of a larger GSN argument and thus some of the questions we put are answered there or are not relevant. We have taken the example out of its original context to illustrate the process of deconstruction. GSN is intended to make the structure of arguments clearer than in free text. Thus it provides a neutral and convenient format for the (de)construction of safety counter-arguments. GSN specifies:

- Goals (best expressed as predicates)
- Goal Decomposition (top down)
- Strategies (for explaining goal decompositions)
- Solutions (direct information sources)
- Justifications (for explaining rationale)
- Assumptions

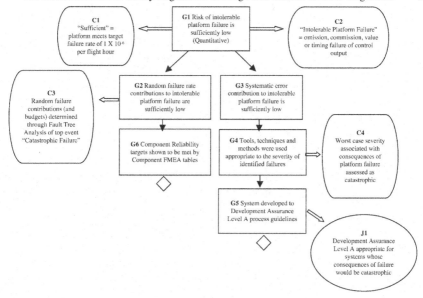

Fig. 1. GSN Example

There are also links to information and factors outside the scope of the argument itself: Contexts (for describing the circumstances of the argument), and links to Models of a system. Hence it is a simple matter to define a "shadow" GSN that provides a starting point for the construction of counter-arguments:

- *Anti-goals* (negations of the stated goals)
- *Anti-goal Deconstruction* (questioning the verifiability of a goal, the consistency between its anti-goal and stated subgoals, and the mutual independence of subgoals)
- *Tactics* (goal decompositions without an explicit strategy)
- *Questions* (to be placed against solutions)
- *Presuppositions* (unexplained rationale behind justifications)
- *Counterassumptions* (negations of assumed facts)

In the reversal stage, GSN contexts and links to system models should be taken as givens. However, during displacement, if a counter-argument proves fruitful, the context in which it is stated may diverge in important ways from the original and this should be recorded in it.

2.1 Reversal

Given that the meanings of "sufficient" and "intolerable platform failure" are made clear in Fig 1, the negation of the top-level goal G1 to give an anti-goal is trivial. Looking at the decomposition of G1 we can see that the argument depends upon a distinction between random and systematic failure contributions, but this distinction is left unexplained. The deconstructor would hypothesize the absence of any explanatory strategy as an argumentative *tactic*. The way in which the two rates have been combined in the example is not clarified: for example, one can ask whether in order to get random failure rates sufficiently low the design has not used a complex scheme for redundancy that has made systematic errors more likely.

Furthermore, the distinction between "random" and "systematic" failures can be questioned. For example, "random" failure rates for hardware vary with intended operating conditions and it could be that Fault Tree Analysis (C3) has not taken account of this.

For "systematic" failure rates the chain of goals G3-G4-G5 could indicate flawed reasoning. For example, the negation of G3 is not in contradiction with G4. A presupposition behind J1 is that Development Assurance Level A and its associated tools, techniques and methods are "appropriate" for systems whose consequences of failure would be catastrophic. This most likely means that Level A development is required where failure is catastrophic; but it probably does not mean that adherence to Level A is considered sufficient to bound the predicted *rate* of systematic failure, or that the prediction must remain below any specific threshold of acceptability. Still less can a process be expected to bound the *measured* rate of catastrophic failure, as this is dependent upon the level of exposure to the system and its hazards that society chooses to accept.

The example argument omits system and environment models from which systematic failure rate predictions must be derived. Instead, it argues that a Level A development process is commensurate with an acceptable systematic failure contribution. However, the best contribution that a development process can make to a systematic failure rate prediction is assurance that it provides the right context for the detection of unreliable systematic failure predictions: historically, it should have supported the derivation of reliable predictions, whatever those predictions might have been. Assuming this to be the case, the argument remains incomplete without the models that justify a specific predicted figure.

We can also speculate that justification J1 would be especially fallacious if the definition of Development Assurance Level A recognised that its tools and techniques – while appropriate for handling catastrophic hazards – were insufficient for the attainment of definite systematic failure rates. In such a case, the goal chain G3-G4-G5 would constitute a non-compliance with Level A and we might consider the argument to be what philosophers sometimes call a *performative self-contradiction* (a noncompliant assertion of compliance).

Such questions would lead to the counter-argument in Fig 2.

2.2 Displacement

The original GSN argument would be considerably improved by:

–   The addition of a specific systematic failure contribution estimate
–   Linking in system specification, test evidence, and hazard models as solution evidence for the systematic failure prediction G3
–   Adding a strategy showing how the systematic failure rates were combined with the random failure estimate to give G1
–   Stressing that goals G1 and G2 are only predicted failure rates in their text

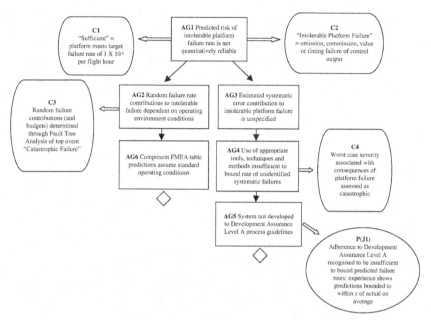

Fig. 2. Example GSN Counter-argument

- Making G5 part of the context of G1
- Combining G4 and J1 into a justification of the systematic failure rate prediction (by attachment to the modified G3)

A general conclusion that emerges from the deconstruction is that even when a top-level safety goal is clearly stated, the conditions of its verifiability might presuppose the acceptance that is supposedly being argued. Evidently no analysis can predetermine a predicted rate as equal to the measured rate; system acceptance is a condition for verifying such a prediction. Thus when a predicted catastrophic failure rate of 10^{-6} is set as a "goal", there is a risk that the safety argument focuses solely on finding a way of expressing the required prediction. The problem with our example argument is that only goals G6 and G4 can be reasonably considered verifiable *before* acceptance, whereas G1 and G2 and G3 have to be understood as predictions that could be verified only after a presupposed acceptance.

Such goals might be better thought of as conditions for continued system acceptability: for example, the system could be temporarily withdrawn for modification if the failure rate ever exceeded the predicted rate. However, it is sometimes the case that a system is withdrawn for modification as soon as it fails catastrophically *within* the predicted rate, or even after a "near-miss". There seems to be an implicit distinction between the acceptability of a predicted rate of catastrophic failure and the acceptability of a near-miss or an actual catastrophic failure, even where the rate prediction admits these possibilities. Put simply, we accept abstract and idealised dangers as they are predicted in safety arguments more readily than we accept the empirical prospect of danger or its actual consequences.

In this case, predictions of catastrophic failure rate are best seen as a basis for assessing and controlling exposure to danger, so that "over-egging" the predictive power of a development process is to be avoided. Since no development process could be shown to bound *measured* systematic failure rates without reference to a specification (which determines which behaviours are considered as failures) and since the process arguably *limits* the reliability of predicted failure rates, to do so might breed false confidence on all sides.

3   A Philosophical Justification for Safety Argument Deconstruction

To have any force, a safety argument must really consist of an argument and a "meta-argument". The argument says that from a certain set of premises $P_1,..., P_n$, the conclusion C follows. The conclusion might consist of a number of claims $C_1,..., C_n$ but we will assume a single conclusion for simplicity. We will use *deductive validity* as the interpretation of "follows" for now, but we do not mean this to be taken too literally: we expect that any kind of inference rule could be used – including rules that allow exceptions, such as Toulmin's (1958) "warrants" with their backing evidence and qualifiers. Thus our safety arguments will be of the form:

$$P_1,..., P_n \vdash C$$

Since deductive validity does not guarantee that the inference is *sound*, the argument must also justify belief in each premise. For now we will not worry about the strength of this justification. Thus the argument being offered is equivalent to:

SA   *justified(P_1),..., justified(P_n) $\vdash$ justified(C)*

To have the force that it has, the argument needs to claim that because the premises are justified and the conclusion follows from them, then the conclusion is also justified. There is usually a constraint on the strength of the claim. We shall consider this matter presently.

The principle relied upon to make inferences of warranted beliefs from warranted premises is called the Deductive Closure Principle (***DCP***). As Olin (2003, p.83) expresses it:

Deductive Closure Principle (DCP). If you are justified in believing $P_1,..., P_n$ and $P_1,..., P_n$ jointly imply Q, and you see this, then you are justified in believing Q.

Olin gives several reasons why this principle is more problematic than it first appears. Her observations relate to the "lottery paradox". In this paradox, we hold a ticket in a thousand-ticket lottery. We know one ticket will win. We assess the probability against winning as 999/1000 and decide that this level of probability justifies us in believing we will not win: but our ticket is just like all the others, and our inference is therefore equally justified for all other tickets; which would mean that no ticket would win. So in making the inference that we will not win we are implicitly accepting contradictory propositions (Olin 2003). We have drawn analogous conclusions from a consideration of the underlying logic of acting upon evidentially justified beliefs that is the basis of the safety process.

Consideration of **DCP** leads to a variant of the lottery paradox that applies to the notion of a "sufficiency" of confidence in a defeatable statement, such as a safety claim. Note the words "and you see *this*" in **DCP**: Derrida's deconstruction is concerned with what happens when one sees "this" but does not see what is opposed to "this". It suggests that we ask what the opposite of "justified" could be. The answer "unjustified" yields a problem: "unjustified" does not mean the same as "unjustifiable". All "justified" means is that a good justification for a statement has been constructed. All "unjustified" means is that no good justification has been offered so far. Ironically, a claim of "unjustifiability" would be itself *unjustified* in the context we are considering: in denying the possibility of empirical justification to a given statement, "unjustifiability" makes an implicit appeal to the absolute truth of the negation of that statement. We are trying to minimize reliance on such appeals for empirical premises; yet we cannot assert the "unjustifiability" of an assertion where, to avoid the charge of scepticism, *all* empirical reasoning has been put on non-absolute and evidential grounds. However, we will continue (at least provisionally) to adhere to the view that non-empirical (i.e. logical) contradictions are unjustifiable.

We have found a number of problems with **DCP** as Olin (2003) formulates it. Firstly, it is not clear whether "implies" is a material implication and if it is, whether we are to believe that the inference $P_1,..., P_n$ *implies* Q is itself justified. Secondly, since *false* implies every statement, **DCP** can be used to deduce belief in contradictions from contradictory premises. We fix these problems by requiring that the set of premises $P_1,..., P_n$ be *satisfiable* (their conjunction is logically consistent) and that there must be a deductive argument from them to the conclusion in question:

Strengthened Deductive Closure Principle (SDCP). Given:
  a)   a set of premises $P_1,..., P_n$
  b)   a justification for each premise in $P_1,..., P_n$
  c)   an argument that $P_1,..., P_n$ is a *satisfiable* set of premises
  d)   that $P_1,..., P_n \mathrel{|-} Q$ is a *deductively valid* inference
  e)   and one sees this,
then one is justified in believing Q.

Below we develop a "deconstructive" schema for dialectical argument that allows different levels of confidence to be assigned to a statement. We follow Toulmin (1958) in allowing that what he calls a "warrant" – an inference rule – itself needs to be justified. It can be strengthened by backing evidence or weakened by data about exceptions. Thus confidence in a justification is a matter of degree. Rather than introduce backing as a separate term, we define the level of confidence in a justification as a function ω that maps the claimed statement to a value n where $0 \leq n \leq 1$. We refer to this as the *warrantedness* of the statement. Warrantedness can be absolute or zero, so that we can include total certainties and unwarranted statements should they be claimed.

We also need to be able to record how far the deductive argument itself is warranted. For example, we might use a proof tool to do a deduction, and have some worries about its reliability; or if the derivation is long and complex, we might have doubts about our own capability to check it. If we accept such possibilities, we have to adopt a logically weakened version of **SDCP**:

Warranted Deduction Schema (WDS). Suppose we have:
   a)   a set of premises $P_1,..., P_n$
   b)   a degree of warrant ω where $0 \leq \omega \leq 1$, for each of $P_1,..., P_n$
   c)   an argument that $sat(P_1,..., P_n)$, i.e. we have a *satisfiable* set of premises
   d)   a deductively valid inference $P_1,..., P_n \mid- Q$
   e)   a degree of warrant ω for the argument in (c)
   f)   a degree of warrant ω for the deduction in (d)
then we are justified in believing $\omega(Q)$, where this is defined as:

$$\omega(P_i) \times \omega(sat(P_1,..., P_n)) \times \omega(P_1,..., P_n \mid- Q_i)$$

where $\omega(P_i)$ is the minimum of the warrants in b): $min(\{ x \mid x = \omega(P_j)$ for all j in $1 .. n\})$

Note that a consequence of **WDS** is that a zero degree of warrant for any statement or deduction immediately nullifies the degree of warrant for the conclusion. The derivation of a certainty would require all statements and deductions to be certain. In bounding confidence in our argument by the least warranted premise, we have adopted a conservative approach. We do not currently allow the mutual consistency of premises to increase confidence in the set as a whole.

A theory of inductive justification requires the idea of a *sufficient* degree of warrant that justifies belief in a defeasible statement. This is analogous to a basic presupposition of probabilistic reasoning that the lottery paradox puts into question (see Olin 2003, p. 79):

Principle of Sufficient Warrant (PSW).
There exists a degree of warrant ω such that $0.5 < \Omega \leq 1$, and such that if statement P has warrant $\omega(P) \geq \Omega$, then we are justified in believing that P.

In what follows, where a statement P has the sufficient degree of warrant Ω, we will simply write $\Omega(P)$. This principle leads to a contradiction analogous to the lottery paradox as we shall show.

Consider the notion of a *least sufficiently warranted argument*. This is an argument in which Ω is attained exactly for all premises and inferences:

LSWA1
   $\Omega(P_1), ..., \Omega(P_n)$ (the premises are all warranted)
   $\Omega(sat(P_1,..., P_n))$ (the satisfiability of the premises is warranted)
   $\Omega(P_1,..., P_n \mid- Q)$ (the deduction is warranted)
   Therefore, by **WDS** we have $\Omega(Q)$.

However, suppose we have *not seen* the following counter-argument:

LSWA2
   $\Omega(A_1), ..., \Omega(A_n)$ (the premises are all warranted)
   $\Omega(sat(A_1,..., A_n))$ (the satisfiability of the premises is warranted)
   $\Omega(A_1,..., A_n \mid- not\ Q)$ (the deduction is warranted)
   Therefore, by **WDS** we have $\Omega(not\ Q)$.

It may be that we could not find such an argument even if we looked for it. However, the possibility of an argument of *LSWA2*'s form is not denied by the mere fact that we found *LSWA1* first: perhaps if we had set out to prove *not Q* we would have found *LSWA2* first and missed *LSWA1*. What justifies the "blindness" when we see that *LSWA1* is valid and claim we are therefore justified in believing *Q*?

For example, a dishonest attempt at persuasion might avoid drawing attention to a sufficiently warranted counter-argument that has already been made. The case where one can sense the possibility of *LSWA2*, but cannot pursue the matter further is a very difficult one and not remote from everyday life. We may feel a particular conclusion is forced upon us by the circumstances we are in. Thus force of circumstances can defeat the requirement for sufficiency of warrant before action. A deconstruction of a safety argument will look for implicit clues to uncontrolled factors, but will also try to understand the nature of the "force" of circumstances where *force majeure* is explicitly claimed: for example, one can ask how far the force of circumstances was a result of previous freely-taken decisions.

Our difficulty derives from the fact that nothing in *WDS* or *PSW* allows us to claim that an argument of the form *LSWA2* cannot exist: all inductive reasoning is *defeatable* in the light of new information, which might make possible an argument of the form *LSWA2*. What we call "twenty-twenty hindsight" sometimes reveals just such an argument. Whilst acting on *LSWA1*, one might claim that the existence of an argument of the form *LSWA2* is highly improbable. However, *LSWA2* is only a schema, so there could be an infinite number of such arguments, or none; in practice, we can at best estimate the amount of effort spent on trying to find a counter-argument and take our assurance from how hard it is to find one. This is why we propose the formulation of the best possible counter-argument to a safety argument before system acceptance.

We can express the dilemma of choosing between equally strong but opposing arguments more explicitly as the decision to accept or reject the following conjecture:

Sufficient Warrant Conjecture (SWC): $\Omega(P)$ *implies not* $\Omega(\text{ not } P)$.

So long as we have *LSWA1* and noone has found any *LSWA2*, we can substitute $\Omega(P)$ into *SWH* in order to state that the opposite conclusion is not sufficiently warranted: *not* Ω (*not P*). But of course this does not mean it is *unwarrantable*. If someone does find an argument of form *LSWA2* and *we have not seen it*, they can then also use *SWH* to argue *not* $\Omega(P)$ and we have a contradiction with $\Omega(P)$.

So perhaps we decide to deny *SWC*, so that we believe: *not*($\Omega(P)$ *implies not* Ω(*not P*)). In that case, one can ask what interpretation should be attached to the following statements:

Insufficiency of Warrant Conjectures:
1. Ω *(P) and* Ω *(not P)* – a statement and its opposite can be sufficiently warranted
2. $\Omega(P)$ *and not* $\Omega(P)$ – a statement can be both sufficiently warranted and insufficiently warranted
3. *not* $\Omega(P)$ *and not* $\Omega(not P)$ – no sufficient warrant exists for either alternative

4. $\Omega(P$ and not $P)$ – warranted belief in contradictions (radical *dialethism*)
5. not $\Omega(P$ and not $P)$ – non-belief in contradictions (the classical principle)

We do not argue for (4) here. Interestingly however, logician Graham Priest (2002) does make a relatively strong case for dialethism; see Olin (2003, Chapter 2) for a critique.

We accept (5) provisionally, but show that doing so leads us to a "meta-problem" in choosing whether to accept (2). The denial of *SWC* makes (1) consistent: we have to accept the possibility that a statement and its negation can both be warranted to a sufficient degree; but suppose that we have derived $\Omega(P)$, and act as if P. The action is an implicit appeal to *SWC* (which we have denied) in order to deny (2). Do we not act *as if* we believe there is no equally warranted argument for $\Omega(not(P))$? Certainly, we can only act confidently in the belief that the sufficiency of our warrant is not defeated even as it is asserted.

The contradiction involved in our thinking comes into sharper focus in a situation where we can actually *see* an adequate counter-argument to P, and have to decide to act as if P or *not P*. In such a case, we are forced to recognise (2), as it follows from (1) and (5): the "sufficient" warrant of the one argument defeats that of the other. Since we cannot tell which argument is at fault, we have a case where (2) seems to be true for each argument.

We interpret this possibility as meaning that where we have equal 'sufficient' belief in arguments for P and for *not P* we have *no* justification for believing either (3). Unfortunately, if we were to capture this principle in an inference rule, we would create an unsound logic that allows (2):

defeatability_of_warrant(dow) $\Omega(P)$, $\Omega(not\ P)$ $|-$ not $\Omega(P)$, not $\Omega(not\ P)$

So far we have assumed that we have arguments for both P and *not P* that meet the requirements for sufficiency exactly. In the more usual case where one claim seems to have a higher degree of warrant than the other, one usually chooses to act according to the more warranted argument; but on what grounds? If the "sufficient" degree of warrantedness really is sufficient for belief, then there is no advantage to be gained from *more* than "sufficient" confidence; the opposed arguments should still disqualify one another. Where we have sufficiently warranted arguments for both P and *not P*, as (1) allows, then we should in practice have *no* confidence in either statement.

If P and *not P* are opposite outcomes of some type of trial, and we decide to test which argument is correct by direct observation, then from our viewpoint and in our circumstances, the outcome is a matter of sheer chance. If we try to justify the undertaking of the trial by means of only one of the arguments, then the warrant for the argument we act against is not only simultaneously sufficient and defeat*able*, it is simultaneously sufficient and defeat*ed*.

For example, say we have equal warrant for *heads* and *tails* in a coin toss – the argument that $\mathbf{P} = 0.5$ for both outcomes; then naturally, we can have no justified confidence that either outcome is more likely. However, say we ended up with arguments of $\mathbf{P} = 0.6$ for *heads* and $P = 0.7$ for *tails*, where we needed $\mathbf{P} = 0.51$ for sufficient belief. Since this is a contradiction according to probability theory and we accept (5), the situation is no different; both arguments must be insufficient for confidence. If we leave the matter at that, we have *no* warrant for predicting what the outcome will be at all.

In practice, other courses of action than trial might be available to us. We could appeal to factors not covered in either argument, effectively trying to find a third which is more warranted than either of the first two; or we could appeal for more work to be done to test one or the other argument, or both. Nonetheless, these courses of action imply that we have invalidated the degree of sufficiency for belief Ω. Indeed, we must invalidate it, for not to do so is to accept the justifiability of belief in contradictory statements (4).

Thus, for any predictive argument at a particular time, if the discovery of an equally good or better counter-argument is possible at that time, then we do not really *know* the degree of sufficient warrant for the argument we have: in acting on it, we merely *assert* belief in it. At best we can claim that we have expended as much effort as possible on trying to find counter-arguments against our prediction and can see no reason why it should go wrong; if noone else can either, that is the most assurance we are ever going to get. Thus our schema illustrates that the "sufficient" level of belief we attach to a statement retains a potential for destabilisation and is itself something that can be renegotiated in the light of experience. This goes some way to explicating the problem behind the oft-asked question "how safe is safe enough?" and why a definitive and context-free answer cannot be given.

In a dilemma such as this, force of circumstances is often offered as a justification for following a certain course of action. Such assertions need to be considered carefully. We can ask the following questions:

a)   How does a party (perhaps ourselves) represent the circumstances they are in to themselves?

b)   Is the representation accurate, e.g. does it symbolise hidden value systems, *emphasise* certain interests and *de-emphasise* or *exclude* others?

c)   When they act, does a party use political power to *change* the circumstances whilst arguing that they are subject to them?

These are key themes of postmodern philosophy and questions that might help safety assessors understand the "safety culture" of an organisation that puts a safety-critical system up for acceptance.

However, they are also questions that assessors should ask of themselves, since to ask a), b) and c) at all presupposes a viewpoint that differs from the viewpoint being assessed.

4   The Politics of Safety Argument Displacement

The safety process sometimes involves 'meta-arguments' about the acceptability of prearranged acceptance criteria as well the adherence of a system to them. In an adversarial approach, the worst-case scenario is formally "warranted" incompatibles. Such an outcome requires that displacement specify how the acceptance criteria need to be evolved and improved. As uncommon as it might be, this scenario is disorienting for all concerned. Differing viewpoints, competing interests, and changes in circumstances only complicate the problem. Common agreement might evade concerned parties: for example, the failure to find a good counter-argument might not be total.

Furthermore, even in the best case, the question of why submission to the test of experience was accepted precisely when it was may arise later if safety problems do occur.

Furthermore, if "warrant" is relative to how much justificatory work is undertaken then, since one could theoretically work on the warrant for a particular statement forever, a politics of "creative inertia" becomes possible: the supplier of a safety argument *SA*, being initially intrigued by a counter-argument *CA*, might agree that *CA* seems strong; but they might then argue that the warrant of one of its statements – say R_j – needs more backing. The supplier of *CA* might agree; but they could also object that one of the premises of *SA* – say P_i – also needs more work, and so forth.

Our suggestion has been that should a reversal succeed well enough to cause a deadlock situation then *neither* argument should be considered valid. Otherwise, the only way to break a deadlock in the dialectic process is through an action that implicitly subordinates one argument to the other. Where there are equally plausible arguments for opposite outcomes, involved parties sometimes cannot see any other option but to make the test of experience.

However, in so doing they assert their cultural values. Thus safety processes depend upon cost-benefit analysis to resolve political deadlocks. Nonetheless, it is not unusual to encounter decisions with benefits to some (e.g. increased profits) that would be costs to others (e.g. increased dangers). The 'resolution' of these dilemmas is often forced by the application of principles that are little more than surreptitious assertions of power. This can been illustrated by the difference between "willingness to pay" (an amount that would *prevent* a loss) with "willingness to accept" (an amount that makes the loss *acceptable*) compensation approaches (Adams 1995, p. 98).

To describe deadlock situations we need to consider the various arguments in the light of implicit assumptions about the urgency of a decision. This suggests that for any outcome *C* we consider:

1. an argument *SA* for doing action *a* because it will probably have the positive outcome (*C*)
2. an argument *CA* against doing *a* because the outcome will probably be *negative* (*not C*)
3. a proposition that *SA* should be accepted *now*, i.e. we should test *C or not C* by doing *a*
4. a proposition that *CA* should be accepted *for now*, i.e. we should not do *a* and not test *C or not C*

Implicit propositions like (3) and (4) are apparent in any "battle of wills": assumption (3) might be made explicit in order to defeat *CA* as a matter of exigency, thus attracting no criticism; but (3) could also be *enforced* by one party on the other. In a case where (3) gives *SA* priority over *CA*, *CA* is in effect given *no* priority, whatever steps have been taken against the failure of *C*. Likewise, (4) can be enforced by the party with the more political power and resources: (4) need consist only of a plea for more evidence (short of testing *C*) used as a delaying tactic to defeat (eventually) *SA* by "putting off the evil day" until the proposer of *SA* either loses interest or runs out of resources to do *a*.

Unsurprisingly, the deadlock situation brings underlying power struggles to the surface: but we can only make sense of the situation through attempts to understand viewpoints that differ from our own, and exposure of our own viewpoint to analysis and criticism. To make sense of the political controversy and hopefully avoid wasteful argument, the displacement stage must consider what factors *in addition* to their belief in their proffered arguments parties might have for whichever of proposition (3) or (4) they favour. Indeed, such factors *must* be operative, since in the absence of unexpressed considerations, the justifications for *both* courses of action would be entirely circular, as follows: to do action *a* is to commit to (3), which presupposes *SA*; to "do" *not a* and commit to (4) presupposes *CA*. *Both* parties must be acting according to preferences and interests not made explicit in their arguments. Trying to make these new criteria explicit, should it prove necessary, will probably be the most difficult and protracted part of safety argument displacement.

5 The Pragmatics of Safety Argument Deconstruction

The DERIDASC project did not set out to assess the advantages and disadvantages of our approach in industrial practice: we felt that experimentation with an immature method might prove obstructive. However, our experimental applications of the Warranted Deduction Schema to example safety arguments suggested the following benefits:

- an approach to safety assessment that is more visibly adversarial, leading to the construction of better safety arguments
- more reliable and unambiguous rejection of unsatisfactory safety arguments
- the ability to monitor the effect of new information and knowledge on accepted safety arguments
- a "ready made" assessment approach for different safety argument notations (through the definition of accompanying "shadow" notations)
- a method by which regulators can explicitly manage the incorporation, comparison, and assessment of different viewpoints on the safety of a system, including arguments addressed to the lay public from differing viewpoints
- a way of explaining the evolution of safety acceptance criteria to the public

The issues yet to be addressed concern practical safety argument deconstruction in an industrial context. These issues are:

- are "in-house" counter-arguments an effective way for suppliers to identify and remedy objections before regulatory assessment takes place?
- what resources need to be set aside for the production of counter-arguments?
- would through-life counter-argument maintenance be cost-effective?
- is public trust enhanced by the explicitly adversarial nature of the approach?

A key question about our adversarial approach is whether it will really prove resistant to the production pressures, unimaginative complacency, and excessive bureaucracy that are generally alleged as the root causes of safety failure. A fascinating and perhaps morally necessary deconstructive exercise would be to apply our strategy to itself, that is, to our own justification for it, in collaboration with independent colleagues.

References

Adams J (1995). *Risk*, Routledge ISBN 1-85728-068-7.

Armstrong (2003). *Danger:Derrida at Work*, Interdisciplinary Science Reviews, Vol. 28, No. 2, June 2003, pp. 83–94.

Armstrong J & Paynter S (2003). *Safe Systems: Construction, Destruction, and Deconstruction*, In: *Proceedings of the Eleventh Safety Critical Systems Symposium*, Bristol UK, Edited by Redmill F and Anderson T, Springer, ISBN 1-85233-696-X, pp. 62–76.

Kelly TP (1998). *Arguing Safety: A Systematic Approach To Managing Safety Cases*. DPhil Thesis, Department of Computer Science, University of York. Available from the author's homepage: http://www-users.cs.york.ac.uk/~tpk/

Olin D (2003). *Paradoxes*. Central Problems of Philosophy Series Editor John Strand, Acumen Publishing, ISBN 1-902683-82-X.

Priest G (2002). *Beyond The Limits of Thought*, Oxford University Press, ISBN 0-19-925405-2.

Toulmin S (1958). *The Uses of Argument*. Cambridge University Press, ISBN 0-521-09230-2.

Using Fuzzy Self-Organising Maps
for Safety Critical Systems

Zeshan Kurd and Tim P. Kelly

High Integrity Systems Engineering Group
Department of Computer Science
University of York, York, YO10 5DD, UK.
{zeshan.kurd,tim.kelly}@cs.york.ac.uk

Abstract. This paper defines a type of constrained Artificial Neural Network (ANN) that enables analytical certification arguments whilst retaining valuable performance characteristics. Previous work has defined a safety lifecycle for ANNs without detailing a specific neural model. Building on this previous work, the underpinning of the devised model is based upon an existing neuro-fuzzy system called the Fuzzy Self-Organising Map (FSOM). The FSOM is type of 'hybrid' ANN which allows behaviour to be described qualitatively and quantitatively using meaningful expressions. Safety of the FSOM is argued through adherence to safety requirements – derived from hazard analysis and expressed using safety constraints. The approach enables the construction of compelling (product-based) arguments for mitigation of potential failure modes associated with the FSOM. The constrained FSOM has been termed a 'Safety Critical Artificial Neural Network' (SCANN). The SCANN can be used for nonlinear function approximation and allows certified learning and generalisation. A discussion of benefits for real-world applications is also presented within the paper.

1 Introduction

Artificial Neural Networks (ANNs) are employed in a wide range of applications. These include areas such as defence, medical and industrial process control domains [1]. A plethora of appealing features are associated with ANNs. One notable benefit includes the ability to learn and adapt to a changing environment. Another advantage is the ability to generalise outputs given novel data. The operational performance of ANNs can also exceed conventional methods [1] in areas of pattern recognition and function approximation. They are good tools for finding quick solutions using little input from designers. These qualities enable applications to provide improved efficiency (in terms of reduced cost) through maximising performance in a changing operating context. However, the continued absence of analytical safety arguments necessary for certification has prevented their use in dependable roles within safety critical applications.

There are several difficulties associated with ANNs that restrict their use to advisory roles in safety related applications. One prominent problem is the inability to understand and control the behaviour of the ANN since they are typically viewed as black-boxes. As a result, little or no arguments can be made about the control or miti-

M. Heisel et al. (Eds.): SAFECOMP 2004, LNCS 3219, pp. 17–30, 2004.

gation of potential hazards. The main thrust of existing approaches justifying ANNs for safety critical systems have focussed on improving validation or performance indexes. One example of such an approach [2] aims to provide guaranteed output within bounds. This approach interprets the ANN as a black-box and uses exhaustive testing to analyse the behaviour. This limits the benefits of ANNs which is dealing with novel inputs. Although the concept of bounding the function is useful, it is not clear how the output bounds are derived from safety analysis. Other limitations include the ANN being prevented from learning post-certification. These restrictions highlight the need for improved neural models which allow white-box style analysis to understand and control behaviour. These qualities permit compelling safety and performance arguments to be made.

Our previous work [3] has identified 'hybrid' neural networks as a potential model for allowing white-box style (decompositional) analysis. It also focussed on other issues such as establishing a suitable development and safety lifecycle [3] (which employs extra tasks [3, 4] involved in developing ANNs). Building on this work, section 2 of this paper will lay out the definition of an existing but suitable neural network along with its learning algorithms (used throughout development and operation). Section 3 argues the potential safety of the neural model by tackling important failure modes. These failure modes are shown to be mitigated by adding constraints to the existing neural model. These constraints contribute to product-based safety arguments for both ANNs and Fuzzy Logic Systems (FLS). Section 4 of the paper reaffirms the feasibility of the approach by maintaining performance and safety whilst making acceptable trade-offs.

2   Fuzzy Self-Organising Maps

This section describes a potentially suitable existing ANN model. Details of its operation are provided including several learning algorithms. Previous work on the safety lifecycle highlighted a number of characteristics for a suitable ANN model. Some of the main points are:

- Exploit decompositional approaches [3] to insert and extract ANN behaviour (Knowledge within the ANN must be highly structured and organised).

- Use qualitative forms of knowledge to express behaviour of the ANN (Such as "IF X is <condition> THEN Y is <condition>"). This helps analyse and comprehend ANN behaviour more easily than solely relying on quantitative representations (which is a common approach [2, 4]).

One potentially suitable model is known as the Fuzzy Self-Organising Map (FSOM) [5]. This model has the ability to fully express its behaviour using a set of fuzzy rules. These fuzzy rules encapsulate both qualitative and quantitative descriptions of the functional behaviour. Since the FSOM represents data in highly structured forms, knowledge can be inserted or extracted using trivial processes [6]. The FSOM is based upon Kohonen's ANN [7] and uses a modified version of its learning algorithm. Two similar variants of the FSOM have been developed, one of which is used for pattern recognition problems [5], and the other for nonlinear function approximation [6]. Results have shown that the FSOM performs well over a range of real-world control theory applications. These include identification of heating process [6], inverted pendulum [6], fault diagnosis of a reactor [6] and several others. The FSOM has also been used for the benchmark 'sinc' problem with results comparable to the well known ANFIS [8] system. Moreover, findings from pattern recognition case studies show that the FSOM is markedly better (in terms of generalisation perform-ance) than Kohonen's LVQ and Nearest Neighbour Networks [5].

Knowledge encapsulated through theoretical or empirical sources are represented in the FSOM as Takagi-Sugeno fuzzy rules [9]. These rules are defined as (1):

$$\Re i: \textbf{IF} \left(x_1 \text{ is } U_{i,1} \textbf{ AND },..., \textbf{ AND } x_n \text{ is } U_{i,n} \right) \textbf{ THEN } y_i = f_i \left(x_1,...,x_n \right) \quad (1)$$

Each fuzzy set is defined as $U_{i,j}$ for the ith rule where $i = 1, 2,..., m$, (m is the total number of rules) and the jth input where $j = 1, 2,..., n$, (n is the total number of input variables). The fuzzy set can be described linguistically using meaningful labels such as {LOW, MEDIUM, HIGH}. These labels can also be described quantitatively as discrete or continuous ranges. The output y_i (actuator) is a linear function of the ith rule inputs. All rules in the FSOM have the same actuator and input variables.

If rules have $n > 1$ inputs then it is known as a MISO (Multiple-Input Single-Output) rule. Single input rules are known as SISO (Single-Input Single-Output). More information about fuzzy logic can be found in [6]. The FSOM topology consists of six layers and is illustrated in figure 1.

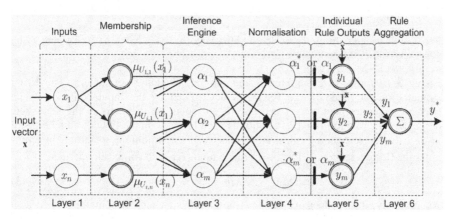

Fig. 1. Fuzzy Self Organising Map adapted from [6] where constrained neurons are denoted by double rings described in section 3.

Layer 1 is the input layer and propagates inputs (from sensors) to layer 2. No pre-processing occurs here and the number of neurons equals number of input variables.

Layer 2 is the fuzzy set membership (distance) function layer. This layer contains a neuron for every fuzzy set $U_{i,j}$. The triangular function (2) is used to describe membership and is illustrated in figure 2(a).

$$\mu_{U_{i,j}}\left(x_j\right) = \begin{cases} \dfrac{x_j - sl_{i,j}}{c_{i,j} - sl_{i,j}}, & sl_{i,j} \le x_j \le c_{i,j}, \\[2mm] \dfrac{x_j - sr_{i,j}}{c_{i,j} - sr_{i,j}}, & c_{i,j} \le x_j \le sr_{i,j}, \\[2mm] 0, & \text{otherwise} \end{cases} \tag{2}$$

The purpose of the membership function is to determine the degree a particular value belongs to a set. Membership degrees for each input range from zero to one. Values within the set all have membership greater than zero. The centre $c_{i,j}$ of $U_{i,j}$ always has a degree of one and can move anywhere within the set during learning. Left and right edges of the spread (or support) are described by $[sl_{i,j}, sr_{i,j}]$ for fuzzy set $U_{i,j}$ and learning is performed by adapting parameters that define the membership.

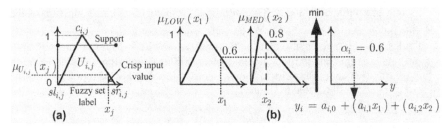

Fig. 2. (a) Triangular fuzzy set membership function. (b) Fuzzy inference & reasoning using Takagi-Sugeno (TS) rules

Layer 3 performs fuzzy inference and has no adaptable parameters. The firing strength for each rule in the FSOM is determined by the input conditions. The strength is greater than zero if and only if all inputs are members of the fuzzy sets defined by the rule (all rule pre-conditions must be true). In the FSOM, all neurons in layer 2 (for corresponding rules) are connected to the minimum operator. This computes the firing strength α_i for the ith rule output (for each firing rule) defined by (3):

$$\alpha_i = \min\left\{\mu_{U_{i,1}}\left(x_1\right), \mu_{U_{i,2}}\left(x_2\right),...,\mu_{U_{i,n}}\left(x_n\right)\right\}. \tag{3}$$

Alternatively, the product operator can be employed which is commonly seen as a more practical approach for real-world applications [10].

$$\alpha_i = \mu_{U_{i,1}}\left(x_1\right) \cdot \mu_{U_{i,2}}\left(x_2\right) \cdot,...,\cdot \mu_{U_{i,n}}\left(x_n\right). \tag{4}$$

Layer 4 is composed of normalisation neurons which have no adaptable parameters. These neurons normalise firing strengths for each rule firing rule α_i^* and is defined by (5):

$$\alpha_i^* = \left| \frac{\alpha_i}{\displaystyle\sum_{p=1}^{m} \alpha_p} \right. \tag{5}$$

Layer 5 computes crisp rule outputs using input values (from layer 1). Each rule will only produce an output (post-condition) if all rule inputs are true (pre-condition).

The rule outputs are Takagi-Sugeno [9] forms defined by (6) and illustrated in figure 2(b).

$$y_i = f_i(x_1,...,x_n) = a_{i,0} + a_{i,1}x_1 + a_{i,2}x_2 +,...,+a_{i,n}x_n. \tag{6}$$

The output is a linear function for the ith rule and the number of rule output neurons is equal to the number of rules. The total number of tunable parameters in this layer for each rule are $n + 1$ or $m(n + 1)$ for all rules.

Layer 6 consists of a solitary neuron whose purpose is to determine a single output value from several firing rules. Multiple rule firing occurs when rules preconditions overlap and is resolved using weighted averaging defined by (7):

$$y^* = \left\{ \frac{\sum_{i=1}^{m} \alpha_i y_i}{\sum_{i=1}^{m} \alpha_i} \right. . \tag{7}$$

Where the weighted average output is y^* for the given input vector **x**. For a single firing rule i, $y^* = y_i$. All FSOM parameters that undergo adaptation and optimisation for the ith rule are defined as (8) and (9):

$$\left\{ sl_{i,j}, c_{i,j}, sr_{i,j} \right\}, \tag{8}$$

$$\{ a_{i,0}, a_{i,1},..., a_{i,n} \}. \tag{9}$$

These parameters are tuned by learning algorithms described in the following section.

2.1 Static Learning Algorithm

The static learning algorithm tunes parameters (8) and (9) using training samples or input data to improve generalisation performance. It is performed in two phases as defined in [6]:

♦ **Phase 1**: Antecedent parameters are frozen and the consequent parameters (9) are refined using the gradient descent algorithm [11] (supervised mode).

♦ **Phase 2**: Consequent parameters are frozen and the antecedent parameters (8) are tuned using the modified LVQ algorithm [6] (supervised or unsupervised mode).

Phase 1 is performed using the well known Least Mean Square (LMS) algorithm [11]:

1. Propagate training sample with input signal vector $\mathbf{x}(t)$ at time t.
2. Determine learning coefficient $g_a(t)$ where $1 > g_a(t) \geq 0$ defined for consequent parameters.
   - This determines the amount the parameter changes and gradually decreases during training resulting in finer parameter adjustments.
3. Determine error between final output y^* and desired output y.
   - Where the desired output is defined by the training sample.
4. All consequent parameters (10) are tuned to reduce error using LMS (11).

$$\boldsymbol{a}_i = \left[a_{i,0}, a_{i,1},..., a_{i,n} \right], \tag{10}$$

$$\boldsymbol{a}_i(t+1) = \boldsymbol{a}_i(t) + g_{a,i}(t) \cdot \alpha_i \cdot [y^*(t) - y(t)]. \tag{11}$$

Phase 2 of learning is triggered when there are multiple firing rules for a given input vector. The first task involves choosing the input fuzzy set of the first runner-up rule r (second most highly activated rule). This is done by selecting the rule with the smallest overlap (with the winner rule w where α_w is the largest) and with the furthest centres. The runner-up spread is defined as $s_{r,k}$ or the edge $sl_{r,k}$, $sr_{r,k}$ which overlaps with the winner rule (where k is corresponding input variable).

After the appropriate spread has been chosen, it is updated and refined using the modified LVQ 2.1 algorithm. This learning law (12) moves the FSOM output y^* closer to the training data output y by increasing or decreasing the influence of the runner-up rule and is described as follows:

- The influence of the runner-up rule is increased by moving runner-up spread edge towards the centre of the winner rule.
- The influence of the runner-up rule is decreased by moving runner-up spread edge away from the winner rule centre and towards $s_{w,k}$.

$$s_{r,k}(t+1) = s_{r,k}(t) + g_{U,r}(t)[c_{w,k}(t) - s_{r,k}(t)], \quad \operatorname{sgn}(y - y^*) = \operatorname{sgn}(y_r - y_w),$$

$$s_{r,k}(t+1) = s_{r,k}(t) + g_{U,r}(t)[s_{w,k}(t) - s_{r,k}(t)], \qquad\qquad \text{otherwise}$$

$$(12)$$

Where the learning coefficient of the fuzzy sets $U_{r,j}$ is defined as $g_{U,r}$.

If a single rule fires then the learning algorithm initiates unsupervised learning. This process tunes the centres of input sets by moving the winner centre c_w (firing rule) towards the input sample (using defined learning rate). Further details on the static learning algorithm for the FSOM can be found in [6].

Static learning algorithms focus on adapting the semantic meanings of the knowledge (expressed by the fuzzy rules). This is in contrast to other approaches which deal with adapting logical representations [12]. Rules in the FSOM may be generated through theoretical knowledge (provided by experts) or empirically using the dynamic learning algorithm.

2.2 Dynamic Learning Algorithm

The self-generation of fuzzy rules is an attractive property as it automatically acquires novel features described by training data. Adding more rules contribute to the function approximation ability of the FSOM. The topology and architecture is automatically adapted (creating new neurons and links) without user intervention. The self-generation method described by Vuorimaa [5], uses three heuristic rules to create new fuzzy rules which are:

1. **Errors are removed in descending order.**
   - Guarantees fuzzy rules are added so that the largest error (between FSOM and training sample outputs) is removed first, which is measured during each training cycle or epoch.
2. **New fuzzy rule is only added once existing fuzzy rules have been tuned.**
   - If the FSOM has difficulty reducing error (using static learning), a new rule is added at the input sample point with default spread width wi.

3. **Interference caused by new rule upon existing rules is minimised.**

   - To prevent forgetting of previously learnt knowledge the width of new rule spread wi is limited.

This process is used during the development lifecycle for ANNs [3] prior to certification. The earliest time which this process can stop is determined by criteria used by Preliminary System Safety Assessment and an additional phase of safety assessment [3]. This includes providing assurance that the input space is covered and rules overlap (described in section 3). Further details on dynamic learning can be found in [6].

3 Safety Constraints and Arguments

Enabling the FSOM described in section 2 for use in safety critical systems requires integrating mechanisms to prevent specific faults (which may lead to potential failures). In previous work [13], the safety criteria were established as a number of high-level goals with a safety argument expressed in GSN (Goal Structuring Notation). These goals or claims were based upon encapsulating different failure modes associated with the behaviour of ANNs. The main claims of the safety criteria focussed on controlling the input-output relationship during generalisation and learning (including unrepresentative training samples).

The constrained FSOM is called the SCANN and is suitable for nonlinear function approximation problems. The approach is to use a series of linear functions to model the desired nonlinear function and is a common technique using fuzzy rules [14]. Moreover, it has been shown that fuzzy logic is a universal function approximator and can approximate any function to any degree of accuracy [15]. Preventing failures modes associated with the FSOM will require constraints and bounds on both the generalisation and learning operations.

Previous work has highlighted that potential failure modes associated with ANNs are not well understood [16]. However, a set of failure modes have been identified for the FSOM that have been derived from HAZOP (Hazard Operability Study) [17] guide words (which originates from the process-control theory domain). The guide words were applied to the FSOM input and output data rate and value. The main identified failure modes are a complete set for many real-world applications and are summarised as follows:

1. **Output is too high or too low for the given input.**
2. **Output omission given valid inputs.**
3. **Output increases when it should decrease (and vice versa).**
4. **Output derivative or rate of change is too high or too low.**

Failure modes 1, 3 and 4 have been derived from guide words 'MORE, LESS and REVERSE' and failure mode 2 from the guideword 'NONE'. The above failure modes tackle issues associated with verification and validation of ANNs and aim to provide correct mapping function over the required input space. Mitigation and control of potential hazards will be performed through identification and removal of related systematic faults associated with each failure mode.

3.1 Fuzzy Rules for Safety Critical Systems

Fuzzy logic attempts to model human reasoning using IF-THEN rules which is typically approximate and linguistic. This makes Fuzzy Logic an invaluable tool for expression and comprehension during design of the SCANN [3]. However, fuzzy sets have various interpretations that may or may not lend well to safety critical applications. There are two interpretations of fuzzy set membership which are known as likelihood [18] and random views [18]. The degree of membership is interpreted probabilistically (from possibility reasoning). These are undesirable for critical applications [19] as satisfaction of rule pre-conditions can potentially lead to hazardous post-conditions (during ANN mappings). This is because it cannot be said with certainty whether an input belongs to a set or not. This type of argument is essential for providing assurance about the pre-conditions and post-conditions of the behaviour.

Other interpretations are measurement [18] and similarity views [18]. These are more appropriate, as set membership for an input (that is precise and non-approximate) can be determined with certainty. The degree of membership is seen as relative to other members within the set. This relationship is discovered through training samples and expressed using triangular, Gaussian, trapezoid or other functions [6].

On the whole, soft-computing is described as a combination of ANNs, Fuzzy Logic Systems (FLS) and probabilistic reasoning. Our area of interest is the combination of ANNs and FLS. Primarily because of the benefits offered by 'hybrid' systems [3] whilst avoiding probabilistic safety arguments.

To justify the safety of the FSOM for SISO rules, the following sections present product-based arguments (extracted from a complete safety case) about various functional properties. This includes tackling hazards associated with the stability of nonlinear system dynamics by exploiting constraints and linearization methods.

3.2 Safety Argument for Function Mappings Using Semantic Constraints

Failure mode 1 is when the output is too high or too low for the current input. This may be caused by flawed training samples resulting in the FSOM diverging from the desired function. Remedial actions for this failure mode include incorporating semantic bounds for each rule. These bounds are used to control the input and output sets during learning (rule pre and post-conditions). This approach is similar to previous work on improving performance using semantic constraints on fuzzy rules [20].

There are two main branches of argument supporting the claim that the FSOM adheres to its bounds. The first is associated with providing assurance that all rule inputs with membership greater than zero lie within prescribed bounds. These bounds are derived from hazard analysis and system safety requirements as discussed in [3].

To provide assurance that failure mode 1 will not occur (during learning post-certification) the input sets parameters (8) for every neuron (in layer 2) are bounded according to (13) and (14). These bounds limit the possible meanings of the input fuzzy sets.

$$\text{Bounded Left Spread } sl_{i,j} = [\min sl_{i,j}, c_{i,j}]. \tag{13}$$

$$\text{Bounded Right Spread } sr_{i,j} = [c_{i,j}, \max sr_{i,j}]. \tag{14}$$

Moreover, the centre of the input fuzzy set is constrained to lie within the set spread as defined by (15). This is to prevent the centre stepping outside spread edges leading to false satisfaction of rules pre-conditions.

$$\text{Bounded Core } c_{i,j} = [sl_{i,j}, sr_{i,j}]. \tag{15}$$

Attempts to violate these bounds may be due to unrepresentative or flawed training samples. Offending training samples are consequently rejected (or used again when the learning rate defined in (12) becomes smaller).

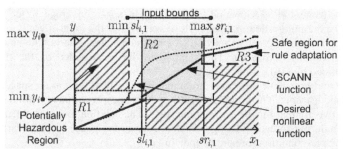

Fig. 3. Semantic safety bounds derived from safety requirements for SISO rules

Having defined input bounds which also encapsulate novel inputs, the next argument is the adherence of set bounds during generalisation. One potential fault is that the output function may attempt to produce a value that is beyond the output bounds (extremes). To avoid over-constraining learning, this problem can be solved by bounding the rule output as described by (16):

$$y_i = \begin{cases} \min y_i, & \text{if } f_i(x_1,...,x_n) < \min y_i, \\ \max y_i, & \text{if } f_i(x_1,...,x_n) > \max y_i. \end{cases} \tag{16}$$

Where $\min y_i$ and $\max y_i$ are output bound extremes for the ith rule and illustrated in figure 3. Acquiring such bounds from safety requirements is simplified because of the comprehensibility offered by fuzzy rules. When attempting to define a bound, output extremes may not be common for the entire rule input range. In this case, the approach is to split the rule so that the output bounds for each rule are uniform. This is one of the tasks performed during the development and safety lifecycle processes [3]. The weighted average will always output a value within the defined output bounds (of at least one firing rule) as long as rules with arbitrary overlap in inputs also overlap in output sets (and all rules must have at least one overlapping rule). To understand how semantic bounds for the SCANN are derived consider the following rule (17):

$$\Re i : \textbf{IF } (x \text{ is LOW}) \textbf{ THEN } y_i = f_i(x) \tag{17}$$

During development phases, LOW may be defined as the discrete range $\{0,...,40\}$. The definition of LOW is a pre-condition of the rule to fire. Using this input range, safe limits for the rule output are acquired from safety requirements (which are associated with control laws of the controlled device). The rule post-condition becomes $[\min y_i, \max y_i]$ and expresses non-changing output extremes. The input set used to derive output bounds then becomes a safety bound. During learning the semantics of LOW is constrained to lie within bounds (13), (14) and (15).

3.3 Safety Argument for Input Space Coverage

Failure mode 2 occurs when there is no output given valid inputs (output omission). This failure is due to faults associated with incomplete knowledge base or faulty input set updating. The input space that must be covered (at all times) is defined from analytical phases during hazard analysis [3] prior to certification. Once the required input space is defined the safety argument can be described as forming two main branches. The strategy is to first argue that the rule base completely covers the defined input space during generalisation. Assurance is provided through Preliminary System Safety Assessment (PSSA) which evaluates input space coverage by checking for "holes (by examining rule input sets). However, even if the input space is covered, an invalid output (missing value) may still be produced, since the output function may partially cover the output set. The solution to this is provided by the rule output bounds defined by (16).

The second branch of the safety argument is concerned with input space coverage during static learning. The argument relies upon the property that no "hole" should be created between input sets of overlapping rules. The solution to this problem is to add a condition during spread updating (which occurs during phase 2 of the learning algorithm). The pre-condition for spread updating is:

- The resultant update maintains an overlap or no gap (between winner $s_{w,k}$ and runner-up $s_{r,k}$ input sets). Otherwise the update is not performed.

This argument contributes to providing assurance about the functional input-output mappings during generalisation and learning phases.

3.4 Safety Argument for Output Function Gradient

Other safety requirements may be expressed for the desired function using fuzzy rules of the form:

$$\Re i : \textbf{IF}\,(x \text{ is } INCREASING)\,\textbf{THEN}\,(y_i \text{ is } DECREASING) \qquad (18)$$

The above rule is expressed for an existing rule i (1) in the knowledge base. The purpose of this rule is to qualitatively express a constraint on the SCANN function (related to failure mode 3).

The safety argument for adhering to these bounds focuses on providing assurance that the gradient sign (as expressed by (19)) is preserved during generalisation and learning. The solution to this argument is that parameter $a_{i,1}$ will always be positive to reflect increasing output (and negative to define decreasing output). A safety requirement trade-off is that the gradient in any case, can be zero because of the rule output bounds defined by (16). During phase 1 of learning, the $a_{i,1}$ is bounded in the following way:

$$
\begin{aligned}
a_{i,1}(t+1) \geq 0, &\quad \text{if output must be increasing or constant,} \\
a_{i,1}(t+1) \leq 0, &\quad \text{if output must be decreasing or constant.}
\end{aligned}
\qquad (19)
$$

Input variations outside normal behaviour described by safety requirements must be assured through other means. Safety processes during the lifecycle must identify any violations of (19) before certification using simple search algorithms. Attempted violations of the gradient during learning (post-certification) can be logged and reviewed during maintenance as described in section 4.

Another aspect of the safety argument is adhering to constraints during rule overlaps (or when the weighted averaging is used). For rule overlaps of arbitrary size, there may overlapping rules with dissimilar gradient constraints. The interpretation of this condition is that bound (19) no longer applies during the overlap and allows weighted average outputs. On the other hand, when two or more overlapping rules have the same gradient direction, then (7) may potentially violate (19). To avoid violating (19) the static learning algorithm is constrained according to (20).

$$y_{i-1}(x_j) \leq y_i(x_j) \text{ and } y_{i+1}(x_j) \geq y_i(x_j), \quad \text{if outputs must be increasing,}$$
$$y_{i-1}(x_j) \geq y_i(x_j) \text{ and } y_{i+1}(x_j) \leq y_i(x_j), \quad \text{if outputs must be decreasing.} \tag{20}$$

Where rule i is proposing adaptation of parameters (9) and overlapping rule $i-1$ is left of rule i (where $sl_{i-1,k} < sl_{i,k}$) and $i+1$ is rule right of i.

These constraints can be enforced through simple boundary testing of set spread edges. This also requires that the fuzzy set centres are frozen during operation in rule overlaps (with common bounds (19)) to prevent the output changing direction. Finally, rules subsumed by other rules must be removed before certification (when inputs are subset of an existing rule).

This safety argument contributes to providing assurance that specific safety requirements are adhered to during learning and generalisation. This also demonstrates the ability to derive arguments about specific functional properties.

3.5 Safety Argument for Output Derivatives

Failure mode 4 describes a condition when the difference between FSOM outputs $y^*(t)$ and $y^*(t+1)$ is too large (the output exhibits fluctuation). This may be problematic in many control theory domains where such sudden changes can be potentially hazardous. For SISO rules parameter $a_{i,1}$ can be constrained by determining the maximum safe output and input rate change (derivatives) resulting in constraint (21).

$$-\max a_{i,1} \leq a_{i,1} \leq +\max a_{i,1}, \qquad \text{if no sign constraint,}$$
$$0 \leq a_{i,1} \leq +\max a_{i,1}, \qquad \text{if output must be increasing,} \tag{21}$$
$$-\max a_{i,1} \leq a_{i,1} \leq 0, \qquad \text{if output must be decreasing.}$$

Similarly, the minimum safe output rate of change (given minimum input rate of change) can be constrained by

$$-\min a_{i,1} \geq a_{i,1} \geq +\min a_{i,1}. \tag{22}$$

The output rate of change extremes can be defined globally (constant for the entire function) or locally (specific to particular rules). Output fluctuations may persist when control is passed from one rule to another. The remedy involves checking for potential faults (present in overlaps) before certification and then constraining the static learning post-certification. The derived safety argument is divided into two main strategies – arguing about the output states during learning and generalisation. The approach is to perform boundary analysis on each fuzzy set spread edge for every rule (to mitigate all related faults before certification). This is performed by enforcing the property:

♦   At any set edge, the difference between rule outputs must be $\min(|\max a_{k,1}|)$ and $\max(|\min a_{k,1}|)$ where k is the index of every firing rule. This applies to rules with arbitrary local (rule specific) gradient constraints.

The first branch of the safety argument relies upon the FSOM adhering to the above property (21) and (22) whilst adapting parameters (8) and (9). However, constraint (16) can violate constraint (22). To prevent this violation all possible rule outputs with (22) must be within $[\min y_i, \max y_i]$. This condition can be checked by simple boundary testing for each input set edge. The second branch of the argument is concerned with generalisation where weighted averaging may violate the above property (with set centre tuning). To prevent this, the weighted averaging produces output only if the above property is true. If not, the weighted averaging function is suspended and the single most highly fired rule allows safe continuation of the function. This argument enables control of the output derivatives using simple parameter constraints.

4   Benefits of SCANN Application

As described in section 2, the FSOM has been successfully employed in a wide range of control domain applications. The SCANN can be used for both industrial control applications (where inputs are sensors and outputs are actuators) and medical systems (where inputs are sensors and output is dosage). Safety constraints are exploited by the SCANN and the approach is more beneficial than safety 'monitors'. For example, the underlying behaviour can be extracted and understood along with attempted constraint violations during learning. Functional properties of the SCANN can be controlled to prevent failure modes without arbitrary degree of safety. Moreover, implementing local constraints (for each rule) can result in overly complex safety monitors.

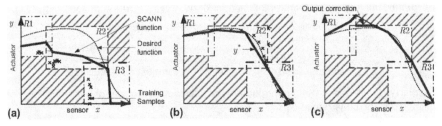

Fig. 4. Static learning algorithm keeps SCANN function within safe regions for both (a) unrepresentative data and (b) representative data. (c) SCANN output is controlled to prevent hazardous conditions inferred by training data

The SCANN can approximate any safe function using dynamic learning as long as safety constraints are not violated. Due to space constraints, a real-world application of the SCANN is not discussed. Instead, benefits associated with SCANN technology are listed below which enable efficiency in terms of cost for many applications:

◆ **Performance:** Generalisation and learning abilities can be exploited to approximate desired function without re-certification as illustrated in figure 4(a) and (b).

◆ **Adaptation:** Performance can be maximised by adapting to a changing operating context. For example, in industrial process control the static learning algorithm can adapt to changing plant states or aero-engine degradation [21].

◆ **Design:** During design, the SCANN can generate human comprehensible knowledge by using empirical techniques to directly interact with the problem. This enables specification to be derived from both theoretical and empirical sources.

◆ **Maintenance:** The SCANN has the ability to detect when the operating context is approaching hazardous conditions. For example, consider figure 4(c). The SCANN function is outside the bounds for rules 2 and 3. This may be due to un-representative training data or changes in the operating context (such as engine wear). All attempted bound violations are logged and used for system health monitoring. This knowledge can be exploited to indicate the need for product maintenance.

5 Conclusions

In this paper we present the SCANN, which exploits parameter constraints to mitigate identified failure modes common to nonlinear function approximation problems. The behaviour of the SCANN is represented by fuzzy logic and is useful for white-box style analysis. Identified failure modes have been derived from HAZOP guide words. The 'transparent' nature of the SCANN offers the prospect to adhere to various safety requirements. Safety constraints are used by the SCANN learning algorithms to prevent introducing systematic faults which may lead to violation of safety requirements. This enables compelling analytical certification arguments required for highly-dependable roles in safety critical systems. Benefits of the SCANN include generalisation and learning abilities post-certification through predicable and controlled behaviour. This allows training data to be of arbitrary integrity whilst providing assurance for safe behaviour. The SCANN offers many incentives which can lead to cost efficiency and make it an invaluable tool for safety critical applications.

References

1. Lisboa, P., Industrial use of safety-related artificial neural networks. Health & Safety Executive 327, (2001).
2. Hull, J., D. Ward, and R. Zakrzewski, Verification and Validation of Neural Networks for Safety-Critical Applications, Barron Associates, Inc. and Goodrich Aerospace, Fuel and Utility Systems (2002).
3. Kurd, Z. and T.P. Kelly, Safety Lifecycle for Developing Safety-critical Artificial Neural Networks. 22nd International Conference on Computer Safety, Reliability and Security (SAFECOMP'03), 23-26 September, (2003).
4. Nabney, I., et al., Practical Assessment of Neural Network Applications, Aston University & Lloyd's Register: UK (2000).
5. Vuorimaa, P., Fuzzy self-organising map. Fuzzy Sets and Systems. 66 (1994) 223-231.

6. Ojala, T., Neuro-Fuzzy Systems in Control, Masters Thesis, Department of Electrical Engineering, Tampere University of Technology, Tampere, 1994
7. Kohonen, T., Self-organisation and associative memory, Berlin: Springer-Verlag (1984).
8. Jang, J.S.R., ANFIS: adaptive-network-based fuzzy inference systems. IEEE Trans. Syst. Man. Cybern. 23(3) (1993) 665-685.
9. Takagi, H., et al., Neural networks designed on approximate reasoning architecture and their applications. IEEE Trans. Neural Networks. 3(5) (1992) 752-760.
10. Brown, M. and C. Harris, Neuro-fuzzy adaptive modelling and control, New York: Prentice Hall (1994).
11. Haykin, S., Neural Networks: A Comprehensive Foundation: Prentice-Hall (1999).
12. Towell, G. and J.W. Shavlik, Knowledge-Based Artificial Neural Networks. Artificial Intelligence,(70) (1994) 119-165.
13. Kurd, Z. and T.P. Kelly, Establishing Safety Criteria for Artificial Neural Networks. In Seventh International Conference on Knowledge-Based Intelligent Information & Engineering Systems (KES'03), Oxford, UK, (2003).
14. Wen, W., J. Callahan, and M. Napolitano, Towards Developing Verifiable Neural Network Controller, Department of Aerospace Engineering, NASA/WVU Software Research Laboratory, West Virginia University, Morgantown, WV, 1996
15. Wang, L., X., Fuzzy systems are universal approximators. IEEE Trans. Syst. Man. Cybern. SMC-7(10) (1992) 1163-1170.
16. Jackson, T.O. and J. McDermid, Certification of Neural Networks. ERA Technology Ltd, Report 97-0365, Project 13-01-4745, (1997).
17. CISHEC, A Guide to Hazard and Operability Studies, The Chemical Industry Safety and Health Council of the Chemical Industries Association Ltd. (1977).
18. Bilgic, T. and I.B. Turksen, *Measurement of membership functions: theoretical and empirical work*, in Handbook of fuzzy sets and systems, In Dubois and Prade (1997).
19. Fox, J. and D. Robertson, Industrial use of Safety Related Expert Systems, Health & Safety Executive 296 (2000).
20. Oliveira, J.V., Semantic Constraints for Membership Function Optimisation. IEEE Trans. Syst., Man., Cybern. Part A: Systems and Humans,. 29(1) (1999).
21. Chipperfield, A.J., B. Bica, and P.J. Fleming, Fuzzy Scheduling Control of a Gas Turbine Aero-Engine: A Multiobjective Approach. IEEE Trans. on Indus. Elec. 49(3) (2002).

Using Formal Methods
in a Retrospective Safety Case

Lars-Henrik Eriksson*

Department of Information Technology
Uppsala University
Box 337
SE-751 05 UPPSALA, Sweden lhe@it.uu.se

Abstract. Today the development of safety-critical systems is to a large
extent guided by standards that make demands on both development
process and system quality. Before the advent of these standards, development was typically done on a "best practise" basis which could differ
much between application areas. Some safety-critical systems (e.g. railway interlockings) have a long technical and economical lifetime so that
today we have many legacy safety-critical systems in operation which
were developed according to practises that would be regarded as unacceptable today. Usually, such systems are allowed to continue operating
by virtue of past performance. If there is doubt about the integrity of
a legacy system, an alternative to replacement could be making a "retrospective" safety case demonstrating that the legacy system is indeed
safe to use. Using as example a case taken from railway signalling, we
will show how formal verification can be used in a retrospective safety
case. In this application of formal methods several particular problems
arise, such as uncertainty about the original requirements and the required safety level of the various system functions. We will discuss such
problems and the approach taken to deal with them in the example case.

1 Introduction

On January 4th 2000 two trains collided head-on near the Norwegian village
of Åsta, causing the death of 19 people and injuries to 30 more. A government
commission [1] was formed to investigate the accident. It was determined that
one of the trains had passed a signal which should have been at "danger". The
commission could find nothing specifically wrong with the signalling system that
could have caused the signal to incorrectly show a "clear" aspect, nor could it
determine with certainty that it did show a "danger" aspect. The conclusion
was that the cause of the accident was either a technical malfunction or a driver
error, but that it was not possible to state which.

---

* The work presented herein was done while the author was employed by Industrilogik
L4i AB, Box 3470, SE-103 69 STOCKHOLM, Sweden. I wish to thank my former
colleagues for their involvement in this work.

M. Heisel et al. (Eds.): SAFECOMP 2004, LNCS 3219, pp. 31–44, 2004.

A question raised by the commission was the reliability of existing signalling systems in view of today's requirements. Today there are a number of standards (e.g. CENELEC EN50126 [10], EN50128 [11], ENV50129 [12]) for the development of railway signalling systems. Previously, development of signalling systems was typically done on a "best practise" basis with relatively few development rules, to a large extent guided by the knowledge of experienced engineers. This is a situation not limited to railway signalling systems but is generally relevant to "legacy" safety-critical systems with long technical and economical lifetime. The continued operation of such systems today is typically motivated by operational experience without incidents, but is that always sufficient?

In the opinion of the Åsta commission a safety review of the existing railway signalling system was necessary. Primarily this concerned the particular signalling system (*interlocking*) in operation on the railway line where the collision occurred (NSB-87) but also – although less urgent – of a different signalling system (NSI-63) which was the most wide-spread system in use in Norway. The result was a decision by the National Norwegian Rail Administration (Jernbaneverket – JBV) to make a "retrospective" safety case for the NSB-87 based on the CENELEC standards for railway signalling systems.

A central part of a safety case according to the standard ENV50129 is the "Technical Safety Report" which presents the arguments that the technical design of the signalling system is sound. The Swedish consultancy Industrilogik L4i AB was employed to develop the Technical Safety Report for the NSB-87 safety case and on their suggestion formal verification was used as the basic means of analysing the interlocking design.

This paper describes the role of formal methods in carrying out the retrospective safety case. In section 2 the general structure and contents of the retrospective safety case is described while the the particular formal methods process used is described in section 3. Section 4 discusses the problems encountered and experiences made while actually carrying out the work. The conclusion section 5 ends the paper.

2   The Safety Case

2.1   General

According to ENV50129, a safety case is "the documented demonstration that the system complies with the specified safety requirements". Already this definition is troublesome for a "retrospective" safety case, in that in all likelihood there are no proper "specified" safety requirements in the sense of the Standard suitable for the existing system. In the case of NSB-87, the safety requirements had to be compiled from a variety of sources.

Of course, this should not be taken to mean that the NSB-87 system was developed without any safety requirements, only that – in retrospect – the safety requirements used were not as complete or well-defined as the Standard requires of new systems. Indeed, it is stated in the Standard itself, that it is intended to be used for the development of new systems, rather than assessment of old ones.

A safety case according to ENV50129 is divided into the following main parts:

System Definition. A precise definition of, or reference to, the system to which the Safety Case refers, including version numbers and modification status of all requirements, design and application documentation.

Quality Management Report. The evidence of Quality Management.

Safety Management Report. The evidence of Safety Management.

Technical Safety Report. The evidence of Functional and Technical Safety.

Related Safety Cases. References to Safety Cases of any sub-systems or equipment on which the main Safety Case depends, if any.

Conclusion. A summary of the evidence presented in the other parts of the Safety Case, and an argument that the system is adequately safe, subject to compliance with the specified application conditions.

The principal parts of the safety case will be discussed in turn.

2.2   System Definition

The NSB-87 is an interlocking type in use at 18 different installations. The installations are generally very similar, differing only in detail. One particular installation, that of Rena railway station, was selected to be the representative system to which the safety case refers. The differences between the installations were deemed to be so small that no separate safety cases were needed for the other installations beside Rena.

The structure of an NSB-87 installation is shown in figure 1.

The interlocking logic is encoded in a PLC (Programmable Logic Controller) program. When the NSB-87 was developed, the use of industry standard PLC's in railway interlocking was unusual and there was doubt both about the safety integrity of the PLC and how to demonstrate the safety of the program and of the PLC itself. Also, a single channel PLC was used with no duplication or redundancy either in software or hardware.

To avoid the safety issues with using a single channel standard PLC, a minimal interlocking based on traditional relay technology was added as a "filter" between the PLC and the trackside objects. Electrical circuits from the PLC to the trackside objects passes through relay contacts in the relay interlocking so that, in effect, 2 out of 2 voting between the PLC and the relay interlocking is done when executing possibly dangerous manoeuvres (clearing signals, reversing points...).

Should the PLC behave in an unsafe manner, the relay interlocking will thus "contain" the fault and protect trains operating in the area controlled by the interlocking. In effect, the burden of maintaining safety integrity is placed on the relay logic. Following this principle, in the formal analysis of the interlocking system the PLC was treated as a "hostile" part of the system which could exhibit arbitrary (i.e. unsafe) behaviour.

Since the manoeuvring system of the NSB-87 is also in the PLC, the relay interlocking receives input from the traffic control centre through the PLC. This function of the PLC is also not considered safety-critical as the purpose of a railway interlocking is reject commands that would be dangerous to carry out.

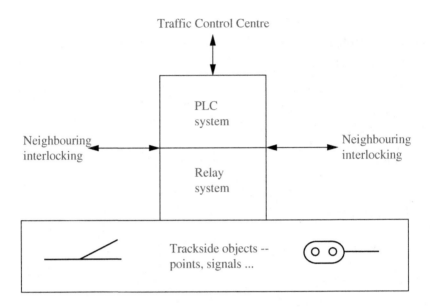

Fig. 1. Structure of a NSB-87 interlocking

2.3   Quality Management Report

At the time the NSB-87 was developed, quality management was done in an informal manner. This section of the safety case briefly describes the practises used. When possible reference is made to more recent documents based on these earlier practises.

2.4   Safety Management Report

At was the case with quality management, safety management was done in an informal manner. Some general principles about "fail-safe" operation were applied. Again, when possible reference was made to more recent documents based on earlier practises.

2.5   Technical Safety Report

This section forms the bulk of the safety case. Most of the contents of the Technical Safety report refers to the formal verification. As there was no "original" safety requirements specification in existence, one had to be compiled anew from various sources. Under those circumstances many minor deviations from the requirements specification could be expected. All deviations found (see section 4.3) were subject to a traditional risk analysis to determine whether or not they posed an acceptable or unacceptable risk. Thus safety properties at the system level were established using a combination of formal verification and risk analysis.

3   The Formal Verification Process

3.1   Basic Principles

As usual, we use the term "formal methods" to refer to the use of mathematically precise notation to describe requirements ("formal specification") and to use mathematically rigourous methods to determine whether the requirements are satisfied of a particular system ("formal verification").

The formal verification process used in the retrospective safety case is based on automated theorem proving in propositional (mathematical) logic. The requirements specification is represented by a number of logic formulae. Likewise, the system to be verified is modelled as a set of logic formulae. The (requirements) specification formulae determines the *permissible* behaviour of the system, while the (system) model formulae determines the *possible* behaviours of the system. The model of a correct system is said to be a *refinement* of the specification.

Clearly, if every possible behaviour is also a permissible behaviour, the system fulfils its requirements specification[1]. It is a result in mathematical logic that this relation is equivalent to the fact that a proof can be made of every specification formula using the model formulae as assumptions.

With modern theorem-proving algorithms such as Chaff [9] and fast computers, very large proofs can be attempted automatically in seconds. Should the proof fail, the algorithms will give a detailed counterexample (countermodel), describing a concrete situation where the requirements fail to hold. In this particular case, the descriptions of such situations were used as input to a traditional risk analysis.

The formal verification process is outlined in figure 2 and its various parts are described in the following sections. The process is described in more detail in [4][5][7].

Model Checking [3] is a different technique which is more commonly used for automatic formal verification and has been very successful in a number of industrial application areas. In the case of railway interlocking systems, though, there is some evidence that model checking works less well compared to theorem proving. [8] describes an application of model checking to formal verification of interlocking systems which was not feasible unless a number of optimisations were made to the model checker input. In our experience, no such optimisations are necessary when doing automatic verification by theorem proving.

We have not made any proper investigation as to why this would be the case, but we believe that the reason why theorem proving works well is that interlockings are typically designed so that most requirements hold even in unreachable states. In the few cases where this is not true, it is usually straightforward to characterise the relevant unreachable states by hand. The important function of a model checker of enumerating or characterising reachable states is thus not needed.

---

[1] As far as the behaviour can be correctly modelled in logic.

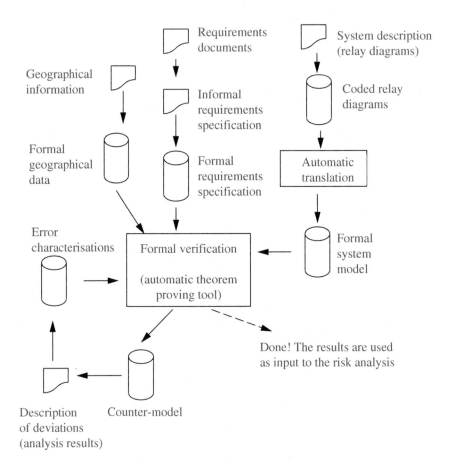

Fig. 2. The formal verification process

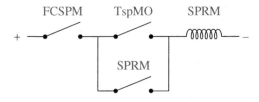

Fig. 3. Sample relay circuit

3.2   Specifications

Safety-critical systems in general (and railway interlocking systems in particular) are governed by a general set of requirements, while the systems have to be configured for any particular installation. It is desirable to have a general formal specification that can be used with any installation to avoid the work (and quality assurance issues!) of writing a separate specification for every installation.

This is done by writing the specification in a logic language (predicate logic) where it is possible to refer to information about a specific installation. In the railway context this information is called the "geographical data" and describes the geographical layout of the particular part of a railway where the interlocking operates (e.g. the location of tracks, signals, points etc.). By combining the general specification with installation-specific data an installation-specific specification is obtained which can be used as input to the formal verification process[2].

Example 1. A typical informal requirement:

"A point is locked when any of the following conditions are met [...] the point is part of a locked train route [...]"

The corresponding logical formula is

```
ALL pt (SOME tr (routelocked(tr) & part_of(pt,tr)) ->
                pointlocked(pt))
```

Here `pt` and `tr` are variables ranging over points and train routes. The subformula `part_of(pt,tr)` is a reference to the geographical data. Part of the geographical data will state precisely which points are parts of which train routes.

3.3   System Model

To make formal verification possible, a representation of the system in logic must be created. In the case of NSB-87, the system to be verified was the relay circuitry of the interlocking. This circuitry was documented by circuit diagrams which were translated into logic to obtain the system model. As the safety case must also demonstrate the safety of the system in the presence of faults, the translation method employed took into account the possibility of failures (single mode in this case) in the circuitry according to a specified set of possible failure modes.

Example 2. Figure 3 shows a sample circuit of the relay interlocking. FCSPM is an output contact of the PLC, while `TspMO` and `SPRM` are relays. The translation into logic is:

```
SPRM <-> FCSPM & (TspMO # PRE SPRM) & ~SPRM_broken # SPRM_stuck
```

---

[2] The combining process includes a step where the predicate logic of the general specification is transformed into propositional logic so that it can be used with automatic propositional theorem provers.

stands for logical disjunction (or). PRE SPRM is an expression referring to a variable representing the state of the SPRM relay at the previous moment in time (see section 3.6). SPRM_broken and SPRM_stuck are variables modelling failures of the circuit. SPRM_broken is true if the relay does not pick up because the electric circuit has been broken or because of a relay fault. SPRM_stuck is true if the relay SPRM does not drop out because it is stuck or its contacts have welded[3].

The translation into logic was carried out automatically. A textual encoding of the relay circuitry was made by hand and stored in a file. A translation program read the file and automatically produced a set of logic formulae representing the behaviour of the relay system. This set of formulae was then used as input to the theorem prover.

Computer software such as PLC programs can also be translated into logic, but for this work the PLC software was not (initially, see section 4.3) considered safety-critical and therefore was not formally verified.

3.4   Counter-Model Analysis

More often than not, a proof fails because the system does not quite follow the specification. The theorem prover algorithm will then automatically generate a "counter-model", a description of a situation where the system exhibits a behaviour which is not allowed by the specification. The counter-model itself is of limited use partly because of its excruciating detail but also because it does not in itself explain the reason for the incorrect behaviour. Most of the information described in the counter-model is coincidental to the particular requirement being violated. E.g. the counter-model will include state information of parts of the interlocking not related to the failing function.

Example 3. Suppose that the system did not satisfy the sample requirements formula of example 1. As part of the counter-model the theorem prover would give information about the particular point and train route involved. Also, the states of all relays – including failures – and other parts of the circuitry in the error situation would be given.

An important step of the process is the analysis of a counter-model to provide a characterisation of the situations where the system exhibits an erroneous behaviour. The analysis is presently carried out by hand and requires a substantial understanding of how the verified system works. The result of this analysis is used as output from the verification process to describe a particular problem with the verified system.

Example 4. In the case of the sample requirements formula of example 1, the conclusion could be e.g. that for point 4 and train route AL, the requirement would not be satisfied if a failure of relay FrLok occurred[4].

---

[3] Since interlocking relays are safety relays with forced contacts all relevant single failure modes can be represented using combinations of values of the _stuck and _broken variables for the various relays.

[4] This is a hypothetical error and does not represent any actual error found in the analysis of the NSB-87 interlocking.

The characterisation is also used to find other situations where the same (or other) requirement is violated. The theorem proving attempt is repeated with the added assumption that the just characterised error situation can not occur. This will cause the theorem prover to disregard this particular error and it will either report that the proof succeeded (in which case all errors have been found), or it will generate a counter-model for a different error situation which can in its turn be analysed. By successively analysing counter-models and retrying the proof in this manner, all ways in which the system violates some requirement will eventually be found.

3.5   Risk Analysis

The risk analysis phase is not properly a part of the formal verification process, but it was an important step in producing the NSB-87 safety case so its relation to the formal verification will be briefly discussed.

In this formal verification process no attempt is made to calculate the frequencies or consequences of failures. Indeed, the logic is discrete and deterministic so the representation of failure modes simply states that the failure of a component of the verified system *may* happen. Also, there is of course always the possibility that the system does not function according to the specification even in the absence of component failures.

To determine whether deviations from the requirements have dangerous consequences and, if so, whether the probability of a deviation actually occurring is too high to be acceptable, a traditional risk analysis can follow the formal verification. Using known or estimated frequencies of component failures and behaviour patterns of the system environment (the railway in this case) the risk analysis can estimate the likelihood and consequences of incorrect system behaviour for each deviation found during the counter-model analysis.

In formal methods, a successful formal verification is normally used by itself as evidence of the safety of the system. When used in conjunction with risk analysis the formal verification need not be "successful" in the usual sense of the word. In contrast, it can serve the purpose of finding possibly dangerous situations which are subject to risk analysis. By using formal methods a much more complete set of findings can be obtained compared to what can be expected using traditional (manual) methods.

3.6   Handling Time

The behaviour at any given point in time of virtually every system found in practise is dependent of what has happened previously. In other words, the formal notation must be able to refer to different moments in time. There are many approaches to handling time. In the present work, the synchronous hypothesis [2] is adopted. This basically means that time can be seen as a sequence of separate infinitesimally small instances and that all actions of the system (e.g. change of output) take place from one time instance to the next. That is, the actions are taken to be instantaneous. This simplification (or abstraction) of real time is meaningful if we assume that the system will always react "quickly enough" to changes in its environment.

The requirements specification as well as the system model are transition relations, describing what states are permissible/possible in the present moment of time given the system state at the previous moment of time.

A drawback with this model of time is that it does not allow for specific time intervals, e.g. that two events are separated by a 5 seconds (say) interval. It turns out that in the present application, there is seldom a need for such specific time intervals. When they do occur they are simulated by assuming the existence of a clock which will signal when the given time interval has elapsed.

3.7 Tools

The process is supported by a software tool, GTO, developed by Industrilogik L4i AB. This tool can "plug in" any automatic propositional theorem prover, and various theorem provers such as SATO [14], zChaff [9] and Prover Technology CL-Tool (based on "Stålmarck's method" [13]) have been used with GTO.

4   Experiences from Developing the Safety Case

4.1   The Requirements Specification

A prerequisite to any verification and validation effort is a requirements speci-fication. In the case of the NSB-87 system no proper requirements specification was made when the system was developed[5]. Instead, the system was designed to generally have the same behaviour as previous systems and to follow the opera-tional rules of the railway. Many of the actual requirements for an interlocking system were simply embodied in the design of previous signalling systems.

In order to carry out the safety case, a proper requirements specification had to be developed. To this end the relevant regulatory documents issued by JBV were studied. These documents were written after the development of the NSB-87 and it was known that they did not always correspond to earlier practise. Also, much information was missing from the regulations. Partly this was because "obvious" requirements were omitted, but also since the style of the documents in many cases was to state requirements by giving examples of correct behaviour, leaving the reader to extrapolate the requirements in situations not covered by the examples.

To address the problems of the missing requirements as well as to save time, an existing formal requirements specification for Swedish railway signalling [4][6] was used as a basis for the requirements specification for NSB-87. Swedish and Norwegian practises are similar so the structure of the specification could be kept while details were changed in accordance with the JBV documents.

---

[5] This is a general phenomenon with older railway interlocking systems and not par-ticular to the NSB-87.

In order to validate the requirements specification, an informal version of the formal specification was made. This informal specification was essentially a direct translation of the logic formulae into plain text, preserving the structure and concepts of the formal specification. The informal requirements specification was turned over to JBV experts for inspection and approval and necessary modifications were made.

During the requirement engineering process, care was taken to maintain traceability from individual requirements formulae back to the documents or other sources motivating each formula.

As the formal verification work began, it turned out that in spite of the inspections and approval, some requirements were incorrect or not applicable, so the specification was further revised after consultation with JBV signalling experts. In our experience, it is typical that domain experts do not always understand the full ramifications of a particular requirement as they are used to follow rules that do not always work and to make ad-hoc deviations from them when circumstances make it necessary.

Creating the geographical data from a description of the layout of Rena station was straightforward.

4.2   The System Model

The relay circuitry was documented using a set of relay circuit diagrams. The manual coding of the circuit diagrams was very time-consuming and tedious. As the diagrams had been written using a CAD system, they were stored on CAD files and in principle the manual coding could have been replaced by an automatic interpretation of the representations of symbols and lines in the CAD files. However, the cost of developing such an interpretation program and uncertainty about how well it would work in practise was too great for a single project.

Occasionally, mistakes were found in that the circuit diagrams did not correctly represent the actual relay circuitry in the interlocking system. The mistakes were in most cases not detected until the verification process gave unreasonable results.

In most cases, an experienced signalling engineer would have spotted the mistakes, but as more time passes since the diagrams were made up the greater is the risk that engineers would fail to spot the mistakes, causing errors to be introduced into the system during modification or repair.

4.3   Verification

The formal verification revealed a large number of deviations from the requirements specification. This was caused partly by the fact that the requirements were made up some 15 years after the system had been initially developed. What today would be considered incorrect behaviour would not necessarily have been seen as such at that time. In some cases, the deviations motivated a revision of the requirements specification. In other cases deviations could be motivated by special circumstances, while the requirements specification applied uniform requirements in all situations.

However, there were a number of cases where the system did not always behave as expected even by the standards applied at the time of development – particularly in the presence of faults.

These remaining cases were subject to risk analysis and in the end it was determined that the risks were acceptable. It was also found that – contrary to the intention when the system was first developed – some safety critical functionality was located only in the PLC system and not also provided by the relay "filter". Once this was realised, the risk analysis was used to determine if the situation was acceptable.

Nothing was found indicating incorrect behaviour that could have caused the accident at Åsta.

The manual analysis of the counter-model generated by the automatic theorem prover was very tedious and time-consuming. It also required a substantial understanding of how the circuits of the verified system actually worked.

A suitably different interlocking design could have simplified the verification and counter-model analysis. E.g. the design could have been structured in a similar way as the specification and with more redundancies in the circuitry – particularly in "don't care" situations. When making new designs it is important to consider how to "design for (formal) verifiability".

5   Conclusions

In summary, the formal verification of the NSB-87 interlocking was quite successful. In spite of some difficulties, the project produced the desired output and was completed within schedule.

Determining the safety requirements was not straightforward – particularly not considering the amount of detail and precision required of a formal specification. The original specifications from the 1980's were not documented in a complete or uniform way and it was also not clear to what extent they are relevant today. On the other hand, if the requirements of today would have been used without changes, it would be certain that in many cases they would not be fulfilled by the system.

For these reasons it was necessary to accept that a large number of deviations from the requirements were found during formal verification. To determine whether or not the deviations were acceptable, they were subject to a traditional risk analysis. In a sense, the main function of the formal verification was to provide input to the risk analysis rather than itself establish the safety of the system. This was the major difference between the use of formal methods in the retrospective safety case compared to using formal methods when developing a new system.

The use of formal verification gave a considerably better verification coverage of the system than would have been expected by a traditional analysis based on manual inspection of circuit diagrams. This was particularly true when the effect of faults was considered as it is difficult for a person to fully consider and grasp the effects of all possible faults on a system.

The manual steps in the formal verification process – the coding of circuit diagrams and the analysis of counter-models were very time-consuming. The coding could in principle have been automated, and in any case modern systems are typically based on computer (e.g. PLC) technology where the program source code is machine-readable from the start and no manual coding is necessary.

The counter-model analysis is a different matter, as it requires insight into the workings of the system to determine what part of the system design contributes to a deviation from a particular requirement. Nevertheless, it is expected that much of this analysis could also be automated – however it is basically a research issue to determine how this could be done.

The involved staff of the Norwegian National Rail Administration were generally quite impressed with the results that could be achieved using formal methods. The same methodology was again used successfully for another retrospective safety review of the different interlocking system NSI-63 (also a recommendation of the Åsta commission). Additionally, the NSB-87 safety case indirectly led to new industrial adoption of formal methods as a component in the development of safety cases for new signalling systems.

References

1. Åsta-ulykken 4. januar 2000 – Hovedrapport, The Norwegian Ministry of Justice and the Police (2000)
2. Benveniste, A. and Berry, G.: The Synchronous Approach to Reactive and Real-Time Systems, Proceedings of the IEEE, Vol. 79 No. 9, pp. 1270–1282 (1991).
3. Clarke, M.E., Grumberg, O. and Peled, D.A.: Model Checking, MIT Press (1999).
4. Eriksson, L-H.: Formalising Railway Interlocking Requirements, Technical report 1997:3, Swedish National Rail Administration (1997)
5. Eriksson, L-H.: Formal Verification of Railway Interlockings, Technical report 1997:4, Swedish National Rail Administration (1997)
6. Eriksson, L-H.: Specifying Railway Interlocking Requirements for Practical Use, In Schoitsch, E. (ed.): Proceedings of the 15th International Conference on Computer Safety, Reliability and Security (SAFECOMP'96), Springer-Verlag (1996)
7. Eriksson, L-H. and Johansson, K.: Using formal methods for quality assurance of interlocking systems, In Mellit, B. et.al. (eds.): Computers in Railways IV, Computational Mechanics publications (1998).
8. Huber, M. and King, S.: Towards an Integrated Model Checker for Railway Signalling Data, In Eriksson, L-H. and Lindsay, P.A. (eds.): FME'2002: Formal Methods – Getting IT Right, pp. 204–223, Lecture Notes in Computer Science 2391, Springer-Verlag (2002).
9. Moskewicz, M., Madigan, C., Zhao, Y., Zhang, L. and Malik, S.: Chaff: Engineering an Efficient SAT Solver, Proceedings of the 38th ACM/IEEE Design Automation Conference (DAC'01), pp. 530–535, ACM/IEEE (2001)
10. Railway Applications: The Specification and Demonstration of Reliability, Availability, Maintainability and Safety (RAMS), European standard EN50126, CENELEC, Brussels (1999)

11. Railway Applications – Communication, signalling and processing systems – Software for railway control and protection systems, European standard EN50128, CENELEC, Brussels (2001)
12. Railway Applications – Safety related electronic systems for signalling, European standard ENV50129, CENELEC, Brussels (1998)
13. Sheeran, M. and Stålmarck, G.: A Tutorial on Stålmarck's Proof Procedure for Propositional Logic, In Gopalakrishnan, G. and Windley, P. (eds.): Proc. 2nd Intl. Conf. on Formal Methods in Computer-Aided Design, FMCAD'98, pp. 82–99, Lecture Notes in Computer Science 1522, Springer-Verlag (1998)
14. Zhang, H.: SATO: An Efficient Propositional Prover, In McCune (ed.): Proc. 14th International Conference on Automated Deduction (CADE-14), Lecture Notes in Computer Science, Springer-Verlag (1997)

A Highly Fault Detectable Cache Architecture for Dependable Computing

Hamid R. Zarandi and Seyed Ghassem Miremadi

Department of Computer Engineering, Sharif University of Technology
Tehran, Iran
zarandi@ce.sharif.edu, miremadi@sharif.edu

Abstract. Information integrity in cache memories is a fundamental requirement for dependable computing. As caches comprise much of a CPU chip area
and transistor counts, they are reasonable targets for single and multiple transient faults. This paper presents: 1) a fault detection scheme for tag arrays of
cache memories and 2) an architectural cache to improve dependability as well
as performance. In this architecture, cache space is divided into sets of different
sizes and different tag lengths. The error detection scheme and the cache architecture have been evaluated using a trace driven simulation with soft error injection and SPEC 2000 applications. The results show that error detection improvement varies between 66% and 96% as compared with the already available single parity in microprocessors.

1 Introduction

Memory hierarchy is one of the most important elements in modern computer systems. In particular, cache memories are simple cost-effective elements to achieve
higher memory bandwidth, which significantly affects the peak throughput [19]. The
performance of the cache depends on several factors such as cache size, block size,
mapping function, replacement algorithm, and write policy [25]. Current modern
processor designs often devote a large fraction of on-chip transistors (up to 80%) to
caches [22]. Consequently, the reliability of caches affects the dependability of the
overall system. The purposes of integrating an error checking scheme in the memory
system such as caches are to prevent errors to propagate to other components and to
overcome the effects of errors locally. This contributes the overall goal of achieving
failure-free computation.

Transient faults can corrupt information in the memory [14], i.e., instructions and
data errors that may result in erroneous computation. In particular, errors in cache
memory that is the closest data storage to the CPU can easily propagate into the processor registers and other memory elements, and eventually cause computation failures. Although the cache memory quality has improved tremendously due to advances
in VLSI technology, it is not possible to completely avoid transient fault occurrences
[18]. As a result, data integrity checking, i.e., detecting and correcting soft errors, is
commonly used in cache memories.

There are two important error checking schemes: parity codes [28] and error-
correcting codes (ECC) [13]. Parity codes can detect odd number of errors and their

M. Heisel et al. (Eds.): SAFECOMP 2004, LNCS 3219, pp. 45–59, 2004.

power consumption is much less than ECC [5], however, ECC can correct errors. Each of these codes has a serious problem, i.e., the parity codes have low error detection capability [32], and the ECC codes incur low performance [24]. Moreover, using each of them in a uniform structure may occupy significant area space [9], [18]. It is due not to flexible in terms of chip area requirements as the area occupied by them is directly proportional to the cache size. For example, 12.5% area overhead is needed to store a parity for 8-bit data and the same overhead is required for an 8-bit SEC-DED (single error correction, double error detection) for a 64-bit entity. It should be noted that these codes could detect or correct only single error and have not good efficiency in the applications that are more prone to multiple-errors e.g., space applications.

This paper proposes a new cache architecture that exhibits a performance near to fully associative but its power and area are less than it. Using this algorithm, a new solution to the mentioned problem can be obtained since it enables us to provide a protection code such as generalized parity for every tag of cache line to detect multiple faults without compromising the performance or increasing significant area. In this scheme, cache space is divided into sets of different sizes, similar to set-associative one, but organized in a hierarchical structure where the size of the set at a given level is twice the size of the set in the next level of hierarchy. Thus, the scheme is called Hierarchical Binary Associative Mapping (HBAM).

The structure of the paper is as follows. Section 2 presents some related work. Section 3 gives an overview of the problem, the proposed cache architecture and fault detection method. Section 4 experimentally studies performance and fault detection of our method. Section 5 discusses hardware complexity and power consumption. Finally, section 6 concludes the paper.

2   Related Work

Sometimes a direct-mapped cache has a high miss rate, resulting in higher memory access time. Increasing cache associativity can decrease the cache miss rate and hence memory access time. For example, the average miss rate for the SPEC92 benchmarks is 4.6% for a direct-mapped 8Kbyte cache, 3.8% for a 2-way 8Kbyte cache and only 2.9% for 4-way 8Kbyte cache [11]. Though these differences may appear small, they in fact translate to big performance differences, due to the large penalty cycles of misses [33]. Higher associativity degree is important when the miss penalty is large and when memory and memory interconnect contention delays are significant or sensitive to the cache miss rate. Both situations may occur in shared-memory multiprocessors [8], [17]. A uniprocessor also may have a large miss penalty when it has only a first-level cache and the gap between processor and memory speed is large. Increasing associativity also has the advantage of reducing the probability of thrashing. Repeatedly accessing m different blocks that map into the same set will cause thrashing. A cache with an associativity degree of n can avoid such thrashing if $n \geq m$ and LRU replacement policy is employed [34]. A hash-rehash cache [1] uses two mapping functions to determine the candidate location with associativity of two and by sequential search, but higher miss rate results from non-LRU replacement. Agarwal et al. [2] proposed the column-associative cache that improves the hash-rehash cash by adding hardware to implement LRU replacement policy. The predicative sequential associative cache proposed by Calder et al. [7], uses bit selection, a sequential search and steering bit table, which is indexed by predictive sources to determine search order. However this approach is based on prediction, which may be incorrect and has slightly longer average access time. Skewed-associative cache [23] increases associativity in orthogonal dimension using skewing function instead of bit selection to determine candidate locations. The major drawbacks of this scheme are a longer cycle time and the mapping hardware necessary for skewing.

Ranagathan [22] proposed a configurable cache architecture useful for media processing which divide the cache into partitions at the granularity of the conventional cache. The key drawback of it is that the number and granularity of the partitions are limited by the associativity of the cache and also it causes to modify the hardware of the cache to support dynamic partitioning and associativity. Another configurable cache architecture has been proposed in [33], which intended for some specific applications of embedded systems. The cache mapping function can be configured by software to be direct mapped, 2-way, or 4-way set-associative caches.

Also, several studies have been done to provide fault-tolerance in caches memories [18], [24], [32]. In [18], a very small cache was proposed to store parity information or to duplicate recently used data with a very good hit rate. In [24], a programmable address decoder was proposed to disable faulty blocks and to remap their references to non-faulty blocks. But area overhead for a typical 16KB cache is 11% of total cache area. Replicating data in the cache to enhance reliability was proposed in [32]. The fault detection scheme was either parity or ECC, and in the case of detecting faults, one of the replications of the affected word in the cache was used. However, this scheme can detect only single transient faults and has significant effects on the performance of the cache such that miss rate of the cache increases up to 4 times.

3 Problem Overview

3.1 Errors in Cache and Their Effect

Use of lower voltage levels, high speed data read/write operations and extremely dense circuitry increase the probability of transient fault occurrence, resulting in more bit errors in cache memories. Moreover, external disturbances such as noise, power jitter, local heat densities, and ionization due to alpha-particle hits can also corrupt the information [16].

Most of transistors in a cache are in memory cells. Hence, the probability that a given defect is in a memory cell (a bit in the data or tag field) is higher than the probability of it being in the logic circuitry.

Furthermore, the faults occurred in a tag field are more serious than those affect on the data field. It is due to 1) the size of a CAM cell is about double as that of a RAM cell [21], 2) each tag entry is responsible for storing/retrieving several words in its corresponded block. This means that a given fault in the tag has B (block size) times crucial effects more than the similar one occurred in a word of the corresponded block, and 3) bit changes in the tag cause the improper cache hit and miss decisions i.e., pseudo-hit, multi-hit, and pseudo-miss, and make the memory references to be invalid. In the case of a pseudo-hit, the processor gets wrong data on a read and updates the data in the wrong location on a write. A pseudo-miss generates an unnecessary main memory access. The multi-hit may be detected by the cache controller but handling is not simple. The controller cannot distinguish between the multiple hit lines to service the processor's request.

Parity codes are extensively used in cache memories of today's modern processors. As an example, the parity checking employed in data cache in the Pentium® processors [26] are: 1) parity bit per byte in the cache storage RAM, and 2) parity per entry in the tag array. However, parity can only detect odd number of errors (coverage of 50%) and is not suitable for the applications which need high reliability. For example, a relatively large fraction of the transient faults caused by alpha-particle radiation or heavy-ion [16] manifests as multiple-bit errors i.e., single-event multiple upsets [4] [27].

3.2 HBAM Cache Organization

Let C be the cache size in blocks. According to the HBAM scheme there are $\log_2 C + 1$ sets. Set i consists of B_i blocks where

$$B_i = \begin{cases} C/2^{(i+1)}, & if \ \ 0 \leq i < \log_2 C \\ 1, & if \ \ i = \log_2 C \end{cases} \tag{1}$$

Size of sets varies in power of 2. The first set has the largest size of $C/2$ blocks while the last two sets contain a minimum of 1 block each. This means if frequently-referenced blocks can be mapped into larger associative-sets, a higher hit ratio can be achieved. Also, the cost of this scheme is less than the cost of fully-associative scheme. Due to the separate logic associated to each set, its operation is relatively faster compared to fully-associative mapping and slower than set-associative mapping. In this scheme, address translation is performed dynamically (value-based) instead of statically (bit selection) in the direct mapping scheme. This means that there is no predefined specified format to determine set number of a memory address in the cache. The set number should be determined using the address pattern coming from the CPU. Figure 1 shows the set organization of a HBAM cache.

Suppose the block size is $B = 2^b$ words. For an n-bit address pattern $A = A_{n-1}A_{n-2}...A_0$, the b low-significant bits determine the offset of the required word in the block containing the word. The set number is given by the number of zero bits preceding the offset. Table 1 portrays the address mapping function and required bits for tag storing.

3.3 The Proposed Protection Code

In the HBAM cache, the reduced area, related to tag storage, was used for a protection code. The utilized protection code is named generalized parity (GParity). A generalized parity in radix r, which also includes the even-parity when the radix is two, is sum of 1's in the word modulo r. It behaves as a checksum for the word and can detect any simultaneously single-event faults where number of faults is not divisible by r. As an example, the following figure show a HBAM tag of a memory address whose 3 bits are not necessary for storing. Its GParity in radix 8, which used for protecting this tag has been shown, as well. Its GParity is 5 since the number of 1's in the memory address is 5.

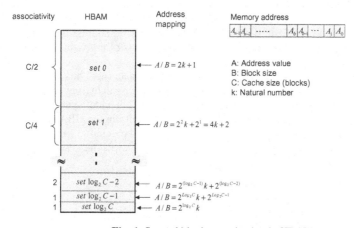

Fig. 1. Set and block organization in HBAM

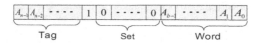

Fig. 2. Memory address format used for mapping function in HBAM

Table 1. Address mapping and required bits for tag in each set

Set #	Logical condition	Tag bits	# of bits in tags	# of dedicated lines in set
0	$A_b = 1$	$A_{n-1} \, downto \, A_{b+1}$	n-b-1	C/2
1	$A_{b+1} \overline{A_b} = 1$	$A_{n-1} \, downto \, A_{b+2}$	n-b-2	C/4
2	$A_{b+2} \overline{A_{b+1}} \, \overline{A_b} = 1$	$A_{n-1} \, downto \, A_{b+3}$	n-b-3	C/8
...	...	...	...	...
$\log_2 C - 2$	$A_{b+\log C-2} \overline{A_{b+\log C-3} ... \overline{A_b}} = 1$	$A_{n-2} \, downto \, A_{b+\log C-1}$	n-b-log C+1	2
$\log_2 C - 1$	$A_{b+\log C-1} \overline{A_{b+\log C-2} ... \overline{A_b}} = 1$	$A_{n-1} \, downto \, A_{b+\log C}$	n-b-log C	1
$\log_2 C$	$\overline{A_{b+\log C-1}} \, \overline{A_{b+\log C-2} ... \overline{A_b}} = 1$	$A_{n-1} \, downto \, A_{b+\log C}$	n-b-log C	1

memory address	GParity	tag in the HBAM
0100 1001 1000 0100	101	0 100 1001 1000 0

Fig. 3. A generalized parity in radix 8 for a memory address used in the HBAM cache

This protection code is more suitable for the HBAM because: 1) it can be easily adjusted to any length of bits, 2) it only depends on the number of 1's in the tag (or memory address) and hence can be calculated in parallel with address decoding, and 3) it can detect more portion of faults due to multiple effects of transient faults are all in the same event e.g., single-event multiple upsets [27].

In HBAM cache, all tags of a set whose number is i, has an $(i+1)$ bits length GParity, i.e., a GParity in radix 2^{i+1}. The cost of adder needed for calculating sum of 1's is negligible in total cost of the cache [10]. For example, a 32-bit adder synthesized via a common synthesis tool, use only 32 LUTs. Using the GParity in the HBAM cause the fault detection coverage to be improved and makes it to be suitable for dependable computing systems such as dependable embedded systems which have serious limitations in the area space.

4 Experimental Study

The cache simulator in [6] was modified to simulate the proposed HBAM cache scheme. Benchmarks used in this trace-driven simulation included several different kinds of programs of SPEC2000 benchmarks [35], namely *bzip2, apsi, swim, vortex, eon_cook, eon_rush, gcc, gzip, parser, sixtrack,* and *vpr.* Each file contains at least 100000000 references. Both data and instruction references are collected and used for the simulation. Three well-known placement schemes, i.e., the direct, set-associative, and fully-associative mapping are chosen for performance comparison and evaluation.

4.1 Performance Analysis

Two major performance metrics i.e., the miss (hit) ratio and the average memory access time are used to evaluate and compare the HBAM cache with other schemes. First the direct-mapped cache is compared in terms of miss (hit) ratio and average memory access time. Second the set-associative and fully-associative caches are compared.

The cache miss ratios for the conventional direct-mapped cache and the proposed HBAM cache are shown in Figure 4. For the direct-mapped cache denoted as DC in the figure, the notation "8k-8byte" denotes an 8KB direct-mapped cache with a block size of 8 bytes. For each benchmark, the miss ratios are shown for various cache sizes and block sizes. Notice the average miss ratio of the HBAM cache for a given large cache size (e.g., 32KB) is about that of conventional direct-mapped caches with a size of four times larger. Another useful measure to evaluate the performance of any given memory-hierarchy is the average memory access time, which is given by

$$\text{Average memory access time} = \text{Hit time} + \text{Miss rate} \cdot \text{Miss penalty} \qquad (2)$$

Here *hit time* is the time to process a hit in the cache and *miss penalty* is the additional time to service the miss penalty. The basic parameters for the simulation are: CPU clock =200 MHz, Memory latency=15 CPU cycles, Memory bandwidth=1.6 Gb/s. The hit time is assumed to be 1 CPU cycle. These parameters are based on the values for common 32-bit embedded processors (i.e., ARM920T [3] or Hitachi SH4 [12]).

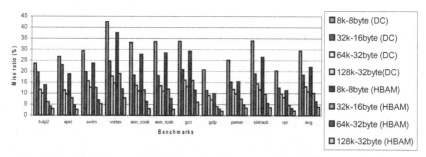

Fig. 4. Miss ratio of the direct-mapped cache and the HBAM cache.

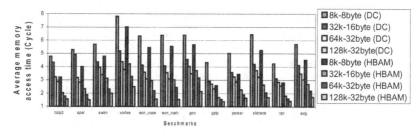

Fig. 5. Average memory access time of the direct-mapped cache and the HBAM cache.

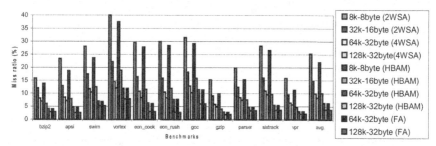

Fig. 6. Miss ratio of the set-associative cache, the fully-associative cache, and the HBAM cache.

The average memory access time for the conventional direct-mapped cache and the HBAM cache are shown in Figure 5. As a result of benchmark analysis, application with high degree of locality like *vpr* shows particularly higher performance improvement in using HBAM cache. Also, the cache miss-ratios and the average memory access time for the conventional k-way set-associative cache ($k = 2, 4$), fully-associative cache, and the proposed HBAM cache are shown in Figure 6 and 7. In these figures the 2-way, the 4-way set-associative, and fully-associative caches are denoted as 2WSA and 4WSA, and FA, respectively. As shown in both figures, HBAM behaves very closely to the fully-associative cache in the miss ratio and the average memory access time instead of the conventional set-associative cache. In the case of large cache size (e.g., 32KB) the average memory access time of HBAM equals these conventional set-associative caches with a size of two times as much as the given cache size for the 4-way set-associative.

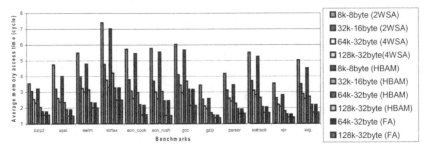

Fig. 7. Average memory access time of the set-associative cache, the fully-associative cache, and the HBAM cache.

In the case of simulating the set-associative cache, N sets, $2 \leq N \leq 512$, have been considered. For brevity, only some selected figures are shown here. Figures 8-11 show the plot of hit ratio against cache size for four selected benchmarks, while figures 12-15 show similar curves for the effects of block size to cache performance. They illustrate comparative performance of the conventional placement schemes (fully-associative, set-associative and direct mapping) and the HBAM scheme. Notice that there is a general trend of the HBAM scheme exhibiting higher hit ratios (except for fully-associative scheme). It can be seen, in figures 8-11, that the HBAM scheme outperforms the set-associative and direct mapping schemes for a wide variety of cache configurations. For instance, Fig. 8 shows the hit ratio of the considered schemes for benchmark *bzip2* (with the set size of 8 blocks in set-associative mapping) where each block contains 8 bytes. Fig. 12 shows the effect of block size to the hit ratio for a cache size of 8 KB for HBAM scheme and other schemes. As can be seen in the figures, the hit ratio of the HBAM scheme is closer to fully-associative cache than the other schemes.

4.2 Fault Injection and Fault Detection Coverage

For evaluation of the proposed protection code, we have simulated the scheme using the benchmarks in the presence of randomly injected faults and fault detection coverage of the protection code has been calculated. A typical cache size 8Kbyte with block size of 64 byte has been used. In this evaluation three cache schemes were equipped by GParity with the same hardware cost, and their performance and coverage were considered.

Table 2 portrays the number of bits and radix of GParity used in these caches and also shows their experimentally calculated fault coverage. The coverage of GParity when the radix is high (in set-associative), is near to 98% while for the HBAM and fully-associative caches are close to 83% and 50%, respectively. It shows that GParity behaves as a good protection code for detecting transient faults.

Though fault coverage of HBAM is less than set-associative cache, but its miss ratio is less than that of set-associative cache, as shown in the Fig. 17. Conversely, the fault coverage of the HBAM is more than fully-associative cache while its performance is less than it. For more precisely consideration, we compared their fractions of coverage by miss-ratio as a good metric which incorporates both of fault-tolerance

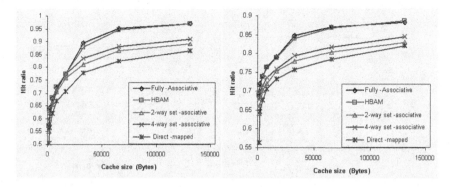

Fig. 8. Hit ratio vs. cache size; block size= 8Byte, benchmark = *bzip2*

Fig. 9. Hit ratio vs. cache size; block size= 8Byte, benchmark = *swim*

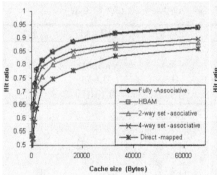

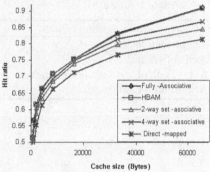

Fig. 10. Hit ratio vs. cache size; block size= 8Byte, benchmark = *parser*

Fig. 11. Hit ratio vs. cache size; block size= 8Byte, benchmark = *gcc*

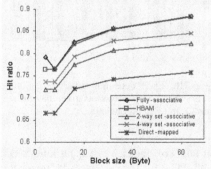

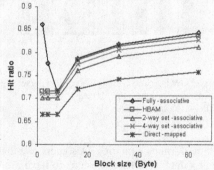

Fig. 12. Hit ratio vs. block size; cache size= 8KByte, benchmark = *swim*

Fig. 13. Hit ratio vs. block size; cache size= 8KByte, benchmark = *bzip7*

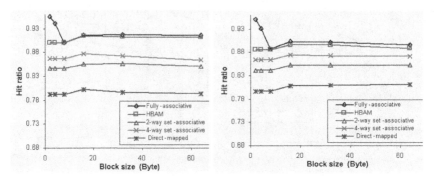

Fig. 14. Hit ratio vs. block size; cache size= 8KByte, benchmark = *gzip*

Fig. 15. Hit ratio vs. block size; cache size= 8KByte, benchmark = *vpr*

Table 2. Fault detection coverage with same hardware cost for 8Kbyte cache

parameters and results	2WSA	HBAM	FA
# of protection bits	6	Variable	1
Radix of GParity	64	Variable	2
Avg. of calculated fault detection coverage	0.98	0.83	0.50
Avg. of miss ratio	0.1718	0.1307	0.126

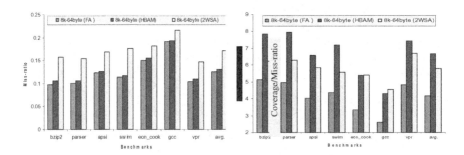

Fig. 17. Miss-ratio comparison of 2-way set-associative cache, the HBAM cache and Fully-associative cache

Fig. 18. Fault detection coverage per miss-ratio for 2-way set-associative, the HBAM cache and Fully-associative cache

and performance metrics. Designers like that fault coverage as well as hit-ratio to take high value. This leads designs to have a high value for the coverage per miss-ratio. Fig. 18 shows the coverage per miss-ratio for the mentioned cache architectures. As shown in the figure, the HBAM cache, specially in the average case, outperforms both of the fully-associative and 2-way set-associative cache, except for the *gcc* and *eon-cook* which present less spatial locality of memory references and cause more miss ratio for the full-associative and the HBAM cache.

5 Cost and Power Consumption Analysis

5.1 Hardware Complexity

In order to reduce latency of tag comparison in fully-associative caches, these memories are constructed using CAM (content addressable memories) structures. Since each CAM cell is designed as a combination of storage and comparison logic, the size of a CAM cell is about double as that of a RAM cell [21]. For fair performance/cost analysis, the performance for various direct and HBAM caches are evaluated. The metric used to normalize cost-area analysis is *rbe* (register bit equivalents).

We use the same quantities used in [19], where the complexity of *PLA* (programmable logic array) circuit is assumed to be 130 *rbe*, a RAM cell as 0.6 *rbe*, and a *CAM* cell as 1.2 *rbe*. The *RAM* area can be calculated as [21]

$$RAM = 0.6 \left[\#entries + \#L_{sense\,amplifiers} \right] \cdot \left[(\#data\,bits + \#status\,bits) + W_{driver} \right] \quad (3)$$

where $\#entries$ is the number of rows in tag array or data array, $\#L_{sense\,amplifiers}$ is the length of a bit-line sense amplifier, $\#data\,bits$ indicates the number of tag bits (or data bits) of one set, $\#status\,bits$ is the state bit of one set, and W_{driver} is the data width of a driver. The area of *CAM* can be given by [21]

$$CAM = 0.6 \left[\sqrt{2} \cdot \#entries + \#L_{sense\,amplifiers} \right] \cdot \left[\sqrt{2} \cdot \#tag\,bits + W_{driver} \right] \quad (4)$$

where $\#tag\,bits$ is the number of bits for one set in the tag array. The total area can be given by

$$Area = RAM + CAM + PLA \quad (5)$$

The area of HBAM cache was calculated by assuming that it is composed of several fully-associative caches, each of which has its specified size and tags. Table 3 shows the performance/cost for various cache sizes. The HBAM cache (2KB with 8-byte block size) shows about 45% area reduction compared to the conventional direct-mapped cache (8KB with 8-byte block size) while showing almost equal closed performance gains. Also higher performance for HBAM scheme may be achieved by increasing the size of caches, compared to direct mapping schemes.

Table 3. Performance and cost of direct-mapped cache and HBAM cache

Cache Configuration	Area (*rbe*)	Average Miss ratio (%)	Avg. memory access time (cycles)
1KB-8byte (DC)	1507	0.45439	8.2703
2KB-8byte (DC)	2944	0.38587	7.1740
4KB-8byte (DC)	5773	0.32477	6.1964
8KB-8byte (DC)	11356	0.29335	5.6936
1KB-8byte (HBAM)	3758	0.34361	6.4977
2KB-8byte (HBAM)	6254	0.28602	5.5764
4KB-8byte (HBAM)	11356	0.24745	4.9592
8KB-8byte (HBAM)	23547	0.22014	4.5222

5.2 Power Consumption

Energy dissipation in CMOS integrated circuits can be mainly caused due to charging and discharging gate capacitance. The energy dissipated per transition is given by [19]

$$E_t = 0.5 \cdot C_{eq} \cdot V^2 \tag{6}$$

To obtain the values for the equivalent capacitance, C_{eq}, of components in the memory subsystem, we follow the model proposed by Wilton and Jouppi [31]. Their model assumes a 0.8um process and a supply voltage of 3.3 volts. To obtain the number of transitions that occur at each transistor, the model introduced by Kamble and Ghost [14], [15] is adapted here. According to this model, the main sources of power are determined to be the following four components: E_{bits}, E_{word}, E_{output}, and E_{input}. These notations denote the energy dissipation for bit-lines, word-lines, address and data output lines, and address input lines, respectively. The energy consumption is then given by

$$E_{cache} = E_{bits} + E_{word} + E_{output} + E_{input} \tag{7}$$

Energy dissipated in the bit lines. E_{bits} is the energy consumption of all the bit-lines when SRAMs are accessed; it is due to pre-charging lines and reading or writing data. It is assumed that the tags and data array in the direct-mapped cache can be accessed in parallel. In order to minimize the power overhead introduced in fully associative caches, first a tag look-up is performed and the data array is then accessed only if a hit occurs. In a K-way set-associative cache, the E_{bits} can be calculated as

$$E_{bits} = 0.5 \cdot V^2 \cdot \left[N_{bp} C_{bp} + K \cdot (N_{hit} + N_{miss}) \cdot (8B + T + S) \cdot (C_{g,Q_{pa}} + C_{g,Q_{pb}} + C_{g,Q_p}) + N_{bw} C_{ba} + N_{br} C_{ba} \right] \tag{8}$$

where N_{bp}, N_{bw}, and N_{br} are the total number of transitions in the bit lines due to precharge, the number of writes, and the number of reads, respectively. B is the size of block in bytes, T is the tag size of one set, and S denotes the number of status bits per block. $C_{g,Q_{pa}}$, $C_{g,Q_{pb}}$, and C_{g,Q_p} are the gate capacitance of the transistor C_Q. Finally, C_{bp} and C_{ba} are the effective load capacitance of each bit line during pre-charging, and reading/writing from/to the cell. According to the results reported in [31], we have

$$C_{bp} = N_{rows} \cdot \left[0.5 \cdot C_{drain,Q_1} + C_{bitwire} \right] \tag{9}$$

$$C_{ba} = N_{rows} \cdot \left[0.5 \cdot C_{drain,Q_1} + C_{bitwire} \right] + C_{drain,Q_p} + C_{drain,Q_{pa}} \tag{10}$$

where C_{drain,Q_1} is the drain capacitance of transistor Q_1, and $C_{bitwire}$ is the bit wire capacitance of a single bit cell.

Energy dissipated in the word lines. E_{word} is energy consumption due to assertion of a particular word-line; once the bit-lines are all precharged, one row is selected, performing read/write to the desired data. E_{word} can be calculated as [31]

$$E_{word} = V^2 \cdot K \cdot [N_{hit} + N_{miss}] \cdot [8B + T + S] \cdot \left[2C_{gate,Q_1} + C_{wordwire} \right] \qquad (11)$$

where $C_{wordwire}$ is the word-wire capacitance. Thus,

$$C_{wordwire} = N_{column} \cdot \left[2C_{gate,Q_1} + C_{wordwire} \right] \qquad (12)$$

Energy dissipated at the data and address output lines. E_{output} is the energy used to drive external buses; this component includes power consumption for both the data sent or returned and the address sent to the lower level memory based on a miss request. E_{output} can be calculated as

$$E_{output} = E_{addr\,output} + E_{data\,output} \qquad (13)$$

where $E_{addr\,output}$ and $E_{data\,output}$ are the energy dissipation at the address and data lines, and are given by

$$E_{addr\,output} = 0.5 \cdot V^2 \cdot N_{addr\,output} \cdot C_{addr\,out} \qquad (14)$$

$$E_{data\,output} = 0.5 \cdot V^2 \cdot N_{data\,output} \cdot C_{data\,out} \qquad (15)$$

where $N_{addr\,output}$ and $N_{data\,output}$ are the total number of transitions at the address and data output lines, respectively. $C_{addr\,out}$ and $C_{data\,out}$ are their corresponding capacitive loads. The capacitive load for on-chip destinations is 0.5pF and for off-chip destinations is 20pF [29].

Energy dissipated at the address input lines. E_{input} is the energy dissipated at the input gates of the row decoder. The energy dissipated at the address decoders is not considered, since this value turns out to be negligible compared to the other components [19]. The actual values of different factors of power dissipation are obtained by using the above-mentioned equations and assumptions. Table 4 shows the various capacitance values.

To obtain the actual power consumption, the tag array of each section in the proposed cache must be considered as a CAM structure. By considering the proposed cache as a collection of several set-associative caches with different tag width, these values were obtained. Now the power consumption of the proposed cache can be compared with that of the associative cache. Any comparison with conventional directed-mapped caches is not provided because of their low performance observed for different cache sizes.

Fig. 19 presents the power consumption of the fully-associative cache and the HBAM cache with the same cache size. As will be shown in later, the fully-associative cache can achieve slightly better performance gain compared to the HBAM cache, but the aspect of power consumption can provide a significant effect. Bit-lines of large block size and a large number of content swaps influence the high power consumption for the fully-associative cache compared to the HBAM cache. Thus it is shown that power consumption of the HBAM cache is reduced by about 3-10% when comparing to that of the fully-associative cache configuration.

Table 4. Capacitance values

Cdrain,Q1	2.737 fF
Cbitwire	4.4 fF/bitcell
Cdrain,Qp	80.89 fF
Cdrain,Qpa	80.89 fF
Cgate,Q1	0.401fF
Cwordwire	1.8 fF/bitcell
Cg,Qp	38.08 fF
Cg,Qpa,	38.08 fF
Cg,Qpb	
Caddroutput	0.5pF(on-chip)
Cdataoutput	20 pF(off-chip)

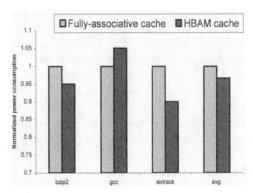

Fig. 19. Power consumption of fully-associative cache and HBAM cache

6   Conclusions

This paper proposed a fault detection scheme namely GParity and a cache architecture based on hierarchical binary associative mapping, called HBAM, which provides sets of different sizes. This architecture enabled designers to utilize the proposed protection code for every tag of cache line to improve fault detection coverage without compromising the performance or increasing significant area. Results obtained using a trace-driven simulator and soft-error injection revealed that HBAM can provide significant performance improvements with respect to traditional schemes and error detection coverage has been improved as compared with the already available single parity microprocessors.

Acknowledgements. The authors would like to thank Hamid Sarbazi-Azad for his contributions in the initial stages of this work and the anonymous referees for providing helpful comments.

References

1.   Agarwal A., Hennessy J., Horowitz M.: Cache Performance of Operating Systems and Multiprogramming. ACM Trans. Computer Systems, Vol. 6, No. 4 (1988) 393-431
2.   Agarwal A., Pudar S. D.: Column-Associative Caches: a Technique for Reducing the Miss Rate of Direct-Mapped Caches. Int'l Symp. on Computer Architecture (1993) 179-190
3.   ARM Company: ARM920T Technical Reference Manual. http://www.arm.com
4.   Asadi G., Miremadi S. G., Zarandi H. R., Ejlali A. R.: Evaluation of Fault-Tolerant Designs Implemented on SRAM-based FPGAs. Proc. IEEE/IFIP Pacific Rim International Symposium on Dependable Computing, French (2004) 327-333
5.   Bertozzi D., Benini L., De Micheli G.: Low Power Error Resilient Encoding for On-chip Data Buses. Proc. of Design, Automation and Test in Europe Conference, France (2002) 102-109
6.   Brigham Young University: BYU Cache Simulator. http://tds.cs.byu.edu
7.   Calder B., Grunwald D.: Predictive Sequential Associative Cache. Proc. 2nd Int'l Symp. High performance Computer Architecture (1996) 244-253

8. Chen H., Chiang J.: Design of an Adjustable-way Set-Associative Cache. Proc. Pacific Rim Communications, Computers and signal Processing (2001) 315-318
9. Faridpour A., Hill M.: Performance Implications of Tolerating Cache Faults. IEEE Trans. on Computers, Vol. 42, No. 3 (1993) 257-267
10. Farooqui A. A., Oklobdzija V. G., Sait S. M.: Area-Time Optimal Adder with Relative Placement Generator. Proc. of Int. Symp. on Circuits and Systems, Vol. 5, (2003) 141-144
11. Hennessy J. L., Patterson D. A.: Computer architecture Quantitative Approach. 2nd Edition, Morgan-Kaufmann Publishing Co. (1996)
12. Hitachi Company: SH4 Embedded Processor. http://www.hitachi.com
13. Imai H.: Essentials of Error-Control Coding Techniques. Academic Press, San Diego, (1990)
14. Kamble M. B., Ghose K.: Analytical Energy Dissipation Models for Low Power Caches. Proc. of Intl. Symp. on Low Power Electronics and Design (1997) 143-148
15. Kamble M. B., Ghose K.: Energy-Efficiency of VLSI Cache: A Comparative Study. Proc. IEEE 10th Int'l. Conf. on VLSI Design (1997) 261-267
16. Karlsson J., Liden P., Dahlgern P., Johansson R., Gunneflo U.: Using Heavy-Ion Radiation to Validate Fault-Handling Mechanisms. IEEE Micro, Vol. 14 (1994) 8-23
17. Kessler R. R., et al.: Inexpensive Implementations of Associativity. Proc. Intl. Symp. Computer Architecture (1989) 131-139
18. Kim S., Somani A.: Area Efficient Architectures for Information Integrity Checking in the Cache Memories. Proc. Intl. Symp. Computer Architecture (1999) 246-256
19. Lee J. H., Lee J. S., Kim S. D.: A New Cache Architecture based on Temporal and Spatial Locality. Journal of Systems Architecture, Vol. 46 (2000) 1452-1467
20. Miremadi G., Torin J.: Evaluating Processor-Behavior and Three Error-Detection Mechanisms Using Physical Fault Injection. IEEE Trans. Reliability, Vol. 44 (1995). 441-453
21. Mulder J. M., Quach N. T., Flynn M. J.: An Area Model for On-Chip Memories and its Applications. IEEE journal of solid state Circuits, Vol. 26 (1991) 98-106
22. Ranganathan P., Adve S., Jouppi N. P.: Reconfigurable Caches and their Application to Media Processing. Proc. Int. Symp. Computer Architecture (2000) 214-224
23. Seznec A.: A Case for Two-Way Skewed-Associative Caches. Proc. Intl. Symp. Computer Architecture (1993) 169-178
24. Shirvani P., McCuskey E. J.: PADded Cache: A New Fault-Tolerance Technique for Cache Memories. Proc. 17th IEEE VLSI Test Symp. (1999) 440-445
25. Smith A. J.: Cache memories. Computing Survey, Vol. 14, No. 4 (1982) 473-530
26. Intel Corporation: Pentium® Family Developer's Manual. http://www.intel.com
27. Reed R.: Heavy Ion and Proton Induced Single Event Multiple Upsets. IEEE Nuclear and Space Radiation Effects Conference (1997)
28. Swazey P.: SRAM Organization, Control, and Speed, and Their Effect on Cache Memory Design. Midcon/87 (1987) 434-437
29. Wilton S. J. E., Jouppi N. P.: An Enhanced Access and Cycle Time Model for On-chip Caches. Digital WRL Research Report 93/5 (1994).
30. Wu A., Meador J.: Fast, Area-Efficient CMOS Parity Generation. Proc. 33rd Midwest Symposium on Circuits and Systems (1990) 874-876
31. Wilton S. J. E., Jouppi N. P.: CACTI: An Enhancement Cache Access and Cycle Time Model. IEEE Journal of Solid-State Circuits, Vol. 31 (1996) 677-688
32. Zhang W., Gurumurthi S., Kandemir M., Sivasubramaniam A.: ICR: In-Cache Replication for Enhancing Data Cache Reliability. In Proceedings of the International Conference on Dependable Systems and Networks (DSN) (2003) 291-300
33. Zhang C., Vahid F., Najjar W.: A Highly Configurable Cache Architecture for Embedded Systems. Int. Symp. on Computer Architecture (2003) 136-146
34. Zhang C., Zhang X., Yan Y.: Two Fast and High-Associativity Cache Schemes. IEEE micro (1997) 40-49
35. Standard Performance Evaluation Corporation: SPEC CPU 2000 benchmarks. http://www.specbench.org/osg/cpu2000

An Empirical Exploration of the Difficulty Function

Julian G.W. Bentley, Peter G. Bishop, and Meine van der Meulen

Centre for Software Reliability
City University
Northampton Square
London EC1V 0HB, UK

Abstract. The theory developed by Eckhardt and Lee (and later extended by Littlewood and Miller) utilises the concept of a "difficulty function" to estimate the expected gain in reliability of fault tolerant architectures based on diverse programs. The "difficulty function" is the likelihood that a randomly chosen program will fail for any given input value. To date this has been an abstract concept that explains why dependent failures are likely to occur. This paper presents an empirical measurement of the difficulty function based on an analysis of over six thousand program versions implemented to a common specification. The study derived a "score function" for each version. It was found that several different program versions produced identical score functions, which when analysed, were usually found to be due to common programming faults. The score functions of the individual versions were combined to derive an approximation of the difficulty function. For this particular (relatively simple) problem specification, it was shown that the difficulty function derived from the program versions was fairly flat, and the reliability gain from using multi-version programs would be close to that expected from the independence assumption.

1 Introduction

The concept of using diversely developed programs (N-version programming) to improve reliability was first proposed by Avizienis [1]. However, experimental studies of N-version programming showed that the failures of the diverse versions were not independent, for example [2, 4] showed that common specification faults existed, and Knight and Leveson [6] demonstrated that failure dependency existed between diverse implementation faults to a high level of statistical confidence. More generally, theoretical models of diversity show that dependent failures are likely to exist for any pair of programs. The most notable models have been developed by Eckhardt and Lee [5] and Littlewood and Miller [7]. A recent exposition of these theories can be found in [8]. These models predict that, if the "difficulty" of correct execution varies with the input value, program versions developed "independently" will, on average, not fail independently. A key parameter in these models is the "difficulty function". This function represents the likelihood that a randomly chosen program will fail for any given input scenario (i.e. the probability that the programmer is more likely to make a mistake handling this particular input scenario).

M. Heisel et al. (Eds.): SAFECOMP 2004, LNCS 3219, pp. 60–71, 2004.
© Springer-Verlag Berlin Heidelberg 2004

While there has been considerable theoretical analysis of diversity, and empirical measurement of reliability improvement, there has been little research on the direct measurement of the difficulty function. This paper presents an empirical analysis of many thousands of "independently" developed program versions written to a common specification in a programming contest. The objectives of the study were:

- to directly measure the failure regions for each program version,
- to examine the underlying causes for faults that lead to similar or identical failure regions,
- to compute the difficulty function by combining the failure region results
- to assess the average reliability improvement of diverse program pairs, and compare it with the improve expected if the failures were independent.

The focus of this study was on diverse *implementation* faults. The correctness, completeness and accuracy of the specification were considered to be outside the scope of this project. However, specification-related problems were encountered in the study, and are discussed later in the paper.

In Section 2 of the paper we describe the source of the program versions used in this study, Section 3 summarises the difficulty function theory, Section 4 describes the measurements performed on the programs, while Sections 5 and 6 present an analysis of the results. Sections 7 and 8 discuss the results and draw some preliminary conclusions.

2   The Programming Contest Software Resource

In the past, obtaining many independently developed program versions by different authors to solve a particular problem would have been difficult. However, with wider use of the Internet, the concept of "programming contests" has evolved. "Contest Hosts" specify mathematical or logical challenges (specifications) to be solved programmatically by anyone willing and able to participate. Participants make submissions of program versions that attempt to satisfy the published specification. These are then "judged" (usually by some automated test system at the contest site) and then accepted or rejected.

We established contact with the organiser of one of these sites (the University of Valladolid) which hosts contest problems for the ACM and additional contest problems maintained by the University [9]. The organiser supplied over six thousand program submissions for one of its published problems. The programs varied by author, country of origin, and programming language. Authors often submitted several versions in attempting to produce a correct solution to the problem. This program corpus formed the basis for our research study.

Clearly, there are issues about realism of these programs when compared to "real world" software development practices, and these issues are discussed in Section 7. However the availability of so many program versions does allow genuine statistical studies to be made, and does allow conjectures to be made which can be tested on other examples. In addition such conjectures can be evaluated on actual industrial software and hence have the potential to be extended to a wider class of programs.

3 Probability of Failure and the Difficulty Function

Two of the most well known probability models in this domain, are the Eckhardt and Lee model [5], and, the Littlewood and Miller extended model [7]. Both models assume that:

1. Failures of an individual program π are deterministic and a program version either fails or succeeds for each input value x. The failure region of a program π can be represented by a "score" function" $\omega(\pi, x)$ which produces a zero if the program succeeds for a given x or a one if it fails.
2. There is randomness due to the development process. This is represented as the random selection of a program from the set of all possible program versions Π that can feasibly be developed and/or envisaged. The probability that a particular version π will be produced is $P(\pi)$.
3. There is randomness due to the demands in operation. This is represented by the (random) set of all possible demands X (i.e. inputs and/or states) that can possibly occur, together with the probability of selection of a given input demand x, $P(x)$.

Using these model assumptions, the average probability of a program version failing on a given demand is given by the *difficulty function*, $\theta(x)$, where:

$$\theta(x) = \sum_{\pi} \omega(\pi, x) P(\pi) \tag{1}$$

The average probability of failure per demand (*pfd*) of a randomly chosen single program version can be computed using the difficulty function and the demand profile $P(x)$:

$$E(\text{pfd}_1) = \sum_{x} \theta(x) P(x) \tag{2}$$

The average pfd of randomly chosen pair of program versions (π_A, π_B) taken from two possible populations A and B is:

$$E(\text{pfd}_2) = \sum_{x} \theta_A(x) \theta_B(x) P(x) \tag{3}$$

The Eckhardt and Lee model assumes similar development processes for A and B and hence identical difficulty functions

$$E(\text{pfd}_2) = \sum_{x} \theta(x)^2 P(x) \tag{4}$$

where $\theta(x)$ is the common difficulty function. If $\theta(x)$ is constant for all x (i.e. the difficulty function is "flat") then, the reliability improvement for a diverse pair will (on average) satisfy the independence assumption, i.e.:

$$E(\text{pfd}_2) = E(\text{pfd}_1)^2 \tag{5}$$

However if the difficulty function is "bumpy", it is always the case that:

$$E(\text{pfd}_2) \geq E(\text{pfd}_1)^2 \tag{6}$$

If there is a very "spiky" difficulty surface, the diverse program versions tend to fail on exactly the same inputs. Consequently, diversity is likely to yield little benefit and pfd_2 is close to pfd_1. If, however, there is a relatively "flat" difficulty surface the program versions do not tend to fail on the same inputs and hence pfd_2 is closer to pfd_1^2 (the independence assumption).

If the populations A and B differ (the Littlewood and Miller model), the improvement can, in principle, be *better* that the independence assumption, i.e. when the "valleys" in $\theta_A(x)$ coincide with the "hills" in $\theta_B(x)$, it is possible for the expected pfd_2 to be less than that predicted by the independence assumption.

4   Experimental Study

For our study we selected a relatively simple Contest Host problem. The problem specified that two inputs, velocity (v) and time (t) had to be used to compute a displacement or distance (d). The problem had defined integer input ranges. Velocity v had a defined range of ($-100 \le v \le 100$), whilst time t was defined as ($0 \le t \le 200$). A set of 40401 unique values would therefore cover all possible input combinations that could be submitted for the calculation. However, this was not the entire input domain, because the problem specification permitted an arbitrary sequence of input lines, each specifying a new calculation. If all possible sequences of the input pairs (v, t) were considered, assuming no constraints on sequencing or repetition, the input domain for the program could be viewed as infinite. However, as each line of input should be computed independently from every other line, the sequence order should not be relevant, so the experiment chose to base its analysis on the combination of all possible values of v and t. This can be viewed as a projection of the input domain (which has a third "sequence" dimension) on to the (v, t) plane.

The experiment set up a test harness to apply a sequence of 40401 different values of v and t to the available versions. The results for each version were recorded and compared against a selected "oracle" program. The success or failure of each input could then be determined. Some versions were found to have identical results to others for all inputs. The identical results were grouped together in "equivalence classes".

In terms of the difficulty function theory outlined, each equivalence class was viewed as a possible program, π, taken from the universe of all programs, Π, for that specification. The record of success/failure for each input value is equivalent to the score function, $\omega(\pi, x)$ for the equivalence class as it represents a binary value for every point in the input domain, x, indicating whether the result was correct or not. For the chosen problem, the input domain, x, is a two-dimensional space with axes of velocity (v) and time (t), and the score function represented the failure region within that input domain.

$P(\pi)$ was estimated by taking the ratio of the number of instances in an equivalence class against the total number of programs in the population. The size of the failure region was taken to be the proportion of input values that resulted in failure. The failure regions can be represented two dimensionally on the v, t plane, but it should be emphasised that this is only a projection of the overall input domain. It is only possible to sample the total input domain.

5   Results

The results revealed that the 2529 initial program versions produced by the authors (the "v1" population) formed 50 equivalence classes. The five most frequent equivalence classes accounted for approximately 96% of the population. The results of the analysis are summarised in Table 1.

Table 1. Population v1 equivalence classes (frequent)

Equivalence Class (π)	Number of versions	P(π)	Size of Failure Region
EC1	1928	0.762	0.000
EC2	201	0.079	1.000
EC3	189	0.075	0.495
EC4	90	0.036	0.999
EC5	27	0.011	0.990

Equivalence class 1 agrees with the oracle program. There are no known faults associated with this equivalence class result, consequently the size of the failure region was 0%.

For equivalence class 2, analysis of the programs revealed a range of different faults resulted in complete failure across the input domain.

For equivalence class 3, failures always occurred for v < 0. This was due to a specification discrepancy on the Contest Host web site. Two specifications existed on the site—one in a PDF document, the other on the actual web page. The PDF specification required a *distance* (which is always positive) while the web specification required a *displacement* which can be positive or negative. The "displacement" version was judged to be the correct version.

Equivalence class 4, typified those versions that lacked implementation of a loop to process a sequence of input lines (i.e. only computed the first input line correctly).

For equivalence class 5, inspection of the program versions revealed a variable declaration fault to be the likely cause.

A similar analysis was performed on the final program version submitted by each author (the "vFinal" population). The results revealed that of the 2666 final program versions could be grouped into 34 equivalence classes. The five most frequent equivalence classes accounted for approximately 98% of the population. The results of the analysis are summarised in Table 2.

Table 2. Population vFinal: equivalence classes

Equivalence Class (π)	Number of versions	P(π)	Size of Failure Region
EC1	2458	0.922	0.000
EC2	70	0.026	1.000
EC3	40	0.015	0.495
EC4	21	0.008	0.999
EC5	13	0.005	0.990

Note that there is some overlap between the "first" and "final" populations as some authors only submitted one version. It can be seen that the dominant equivalence classes are the same as in the first version, but the proportions of each equivalence class have decreased (apart from EC1) presumably because some programs have been successfully debugged.

Figure 1 shows examples of the less frequent equivalence class failure regions.

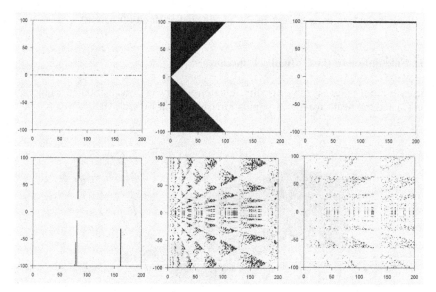

Fig. 1. Failure regions for some of the infrequent equivalence classes

These graphs show that there is a remarkable variation in the failure regions even for such a simple problem. The failure regions for the frequent EC1 to EC5 equivalence classes are simpler in structure, i.e. all "white" for EC1, almost all "black" for EC2, EC4 and EC5 and a black rectangle for EC3 covering the negative portion of the input domain.

6 Analysis

The "score functions" and frequency data of the equivalence classes can be combined to estimate the difficulty function for the specific problem. Note that this is an approximation to the actual difficulty function which should be an average taken over the population of all possible programs. It is unlikely that the set of all possible programs (Π) are limited to the 50 equivalence classes identified in this study. However, a computation of $\theta(x)$ based on the known equivalence classes should give a good approximation to the difficulty function, as 95% (v1) and 97% (vFinal) of the program versions belonged to four of the most frequently occurring known equivalence classes so uncertainties in the "tail" of the population of programs will only have a marginal effect on the difficulty function estimate.

One issue that needed to be considered in the analysis was the effect of the specification discrepancy. The discrepancy will bias the estimate of implementation difficulty as equivalence class EC3 might not have occurred if the specification had been unambiguous. On the other hand, such specification problems might be typical of the effect of specification ambiguity on the difficulty function. We therefore calculated the difficulty function in two ways:
- including all equivalence classes
- all equivalence classes except EC3 (the adjusted difficulty function).

6.1 Calculation of the Difficulty Function

For each input value, x, the difficulty function value $\theta(x)$ was estimated using equation (1) and the result for the v1 population is shown in Figure 2.

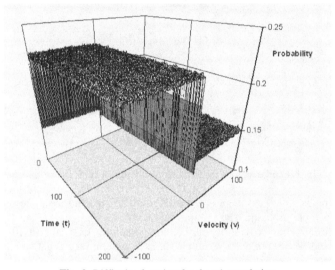

Fig. 2. Difficulty function for the v1 population

This calculation assumes that π is the same as an equivalence class, the score function $\omega(\pi, x)$ is the same as the observed failure region and $P(\pi)$ is the relative frequency of the equivalence class in the population. Effectively the calculation takes a weighted average of the individual failure regions in the v1 population.

Note that the difficulty function shown in Figure 2 has not accounted for any bias introduced by the specification discrepancy and the "step" in difficulty for $v<0$ is due to the specification ambiguity.

The probability of failure also decreases for certain "special" values—the velocity axis $v=0$, and time axis $t=0$. This might be expected since an incorrect function of v and t might well yield the same value as the correct function for these special values (i.e. a displacement of zero). There is also a low probability value at $v=-100$, $t=0$ which is due to faults that fail to execute subsequent lines in the input file, and the first test input value happens to be v=-100, t=0. If the test input values had been submitted in a random order, this point would have been no more likely to fail than adjacent points.

It can also be seen that there is a certain amount of "noise" on the two "flat" regions of the difficulty surface. This is caused by some of the highly complex failure patterns that exist for some of the infrequent equivalence classes (as illustrated in Figure 1).

The results were adjusted to account for specification bias by eliminating the equivalence class EC3 and Figure 3 shows the adjusted difficulty function.

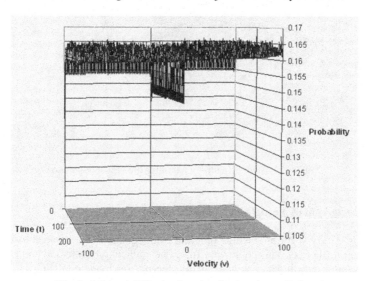

Fig. 3. Adjusted difficulty function for the v1 population

With the adjustment for specification bias, the difficulty function is now almost "flat" apart from the "special case" values on the velocity axis, v=0, and time axis, t=0.

The difficulty functions for the final version populations (adjusted and unadjusted) are very similar in shapes observed in the v1 population. The adjusted vFinal difficulty function is shown in Figure 4.

While the difficulty functions are similar in shape to the v1 population difficulty functions, the mean value of $\theta(x)$ is about one third that of the v1 population—mainly because the vFinal population contains a higher proportion of correct program versions.

The mean values for $\theta(x)$ are summarised in the table below.

Table 3. Mean difficulty values for different program populations

| Program | Mean Value of θ | |
Population	Unadjusted	Adjusted
v1	0.186	0.161
vFinal	0.064	0.058

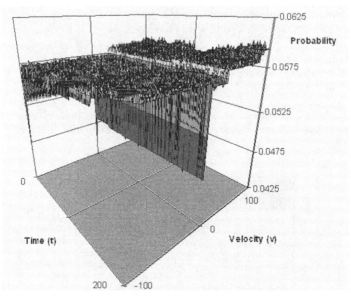

Fig. 4. Adjusted difficulty function for the vFinal population

6.2 Expected *pfd* of a Single Version and a Pair of Versions

To compute the *pfd* for an average program from equation (2), we need to know the execution profile P(x). This could vary from one application context to another. However, assuming any input is equally likely, the *pfd* of a single version is the mean value of θ, while the dangerous failure rate of a fault-detecting pair, pfd_2, given in equation (4) reduces to the mean of $\theta(x)^2$ averaged over the input space. Note that this assumes the same difficulty function for both programs, i.e. they are drawn from the same population (the Eckhardt and Lee assumption [5]).

The expected *pfd*s for a single version and a pair of versions were computed for the v1 and vFinal program populations (and the adjusted versions). The results are shown in the table below and compared with the pfd expected from the independence assumption (pfd_1^2).

Table 4. Comparison of expected probability of failure on demand

Program Population	pfd_1	pfd_2	pfd_1^2
v1	0.186	0.0361	0.0347
v1 adjusted	0.161	0.0260	0.0260
vFinal	0.064	0.0042	0.0041
vFinal adjusted	0.058	0.0033	0.0033

The increase in the *pfd* of a diverse pair (pfd_2) relative to the independence assumption (pfd_1^2) was relatively small for all populations, and for the adjusted populations, the difference between pfd_2 and the independence assumption is almost negligible. The worst-case increase relative to the independence assumption was observed to be 1.04 (for the unadjusted v1 population). This is consistent with expectations, as the difficulty surface was much flatter for the adjusted versions.

7 Discussion

While the results are interesting, we have to be cautious about their applicability to "real world" programs. Programming contests can provide many thousands of versions and this is a clear benefit for statistical studies. On the other hand, the results may be unrepresentative of software development in industry, especially in that:

1. many of the developers are probably amateurs or students rather than professional developers;
2. the program specifications are not overly complex, so that the programs are not typical of software developed in industry, and whole classes of faults that arise in the development of complex software may be missing;
3. the development process is different from the processes applied in industry;
4. there is no experimental control over program development, so independence could be compromised, e.g. by copying other participants' programs, or by submitting programs produced collectively by multiple people.

Discussions with the contest organiser suggests that plagiarism is not considered to be a major issue and, in any case, the main effect of plagiarism of correct versions would be to increase the number of correct versions slightly. In principle, it should be feasible to trap programs from different authors that are identical or very similar in structure.

With regard to programming expertise, the top participants are known to take part in international programming contests under controlled conditions (in a physical location rather than on the internet). So it seems that there is a very broad range of expertise. In future studies we might be able to obtain more information about the participants so that the level of expertise can be more closely controlled.

The example we have studied is "programming in the small" rather than "programming in the large". It is therefore likely that there are classes of "large program" fault, such as integration and interface faults, that will not be present in our example. In addition the processes used differ from industry practice. However experience with quite large programs indicates that many of the faults are due to localised programming errors that remained undetected by industrial verification and validation phases. So it is likely the errors committed in small contest-derived programs will also arise in large industrial programs, although we have to recognise that the set of faults will be incomplete and the relative frequency of the fault classes is likely to differ.

From the foregoing discussion, it is clear that we cannot make general conclusions from a single program example. However, the results can suggest hypotheses to be tested in subsequent experiments. One clear result of this experiment is that the difficulty surface is quite flat. The specification required a single simple "transfer function" that applies to the whole of the input domain. One might conjecture that, for a fixed transfer function, the difficulty would be the same for all input values. Similarly where the program input domain is divided into sub-domains which have different transfer functions, we might expect the difficulty to be flat within each sib domain. If this conjecture is correct, we would expect diverse programs with simple transfer functions to have reliability improvements close to that predicted by independent failure assumption. Indeed, diversity may be better suited to simple functions rather than entire large complex programs. However we emphasise that this is a conjecture, and more experiments would be needed to test this hypothesis.

It should also be noted the *pfd* reduction derived in Table 4 is the *average reduction*. For a specific pair of program versions it is possible for the actual level of reduction to vary from zero to complete reduction. A zero reduction case would occur if a pair of versions from the same equivalence class are selected. Conversely, complete reduction occurs if an incorrect version is combined with a correct version. In Table 2, for instance, 92% of versions in the final population are correct so the chance that a pair of versions will be faulty is $(1-0.92)^2$, i.e. 0.64%. It follows that the chance of a totally fault detecting pair (where at least one version is correct) will 99.36%. Pairs with lower detection performance will be distributed within in the remaining 0.64% of the population of possible pairs and some of these versions will behave identically and hence have zero failure detection probability.

Another issue that we did not plan to examine was the impact of specification problems. However it is apparent that the problem we encountered was a particular example of specification ambiguity that arises in many projects. This illustrates how N-version programming can be vulnerable to common specification problems, and the need for appropriate software engineering strategies to ensure that specifications are sound.

At a more general level, we have to ask whether such experiments are of practical relevance to industry. As discussed earlier, the examples we use are not typical as they are not as complex as industrial software and the development processes differ. However, the experiments could lead to conjectures that *could* be tested on industrially produced software, (such as the assumption of constant difficulty over a sub-domain). If such conjectures are shown to be applicable to industrial software, this information could be used to predict, for example, the expected *variation* in difficulty over the sub-domains and hence the expected gain from using diverse software. It has to be recognised that relating the research to industrial software will be difficult and, at least initially, is most likely to be applicable to software implementing relatively simple functions (like smart sensors). We hope to address this issue in future research.

8   Conclusions and Further Work

We conclude that:
1. One significant source of failure was the specification. We were able to allow for the specification discrepancy in our analysis, but it does point to a more general issue with N-version programming, i.e. that it is vulnerable errors in the specification, so a sound specification is an essential prerequisite to the deployment of N-version programming.
2. For this particular example, the difficulty surface was almost flat. This indicates that there was little variation of difficulty and a significant improvement in reliability should (on average) be achieved, although the reliability of arbitrary pair of versions can vary significantly from this average.

We conjecture that for programs with a single simple transfer function over the whole input domain (like this example), the difficulty function might turn out to be relatively flat. In that case, reliability improvements close to the assumption of independent failures may be achievable. However, more experiments would be needed to test this hypothesis.

There is significant potential for future research on variations in difficulty. The possibilities include:

1. Variation of difficulty for *different* sub-populations (e.g. computer language, author nationality, level of expertise, etc). The extended Littlewood and Miller theory suggests it is possible to have reliability better than the independence assumption value. An empirical study could be envisaged, to determine if this is observed when versions from different populations are combined.
2. Extension to other contest host program examples, and more wide-ranging experiments to assess conjectures like the flat difficulty conjecture discussed above.
3. Relating the hypotheses generated in the experiments to industrial examples.

Acknowledgements. This work was supported in part by the U.K. Engineering and Physical Sciences Research Council via the *Interdisciplinary Collaboration on the Dependability of computer based systems*, (DIRC), and via the *Diversity with Off-The-Shelf Components* Project (DOTS), GR/N24056. The authors would like to thank Miguel Revilla, University of Valladolid, Spain, for providing the program versions and information relating to the programming contest.

References

[1]   A. Avizienis and L. Chen, "On the Implementation of N-version Programming for Software Fault Tolerance during Execution", Proc. the First IEEE-CS International Computer Software and Applications Conference (COMPSAC 77), Chicago, Nov 1977.

[2]   A. Avizienis and J. P. J. Kelly, "Fault Tolerance by Design Diversity: Concepts and Experiments", Computer, Vol. 17, No. 8, August 1984.

[3]   A. Avizienis, "Software Fault Tolerance", Information Processing (G.X. Titter, Ed.), pp. 491-498, Elsevier Science Publishers, Holland, 1989.

[4]   P.G. Bishop, M. Barnes, et/ al., "PODS a Project on Diverse Software", IEEE Trans. Software Engineering, Vol. SE-12, No. 9, 929-940, 1986.

[5]   D. E. Eckhardt, L. D. Lee, "A theoretical basis for the analysis of multiversion software subject to coincident errors", IEEE Transactions on Software Engineering, SE-11 (12), pp.1511-1517, 1985.

[6]   J. C. Knight and N. G. Leveson, "An Experimental Evaluation of the Assumption of Independence in Multi-Version Programming", IEEE Transactions on Software Engineering, SE-12 (1), pp. 96-109, 1986.

[7]   B. Littlewood and D. R. Miller, "Conceptual Modelling of Coincident Failures in Multiversion Software", IEEE Transactions on Software Engineering, Vol. 15, No. 2, pp. 1596-1614, December 1989.

[8]   B. Littlewood, P. Popov and L. Strigini, "Modelling software design diversity - a review", ACM Computing Surveys, vol. 33, no. 2, 2001, pp.177-208.

[9]   S. Skiena and M. Revilla, Programming Challenges, ISBN: 0387001638, Springer Verlag, March, 2003, (http://acm.uva.es/problemset/)

Towards the Integration of Fault, Resource, and Power Management

Titos Saridakis

NOKIA Research Center
NOKIA, PO Box 407, FIN-00045, Finland
tel: +358 7180 37293   fax: +358 7180 36308
titos.saridakis@nokia.com

Abstract. The runtime management of faults, resources and power have
been traditionally dissociated in the development of embedded software
systems. Each of them copes with unsolicited events of different types
(i.e. errors, resource saturation and power alarms), and operates independently of the other two. In this paper we study the case of using
alarm events generated by the resource and power management mechanisms to trigger a graceful degradation mechanism that is otherwise used
for fault management purposes. The occurrence of an unsolicited event is
reported to the graceful degradation mechanism, which removes from the
running system those parts necessary to eliminate, or lessen, the source
of the event, while at the same time allow the system to deliver the basic
functionality for each of the tasks that it runs. As a consequence, the reliability, robustness, and performance qualities of the system under study
improved significantly, for a negligible increase in the complexity of the
graceful degradation mechanism.

1   Introduction

The runtime management of faults, resources and power deal respectively with
the treatment of errors, the allocation of system resources (e.g. CPU and memory), and the handling of the energy source(s) of the system. The analysis of
the tasks and the conception of the software mechanisms that perform these
three types of runtime management has been traditionally dissociated from each
other in embedded systems development, following the *"separation of concerns"*
principle.

This dissociation is justified for various reasons. First, the occurrence of the
events that one type of management is dealing with are considered independent from the occurrence of events that the other two handle. Second, each of
the aforementioned types of runtime management regards system aspects that
belong to different domains, and each aspect needs to be elaborated in depth
by different domain experts. Third, for each of the above three types of management, the analysis of the requirements, the conception of the appropriate
management technique and the implementation of the corresponding mechanism
are fairly complex, which discourages consolidation thoughts. Finally, while the

M. Heisel et al. (Eds.): SAFECOMP 2004, LNCS 3219, pp. 72–86, 2004.

complexity of the development process remains bearable, the requirements of the resulting system can be (and are in most cases) met by the non-overlapping fault, resource and power management mechanisms.

These valid reasons led us to dissociate the design of the fault, resource and power management from each other, when we started our work on a runtime framework for component-based embedded software. However, once the independently designed mechanisms for these areas of runtime management were ready and the three design teams came together to study their impact on the execution framework, we realized that the fault management mechanism could be extended to react to unsolicited events reported by the resource and power management mechanisms. This paper reports on our work to integrate fault, resource and power management issues within a runtime mechanism that supports the graceful degradation of the system functionality in the presence of unsolicited events related to error, resource saturation and power alarms.

The starting point of our work is a system composed of components, where each component provides either basic or optional functionality. Basic functionality is the functionality for which the system was built in the first place, e.g. making a phone call for a mobile phone. Optional functionality is the functionality that increases the friendliness of the system operation without being essential for the correct functioning of the system, e.g. a graphical user interface with 3D shadow effects. Our approach is based on removing optional functionality from the system in the presence of unsolicited events like error occurrences, resource unavailability or saturation, and low power threshold or overheat. The removal of optional functionality helps to eliminate the part of the system that suffered the error, or to reduce the computing- or power-resources that the system needs in order to continue or complete its execution.

The remainder of this paper is structured as follows: the next section contains a summary of the system model and execution framework to which our work applies. Section 3 contains a summary of independently designed mechanisms for runtime management of fault, resources, and power. Section 4 presents the extension of the graceful degradation mechanism, which was initially designed for fault management, to react to unsolicited events reported by the resource and power management mechanisms. A discussion on the applicability of the the integration of fault, resource and power management can be found in Section 5. The paper concludes with a summary of our approach and a mention to our current and future work.

2   Background

Our system is a composition of components, where a component is a container of functionality. The functionality (or a part of it) contained by a component is offered to the component's environment, i.e. other components, other systems or a human user. Also, in order for a component to perform correctly the functionality it contains, it may rely on functionality offered by other components in its environment. The functionality that a component offers to its environment is described in the component's interfaces, in terms of the signature of the operations it implements. The interfaces of a component also describe the functionality offered from the environment on which the component relies for performing its designated functionality.

A component has one or more interfaces each consisting of three parts: the **provides**, **requires**, and **uses** parts. The **provides** part describes the functionality provided by the component in question. The **requires** part contains a description of the functionality that the component in question needs from its environment in order to function correctly. This description is used to identify other components whose presence is mandatory for the correct functioning of the component in question. Finally, the **uses** part contains a description of the functionality that the component in question may employ, when available, in order to increase the quality of certain aspects of the functionality it offers to its environment. This description is used to identify components whose presence is optional for correct functioning of the component in question, i.e. if they are not present then the component in question will still function correctly, possibly offering functionality of lower quality.

The information found in the **requires**, **uses**, and **provides** parts of component interfaces indicates endpoints of communication channels among the components. Coupling these endpoints, i.e. a **requires** or **uses** endpoint with its corresponding **provides** endpoint, creates the necessary connections that link together the components and compose a component-based software system. Hence, a set of components can be used to compose a system that will function correctly, if and only if every **requires** endpoint has a matching **provides** endpoint in that set. On top of that, the more **uses** endpoints have their matching **provides** endpoints in the set, the more complete (or of higher quality) will be the functionality performed by the system.

The goal of building a component-based system as described above is to develop embedded software, where the execution framework is that of a single process with multiple, fail-safe threads (i.e. an error in one thread does not affect directly other threads). The code that implements the functionality contained by components resides in libraries, which are linked with the applications that run in the embedded device. Each application runs in a separate thread. The runtime instance of a component executes in the thread of the application that calls it and it can invoke other components within the same thread. Different threads are used to execute concurrent applications or inherently parallel applications.

In the single address space of one executable process, the components are linked together by means of a *v-table*. A v-table is a structure that maps the symbolic addresses present in the code of a caller-component to the actual address where the callee-component is found in the same address space. When a caller-component needs to call a callee-component it uses a pointer to the v-table entry that contains the memory address where the callee-component is placed. The mappings found in the v-table from symbolic to actual addresses represent the bindings between components.

Finally, the execution framework provides for evolutionary system reconfiguration. An application can be launched even though not all **uses** endpoints of the components that are linked with it are matched with their corresponding **provides** endpoints. In the v-table, these unmatched **uses** endpoints are mapped to the function no_binding(), which is implemented by the execution framework. When this function is called, it returns immediately the execution control to its caller and it raises an exception indicating the lack of the requested binding. During the execution of the application, the components that provide the missing **provides** endpoints may become available (e.g. as dynamically linked libraries that are downloaded in the course of the system execution). At that time, the evolutionary reconfiguration mechanism provided by the execution framework replaces, where appropriate in the v-table mappings, the address of the no_binding() function with the address of the functions that correspond to the newly acquired **provides** endpoints.

3   Fault, Resource, and Power Management

This section presents an overview of the independently designed mechanisms for runtime fault, resource, and power management. Emphasis is given to the aspects of those mechanisms that are relevant to their integration under graceful degradation of system functionality.

3.1   Fault Management

The intention of our runtime fault management for embedded software is to ensure that an error affects the smallest possible part of the system. In terms of the model of a component-based system presented in the previous section, this means that an error affects only the component where it occurs and those components which require the functionality provided by it. The selected approach for achieving this type of runtime fault management was to gracefully degrade the system functionality by removing the failed component and those that, directly or indirectly, require it. A detailed presentation of this approach can be found in [15].

The term *graceful degradation* has been used in a number of domains to describe the smooth changing to a lower state of some system aspect. The system aspect that degrades to a lower state ranges from the content quality in image processing [3,6,11] and in telecommunications [18], to the system performance in shared memory multiprocessors [14,16], multi-modular memory systems [4, 5,12] and RAID systems [2], and to the delivered functionality in distributed agreement protocols [13] and formal system specification [7,17]. Table 1 contains a summary of the different domains where graceful degradation has been applied. In our approach, graceful degradation refers to the decrease of the system functionality in the presence of errors.

The cornerstone of our graceful degradation mechanism is a *component dependency graph (CDG)*, which is a weighed, directed graph whose nodes represent the components of the system and the arcs represent the communication

Table 1. Summary of domains where graceful degradation has been applied.

DOMAIN (ASPECT)	INTERPRETATION
Image processing (Image quality)	Rather than discarding a compressed image that cannot be reconstructed to its original resolution, the image quality can be gracefully degraded to lower levels [3,6,11]
Telecom. (Voice quality)	Rather than closing a connection that is dropping some packets of voice data, the voice quality delivered to the end-points is gracefully degraded to lower levels [18].
Shared memory multiprocessors (Computational power)	Rather than stoping a computation on a multiprocessor system when one of the processors fails, the tasks assigned to the failed processor can be rescheduled on the remaining processors resulting in the graceful degradation of the computational power of the system [14,16].
Multi-modular memory (Memory throughput)	Rather than rendering inaccessible the memory when a one of its modules fails, the data of the failed module are recovered from stable storage and distributed among the remaining modules resulting in a graceful degradation of the memory access throughput of the system [4,5,12].
RAID (Disk access throughput)	Rather than rendering the RAID system inaccessible when one of the disks fails, the data of the failed disk are reconstructed from the error correction codes on the remaining disks and distributed among those resulting in the graceful degradation of the disk access throughput of the RAID system [2].
Distributed agreement (Computational accuracy)	Rather than failing to reach an agreement when one or more members of the distributed agreement group fail, the group can reach an agreement on a value less close to the expected one resulting in a graceful degradation of the accuracy of the agreed value [13].
ABFT (Computational throughput)	Rather than dropping the degree of fault tolerance that an ABFT system provides when one of the processors fails, the remaining processors are reorganized in a smaller number of fault tolerant groups with the same degree of fault tolerance resulting in the graceful degradation of the computational throughput of the ABFT system [17].
O-O systems (Failures of derived classes)	In fault tolerant object-oriented system, graceful degradation qualifies a system any object cannot suffer failures that are more severe than the failures suffered by its superclasses. This implies that the severity of failure gracefully degrades with inheritance [10].
Formal specification (Constraints strictness)	Rather than causing a system failure when a set of constraints that enable some system functionality is not met, an alternative, weaker set of constraints that still hold can enable an alternative system functionality resulting in the graceful degradation of the constraint strictness satisfied by the system during its execution [7].

channels among them. The direction of an arc is from the component with a
requires or **uses** endpoint to a component with the corresponding **provides**
endpoint. Hence, the direction of an arc in the CDG represent a dependency
relation from the component represented by the starting node to the component
representing by the ending node. The weight of an arc is a boolean value set to
TRUE when the arc represents a communication channel between a **requires**
and a **provide** endpoint, i.e. a communication channel that contributes to the
soundness property of the system. The weight of an arc is set to FALSE if the arc
represents a communication channel between a **uses** and a **provides** endpoint,
i.e. a communication channel that does not affect the soundness property of the
system.

When an error occurs on some component, it is reported to the graceful
degradation mechanism. The graceful degradation mechanism, which holds an
up-to-date CDG of the system composition, starts by locating the failed component on the CDG and marks it for removal. The removal of the failed component may violate the correct functioning of the system, if there are component
in the system that require the removed one. To avoid this, the graceful degradation mechanism performs a reverse depth-first traversal of the CDG starting
from the node that corresponds to the failed component and progressing along
the arcs with weight TRUE. Each node visited during the reverse traversal is
marked for removal. Once the reverse traversal is finished, all marked nodes are
removed from the running system. The dangling v-table mappings, which are a
side-product of this removal, are replaced by the address of the **no_binding()**
function, which informs the calling component about the missing binding.

3.2   Resource Management

The runtime resource management is responsible for allocating CPU and memory resources to components running in the system. In order to do that, each
component that needs to have guaranteed access to resources must describe the
amount of CPU and memory bandwidth that it requires for its execution. Components that have such descriptions of the resources they required are called
resource-aware components. The runtime instance of a resource-aware component contains the resource requirements of the component in question.

At the initialization of such a component, the resource management mechanism, which supervises the allocation of system resources, can verify whether
the required resources can be allocated for the execution of the component in
question. If the required resources are available, then they are allocated to the
component in question and the resource management mechanism guarantees that
they will be available throughout the component's execution. If the required resources are not available, then the initialization of the component in question
fails and its runtime instance is not scheduled for execution.

In addition to resource-aware components, a system may be composed of
components that do not have any explicit requirements about the resources
they need for their execution. During their execution, these non-resource-aware

components are allocated resources on a best-effort basis, i.e. the non-resource-aware components use for their execution the remaining system resources after the requirements of the resource-aware components are satisfied. Following the best-effort resource allocation policy, the execution of non-resource-aware components can be arbitrarily delayed when the running resource-aware components saturate the available system resources.

It follows that the reaction of the resource management mechanism to unsolicited events, such as resource saturation or unavailability, is less graceful than the reaction of the fault management on error occurrences. For resource-aware components, the reaction is binary: either required resources are available, in which case they are reserved for a given component and that component is scheduled for execution, or they are not and the initialization of the given component fails. For non-resource-aware components there is no reaction from the resource management to unsolicited, resource-related events. If resources are saturated or not available, then the non-resource-aware components will have to wait until they become available (best-effort policy).

3.3   Power Management

The power management is responsible for monitoring the energy sources that powers up the system, detecting alarming events such as low energy levels or overheated power sources, and taking action to eliminate the cause of the alarms or to reduce their severity. Such actions range from disabling the screen back-light or starting the fan mechanism when such is available, to scheduling the system shutdown or decreasing the voltage produced by the energy source, which results in lowering the frequency in which the CPU of the system operates.

Contrary to fault and resource management, power management does not distinguish components or applications in the running system, but rather views the running system as a single entity that consumes energy sources. In addition, the actions taken by the power management mechanism are not targeted at executing components but at the energy sources. Hence, the reaction of the power management mechanism to unsolicited events, such as power source overheating or low energy source levels, is less graceful than the reaction of the fault management on error occurrences. When such events occur, the actions taken by the power management mechanism affect the whole running system and not individual components within it.

4   Extended Graceful Degradation

The main observation, from the quick overview of the fault, resource and power management given in the previous section, is that the latter two have a less graceful reaction to unsolicited events than the former one. The motivation for the work reported in this section is to extend the graceful degradation mechanism employed by the fault management so it can be used by the resource and power management. For the resource management, the use of graceful degradation would be triggered when system resources are saturated or unavailable and it would remove from the running system the non-resource-aware components whose functionality is optional in the current system execution. For the power management, the use of graceful degradation would be triggered when a low level threshold of energy sources is reached or when the energy sources are overheated and it would remove from the running system all those components whose functionality is optional in the current system execution. In both cases, the result would be that the system will be able to continue executing correctly and performing its basic functionality.

To extend the graceful degradation mechanism described in subsection 3.1 in the aforementioned way, we have to solve two problems. First, we need to design and setup the mechanisms that would detect the occurrence of unsolicited events related to resource and power management. These detectors of unsolicited events would complement the error detection employed in fault management in triggering the graceful degradation mechanism. Second, we must modify the part of the graceful degradation mechanism that traverses the CDG in order to identify the components with optional functionality that must be removed from the system. When the graceful degradation mechanism is triggered by error detection, the traversal starts from the component on which the error was reported. However, such a starting point is not available when an unsolicited event related to resource or the power management is reported.

4.1   Detecting Unsolicited Events

Unsolicited events related to fault management, i.e. error occurrences, are detected by means of exceptions and timeouts. All operations provided by components have a set of exception that they may raise. The component that invokes an operation provided by another component may catch some of the exception and invoked component may raise, and deal with them in its own specific way. However, exceptions that are not caught by the invoking component are reported by the error detection mechanism to the graceful degradation mechanism. In addition to relying on exception for detecting errors, when a component invokes an operation provided by another component, it can set a timer on that invocation, which timer is defined at compile time of the invoking component. If this timer expires before the invoked component returns the results of its invocation to its caller, the error detection mechanism reports an error on the invoked component to the graceful degradation mechanism. In both error reports, the information communicated by the error detection to the graceful degradation is the runtime id of the component where the error occurred.

Unsolicited events related to resource management, such as saturation or unavailability of CPU or memory, are detected by the runtime mechanism that performs resource management only when a resource-aware component requests resources for its execution. In that case, if the requested resources are not available (i.e. some of the system resources have reached saturation levels or are otherwise unavailable) the resource management does not allow the requesting component to get initialized and start executing. However, the allocation of requested resource to resource-aware components has an impact on the execution of non-resource aware ones. Components in the latter category execute on the resources that remain unallocated to components in the former category. Hence, when the unallocated system resource are running very low, the non-resource-aware components get less chances of executing and completing their designated functionality.

The intention of our work is not to interfere with the management of resource-aware components. Instead, we aim at using the graceful degradation mechanism to remove non-resource-aware components, which are optional for the system execution, when the system resources available to them go below a certain threshold. This threshold is a function of the number of the executing non-resource-aware components that use the resource and the percentage of each resource that has already been allocated to resource aware components[1]. To detect when this threshold is reached and the graceful degradation mechanism must be activated, we need to monitor the two parameters that influence it, i.e. the number of executing non-resource-aware components and the usage of system resources.

The mechanism that detects the reaching of the resource saturation threshold, communicates with the resource management mechanism and the execution framework. The former provides information about the number of resource-aware components executing in the system and the usage percentage of CPU and memory. The latter provides information regarding the total number of executing components in the system, which it has since it is responsible for the initialization of every component in the system. The resource saturation detector requests periodically this information from the the resource management and the execution framework. Based on it, the resource saturation detector can deduce the number of executing non-resource-aware components and, subsequently, the percentage of system resources that each of the can use. When this percentage is below a value that has been specified at the system configuration phase, the resource saturation detector reports to the graceful degradation mechanism the occurrence of a resource saturation event.

Unsolicited events related to power management, such as low energy source levels or energy source overheating, are detected by the runtime mechanism that performs power management. When such events are detected, the power management reacts in various ways that depend on the type of event that has been detected. For example, low energy level may lead to disabling the screen back-light or start the system shutdown, and energy source overheating may lead to starting the fan mechanism when such is available or to decreasing the voltage produced by the energy source. Our intention is not to interfere with the power management system when it comes to deal with the above unsolicited events. Rather, we aim at using the graceful degradation mechanism for preventing the occurrence of these events that activate the power management reactions.

---

[1] We assume a uniform allocation of available system resources to non-resource-aware components.

The mechanism that detects alarming conditions on the energy sources is based on information provided by the runtime mechanism that performs power management. This information relates to the current values of energy source characteristics (e.g. energy levels, current temperature of energy source, etc), as well as statistical information about these values in the recent system execution history (e.g. the percentage of change in these values over a specified period of time). The latter information can be used to calculate the current drain rate and heat-increase rate of the energy sources of the system. Comparing the received and the calculated information to the thresholds of acceptable energy source behaviors, which have been specified at system configuration, is used to detect energy source alarms. Then, the energy source alarm detector reports to the graceful degradation mechanism the occurrence of an energy source alarm event. At this point, the removal of a subset of the running components by the graceful degradation mechanism could eliminate, or at least postpone, the occurrence of the events that would trigger the radical reactions of the power management mechanism.

4.2   Alternative CDG Traversals

The activation of the graceful degradation mechanism by an error report leads to a CDG traversal, which starts from the CDG node that corresponds to the runtime instance of the component where the error occurred. This traversal identified all the components in the running system that require, either directly or indirectly, the failed components for their correct execution. At the end of the CDG traversal, the set of identified components are marked for removal. As a result, the running system loses only the functionality (i.e. the components) that was affected by the error. An example of such a CDG traversal and the produced set of components to be removed from the running system is graphically illustrated in Figure 1(a). There, the error is reported on component C, which is immediately marked for removal indicated by a check mark, and the traversal that starts from it and follows the inverse direction of the thick solid-line arrows marks three more components for removal.

However, when the graceful degradation mechanism is activated by a report on resource saturation or an energy source alarm, the starting point of the CDG traversal is not specified. Consequently, we must define a meaningful convention for the starting point of the CDG traversal when it is triggered by unsolicited events related to resource or power management. Our choice is based on the motivation for using the graceful degradation, which is to remove the optional functionality of the system and allow better probabilities for the basic functionality of the system to continue executing and potentially reach completion.

We consider that system applications, which are started either at system startup or explicitly by the operator of the system, are part of the basic system functionality that must not be removed by the graceful degradation. The top-level components that correspond to system applications are those that no other component in the system depends on them. This assumption is not always valid in component-based software, but Section 5 explains why this assumption is valid in our work. Identifying those top-level components, it is sufficient to check all the nodes in the CDG and find those that have no dependencies on them from other nodes. Each of the identified top-level component is a starting point for a distinct CDG traversal. In the example CDG depicted in Figure 1(b), the starting points for the CDG traversal are the components A and B.

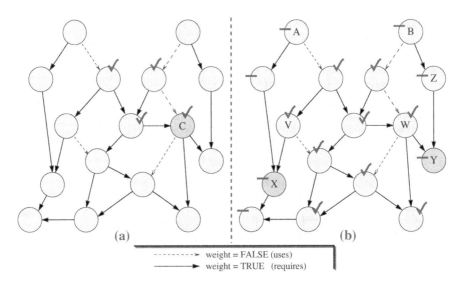

Fig. 1. (a) CDG traversal triggered by error detection on C; (b) CDG traversal triggered by resource saturation report.

Having selected the starting points, the only constraint for performing a CDG traversal, which identifies the components to be removed from the running system, is that the identified components must be optional for the current system execution. Satisfying this constraints is a straightforward task. Opposite to the CDG traversals performed after an error report, a CDG traversal that starts from the aforementioned identified components follows all the arcs of the CDG (and not only those with weight TRUE). The starting point of the traversal and every node reachable from that starting point over a path of arcs with weight TRUE are marked to be kept in the system. On the other hand, the first node reached over an arcs with weight FALSE is marked for removal, if and only if it has not been already marked to be kept by a previous traversal or previous steps of the same traversal. All nodes that satisfy the above condition and are reachable from a node marked for removal, are also marked for removal.

In Figure 1(b), the first time node X is reached in a depth-first traversal starting at node A, it will be marked to be kept. The same node will be reached again during the same traversal from node V that is marked for removal, but since node X is marked to be kept, its marking does not change. Notice that when a node is reachable from a starting point over a path of arcs with weight TRUE, it is marked for keeping independently of any previous marking it may have. For example, node Y in Figure 1(b) will be first reached from node W in a traversal starting at node B and marked for removal. However, later in the same traversal, node Y will be reached from node Z again, and will be marked for keeping. Hence, Figure 1(b) depicts the markings of all nodes in the CDG for two traversals started at nodes A and B, where a check mark indicates removal and a minus mark indicates keeping.

To complete the extension of the graceful degradation mechanism to serve for the desired reaction to unsolicited events related to resource management, a last constraint must be considered: resource-aware components must not be marked for removal. This restriction is because we chose not to have the graceful degradation interfering with the resource management. To force this constraint, once a resource-aware component is entered in the CDG, it is immediately marked for keeping. This ensures that it will not be marked for removal by any CDG traversal that follows the rules described above. The information about the resource-aware components that are scheduled from execution is obtained from the run-time mechanism that performs resource management.

5   Discussion

The extended graceful degradation mechanism that can respond to unsolicited events related to fault, resource, and power management cannot be applied on a general component-based software system. A number of characteristics of embedded software are essential assumptions for the applicability of our approach. In this section, we present in clear the assumptions under which the presented approach can be applied.

First, the distinction between mandatory and optional components in a system composition is a prerequisite. If the component interfaces are do not contain clauses such as **requires** and **uses** with the semantics described in Section 2, other means must be employed for distinguishing the mandatory from the optional components, and this task may not be easy or even feasible. Second, the semantics of the information in the **requires** and **uses** clauses of components interfaces must be verified. This means that when a component claims that it **uses** an operation provided by an other component, then it is able to operate correctly even when the latter component is not present. Such verification, which is common practice in embedded software development, can be achieved via thorough testing of component execution in different execution environments.

The use of the dynamic reconfiguration mechanism for handling the removal of components and the replacement of dangling bindings due to component removal with a binding to the **no_binding()** function is not applicable in the general case of component-based software systems. In case of distributed objects, for example, simply the preparation of the system for a reconfiguration may require the use of a complex mechanism (e.g. see [1]). On top of that, the equivalent of the no_binding() function must be provided and it must be verified that components function correctly when calling it.

Finally, the assumption that the top level application components are those that no other component in the system depends on them is not valid in the general case of component-based software. It is possible, although of doubtful value, to have a low-level component (implementing some intrinsic system functionality) depending on a top-level component implementing the front-end of an end-user application. This case would create dependency loops in the CDG and would not allow the identification of the application components in the way described in subsection 4.2. However, in the context of software for embedded systems often a layered architecture is strictly enforced. Hence, the top-most layer that contains the application components does not have any dependencies from lower layer.

6   Conclusion

The presented approach towards the integration of fault, resource, and power management under the graceful degradation mechanism improves the robustness, reliability and performance of the basic system functionality under the occurrences of a variety of unsolicited events. When an error occurs, only the affected part of the system is removed, ensuring the robust operation of the remaining part of the system. When system resources (CPU and memory) are saturated beyond a predefined threshold, the removal of the optional system functionality allows a better performance for the basic system functionality. Finally, in the presence of energy source alarms, the removal of optional system functionality allow the system to continue delivering its basic functionality, ensuring its reliability.

A topic of ongoing work is related to the interfacing between the graceful degradation mechanism and the resource management, and whether graceful degradation should include resource-aware components too. Our current approach described in subsection 4.2, which is to mark in advance all resource-aware components for keeping, makes possible that after graceful degradation is employed as a reaction to an unsolicited event related to resource management, a resource-aware component does not have any other component in the system depending on it. This can happen if the components that depended on it are removed during the graceful degradation. As a result, that component plus a number of other components on which this one depends on, will remain in the executing system although no system application uses them, hence they are no longer part of the basic system functionality. A solution to this problem is to use a different marking for the resource-aware components in the CDG, which would allow subsequent traversals to mark these components for removal.

As part of the ongoing work, we are testing the extended graceful degradation mechanism in a simulation environment, where reports on unsolicited events from resource and power management are created by the testers. The implementation of the detection mechanisms for these types of unsolicited events, as they are described in subsection 4.1, is scheduled for late 2004.

In our future plans we intend to study various possibilities of complementing the graceful degradation mechanism with a mechanism that detects conditions which allow the system to (re-)instantiate components that provide optional functionality. Such conditions would be the repair of the failed components, the low load of system resources and the recharge or cooling of the energy sources. When such conditions are met, the components providing optional functionality in the system can be deployed again.

Our work on graceful degradation of system functionality in the presence of unsolicited events related to fault, resource and power management is performed in the context of the ITEA project SPACE4U [9]. This project leverages the execution framework for embedded component-based software and the resource management scheme of another ITEA project called ROBOCOP [8] with runtime support for fault, power and terminal management.

References

1. C. Bidan, V. Issarny, T. Saridakis, and A. Zarras. A Dynamic Reconfiguration Service for CORBA. In *Proceedings of the 4th International Conference on Configurable Distributed Systems*, pages 35–42, May 1998.
2. P.M. Chen, E.K. Lee, G.A. Gibson, R.H. Katz, and D.A. Patterson. RAID: High-Performance, Reliable Secondary Storage. *ACM Computing Surveys*, 26(2):145–185, June 1994.
3. Y.-C. Chen, K. Sayood, and D.J. Nelson. A Robust Coding Scheme for Packet Video. *IEEE Transactions on Communications*, 40(9):1491–1501, September 1992.
4. V. Cherkassky and M. Malek. A Measure of Graceful Degradation in Parallel-Computer Systems. *IEEE Transactions on Reliability*, 38(1):76–81, April 1989.
5. K. Cheung, G. Sohi, K. Saluja, and D. Pradhan. Organization and Analysis of a Gracefully-Degrading Interleaved Memory System. In *Proceedings of the 14th Annual International Symposium on Computer Architecture*, pages 224–231, June 1987.
6. P.P. Dang and P.M. Chau. Robust Image Transmission over CDMA Channels. *IEEE Transactions on Consumer Electronics*, 46(3):664–672, August 2000.
7. M.P. Herlihy and J.M. Wing. Specifying Graceful Degradation. *IEEE Transactions on Parallel and Distributed Systems*, 2(1):93–104, January 1991.
8. ROBOCOP / ITEA-00001. Robust Open Component Based Software Architecture for Configurable Devices.
   http://www.extra.research.philips.com/euprojects/robocop/.
9. SPACE4U / ITEA-02016. Software Platform and Component Environment for You. http://www.extra.research.philips.com/euprojects/space4u/.
10. P. Jayanti, T.D. Chandra, and S. Toueg. Fault-Tolerant Wait-Free Shared Objects. *Journal of the ACM*, 45(3):451–500, May 1998.
11. G. Lafruit, L. Nachtergaele, K. Denolf, and J. Bormans. 3D Computational Graceful Degradation. In *Proceedings of the IEEE International Symposium on Circuits and Systems*, pages 3.547–3.550, May 2000.
12. Y.-H. Lee and K.G. Shin. Optimal Recon.guration Strategy for a Degradable Multimodule Computing System. *Journal of the ACM*, 34(2):326–348, April 1987.

13. S.R. Mahaney and F.B. Schneider. Inexact Agreement: Accuracy, Precision, and Graceful Degradation. In *Proceedings of the 4th Annual ACM Symposium on Principles of Distributed Computing*, pages 237–249, August 1985.
14. F. Saheban and A.D. Friedman. Diagnostic and Computational Reconfiguration in Multiprocessor Systems. In *Proceedings of the 1978 Annual Conference*, pages 68–78, December 1978.
15. T. Saridakis. Graceful Degradation for Component-Based Embedded Software. In *Proceedings of the 13th International Concerence on Intelligent and Adaptive Systems and Software Engineering (IASSE)*, July 2004.
16. A. Thomasian and A. Avizienis. A Design Study of a Shared Resource Computing System. In *Proceedings of the 3rd Annual Symposium on Computer Architecture*, pages 105–112, January 1976.
17. S. Yajnik and N.K. Jha. Graceful Degradation in Algorithm-Based Fault Tolerant Multiprocessor Systems. *IEEE Transactions on Parallel and Distributed Systems*, 8(2):137–153, February 1997.
18. G.V. Zaruba, I. Chlamtac, and S.K. Das. A Prioritized Real-Rime Wireless Call Degradation Framework for Optimal Call Mix Selection. *Mobile Networks and Applications*, 7(2):143–151, April 2002.

Modeling Concepts for Safety-Related Requirements in Sociotechnical Systems

Michael Cebulla

Technische Universität Berlin, Fakultät für Elektrotechnik und Informatik,
Institut für Softwaretechnik und theoretische Informatik,
Franklinstr. 28/29, 10587 Berlin
phone: +49 30 314-24244   fax: +49 30 314-73623
mce@tu-berlin.de

Abstract. In this paper we focus on modeling concepts for safety-critical sociotechnical systems. First we claim that there is a great need for model-based reasoning about sociotechnical safety-critical requirements in system design and management. After this we take our starting point from formal methods, requirements engineering, and software architecture. We provide special extensions for these methods which are well-suited for the special challenges of sociotechnical systems: structural dynamism, uncertainty and the behavioral relevance of cognitive parameters. We maintain the visual style of modeling concepts as known from software architecture and provide an easy to use notation for reasoning about the features of specific decision situations. Finally we provide concepts to deal with adaptive system behavior and human error.

Keywords: Formal Methods, Human Factors, Analysis and Modeling.

1 Introduction

In this paper we present an approach for the analysis and modeling of complex sociotechnical systems. Due to the complexity of these systems their analysis and understanding is very difficult. But on the other hand for various reasons (safety, efficiency, organizational learning, change management) there is a strong need for a greater transparency of the related processes.

In our approach we develop a visual notation for the modeling of complex sociotechnical systems. Starting from formal methods and the experiences of *requirements engineering* [10] we provide concepts which are well suited for the description of specific sociotechnical features. Especially the aspects of systemic adaptation, the relevance of cognitive states and the uncertainty of descriptions are traditionally hard to grasp by formal notations.

We claim that a visual modeling notation significantly increases system transparency, support interdisciplinary system analysis, and is well-suited to support measurements of further education. We provide different systemic stakeholders with a simple means for scenario-based system analysis. Hence, we consider our approach as a contribution for an integrated safety management of sociotechnical

M. Heisel et al. (Eds.): SAFECOMP 2004, LNCS 3219, pp. 87–100, 2004.
© Springer-Verlag Berlin Heidelberg 2004

systems. In addition we support simple procedures of domain-specific reasoning by embedding our notation into a standardized framework. For this sake we use a simple logical calculus [1].

After some general considerations (section 2) we describe the critical features of sociotechnical systems in section 3. After presenting the basics of our approach (sections 4 and 5) we introduce concepts for modeling cognitive features (section 6). Afterwards give two examples for the description of adaptive behavior under consideration of contextual dependencies (sections 7 and 8). Finally, we show how to integrate cognitive features into fault trees for a model-based treatment of human error (section 9).

2   A Model-Based Approach to Complexity and Safety

Complex sociotechnical systems have evolved to control high risk technologies by teams of highly qualified specialists. Sociotechnical systems can be defined as *complex* safety-critical systems where *teams* of human operators cooperate with *ensembles* of technical units and devices. Usually, the resulting processes are significantly more complex than in systems consisting solely of technological components. Thus, a model for this kind of systems has to take into account not only technology but also the specific characteristics and risks of human and social behavior. Examples for this kind of systems are nuclear power plants, medical operation theaters and air traffic control.

This new class of system complexity and its related risks have established new requirements for system design and system safety. This is documented by the sad history of catastrophes from Three Miles Island (1979) to Überlingen (2002). The analysis of such complex systems has proven too multi-faceted for the traditional single-disciplinary approach. For a better understanding of safety-critical interactions it is important to possess an integrated modeling method which allows the analysis of all system aspects. The goal of our research is such a framework for modeling and analysis.

A model-based interdisciplinary system analysis is a promising strategy against what Leveson calls *intellectual unmanageability* of high risk systems [5]. The increasing complexity and tight coupling in contemporary high risk systems make a safe and efficient management difficult if not impossible. The main source of failure in complex systems is not human error or an erroneous component, but the *complex interactions* between components which is not understood to a sufficient degree [11]. To increase the level of understanding we choose an model-based approach which is open for results of interdisciplinary research.

The use of modeling concepts is meant to support the intra-organizational discussion process between different stakeholders as well as interdisciplinary system analysis. In any case a conceptual framework of well defined concepts is provided which are taken from the domain. Such a common vocabulary is an important precondition for a structured system analysis. Moreover, since these concepts are formally defined in the framework they may be subject for automatic reasoning. Thus, consistency, completeness and satisfiability of domain models may be automatically checked. To reach these goals we are following an *ontological* approach.

Domain models are well-suited to make domain knowledge plausible and to disseminate it among the participants, thus contributing to the quality and safety of processes. Due to their well-definedness they can be used as foundations for simulations and visualizations.

3   Special Features of Sociotechnical Systems

We observed some specific features of sociotechnical system which can be conceived as challenges for traditional modeling concepts. Basically, these challenges can be originate from an intensified contextual embedding which is typical for sociotechnical systems as well as for advanced software systems as for example pervasive services. All these systems have to provide a high quality of service and high safety given dramatically changing situations. Thus, their adaptive capabilities and their context awareness have to be developed to a very high degree. We claim that research concerning the adaptive features of sociotechnical system can be fruitful also for the development of advanced applications which are characterized by a high degree of contextual embedding.

3.1   Uncertainty

Sociotechnical systems tend to reduce the load of information processing by using *vague concepts*. So human experts normally don't use exact mathematical numbers but vague expressions from natural languages. We claim that the resulting vagueness is an important precondition for the systems' adaptivity and safety. In our approach we use fuzzy sets and fuzzy logic to specify uncertain information [4] (cf. section 5).

3.2   Structural Dynamism

One important feature of sociotechnical systems is their *structural dynamism*. The internal structure of systems like the medical operation theatre can be rapidly changing from one phase of the process to another according to environmental changes. For the description of this *structural dynamism* powerful concepts from dynamic architectures [9] are necessary. We handle this problem by introducing *transformation rules* (cf. section 7).

3.3   Relevance of Cognitive Features

In sociotechnical systems the agent's attitudes are critical factors with respect to system safety. Consequently we provide concepts for the description of cognitive states [14] (cf. section 6).

4   Basics of Architectural Description

For the description of a system's structure we use the concepts known from software architecture [13,8]. As an example we choose the setting of a medical operation theatre. While this special system is characterized by a great variety of behavioral alternatives we have to content ourselves with describing exemplary scenarios taken from anesthesia.

In this section we describe our visual notation which we use for scenario-based analysis. We support different kinds of domain-specific reasoning by mapping parts of the visual notation to the syntactic constructs of *description logic*.

4.1   Systemic Agents

As we show in Figure 1 we conceive *agents* (shown as soft boxes) as constitutive parts of sociotechnical systems. Agents represent human actors as well as technical devices. Since this kind of modeling is quite common for devices we focus on human actors in our examples.

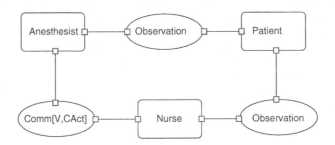

Fig. 1. Visual notation for systemic agents

From a formal point of view agents define an identity and publish a set of *interfaces* which are denoted as little squares in our visual notation. Formally we describe interfaces using signatures.

Definition 1 (Agent Signature). *An agent signature is a quadruple* $\langle \Sigma, I, O, A \rangle$ *where* Σ *is a data signature* $\langle S, Op \rangle$ *in the algebraic sense, O is the set of output attributes (the agent variables), I is the set of external attributes that the agent has to read from it's environment and A is a set of action names.*

More intuitively a signature describes the capabilities of sensing and reacting of (for example) a human actor (represented by the sets I resp. O) as well as the services it provides to its environment (represented by the set A). We use linguistic variables to describe the physical features of agents and connectors. The left hand of an actor or the display of a technical device are examples for this kind of variable.

4.2 Connectors

As we show in Figure 1 agents interact with each other using connectors (which are shown as ovals).

Definition 2 (Connector). *A connector consists of a set of roles and a* glue *which defines the relation between the roles.*

Again we describe roles using agent signatures (denoted by squares in our visual notation). If an agent uses a connector one of his interfaces is connected with a role of this connector by a *link* (denoted by a black line in our visual notation). A prominent applications for links is the assignment of tasks to agents.

5 Basics of Sociotechnical Behavior

Our approach for the description of sociotechnical behavior is based on well known transition systems which are very common in formal specification [2]. In this section we present our visual style for the transition rules which specify sociotechnical behavior.

Behavior IntroTube				
Precond	vis	pale	★	nrm
	acc	★	low	high
	expertise	h/m	low	★
Goals	bodytalk	calm	nerv	★
	introTube	low	low	high

Fig. 2. Behavioral Transition

In figure 2 we show a transition table describing possible behaviors of the agent from our example as a relation between input and output vectors of events. Each of the three columns describe a specific situation an a specific behavioral choice.

- In the left column of the AND/OR-table we describe a situation where the fuzzy probability that the anesthesist introduces the tube into the patient's throat is low because he observes that the color of the patient's face is pale. Since in this situation his expertise is high he remains calm.
- In the second column we refer to the situation where an anesthesist aborts the process of intubation because the low pitch of an alarm tone signalizes to him that the patient's oxygene saturation is too low. Because in this situation his expertise is low he is getting nervous.

– The normal case finally is described in the right column. In this case the values of the input variables express that the situation is normal and the anesthesist can proceed with intubation.

In our table-based notation we use stars ($\star$) to express that we don't care about the value of a parameter in a given context.

We claim that this visual style of reasoning is well-suited to support people with weak mathematical background to specify systemic behavior in a formal way. Moreover, this notation supports simple checks for completeness and correctness. In addition, soft system features (like bodytalk or expertise) can be included. In our approach these features are described by fuzzy semantics.

6   Mental Models: A Cognitive Approach

In our approach we provide a *cognitive perspective* which takes into account the agents subjective motivations and their influence on the global system's behavior. We claim that this allows for a better understanding of the human factors and organizational features of sociotechnical processes. For this sake we use the concept of *mental models,* which describes an agent's internal representation of his environment [14].

A mental model consists of:

– The agent's *intentions:* usually a decision aims at a certain goal. That means that the agent tries to achieve a certain system state by selecting between alternative behavioral options.
– The agent's *beliefs:* a decision is highly influenced by the agent's belief concerning the system's actual state and its further behavior.
– The agent's *desires:* usually the agent has a subjective preference for a certain behavioral option which may or may not interfere with the real situation.

These factors may influence human behavior to a high degree and thus determine global system behavior. Especially the complex configurations of cognitive attitudes in teams is only accessible by a cognitive approach. Moreover subjective factors are subject to a large scale of organizational measures like further education and simulator training.

We represent this internal information using fuzzy sets. This gives us the possibility to represent the *subjective relevance* [15] of a proposition by the membership relation μ.

We notate fuzzy sets by using *calligraphic font.* The function of the three fuzzy sets in figure 3 consists in the mental representation of the relevant contextual features [3].

In figure 3 we use a mental model to reason about the adaptation of an agent in a given situation. We define *adaptation* as a relation between a *Context* and an agent. As relevant features of a context we conceive the situational goal, the behavioral alternatives, and the relevant preconditions of decision making.

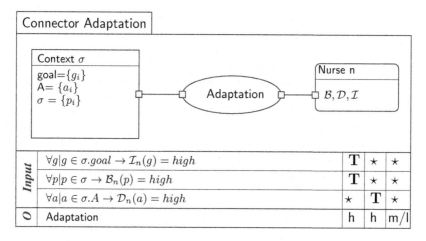

Fig. 3. Example: model for adaptation

In general, we claim that an agent's contextual adaptation is good if he has an intensive representation of the relevant features. Again, we use an AND/OR-table to reason about different configurations and their consequences for the quality of adaptation. For organizational purposes there are some interesting features of contexts. Thus, the cardinality of set A describes the free room of an agent's decision. If it is small this has inhibiting effects on his motivation. If it is too great the agent may be overstrained. Moreover, another important feature of a given context consist in the possibility of differentiation of behavioral alternatives.

We consider an integrated cognitive approach to sociotechnical modeling as a major contribution to an adequate safety management of sociotechnical systems. Frequently, critical situations can be often traced back to missing knowledge in specific contexts. Following a cognitive approach enables us to specify the situational requirements concerning knowledge. The resulting models can be used to detect systemic flaws related to communication procedures.

7   Application: Observing

In this section we describe the interaction of contextual conditions with the systemic task. Especially we focus on the relation between the employment of certain strategies and task assignment. Frequently the *shaping* of processes by contextual conditions can be observed in the medical setting. We consider this shaping as an important adaptive capability of sociotechnical systems. In this section we identify the systemic variables which determine these adaptations and describe the resulting behavior using transformation rules.

During a medical operation the anesthesist has to control the patient's state and the course of anesthesia. Consequently we define as an abstract task that

the anesthesist has to observe the patient. For this sake both, the patient and
the anesthesist have to be members of the initial configuration. And they have
to be connected by an observation connector.

In Figure 4 we use this configuration as a the start configuration of a transformation rule. (For the sake of this presentation we are leaving aside the role
of interfaces.) In our first rule we state that the abstract task of observation
may be mapped to the context-specific configuration on the right hand side of
the rule. In some contexts the anesthesist may delegate the responsibility for the
patient's observation to the nurse and communicate with her about the patient's
actual state. A precondition for the application of this rule is that the nurse has
an adequate qualification.

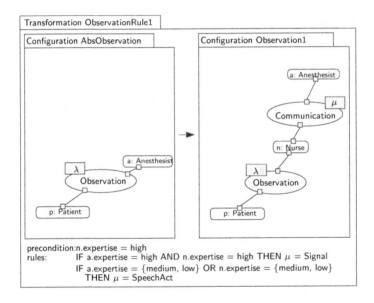

Fig. 4. Transformation Rule 1

Another typical way to process the abstract task of patient observation consists in the usage of a monitoring device which controls the characteristic parameters of the patient's state. The corresponding rule is frequently applicated
in situations where the patient's state is already stabilized.

By using simple relations about the sensual capabilities of human agent's we
are able to reason about the consequences of task assignments.

```
Assignment(acc)≤ 3
Assignment(vis)≤ 1
Assignment(lman)≤ 1
```

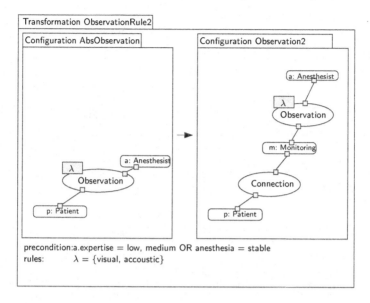

Fig. 5. Transformation Rule 2

For example we claim that for the visual capability of an agent only unary assignments are possible, while the acoustic sense may be used in more than one assignments. For this sake we exploit *numeral description* as known from description logic.

For our example we can conclude that an acoustic observation leaves more flexibility for an agent than a visual engagement. Consequently the configuration in Figure 6 is only legal with $\lambda = \texttt{acc}$. The binding of variable λ with **vis** would violate the assignment constraints. Thus an anesthesist is not able to check another patient when he is occupied with the visual observation of the monitoring device. On the other hand when it is sufficient to control the acoustic alarm tones he can move to another room to assist his colleagues.

8   Application: Behavior and Context

In section 7 we analyzed how different configuration can be substituted in order to process an abstract task given a certain set of context conditions. In this section however we consider that are closer interwoven which each other. In fact they constitute a *cascade of redundancy*.

In this section we study a very simple case of behavioral decision making demonstrating that a cascade of redundancy mechanisms is available if the original configuration fails to behave properly. We consider a scenario where a systemic agent (a nurse) has to decide if she handles a certain device (in this case a laryngoscope) to the anesthesist. Alternatively she simply can do nothing. For

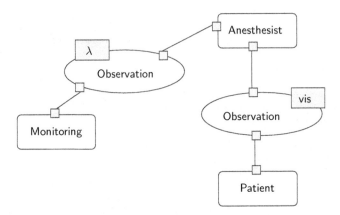

Fig. 6. Parametric Configuration

Behavior Laryngoscopy				
Precond	Adaptation(n)	h/m	⋆	⋆
	Hierarchy(n,a)	⋆	h/m	h/m
	$\mathcal{B}_n(\mathcal{I}_a(n \text{ give } l))$	⋆	h/m	⋆
	Com(a,n) and a snd m	⋆	⋆	**T**
Goals	n **give** l	h/m	h/m	h/m
	nop	l/m	l/m	l/m
	Atmosphere	high	med	low

Fig. 7. Fuzzy enabling relation

the sake of brevity we describe the original situation as well as the cascade of compensatory mechanism in a simple tabular notation (cf. Figure 7).

We selected this scenario because it is understandable without recourse to medical knowledge. Although it is very simple it is not irrelevant. In fact the behavior in this kind of situation is often taken as a criteria for the quality of team performance and for the adaptation of agents. Behavioral failures in these situations are frequently the source of serious irritations which may result in persistent intra-team conflicts.

From a systemic point of view we claim that the cascade of redundancy mechanism plays a crucial rôle concerning the stabilization of human behavior.

8.1 Simple Decision Making

In the first column of figure 7 we describe the simplest configuration w.r.t. our scenario. We argue that the probability for the nurse to show the desired behavior is high or medium if her adaptation to the given context is high or medium.

As we already argued in section 6 we use the concept of adaptation as a shortcut to describe the set of mental models which enables the nurse to show the correct behavior. So for instance she has to know that the anesthesist should become the owner of the device (in this situation) and she should be aware of the fact that he doesn't possess this instrument at the moment. If these mental attitudes are developed to a sufficient degree the nurse will show the correct behavior with a high probability.

8.2 Coordination Mechanisms: Hierarchy

Imagine the case that the nurse's situational awareness is not as good as in our recent example. In this situation she has to rely her decision on further information. Fortunately the contextual information is provided to her by a net of relationships to other agents. In this section we briefly review the coordinational function of hierarchical relations [7].

We assume that the nurse's internal information is not sufficient to provide the foundation for a correct decision. According to our model, possible reasons may be an insufficient internal goal representation or a subjective preference for the wrong behavioral option.

As we show in column 2 and 3 of figure 7 the nurse's decision may be moderated by a hierarchical relation to the anesthesist. According to the second column of our diagram the nurse's correct behavior may be triggered by a complex mental attitude which refers to the cognitive representation of another agent. Thus, if the nurse believes that the anesthesist expects her to give him the laryngoscope (and he is in fact her superior) the probability is high that she will conform to his expectations. Teams of human agents frequently coordinate their activities by higher-order mental representations, i.e. assumptions about the cognitive state of other agents [6].

8.3 Coordination Mechanisms: Communication

Finally, in the last version of our scenario all of the coordination mechanisms considered fail to be effective. In this case the anesthesist has to manipulate the nurse's cognitive representation by a directive communication act. Provided that there is a physical communication channel between the two agents he can induce the belief that he needs the laryngoscope in the nurse. Again there are several ways to do this. For example he has the choice between verbal and non-verbal communication. Each of these alternatives influences the system's performance in a characteristic way.

A crucial aspect in systemic performance is described in the last row of figure 7. By the variable *atmosphere* we describe the consequences of different styles

of behavior for the global temper among the team members. We argue that
an unobstructed way of task processing results in a good working atmosphere
while the need to employ compensatory mechanisms frequently is a source of
irritations and tensions.

9   Uncertain Behavior and Human Error

Since we have a special interest in sociotechnical risks related to human error
we reason about errors using fuzzy fault trees. Using fault trees we can reason
about *knowledge-based type* of human errors *(mistakes)* using propositions about
mental models[12]. Mistakes may occur when the beliefs of an agent are not
adapted to the given context. For example a nurse may have the correct goals
but fail to act properly because she doesn't see the need to act. Another error-
case occurs when an agent's goals do not fit well into the given context.

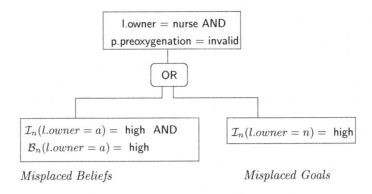

Fig. 8. Fault tree for human error

In Figure 8 we show an error situation where the laryngoscope wasn't given to
the anesthesist in time. Consequently the patient's preoxygenation has become
invalid. From our (simplified) analysis of the situation we can conclude that
there may be two causes of error related to the agents mental representations.

- The nurse may have the correct goal (the anesthesist should be the owner of
  the laryngoscope) but the wrong expectation about the environment. When
  she believes that the anesthesist already has the laryngoscope she will make
  the wrong decision and do nothing *(misplaced beliefs)*.
- The nurse may represent an incorrect intentions *(misplaced goals)*.

Although we have to refine our descriptions in further interdisciplinary research we claim that our method provides a smooth integration of formal modeling and human factors. The consideration of mental models and internal representations in systems engineering provides new possibilities to reason about
soft systemic parameters which so far have frequently escaped formal reasoning.

We claim that the methodical integration of cognitive parameters into model-based reasoning about systemic safety provides a structured way of interdisciplinary system analysis. We think that in sociotechnical settings it is highly important to make explicit the impact of knowledge distributions on safety and process quality.

10   Conclusion

In this paper we provided a visual notation for the modeling of safety-critical sociotechnical systems. We started with structural description, dynamic architectures, and transformation rules for reasoning about adaptive system behavior.

We then took a *cognitive perspective* by introducing the concepts of mental model and decision-making. This type of behavior is observable in systems where human and organizational agents are involved. We introduced visual concepts for the description of decision situations. Using fuzzy concepts we modeled the influence of several factors on decision making and thus on the global system's behavior.

On this platform we are able to describe the adaptive behavior of sociotechnical systems and its specific contextual embedding. We provide concepts for the construction of models that contribute to a better understanding of complex interactions and the impact of contextual parameters.

In the future we will work on the formal foundation of our notation and the implementation of the corresponding semantics in tools for automated reasoning. In addition we will exploit our results as contributions to the design of *context aware* and autonomic systems. In order to make our notation practical and to provide adequate support for real life situations we plan case studies and interdisciplinary cooperations.

Acknowledgements. This work was founded by *Technische Universität Berlin* as part of an interdisciplinary research focus titled *Cooperation and Safety in Complex Sociotechnical Systems*. Many of our arguments were influenced by the discussions and cooperations which researchers from ergonomics, psychology, semiotics and sociology. We are also very grateful for the comments of the anonymous reviewers.

References

1. Franz Baader, Diego Calvanese, Deboray McGuiness, Daniele Nardi, and Peter Patel-Schneider. *The Description Logic Handbook. Theory, Implementation and Application.* Cambridge Unversity Press, Cambridge, 2003.
2. David Harel. Statecharts: a visual formalism for complex systems. *Science of Computer Programming*, 8:231–274, 1987.
3. Janusz Kacprzyk. *Multistage fuzzy control.* Wiley, Chichester, 1997.
4. George J. Klir and Bo Yuan. *Fuzzy Sets and Fuzzy Logic. Theory and Applications.* Prentice Hall, Upper Saddle River, N.J., 1995.

5. Nancy Leveson. *Safeware. System safety and computers.* Addison Wesley, Reading, Mass., 1995.
6. David Lewis. *Convention: A Philosophical Study.* Havard Univ. Pr., Cambridge, Mass., 1969.
7. Henry Mintzberg. *Structures in fives: designing effective organizations.* Prentice Hall, Englewood Cliffs, 1983.
8. Peter Pepper, Michael Cebulla, Klaus Didrich, and Wolfgang Grieskamp. From program languages to software languages. *The Journal of Systems and Software,* 60, 2002.
9. Peter Pepper, Ch. Frank, W. Holfelder, D. Jiang, and G. Matylis. Dynamic software architectures for a "sometimes somewhere" telematics concept. Technical report, Technische Universität Berlin, 2003.
10. Peter Pepper and Martin Wirsing. A method for the development of correct software. In Manfred Broy and Stefan Jähnichen, editors, *KORSO: Methods, Languages, and Tools for the Construction of Correct Software,* pages 27–57. Springer, 1995.
11. Charles Perrow. *Normal Accidents. Living with High-Risk Technologies.* Basic Books, New York, 1984.
12. James Reason. *Human Error.* Cambridge Univ. Pr., 1990.
13. Mary Shaw and David Garlan. *Software Architecture. Perspectives on an emerging discipline.* Prentice Hall, Upper Saddle River, N.J., 1996.
14. Munindar P. Singh. *Multiagent Systems. A Theoretical Framework for Intentions, Know-how, and Communications.* Springer, Berlin, Heidelberg, 1994.
15. Dan Sperber and Deidre Wilson. *Relevance. Communication and cognition.* Basil Blackwell, Oxford, 1986.

Analysing Mode Confusion:
An Approach Using FDR2

Bettina Buth[1,2]

[1] BISS, Bremen Institute for Safe Systems
bb@tzi.de
[2] EADS SPACE Transportation, Bremen

Abstract. Mode confusion situations or more general automation surprises can arise in the context of sophisticated control systems which require the interaction with human operators as for example flight monitoring systems in airplanes. A "mode" is defined by a subset of system variables the values of which determine distinguishable forms of system behaviour. Critical situations can arise if the operator interacts with the system assuming a wrong mode. The identification and analysis of such situations needs to take into account both the system design and the operators mental model of the system. Recent research showed that model-checking techniques are useful for identifying mode-confusion situations. Two different approaches can be found: the first tries to identify mode confusion potential in system design, the second analyses actual mode confusion situations to identify the discrepancies between the mental model of operators and the system design. This paper reports an experiment in using the model-checker FDR2 for comparing system and mental models based on CSP refinement. In contrast to earlier attempts using model-checkers for this task, this approach allows a direct comparison of the two models which can be easily derived from a rule-based description.

1 Introduction

The ever-increasing complexity of computer-based systems has lead to a changed role of human operators, especially in safety-critical applications such as air-craft and train control, chemical and nuclear plants, medical equipment, or automobile components. The use of computers in such systems has a high potential for automation as well as extended functionality, but also requires sophisticated control and monitoring mechanisms due to the inherent complexity. These themselves can be implemented as computer-based processes which allow to take away the strain from human operators who would otherwise have to cope with a multitude of information and a higher demand on reaction times required for the interaction with such systems.

Nonetheless, in many applications a total automation of the system control is not accepted or (not yet) possible. Human operators are often the ultimate instance for dealing with emergencies or have to provide necessary information not directly available to the computer-based kernel systems. Research activities

M. Heisel et al. (Eds.): SAFECOMP 2004, LNCS 3219, pp. 101–114, 2004.

in the Human Factors community focus on human-computer interfaces based on psychological as well as design-oriented considerations. As Sarter, Woods and Billings [1] and Leveson et.al. [2] point out, technology-centred automation potentially leads to designs which are problematic for the human interaction.

One area which has found attention during the last years is the investigation of so called *automation surprises*, particularly *mode confusion*. This paper discusses the use of model-checking for the comparison of abstract system models and mental models with the objective to analyse mode confusion situations. The emphasis is on the specification and model-checking aspects rather than on the socio-technological perspective. The remainder of the introduction provides the background for the approach as well as an informal description of the example, a *kill-the-capture* scenario. Section 2 describes one possible approach to the analysis of this example using FDR2. Section 3 summarizes the experiences and tries to generalize the results.

1.1   Mode Confusion Analysis – Background

Modes are identifiable and distinguishable states of a system which differ with regard to the effect of interactions. The complexity of a system is reflected in a large number of different modes and complex rules for mode transitions as well as functionality in a mode. Mode confusion scenarios or in general automation surprises describe situations where the operator's assumption about the system mode differs from the actual mode of the system and actions performed under this assumption result in critical situations. In order to detect and eliminate mode confusion, a thorough analysis of the system design and functionality as well as the human-computer interface is required.

Techniques from the formal methods field prove to be useful for mode confusion analysis. Several approaches based on abstract models of the system are documented; see e.g. Leveson et.al. [2], Miller and Potts [3], or Lüttgen and Carreño [4]. These experiments focus on the identification of situations that potentially lead to mode confusion, particularly the identification of categories of indicators for mode-confusion situation and use an abstract model of the system as starting point. Rushby [5,6] suggests a complementary use of model-checking based on two different models of the system. The actual model is an abstract model of the actual system behaviour; the second reflects the mental model of the operator which may be a reduced version of the full model or even may contain wrong assumptions about the system.

In contrast to the approaches of Leveson and Miller and Potts, Rushby's approach aims at identifying critical discrepancies between the models rather than investigating the mode confusion potential of the actual model. Such differences reflect deviations in the observed behaviour of the models which can point to potential mode confusion situations. Rushby formalizes the models in the Murϕ [7] model-checker notation and employs Murϕ to perform a full state exploration. The system not only uncovers the flaw already known from the analysis by Leveson, but also detects several other problems of the suggested corrections. The model can also be enhanced by incorporating a more specific operator behaviour.

Since Murφ is not able to compare two models directly, a usual trick is used: both models are merged into one by renaming the relevant state components such that these have disjoint names. The Murφ rules then are used to describe the effect of inputs or events to the full set of state variables.

This is slightly unsatisfactory, since an untrained person will not be able to determine such a specification from the distinct views of the actual and mental models respectively, even if the Murφ rules can be easily understood with a basic knowledge of state transition machines or simple automata. Similarly, the formalization of invariants as criteria for the absence of mode confusion will in general require some explanation or even a manual analysis of the models (which may very well uncover the problems in the models). Rushby himself [5,6] suggests to employ a different type of model-checker, namely the CSP-based tool FDR2 as an alternative, since FDR2 allows to compare models in a more direct way. In the following, this suggested approach is investigated, taking the Murφ model as a starting point.

1.2   The Example

The example in Rushby's papers [5,6,8] is taken from an article by Palmer [9], which reports two cases of altitude deviation scenarios. These cases and three others were observed in a NASA study in which several crews flew realistic missions in DC-9 and MD-88 aircraft simulators. This example has previously been investigated by Leveson [10].

In the following, the scenario description as stated by Rushby [5,6] is presented, which is the starting point for the Murφ model. In order to follow the scenario it is necessary to explain some features beforehand. The PITCH mode is a control element for the autopilot which determines the climbing behaviour of the aircraft. The modes are

VERT SPD vertical speed; climb at a specified rate (feet per minute)
IAS   indicated air speed; climb at a rate which is consistent with holding the air speed (knots)
ALT HLD   altitude hold; hold current altitude
ALT CAP   altitude capture; provide smooth levelling off when reaching desired altitude

The second relevant component is the ALT capture mode (one of several possible capture modes) indicates that the aircraft should climb to the the desired altitude and then hold that altitude. For the example it suffices to imagine this mode as a binary value which reflects whether the mode is set (armed) or not.

The interaction between the modes is of particular interest:

– if ALT capture is armed and the desired altitude is reached, the pitch mode is set to ALT HLD.

- the ALT CAP pitch mode is entered automatically when the aircraft gets near the desired altitude under the condition that ALT is armed; it switches off the ALT capture mode
- if ALT CAP pitch mode is set and the desired altitude is reached, the aircraft levels off and pitch mode is changed to ALT HLD.

The scenario as reported by Palmer [9] describes a potentially critical situation where an aircraft leaves its assigned flight corridor and enters a flight altitude which could be assigned to other aircrafts. The cause for this situation is obviously that the ALT capture was switched off without the Captain noticing it (the only information provided is that the ARM window switches to blank). Analysis of the situation shows that the interaction between pitch modes and ALT capture mode is more complex than first assumed.

Leveson and Palmer [10] present the essential information of this incident as presented in Fig. 1. Note that the information presented is only part of the overall interface of the pilot, especially the control instruments for setting speed and target altitude are placed on a separate panel (the Mode Control Panel) which also presents some of the information available from the FMA.

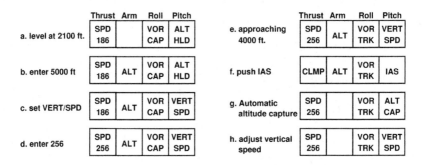

Fig. 1. FMA Displays for the Example Incident

Rushby [8] also derives a state machine representation of the abstract behaviour of the autopilot with regard to pitch mode and altitude capture mode. This model takes into account the relevant modes and the inputs of both the plane crew and the events from the environment. This model, which is shown in Fig. 2 abstracts from the general status of the plane, as for example altitude, speed, motion or similar and from related values the pilot could enter. What remains is an abstraction of the behaviour focused on pitch mode and capture mode restricted to ALT. Similarly, Rushby provides a state machine representation of the mental model as derived from the case study. This is shown in Fig. 3.

The obvious difference between the two models is the number of states. The mental model does not contain an explicit state for ALT CAP, the pitch mode which is entered automatically without pilot interaction. This omission models the fact that the pilot was not aware of this particular mode and the related

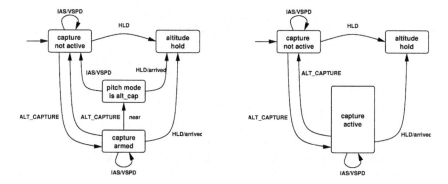

Fig. 2. State Machine for Actual Model   **Fig. 3.** State Machine for Mental Model

changes to the ALT capture mode. A formal analysis of these automata models with regard to their language equivalence will also reveal deviations in the possible mode transitions, but further analysis is required to examine whether these differences are indeed critical.

2   FDR2 Formalization and Analysis

This section presents an approach of employing FDR2 [11] for the investigation of the mode confusion situation reported by Palmer [9]. The Murφ specification described by Rushby provided the starting point. The main objective of the experiment is to evaluate the benefits of FDR2 with regard to its ability to compare two models.

For this purpose several alternative approaches were investigated, which involved both rule-based and automata-based models, where the latter is based in the automata for actual and mental model as presented in Fig. 2 and 3. For the experiment the error situations uncovered by FDR2 were compared to the problems found using the Murφ system. In the following, the rule-based description of separate actual and mental model are presented and analysed. A full report of this and the other approaches can be found in Buth [12].

2.1   Actual and Mental Model – A Rule-Based Specification

The objective of this subsection is to investigate the possibilities of checking mental and actual model by comparing them with regard to refinement properties of CSP models.

The specification language employed by FDR2 is CSP_M, a machine-readable version of CSP. The core concepts of these specifications are processes which communicate over synchronous channels. State spaces in form of global variables are not directly available in CSP, but CSP_M allows the parametrized specification of processes.

The first definitions of the specification introduce the data type pitch-mode similar to the type in the Murφ specification and a set of channels, which in this case represent the possible events from the environment (pilot input and external events). The event names are chosen to correspond to the rule names in the Murφ specification.

```
datatype pitch_modes = vert_speed | ias | alt_cap | alt_hld
channel ALT_CAPTURE, HLD, IAS, VSPD, near, arrived
channel obs : pitch_modes.Bool
```

The additional channel obs of observables is introduce to make the mode transitions visible in the model traces. It is required in addition to the usual observable event traces over the channels to monitor the progress of the system. The motivation is that the information about the state transitions is essential for identifying the causes for error situations in the check.

Two distinct processes ASYS and MSYS are specified for the actual and the mental model, respectively. The state spaces of both models are determined by the pitch-mode and the capture-mode, which are stated as parameters of the processes. Note that the changes of these two state components are observed via the above mentioned channel obs. The initial value is a non-deterministic selection from the set of pitch-modes without the alt_cap mode for the pitch-mode and false for the capture-mode.

```
ASYS = |~| p: diff (pitch_modes, alt_cap) @ ASYS1 (p, false)

ASYS1 (pitch_mode, capture_armed) =
   obs!pitch_mode.capture_armed ->
   (
    ALT_CAPTURE -> ASYS1 (pitch_mode, not capture_armed)
    []
    HLD          -> ASYS1 (alt_hld, capture_armed)
    []
    IAS          -> ASYS1 (ias, capture_armed)
    []
    VSPD         -> ASYS1 (vert_speed, capture_armed)
    []
    (capture_armed) & near -> ASYS1 (alt_cap, false)
    []
    ((pitch_mode == alt_cap) or capture_armed) & arrived
            -> ( let pm = if ((pitch_mode == alt_cap) or capture_armed)
                          then alt_hld
                          else pitch_mode
                 within
                   ASYS1 (pm, false)
               )
   )
```

Note the way the boolean guards are used to express that certain transitions are not possible under all circumstances. Here, additional constraints as derived from the automata model in Fig. 2 have been used to provide a more complete model. The event **near** only has effect if the capture-mode is active. Similarly **arrived** is regarded if the capture-mode is active or the pitch-mode already is alt_cap.

The mental model works with a reduced set of pitch-modes, which does not include the alt_cap mode; here a subset of the full set of pitch-modes is defined. The process MSYS then is defined analogously to the process ASYS, omitting the **near** event and the behaviour in the ignored alt_cap pitch-mode.

```
pm_ideal = {pm | pm <- pitch_modes, pm != alt_cap}

MSYS = |~| p: pm_ideal @ MSYS1 (p, false)

MSYS1 (pitch_mode, ideal_capture) =
  obs!pitch_mode.ideal_capture ->
    (
    ALT_CAPTURE -> MSYS1 (pitch_mode, not ideal_capture)
    []
    HLD          -> MSYS1 (alt_hld, ideal_capture)
    []
    IAS          -> MSYS1 (ias, ideal_capture)
    []
    VSPD         -> MSYS1 (vert_speed, ideal_capture)
    []
    (ideal_capture) & arrived
                 -> MSYS1 (alt_hld, false)
    )
```

This specification of the mental model could easily have been derived from a set of rules or an automata representation such as the one in Fig. 3. In particular, it can be derived without information about the actual model. Note that for the analysis of the mode-confusion situation such a rule-based or automata model will originally needs to be derived from the understanding of the operator rather than other material. For this study, the mental model was taken from the Murφ example.

In order to prove that the models are equivalent, it is necessary to map them to a common set of observable events. This means that the event **near** which is not visible in the mental model as well as the artificial events related to the invisible pitch-mode alt_cap need to be hidden from the interface of the actual model. This is done using the hiding construct in CSP_M:

```
Mental_Model = MSYS
Actual_Model = ASYS \ {|near, obs.alt_cap|}
```

Now it is possible to specify the desired equivalence. Since FDR2 only allows to check refinement in any of the three models (traces, failures or failure-divergence; see [13,11] for details), it is necessary to prove the two directions of the equivalence separately. Furthermore, it is of interest to prove equivalence both in the trace as well as in the failures model. Trace equivalence which is checked as mutual trace refinement ([T=) in FDR2, only ensures that both systems are able to perform the same sequences of events. For the given example this ensures that both systems are able to react to external inputs in the same way and that the state changes are performed accordingly (by observing the obs events). In addition, it is of interest to know whether at any point in time one of the models could refuse an event which can not be refused by the other. This is not of direct interest for the artificial state events, but could point to a problem with the inputs and external system events. Refusal properties are checked using failures refinement ([F=) in FDR2. The following checks were performed in the example:

```
assert Actual_Model [T= Mental_Model
assert Mental_Model [T= Actual_Model
assert Actual_Model [F= Mental_Model
assert Mental_Model [F= Actual_Model
```

Of these checks, the first and third succeed, while the second and fourth fail. FDR2 reports the following error scenarios, which are the same for the two failing checks. The process the behaviour of which is reported in the following is the process ASYS. The behaviour of MSYS is not explicitly reported for these errors, which shows that MSYS is able to perform the same traces except for the last event. Note that the traces of Actual_Model are subtraces of these traces, namely those where the hidden events are removed.

```
BEHAVIOUR:
Performs        <_tau, obs.ias.false, ALT_CAPTURE, obs.ias.true,
                near, obs.alt_cap.false, IAS, obs.ias.false>
```

Analysis of this first error in connection with the specification of MSYS shows that the event obs.ias.false is not a possible event since the capture-mode is still true after ALT_CAPTURE, which is the last relevant event from the perspective of MSYS. This means that FDR2 detects the same kind of error as was found be Murφ and the combined specification. The advantage of this usage of FDR2 is the documentation of other possible errors. The following two are but variants of the first case, where the final state is related to the pitch-modes vert_speed and alt_hld instead of ias.

The next three cases require further analysis of both actual and mental model. The first such error trace of ASYS is reported as follows:

```
BEHAVIOUR:
Performs        <_tau, obs.ias.false, ALT_CAPTURE, obs.ias.true,
                near, obs.alt_cap.false, ALT_CAPTURE,
                obs.alt_cap.true, IAS>
```

The other two traces vary in the initial state, where the different pitch-modes are taken. All of them show the same sequence of external events, namely

```
<ALT_CAPTURE, near, ALT_CAPTURE, IAS>
```

where IAS is the event which is refused by MSYS and thus Mental_Model. Without regarding the auxiliary obs events it is not possible to understand the underlying problem. Thus it helps to have a look at the trace of Actual_Model:

```
BEHAVIOUR:
Performs        <_tau, obs.ias.false, ALT_CAPTURE, obs.ias.true,
                _tau, _tau, ALT_CAPTURE, _tau, IAS>
```

This perspective reveals that Actual_Model is able to perform the IAS event directly after the ALT_CAPTURE event, without an intermediate obs event. This is definitively not possible for MSYS respectively Mental_Model. The essential question here is how to interpret these error situations.

Obviously, the problem is connected to hiding the obs.alt_cap events, which means that it is related to the problem that one of the pitch-modes is invisible. Since the ALT_CAPTURE event only changes the capture-component of the state space but does not lead to a state transition, the full effect is hidden. Investigation of the behaviour of MSYS shows that the second ALT_CAPTURE event leads to the event obs.alt_hld.false in the mental model for the first error case and similar for the other cases. Several things need to be considered here:

- the mode-confusion problem is not only related to the inconsistency in the pitch-modes of the models; the different capture-modes pose a problem in itself. Although the invariant used in the Murϕ model would not be violated if the pitch-modes were the same, a following IAS event would immediately lead to an error trace as the first three reported above.

- what is the desired reaction to an ALT_CAPTURE during the alt_cap pitch-mode? The Murϕ model does allow changes of the capture-mode during the approaching phase after near, but is that a suitable abstraction of the behaviour? Comparison with the models as described in Fig. 2 and Figure 3 does provide a hint that this abstraction could indeed be a problem. While the mental model allows to switch between the "capture active" and "capture not active" state, this is not allowed for the "pitch mode is alt_cap" state. This suggests that the second ALT_CAPTURE event should not have been possible in ASYS. Actually, Rushby detects this problem in one of the later versions of the Murϕ model and assumes that ALT_CAPTURE should not be possible in pitch-mode alt_cap. The FDR2 specification can be corrected in a similar way:

```
...
    (pitch_mode != alt_cap) & ALT_CAPTURE
            -> ASYS1 (pitch_mode, not capture_armed)
...
```

By guarding the event ALT_CAPTURE in the actual model in this way, the error cases can indeed be reduced to the original three which are directly related to the mode confusion situation as related to the capture-modes.

- can the specification be modified in a way that allows to cope with such missing events; more generally: is there a way to deal with hidden state changes in the case where events lead to explicit state changes in the second model? Up to now no general solution has been found for this problem.

After performing the corrections analogously to the suggestions for the Murφ model, the resulting specification still shows an error, a refusal error for the check

```
Mental_Model [F= Actual_Model
```

Checking the traces and refusals reveals that while the actual model could engage in any external event but ALT_CAPTURE or near, the mental model could also engage in ALT_CAPTURE. Further analysis of this situation in comparison with the error-free Murφ model reveals a flaw in that model: rule ''ALT CAPTURE in the Murφ specification reads as follows:

```
rule "ALT CAPTURE" pitch_mode != alt_cap ==>
begin
  capture_armed := !capture_armed;
  ideal_capture := !ideal_capture;
end;
```

But this means that the behaviour of the mental model, namely the changes to state variable ideal_capture are influenced by the value of pitch_mode, which is not part of the mental model. The FDR2 error shows the effect of the change to the actual model alone and reveals a new error situation. This error-situation is due to the the change with regard to the error found above: guarding ALT_CAPTURE in the actual model prevents a second such event in pitch-mode alt_cap, but in the mental model such a change is allowed. Thus the corrections still do not capture the problems arising from the hidden state properly.

3   Lessons Learned

The previous section discusses one possible approach to the analysis of the case study presented by Palmer [9] using CSP specifications and FDR2 for checking them. The specifications are based on the idea of Rushby [5,6,8] to compare abstract formalizations of actual system and mental model. This section tries to summarize and generalize the experiences using FDR2 the suitability of model-checking for mode-confusion analysis in general and the exploitation of mode-confusion analysis for system design.

3.1   Evaluating the FDR2 Approach

The essential difference between the Murφ and the CSP_M specification is the way in which the models are compared. The FDR2 specifications allow a separate specification of actual and mental model, while the Murφ specification presents a view of the combined models with a partially shared state space.

For both approaches it is necessary to determine how mode confusion situations can be identified, which parts of the specifications need to be observed to detect such a critical situation. The study presented Buth [12] contains three different variants for the example: the first directly corresponding to the Murφ version, a second separating the actual and mental model but still using the rule-based description as basis, and a third directly derived from the automata representation as given in Figures 2 and 3.

The overall experience with modelling these versions in FDR2 is quite encouraging: each of the models requires little effort for a CSP expert or even someone with a general specification background. Similarly, the evaluation of error scenarios reported by FDR2 does not pose any particular obstacles assuming a basic understanding of the overall system functionality. The following paragraphs summarize the experience with the different models.

The combined as the original Murφ model requires the formalization of an invariant. The definition of such invariant properties already requires some form of analysis in order to correlate the state spaces of the two models. The approach of specifying two independent models seems to provide a more direct way for the comparison. It is not necessary to define the invariant explicitly; the models can be compared with regard to their external behaviour or - as shown above - additionally with regard to the values of their state components. The general assumption for this approach is that a critical situation only arises if the models react in a different way to their environment. The errors found are essentially the same as by Murφ. The interesting error from the point of view of the comparison is the one not found by Murφ. This error can not be detected in the Murφ model due to the introduction of a dependency between the state transitions of mental and actual model in rule **ALT CAPTURE** of the combined model. The dependency does not exist in reality where the models can not influences each other. This modelling error can not occur in a model using two separate processes, since the state spaces of the processes are not directly related.

The difference of the automata model to the rule-based FDR2 specifications and the Murφ model is the handling of states. The automata model does not work with the full state-space as defined by the cross-product of the possible values of the modes, but starts from a more realistic view where similar states are combined into one state and labelled according to their meaning. The specification of such models from given automata models is straightforward and could even be done automatically provided a suitable presentation of the automata is available.

While the automata-based approach does not have any disadvantages with regard to the errors found, the decision for the automata style does essentially depend on the availability of such a model. Often, it will be easier to capture a set of rules in the style of the rule-based FDR2 specification than to develop the automata view if it is not already available. The capture of rules in this way has the advantage of allowing incompleteness and non-determinism without explicit consideration - at least for an initial version of the specification. A refinement of the specifications in order to exclude unrealistic behaviour will in both cases require the same kind of considerations.

Note that a combination of the rule-based and automata-based specification styles is in general possible. This would allow to use an automata model for the actual system, where such automata presentations may be available from the system design documents, while specifying the mental model based on rules. In general, the main problem for the comparison of models will be the definition of the interrelation between the two systems; this includes the identification which events must be hidden and which renaming should be used to facilitate a comparison. But this is independent from a particular specification style.

3.2   Model-Checking for Mode Confusion Analysis

A first conclusion from the experiments with FDR2 is the confirmation of Rushbys résumé: model-checking provides a relatively easy approach to investigating models with regard to mode confusion situations. One particular benefit is the ease with which the models can be adapted and extended in order to check potential corrections. At least with the given example the model-checker provides almost immediate feedback on error situations.

Two essential questions need to be discussed with regard to the general usage of model-checking for this kind of task:

- How can the specifications for mental and actual model be derived in a systematic way and on basis of which input?
- How can the errors found by model-checking be related to situations in the real system?

Both questions are strongly connected to the topic of suitable abstraction for both the real system and the operators understanding of the system. With regard to the application of a model-checking tool, the specifications should be as abstract as possible, restricted to the minimal set of state and environment information. This is a prerequisite for a successful application of a model-checking tool since too much information will in general lead to a state explosion and thus to potential problems with the state-exploration approach.

A discussion of the questions concerning abstraction and error analysis in relation to the adequacy of the models for the presented example can be found in Buth [12]. The general conclusion is that the suitability of the abstraction and form of specification depends on the concrete application and the knowledge of the people involved; a systematic approach will only be possible when more experiences with this use of formal methods in the framework of human-computer interfaces are available.

3.3   Evaluating the Results from Mode Confusion Analysis

One essential topic not yet addressed is how the results of mode confusion analysis such as presented above could be used. This question is directly related to the goals of such an analysis and these need to be correlated to the development phase in which the analysis takes place. Essentially there are two possible objectives:

- using mode-confusion analysis during the design phase of a system to ensure an adequate design without or at least with a minimum of mode-confusion potential
- analyse critical situations encountered during the integration, acceptance or operation phase of such a system.

A comparative approach as presented in this paper requires the existence of two models. A mental model will not generally be available during the design of a new system. It may be available for new developments in domains where the user interfaces are standardized to a certain extent, as for example aircraft instrument panels, automobile or train control elements. A mental model can also be derived from training material of an existing system or from rules captured in interviews. In most cases a mental model will be derived from discussions with an operator, i.e. after deployment of the system under investigation.

If no such models are available during the design phase, two further alternatives are possible. Model-checking can also be employed to check for mode confusion indicators in an abstraction of the system design as suggested by Lüttgen and Carreño [4], an idea which is influenced by the approach of Leveson [2]. Alternatively, mode confusion analysis could also be used to derive a minimal mode confusion free mental model of new or existing systems. The idea has already been presented by Rushby [5,6,8]. He outlines the use of such minimal models for the evaluation of designs: if even the minimal mental model is very complex this could be an indicator for the inadequacy of the system design from the point of view of the human-computer interface.

In any case identified mode confusion situations should lead to changes in the design; the objective is to prevent the introduction of mode confusion potential in the implementation. For the necessary modifications of the interface, the design, or the operation procedures, results from the human-computer-interfaces community should be taken into account.

3.4   Limits of the Model-Checking Approach

Although the results presented in this study are very exciting and point to a very interesting direction of using model-checking and formal methods in general, some remarks are due with regard to the applicability of this approach. The example considered here as well as those discussed by the other authors, are fairly small parts of larger and more complex systems. It requires more examples to prove that the approach scales to realistic applications. This is essential for many of the potential uses of the mode confusion analysis discussed above, but particularly for the validation of designs.

References

1. Sarter, N., Woods, D., Billings, C.: Automation surprises. In Salvendy, G., ed.: Handbook of Human Factors and Ergonomics. Second edition edn. John Wiley and Sons (1997)

2. Levevson, N.G., Pinnel, L.D., Sandys, S.D., Koga, S., Rees, J.D.: Analyzing software specifications for mode confusion potential. In Johnson, C.W., ed.: Proceedings of a Workshop on Human Error and System Development, Glasgow, Scotland. Glasgow Accident Analysis Group, Technical Report GAAG-TR-97-2 (March 1997) p. 132–146

3. Miller, S., Potts, J.: Detecting mode confusion through formal modeling and analysis. Technical Report NASA/CR-1999-208971, NASA Langley Research Center (January 1999) available at
http://shemesh.larc.nasa.gov/fm/fm-pubs-larc.html.

4. Lüttgen, G., Carreño, V.: Analyzing mode confusion via model checking. Technical Report NASA/CR-1999-209332, ICASE Report No. 99-18, ICASE - NASA Langley Research Center (May 1999) available at
http://shemesh.larc.nasa.gov/fm/fm-pubs-icase.html.

5. Rushby, J.: Using model checking to help discover mode confusions and other automation surprises. In Javaux, D., ed.: Proceedings of the 3rd Workshop on Human Error, Safety, and System Development (HESSD'99), University of Liege, Belgium (1999)

6. Rushby, J.: Using model checking to help discover mode confusions and other automation surprises. Reliability Engineering and System Safety 75 (2002) 167–177 Available at http://www.csl.sri.com/users/rushby/abstracts/ress02.

7. Dill, D.: The Murφ verification system. In Alur, R., Henzinger, T., eds.: Computer Aided Verification, CAV'96. Volume 1102 of LNCS., Springer-Verlag (1996)

8. Rushby, J., Crow, J., Palmer, E.: An automated method to detect potential mode confusions. In: 18th AIAA/IEEE Digital Avionics Systems Conference, St Louis, MO (1999)

9. Palmer, E.: "Oops, it didn't arm." A case study of two automation surprises. In Jensen, R.S., Rakovan, L.A., eds.: Proceedings of the Eightth International Symposium on Aviation Psychology, Columbus, OH. The Aviation Psychology Department of Aerospace Engineering, Ohio State University (April 1995) p.227–232 available at http://human-factors.arc.nasa.gov/IHpersonnel/ev.

10. Leveson, N.G., Palmer, E.: Designing automation to reduce operator errors. In: Proceedings of the IEEE Systems, Man, and Cybernetics Conference. (1997)

11. Formal Systems (Europe) Lts: FDR2 User Manual. (1997) Available under
http://www.formal.demon.co.uk/fdr2manual/index.html.

12. Buth, B.: Formal and Semi-Formal Methods for the Analysis of Industrial Control Systems. Volume 15 of BISS Monographs. (2002) (Habilitationsschrift submitted May 2001).

13. Roscoe, A.W.: The Theory and Practice of Concurrency. Prentice-Hall International (1998)

Handling Safety Critical Requirements in System Engineering Using the B Formal Method

Didier Essamé

Siemens Transportation Systems.
50, rue Barbés. BP 531, 92542 Montrouge Cedex, France
Tel: 01 49 65 72 90
Didier.Essame@siemens.com

Overview

The IEEE standard "std 1220-1998" defines system engineering as a collaborative and an interdisciplinary approach to transform customer needs into a system solution. The fundamental system engineering objective is to provide high-quality products and services, with the correct people and performances features, at an affordable price, and on time. Building critical system involves stringent management of safety critical requirements. In particular, the engineering process must guarantee that resulting technical requirements do not jeopardize customer safety needs.

Introduced by Jean Raymond Abrial in 1998, "Event B" is an extension of the B formal method. Several studies and publications showed the significance of Event B for system level modelling and analysis. However, the approach still needed to be put to the test in an industrial context. Research at Siemens Transportation Systems (formerly MATRA Transport International) defined a methodology of use of Event B in system engineering based on the IEEE 1220 and EIA 632 standard that govern system engineering processes. These standards define a set of processes and activities and give recommendations about how to achieve systems studies. Since Event B has to improve system engineering work, it must:

- Be integrated in the existing system life cycle
- Respect the documentary chain that accompanies the system life cycle.

It must also be accessible to non-specialists and allow systematic practices.

Siemens Transportation Systems defined a set of activities concerning the main disciplines of system engineering where formalization and in particular the B-Method can be applied. This research resulted in two major processes of engineering namely:

- Transparent integration of the formal B-method in systems studies to meet safety critical customer requirements.
- Systematic formal system modelling to prove that resulting technical requirements do not jeopardize customer safety needs.

This talk presents the methodological elements for the application of these two processes in an industrial context with technical and economic constraints. I present a case study of a railway train protection system. I show how to analyse the conditions of the contract and formally derive system's specifications that respect customer safety needs.

M. Heisel et al. (Eds.): SAFECOMP 2004, LNCS 3219, p. 115, 2004.
© Springer-Verlag Berlin Heidelberg 2004

A Hybrid Testing Methodology for Railway Control Systems

Giuseppe De Nicola, Pasquale di Tommaso, Rosaria Esposito,
Francesco Flammini, and Antonio Orazzo

ANSALDO SIGNAL - Ansaldo Segnalamento Ferroviario S.p.A.
Via Nuova delle Brecce, 260
80147 Napoli, Italy
Phone: +39.081.243.2981 – Fax: +39.081.243.7089
{denicola.giuseppe,ditommaso.pasquale,esposito.rosaria,
flammini.francesco,orazzo.antonio}@asf.ansaldo.it

Abstract. International standards for V&V processes prescribe systematic test-ing as a fundamental step of safety-critical systems life-cycle, in order to prove the fulfilment of their requirements. However, proposed approaches are quite general and, for complex systems, imply an excessive number of test-cases to ensure the correctness of system behaviour in any operating scenarios, includ-ing unexpected ones. A more detailed methodology is needed to extensively test all the aspects of a complex system, while keeping the number of test-cases be-low a reasonable threshold. This paper describes the ASF hybrid testing meth-odology, combining black-box and white-box techniques, based on the identifi-cation and reduction of influence variables. Such an approach was successfully applied to validate ASF implementation of the SCMT system (an Italian Auto-matic Train Control specification), showing its time effectiveness and full achieved coverage. The same methodology, with the related customization, is now being improved in order to test the new ERTMS/ETCS systems.

1 Introduction

Testing is one of the most complex and time consuming activities within the devel-opment of dependable real-time systems [2]. A systematic functional testing (black-box) [4] consists in verifying the integration of already validated subsystems, in order to check if the overall system complies with the specification (verification spectrum). Various techniques have been proposed in the literature to deal with functional testing issues. Most approaches are based on the idea of partition testing [5], where the input domain of the system under test is divided into subsets according to various criteria; for each subset one test is selected. Popular approaches are equivalence partitioning, cause-effect graphing [3], category-partition testing [6] and the classification-tree method [7].

A hard to solve problem is that functional testing techniques are based on applica-tion specifications, which however could be incoherent and/or incomplete. Moreover it is very difficult to identify the level of accuracy achieved by the test-set. For these reasons, structural test methods (white-box) have been shown [8] to be an important

M. Heisel et al. (Eds.): SAFECOMP 2004, LNCS 3219, pp. 116–129, 2004.
© Springer-Verlag Berlin Heidelberg 2004

complement to functional testing, allowing to measure the coverage achieved by the test-set. In fact, in safety-critical systems it is very difficult to cover all the code structures, because of the great amount of defensive programming, and identify the functional tests that are needed to exercise a specific uncovered piece of software.

To overcome these problems and to perform not just the verification of the fulfilment of requirements but also the validation of the specifications, a new approach has been developed in Ansaldo Segnalamento Ferroviario (ASF) for the verification and validation of a complex railway control system, the SCMT system. This approach combines the advantages of different methodologies, stands both on empirical and theoretical basis and, above all, has proven to be very effective during our testing experience. In fact, by decomposing the system under test into logic sub-blocks and by stimulating each block with the properly generated input sequences (at the global input ports), we have been able to run all the defined tests within a reasonable time. In the following sections, we will show how the system has been decomposed, stimulated and probed, in order to read its internal status (a "white-box" aspect), and we will describe the reduction techniques applied to the input sequences.

The paper is organised as follows: Section 2 describes the target system, the testing objectives prescribed by the international standards and the context diagram of the system under test; Section 3 describes in detail the testing methodology, based on a logical decomposition of the target system aimed at reducing the complexity of the testing phase, and the combination of white-box and black-box testing methods; Section 4 outlines the results achieved and gives a brief description of the future developments and applications of the testing methodology.

2 Background

Description of the target-system. SCMT[1] is an Italian specification for an ATC (Automatic Train Control) system to be used on the existing rail lines. It can be roughly divided into two parts: an on-board system, which is located on the train, and a ground system, which is installed along the trackside. The ground system is made up by two classes of entities: track-circuits, that is transmission sub-systems which use the rail-lines as the physical medium to connect to the train, and balises, which are antennas used to transmit data to the train via radio through a little air-gap. Track-circuits are meant to send in anticipation to the on-board system the status of the signals which the train is going to reach. Such information will be constant during the time the train takes to travel along the loop made up by the rail-lines (typically, 1350 meters long). The balise sub-system, instead, transmits data in a discontinuous way, just during the time the train is located near and above the apparel. Balises can transmit either static or dynamic data, which contains much more information than the one transmitted by track-circuits. Dynamic balises are connected to an encoder which sends them data telegrams, coherently with the actual state of the line. With such a ground sub-system, the train can get all the information it needs to travel in a safe condition, by adopting two receiving devices: LTM (Loop Transmission Module), meant to read codes from track-circuits, and BTM (Balise Transmission Module),

---

[1] SCMT is the acronym of "Sistema Controllo Marcia Treno", that is the Italian for "Train Movement Control System".

meant to read telegrams from balises. The on-board sub-system is the core of the SCMT system, interpreting and combining all the available information in order to build up the train protection curves, which represent the speed profiles the train must respect. If the train driver does not respect the allowed maximum speed, the on-board system automatically activates brakes to either slow-down or completely stop the train. The overall system architecture is depicted in Fig. 1.

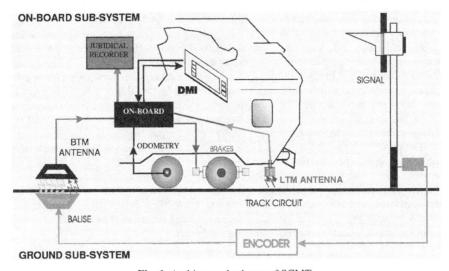

Fig. 1. Architectural scheme of SCMT.

Testing objectives. The objective of the final testing phase for SCMT was the validation of the target system, which comprised the verification of its correct behaviour in both normal and abnormal operating conditions (not always covered by the specification). As already mentioned, functional testing is based only on system specification. However, system requirements tell us what the system must do, but they do not say what the system must not do. Moreover, specification, normally expressed in natural language for railway systems, is often incomplete even when dealing with normal working conditions.

Thus, a more accurate analysis was needed to prove system implementation against its functional specification and safety requirements.

Context diagram. In order to partition the system into independent entities we identified the core logic of the system, located in the on-board sub-system, and the interface managers, that is the blocks interacting with the driver, the train and the ground sub-system. Such a distinction is graphically shown in the context-diagram of Fig. 2 which illustrates functional-level interactions[2].

Any block is seen as a source of information in normal conditions and a potential cause of faults in negative tests.

---

[2] In the following, by using the acronym "SCMT" we will refer to the SCMT on-board sub-system.

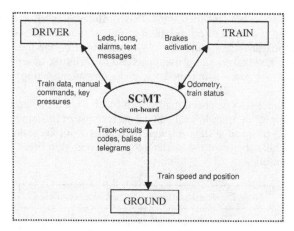

Fig. 2. Context diagram for the SCMT on-board sub-system.

Testing issues. In the systematic testing performed using a black-box approach, the system is stimulated and verified at the global input/output gates. Referring to the above context-diagram, the black-box testing scheme of the SCMT system is depicted in Fig. 3.

Fig. 3. Black-box testing.

In "pure black-box" approach we would rapidly achieve a huge number of test-cases as the system should be tested for each combination of values of the input variables, thus making exhaustive testing unfeasible, in reasonable times, for any complex system. For instance, if we had 10 input variables and each of them could assume 10 different values, the number of possible input combinations would be 10^{10}.

In the following chapter we will start from the shown context diagrams and, applying appropriate reduction techniques, we will achieve a reasonable number of test cases to validate the system.

3 The Testing Methodology

One way to reduce the complexity of the testing phase, while maintaining its efficiency, is to implement a "divide et impera" approach, dividing the system into logical sub-parts and partly breaking the black-box rules. Starting from the specification, it is possible to isolate logical independent blocks interacting with each other through well defined input/output gates. Any decomposition should then be validated by a proper structural analysis ensuring that the actual implementation of the macro-functions does respect such independence. This verification is based on the analysis of function call-graphs as well as on structural testing of functional modules [12, 13]. In fact, the white-box analysis, which is always performed on the basic software modules before the functional testing phase, is needed to verify the absence of side effects that could break the partitioning model, e.g. a component acting in an unguarded manner.

Once a decomposition has been made, each block should be stimulated by an exhaustive set of inputs in order to evaluate the correctness of its outputs, which have to be read from the physical system through non intrusive probes and diagnostic software. The waterfall scheme of the methodology is reported in Fig. 4 and is described in the following sections.

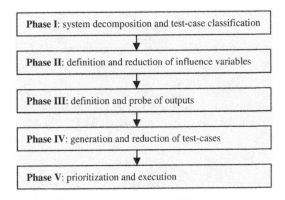

Fig. 4. Methodology waterfall scheme.

3.1   Phase I: System Decomposition and Test-Case Classification

In order to divide the system into macro-functions (or logic blocks) that can be independently tested, we follow two directions (see Fig. 5):

- Horizontal decomposition, which is based on input-output relations;
- Vertical decomposition, by superposition of different complexity levels.

In the horizontal decomposition it is supposed that there is a well defined data path from input to output. The required information travels along the various blocks that are meant to elaborate it. A generic block is influenced in general by both external inputs and the output of the previous block. If an external variable is not changed by a certain logic block, then it is passed as it is to the following block.

Vertical decomposition consists in progressively considering the system working level, from the simplest to the most complex, in a bottom-up way. The upper levels introduce new functionalities that depend on a different set of influence variables. Such a set will contain new variables as well as a (possibly empty) sub-set of the lower levels variables.

In such a way, the system will be divided in distinct logic blocks, as shown in Fig. 6.

For instance, Block 1.2 represents Braking Curve Elaboration (horizontal level) for Complete SCMT (vertical level).

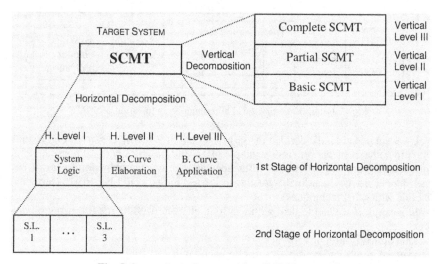

Fig. 5. System logic decomposition (SCMT example).

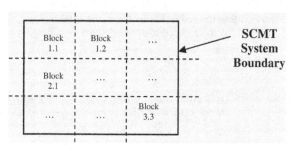

Fig. 6. Logic blocks obtained by decomposition.

Each logic block is sensible to a well defined set of inputs and reacts with outputs that can be visible or not at one of the system output interfaces. In case the output is invisible, system hardware must be probed to obtain the part of the state we are interested in. Finally, it is possible to make a test-case classification according to the introduced logic blocks.

In the SCMT specific example, the first level horizontal decomposition will be as follows (see Fig. 7):

1. Application of the correct "work plane";
2. Construction of the proper braking curve;
3. Control of the braking distance.

In SCMT, vertical working levels are related to the completeness of the information received from the ground sub-system. At the Basic SCMT level, on-board sub-system only reads codes from track-circuits. At the Partial SCMT level, only information from static balises are added to the codes. Finally, in Complete SCMT level all ground transmission devices are used by the train to collect data. It is important to underline that SCMT vertical levels shown in Fig. 5 have to be intended as working levels containing functionality that are complementary to the ones contained in the lower levels.

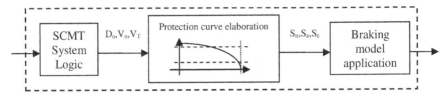

Fig. 7. Detail of the first-level horizontal decomposition of SCMT

If we suppose to have divided the target system in 9 sub-blocks, as in Fig. 6, in the same hypothesis of the previous example (10 input variables with 10 possible values for each one) and considering an influence variable average reduction factor of 2 for each block, the new cardinality of the set of test-cases would be $9 \cdot 10^{10/2}$ (further reducible with other techniques).

In general, if we had to deal with a system characterized by the following parameters:

N: total number of input variables;
m: average number of possible values for each input variable;
s: number of logic blocks in which the system has been divided;
r: average reduction factor in the number of input variable for each logic block[3];

then it could be showed that the reduction factor in the total number of test-cases (and thus in the time required for their execution) would be:

$$\frac{1}{s} \cdot m^{N(1-\frac{1}{r})} \tag{1}$$

As we can see, the overall reduction factor grows exponentially with N (being $r > 1$), so the technique is much more effective with complex systems, characterized by a large number of input variables.

3.2 Phase II: Definition and Reduction of Influence Variables

An influence variable is a variable that has a certain influence on the output of the target (sub)system. We divide influence variables into the following two classes:

- Scenario variables, which represent operating conditions;
- Test-case variables, which represent specific inputs for each scenario.

In order to reduce the number of influence variables for each logic block, we developed the procedure of variable-selection, with a step-by-step independence checking, shown in Fig. 8. If the value of a certain variable is directly deductible from the others, then it is excluded from the set of influence variables because the related test cases are equivalent to the already developed.

For instance, for the proper working of the SCMT logic blocks, it is necessary to define a set of variables to express at least the following information: the completeness of the ground equipment (only track-circuits, track-circuit and static balises or track-circuit and dynamic balises), the type of installed balises and the consistency of

---

[3] The r parameter could be more rigorously defined as follows: $r = 1/s \sum_i N/n_i$, where n_i represents the number of input variables for block i.

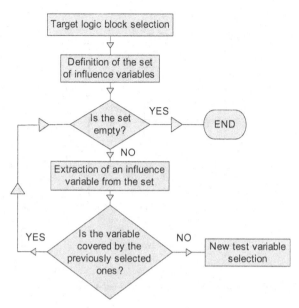

Fig. 8. Variable scanning and selection flow-chart.

the information contained in balises. It could be shown, on the basis of the requirements contained in system specification, that the variable that expresses data consistency of balises is always dependant on the first two variables. Thus, such a variable can be excluded from the set of influence variables.

3.3 Phase III: Definition and Probe of Outputs

Output variables classification is done with reference to the logic block(s) they influence. In particular we are interested in "hidden outputs" that is outputs that are not normally accessible by the interacting entities (see Fig. 2), but are part of the system internal state. To probe such variables, we need to know the system physical structure, which obviously depends on the particular implementation of the specification. This was one of the reasons we defined our methodology as a hybrid between black-box and white-box techniques.

As an example, we could refer to the first level horizontal decomposition shown in Fig. 7. In such a case, as in all similar situations that relate to "internal" blocks, we need to access the variables that are exchanged between blocks. The stimulating variables will be D_o, V_o, V_T, while the output variables to be probed will be S_n, S_a, S_c. The former variables will be assigned values by properly acting on external accessible inputs, while the latter can be read from the log files generated by the diagnostic software that manages probe captions.

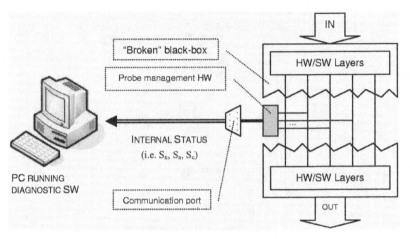

Fig. 9. Hardware probing.

3.4 Phase IV: Generation and Reduction of Test-Cases

We adopted a tree-based test-case generation approach for each logical block. At each depth level, every influence variable is assigned all the significant values of its variation range, according to the criteria that will be described later in this section. Such a generation can be divided into two macro-steps, one for scenario variables and one for test-case variables. In Fig. 10 the process is graphically shown, assuming to deal with *i* scenario variables and *j* test-case variables. The combination of values is performed automatically by a tool that applies a set of reduction rules (described later on in this section), for a "a priori" pruning of pleonastic tree branches. With such an approach, tree leaves represent test-cases which have to be actually executed.

The main reduction criteria adopted for scenarios are:

- Incompatible combination of scenario variables
- Not realistic operating conditions
- Equivalence class based reductions (considering parameter variation ranges)

For test-cases, the main reduction rules are:

- Incompatible combination of test-case variables
- Equivalence class based reductions (considering input variation ranges)
- Context specific reductions (i.e. code-based static independence checking, mapping on test-cases already defined for a different logic block, context-specific dependencies, etc.)

For scenario variables, the conditions to assess "incompatibility" are usually based on constraints coming from physical environment, while "real" operating conditions refer to the railway national or international norms prescribing a set of requirements that must be necessarily respected [11, 14].

In test-case variables, context specific dependencies are very frequent and can be found when the assignment of some particular values or ranges of values to a specific set of variables implies a fixed value assignment for another distinct set of variables.

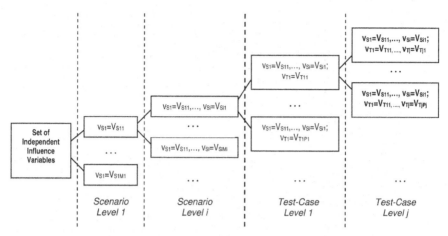

Fig. 10. Tree-based test-case generation.

Even though the previous reduction techniques proved to be very useful to reduce the number of tests, the most complex and efficient techniques was based, for scenario as well as for test-case variables, on equivalence classes.

An equivalence class represents a set of valid or invalid states for a condition on input variables. The domain of input data is partitioned into equivalence classes so that if the output is correct for a test-case corresponding to an input class, then it can be reasonably deducted that it is correct for any test-case of that class. By tree-generating the combinations of influence variables and reducing them with an equivalence class based approach, we implement what is called an extended SECT coverage criterion[4].

Generally speaking, when we have to select input values for influence variables, then for each variation range we will choose at least one test-case for each of the following classes of values assignment:

- internal values
- high-boundary values
- low-boundary values
- near high-boundary values
- near low-boundary values
- over high-boundary values
- below low-boundary values
- special values (only for discrete variables)

The last three classes are very important to test robustness, and thus to verify the safety of system operation against illegal input sequences. All in all, a not Boolean variable will assume, in the final set of test-cases, at least three different values, belonging to the first three categories. The shown general approach includes "Boundary

---

[4] SECT stands for "Strong Equivalence Class Testing" and consists in verifying all kinds of class interactions. Its extension comprises robustness check, that is verification against non valid input classes.

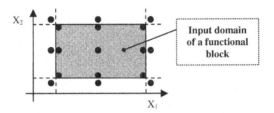

Fig. 11. Example of robust checking for 2 influence variables.

Analysis", "Robustness Testing" and "Worst Case Testing" (WCT) techniques[5]. In some cases, according to system specifications, we can merge the three methods by thrashing the "nearness" conditions while keeping into consideration boundary, robustness and worst-case ones, as shown in Fig. 11 for a two variable example.

Other test-case reduction techniques (i.e. category partitioning, decision tables, cause-effect graphs, etc.) are somehow implicit in our methodology. In fact, they are a consequence of the preliminary system logic decomposition and influence variable classification. The advantage of the tree-based exhaustive generation and contemporary reduction, compared to the "ad hoc" construction, consists in a safer coverage. In other words, with our method we could fail to reduce something reducible, but we can not miss to consider something not yet considered.

The next stage consists in determining expected outputs for each test-case. System behaviour is modelled in terms of significantly varying outputs and their expected values or range of values. Such a behaviour, in normal situations, can be derived directly from system specifications, while in particular cases it must be obtained by means of a parallel independent model. For instance, in Fig. 12 we show an example of using a parallel model for the braking curve prediction in SCMT.

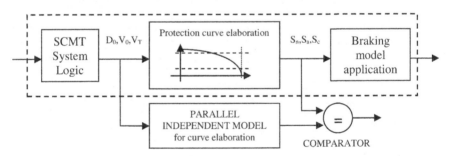

Fig. 12. Example of using a parallel model in SCMT.

As the proposed approach is able to highlight incompleteness in specifications, it is not always possible to identify the expected output. In such a case, it is necessary that the responsible of system specifications (user, client, standard committee) analyze the identified scenario and decide how the system should act in those conditions.

---

[5] Such techniques are based on empirical studies. For instance, it has been noted that most errors generate in correspondence of extreme values of input variables.

3.5 Phase V: Prioritization and Execution

When a big amount of tests have to be executed on a system in a multi-month activity, it is necessary to assign a priority level to the test sets. The main criteria are related to the safety criticality of functions/blocks, identified by the hazard-analysis processes [9], aimed at validating system specifications against the most critical causes of dangerous failures. For instance, the correctness of system behaviour is firstly tested against the so called "restrictive input sequences", namely track-circuit code sequences that should activate one or more train protection mechanisms. Moreover, in testing the system for any new software version, we adopted a "width-first" coverage strategy, which consisted in executing the most significant test-cases for each block and category, in order to quickly discover and notify macroscopic non conformities or dangerous behaviours.

Test-cases have been executed in a simulation environment, made up by the target system, hardware devices simulating external interactions and software tools aimed at the automation of the testing process through batch-files.

In order to speed up the test process, the preparation, execution and output verification activities have been pipelined, allowing more test-engineers work in parallel.

Comparison of the output log-files with the expected outputs had to proceed manually because Pass/Fail criteria were often based on time/speed ranges, very difficult to validate in a complete automatic environment.

In all the cases in which a faulty behaviour has been observed, a proper notification[6] was sent to the engineering department, describing diagnostic and contextual information for programmers to identify what needed to be fixed. Once verified the correction was implemented, non regression tests have been executed on the logic module(s) containing repaired software components.

The testing environment used for SCMT has been depicted in Fig. 13.

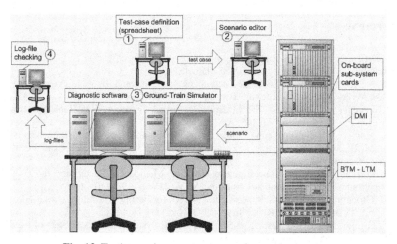

Fig. 13. Testing environment: set-up and execution process.

---

[6] Such a notification is formalized in a document named System Problem Report (SPR).

4   Conclusions and Future Work

The validation of the SCMT system have been a multi-month activity involving several highly specialised resources. The methodology described in this paper allowed them to define and execute about 2000 test-cases, covering the functionalities of the system in normal as well as in degraded states of operation.

The test results revealed a number of errors of different nature (implementation, specification, etc.), and thus also contributed in a relevant way to improve system specifications in terms of both completeness and correctness. While specification completeness verification was within the objectives of the methodology, correctness checking constituted an important collateral effect.

The test process has been accompanied by an extensive documentation activity (test plan, test design specification, test case specification, etc.) that revealed the importance of test organization in order to speed up execution and to allow easy test reproducibility.

The test execution phase, however, is far from being perfect: we are developing techniques and tools to further automate the testing process, above all by developing and validating an automated output checker. Another step which is currently in progress is the verification of coverage by code instrumentation.

The new testing environment is presently being applied, together with the methodology presented in this paper, to the new ERTMS/ETCS[7] [10] system.

Acknowledgments. The authors wish to thank Arturo Amendola, Pietro Marmo and Daniele Ricci for their invaluable collaboration, and the anonymous reviewers for the suggestions they gave us in order to improve this paper.

References

1.   CENELEC: EN 50126 Railway Applications – The specification and demonstration of Reliability, Maintainability and Safety (RAMS)
2.   W. S. Heath: Real-Time Software Techniques. Van Nostrand Reinhold, New York (1991)
3.   G. J. Myers: The Art of Software Testing. Wiley, New York (1979)
4.   J. Wegener, K. Grimm, M. Grochtmann: Systematic Testing of Real-Time Systems. Conference Papers of EuroSTAR '96, Amsterdam (1996)
5.   B. Jeng, E.J. Weyuker: Some Observations on Partition Testing. In Proceedings of the ACM SIGSOFT '89 Third Symposium on Software Testing, Analysis and Verification, Key West (1989)
6.   T. Ostrand, M. Balcer: The Category-Partition Method for Specifying and Generating Functional Tests. Communications of the ACM, 31 (6), (1988) 676-686
7.   M. Grochtmann, K. Grimm: Classification-Trees for Partition Testing. Journal of Software Testing, Verification and Reliability, Vol. 3, No.2, (1993) 63-82
8.   K. Grimm: Systematic Testing of Software-Based Systems. In Proceedings of the 2nd Annual ENCRESS Conference, Paris (1996)

---

[7] ERTMS/ETCS stands for European Rail Traffic Management System / European Train Control System, an ATC standard, aiming at the improvement of safety and interoperability of European railways, which is being used in Italy for high-speed lines.

9. P. di Tommaso, R. Esposito, P. Marmo, A. Orazzo: Hazard Analysis of Complex Distributed Railway Systems. In Proceedings of 22nd International Symposium on Reliable Distributed Systems, Florence (2003) 283-292
10. UNISIG ERTMS/ETCS – Class1 Issue 2.2.2 Subset 026-1
11. Ministero dei Trasporti – Ferrovie dello Stato – Direzione Generale: Norme per l'Ubicazione e l'Aspetto dei Segnali
12. Sommervill: Software Engineering, 6th Edition. Addison Wesley (2000)
13. Telelogic Tau Logicscope v5.1: Basic Concept. (2001)
14. RFI: Applicazione dell'SCMT: caratteristiche di codificazione degli impianti BACC ed integrazioni tecnico-normative. Roma (2003)

Actuator Based Hazard Analysis
for Safety Critical Systems

Per Johannessen[1], Fredrik Törner[1], and Jan Torin[2]

[1] Volvo Car Corporation, Department of Electrical Architecture, ELIN-94221,
SE-405 31 Gothenburg, Sweden
{pjohann1,ftorner}@volvocars.com
[2] Chalmers University of Technology, Department of Computer Engineering,
SE-412 96 Gothenburg, Sweden
torin@ce.chalmers.se

Abstract. In the early stages of a design process, a detailed hazard analysis
should be performed, particularly for safety critical systems. In this paper an actuator based hazard analysis method is presented. Since it is the actuators that
affect the systems environment, this actuator based approach is the logical approach for an early hazard analysis when only limited information of the system
implementation is available. This approach is also unique since all identified
failures are distributed on four different severities. A criticality ranking is assigned to each failure as a combination of the severities and their distribution.
This ranking is also used to give an indication of the preferred fail states. For
the hazards resulting in a high criticality that needs to be handled, the method
supports a solvability analysis between different design solutions. This solvability analysis rewards design concepts that handles hazards with high criticality
numbers.

1 Introduction

There is an ever increasing demand in the automotive industry in areas like safety
functionality, driving experience, and environmental care which requires new complex functionality to be implemented in cars. In the automotive industry, many of
these demands can be fulfilled with mechatronical drive-by-wire systems. This technology step is similar for other engineering disciplines like commercial aircrafts and
trains. Since mechatronical systems involve electronics, mechanics, and software,
they are inherently complex and often safety critical. Further, there will be strict dependability requirements on the electrical by-wire system. The automotive industry
also has requirements on low development cost, low product cost, and short development time. To develop these mechatronical systems with such requirements, there is a
need for structured design methods and design principles.

In [1], Eben and Saermisch refer to an estimate that 70-90% of the safety-related
decisions for a system are made in the early design phase. Hence, it is critical that the
appropriate information support is available during this phase. One type of supportive
information can be derived from a hazard analysis. Consequently, the need for a hazard analysis that could be used at a conceptual level was identified. Such a hazard

M. Heisel et al. (Eds.): SAFECOMP 2004, LNCS 3219, pp. 130–141, 2004.
© Springer-Verlag Berlin Heidelberg 2004

analysis will develop safety requirements on the subsystems. These requirements will help the engineers designing their systems. The value of early hazard analysis has been thoroughly discussed by Leveson [2] and Storey [3].

The most commonly used method for dependability analysis in industry today is Failure Mode and Effect Analysis, FMEA, [4]. An FMEA is based on detailed knowledge about the system design and the system implementation, which is not available in the early design phases. Therefore, a traditional FMEA is hard to do at this phase. However, to avoid costly design iterations a hazard analysis must be done early in the product design.

The automotive industry can learn from the aerospace industry when designing safety critical systems. The SAE ARP-4761 standard [5] describes a safety assessment process for airborne systems. A part of the process is the Functional Hazard Assessment method, FHA, which is used to identify safety hazards at a functional level. It is a powerful method that gives important input when structuring the requirements.

In HiP-HOPS [6], Papadopoulos developed the Functional Failure Analysis method, FFA, by extending FHA with fault classes, similar to the fault classes used in HAZOP [7]. The FFA has the advantage of consistent fault classes. This gives a systematic analysis and the possibility of integrating other dependability analysis methods when analyzing the complete system. The hazards identified in an FFA can for example be used as top events in a Fault Tree Analysis as described in [6]. In HiP-HOPS, the focus of FFA is on functional hazards and the method is very usable for this purpose.

In mechatronical systems, the actuators that will be used are usually known very early in the design process. Since it is only the actuators in the system that affect the environment, all hazards has to origin from the actuators. Hence, an actuator based hazard analysis approach would be very valuable in the design process of mechatronical systems. This paper proposes such an analysis. The analysis modifies the FFA to focus on actuators instead of functions. Further, the analysis is extended with a unique criticality ranking and a solvability analysis for different design concepts.

This paper starts with describing the proposed actuator based hazard analysis method in Section 2. Section 3 continues with presenting an overview of the system onto which the method was evaluated and also an extract of the analysis. In Section 4 the results from the case study is presented and the analysis approach is discussed in Section 5.

2   Analysis Method

The hazard analysis method presented here focuses on actuators. It is a table based analysis approach similar to traditional FMEA and FHA. The analysis is divided into two separate analyses, a hazard analysis and a solvability analysis. The integration of the different analyses uses the criticality ranking as illustrated in Fig. 1.

The hazard analysis is based on three different stages. In the first stage, three standard fault classes are applied to each actuator and a system effect is determined. The second stage assigns severity classes to the individual failures to quantify the analysis.

In the third step, the criticalities are ranked and a preferred fail state can be determined. The criticality numbers are used to guide the continued design of the system. An example of a hazard analysis is shown in Table 4.

In the solvability analysis, different design concepts can be analyzed to determine the concept that is most suitable to handle the identified failure. The analysis is based on comparing different concepts to choose the most promising concept to continue with in the product design. An example of a solvability analysis is shown in Table 5.

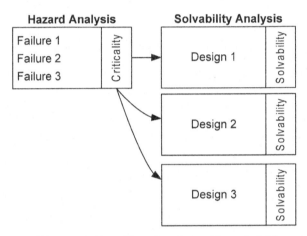

Fig. 1. The concept of the actuator based hazard analysis with a solvability analysis. The criticality numbers from the hazard analysis is used in the solvability analysis.

In most situations there are dependencies between failures and there are not only single faults occurring, an example is common cause faults. Therefore, a failure analysis that focuses on actuators should also consider multiple failures. In the work by Papadopoulos [6], one approach for considering multiple faults is presented. This approach uses tables with combinations of the different faults. There is one new table for each new dimension of faults that is introduced in the analysis. For few faults, this is a durable approach. However, for many faults this approach becomes complicated.

2.1 Fault Classes and Actuator Failures

The proposed hazard analysis method focuses on the system's actuators and the fault classes are chosen for this purpose. It was decided to use a reduced set of the fault classes Papadopoulos provided in [6]. The fault classes used are; *omission, commission,* and *stuck.* When using more fault classes, it is difficult to tell them apart in this early design stage, e.g. there is little difference between *late* and *omission*. Our experience also shows that using other fault classes at this stage do not add any value to the analysis.

The three chosen fault classes propagate to the worst case failures for any mechanical actuator. The class *omission* is interpreted as no force is available at the actuator, *commission* is interpreted as maximum force is applied to the actuator, and *stuck* is interpreted as a mechanical locking. These fault classes are considered as permanent faults. Intermittent faults are less severe.

The combination of actuator and fault class is described in the analysis. This is further used for the system effect analysis. If e.g. *omission* is applied to a brake actuator, this would be described as *no brake force available*.

To interpret the system effect of these failures it is vital to consider if there is intent or not. The class *omission* is only considered when there is intent from the user. Otherwise the fault is latent and not propagated to an actuator failure. For the other fault classes, the system effect is interpreted differently depending on the user's intent to activate the actuator or not.

The system effect is the result of the combination between the analyzed actuator, the fault class, and the user's intent. At this stage in the design process there are several options to decide on the correct system effect: experience, experiments, and simulations. It is a tradeoff between accuracy, cost, and available analysis resources for which alternative to chose.

One additional advantage of using these fault classes is that an actuator can fail or actively be disabled in a *commission, omission*, or *stuck* state. Hence, this can be used to evaluate which failure state is preferred for specific actuators. This evaluation results in a design requirement of the actuator's implementation, e.g. a brake system could be mechanically designed such that it fails in a stuck state in case of power loss.

2.2 Severity Classes

The severity classes used in this specific analysis are taken from IEC-61508 [8]. They are *Catastrophic, Critical, Marginal,* and *Negligible.* The severity classes are coupled to the system effect by using experience, experiments, or simulations.

As for the severity classes used, there are four different levels. Since the analysis is performed at an early stage in the design process, there is only conceptual information for different solutions available. There also exists a high degree of uncertainty of the different solutions. Therefore, it is not feasible to use more than these four severity classes. Using more classes would only result in uncertainties in the assignment process without adding any value to the failure analysis.

All four severity classes are applied to each analyzed actuator failure. A percentage related to the distribution between the different severity classes is assigned for each class to enhance the value of the analysis. The distribution is combined from estimation on the situation when a failure could occur and if there is driver intent or not. However, the probability of occurrence is not considered in the analysis since this depends on the failure rates of components in the implementation. At this stage in the design, the implementation is not known. In Table 1 an example of the distribution between the different severity levels for one actuator failure is shown. The table further includes the criticality ranking.

2.3 Criticality Ranking

To rank the failures for an actuator, and the three different fault classes, the hazard analysis uses a *Criticality* factor. A high value of the *Criticality* factor indicates that the actuator failure should be analyzed in more detail and redundancy might be required in the implementation.

To calculate the *Criticality* factor, it is required to assign weights to the different severity classes. This is however very dependant on the application domain. For a military aircraft, *Catastrophic* could be ranked lower than for a commercial aircraft due to the number of lives involved. For a consumer product, *Negligible* is probably ranked higher than for an industrial product. In the end, the weights assigned to the different severity levels are for the analysis engineer to decide and increase the possibilities with this hazard analysis approach. The weights should typically be identical for all analyses within a certain domain. One example of the assignment of the weights to the severity levels is shown in Table 1.

The criticality of each failure is calculated as the sum of the four products with the severity class' weight and severity distribution. An example of these calculations is shown in Table 1.

Table 1. Example of an actuator failure in omission fault mode with criticality calculation

Failure	...	System severity	Weight	Distribution	Product	Criticality	...
Omission		Catastrophic	10	60%	6.0		
		Critical	6	30%	1.8	8.0	
		Marginal	2	10%	0.2		
		Negligible	1	0%	0.0		

2.4 Design Requirements and Preferred Fail State

In the design process the identified failures should be handled by the designer. There is a possibility to have design requirements such that all actuator failures that exceed a pre-specified threshold should be handled, e.g. to require that the actuator has a fail-safe state.

By comparing an actuator's three different criticality numbers, one for each fault class, it is possible to identify the actuator's preferred fail state. If e.g. the brake actuator has the lowest criticality for *Omission*, its preferred fail state is an inactive state that could be achieved by removal of the actuators energy supply.

2.5 Solvability Analysis and Design Selection

Once the actuator failures have been identified and ranked, the hazard analysis method supports a solvability analysis for different design concepts. The purpose of the solvability analysis is to choose one design concept that is most likely to handle the hazards that were detected in the hazard analysis.

It is desired to choose the concept that is most likely to fulfill the safety requirements early in the design process. An example of a solvability analysis can be seen in Table 2, where a high *Priority* value is preferred. The *Priority* value is calculated according to Equation 1.

Table 2. Example of a solvability analysis with three competing design alternatives

Failure	…	Criticality	Design 1	Solvability			
			Fault handling	Complexity	Cost	Controllability	Priority
Omission		7.2	Redistribute force			2	14.4
Commission		6.9	Disable actuator	1	1	3	20.7
Stuck		4.5	Disable actuator			3	13.5
							48.6
			Design 2	Solvability			
			Fault handling	Complexity	Cost	Controllability	Priority
			Redistribute force			3	5.4
			Disable actuator	2	2	4	6.9
			Disable actuator			4	4.5
							16.8
			Design 3	Solvability			
			…				

Each concept is ranked according to four parameters; *Criticality*, *Complexity*, *Cost*, and *Controllability*. The *Criticality* parameter is from the first part of the hazard analysis. Design concepts that have better controllability for actuator failures with high criticality should be ranked higher than for failure with low criticality.

The *Complexity* parameter is related to the complexity of the design concept. A complex solution is more error prone and requires a larger effort in the design process. In the *Cost* parameter it is the components' cost that is considered, not development cost. Development cost is connected to the complexity measure. The aim of the different designs is to control possible actuator failures. This can be seen in the *Controllability* parameter. A design that can resolve more critical faults have a higher value of the *Controllability* parameter.

For the *Complexity* and *Cost* parameters in the analysis, there are numerous approaches to apply values. In the approach presented here it was chosen to have a relative ranking of these parameters. For *n* different design concepts, the least complex and costly concept is given a value of 1 and the most complex and costly is given the value *n*. Further, *Controllability* has an absolute ranking in this approach as seen in Table 3.

Table 3. Example of controllability weights in the solvability analysis

Controllability	Controllability weight
Resolves no faults	1
Resolves few faults	2
Resolves some faults	3
Resolves most faults	4

The priority value of each design is calculated and the design with the highest value should be the design that most probably solves the actuator failures. However, further analysis and quantification of the different concepts may be needed. To calculate the priority value a generic equation is used,

$$Priority = Criticality \cdot \frac{Controllability^a}{Complexity^b + Cost^c} \ . \tag{1}$$

This equation can easily be modified to adjust the sensitivity of the parameters for the system. For instance a high value of a is appropriate for safety critical system while a high value of c is appropriate for cost sensitive consumer products. These constants should be modified to adapt to the specific domain where the analysis is used.

It is important to note that the presented weights and equation is one possible approach. There is a significant possibility for the designer to easily modify the weights and the constants in the equation such that designs suitable for particular application areas are rewarded. Further, the equation itself and the ranked parameters can be modified to better suit specific application areas.

2.6 Combinational Failures

The focus of this analysis has not been on combinational failures. However, one approach to cover multiple failures in the analysis is to include these failures in the Failure column. One other possibility is presented by Papadopoulos in [6]. Further, there is one challenge to determine the preferred fail state and most suitable design based on the Criticality ranking and Priority values for single as well as for multiple failures.

3 Evaluated Case Study

During the development of this actuator based hazard analysis method, a case study of the method was performed in parallel. The evaluated system was a prototype car that originally was developed within the FAR project [9]. The project was performed in cooperation with the Royal Institute of Technology in Sweden and financed by the Program Board for the Swedish Automotive Research Program at the Swedish Agency for Innovation Systems.

3.1 FAR Car

The analyzed car prototype is a drive-by-wire car in scale 1:5 and has four-wheel steering, individual braking and four-wheel drive, with a total of three actuators per wheel. The car can be programmed into several modes of operation, including steering on two or four wheels and two or four wheel drive. The car is shown in Fig. 2.

Fig. 2. The prototype car in scale 1:5 that was used as a test case for the actuator based hazard analysis method

The hardware used in the FAR car is shown in Fig. 3. There are six Motorola 68340 microcontrollers connected with a TTCAN network. The microcontrollers run at 25 MHz and are equipped with external A/D and D/A converters.

Each wheel has a dedicated node and there is one node for environment sensors. To coordinate the whole system there is one driver node that is connected through a radio link to a HMI node. The HMI node is further connected to a joystick or a steering wheel and pedals.

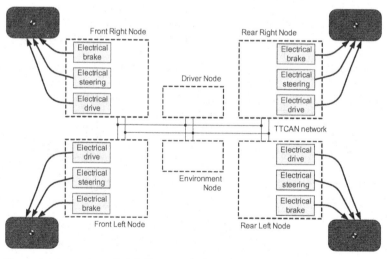

Fig. 3. The prototype car in scale 1:5 that was used as a test case for the actuator based hazard analysis method

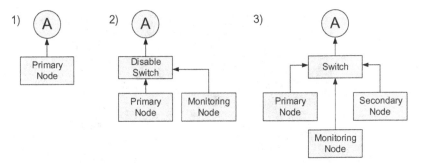

Fig. 4. The three design concepts for the brake actuator in the case study for the solvability analysis

3.2 Hazard Analysis

In this section, an excerpt of the analysis for the FAR car is described. The example is a single failure analysis for one actuator in the brake system. Further, three different design solutions as shown in Fig. 4 are included in the solvability analysis.

The first step in each analysis is to apply the fault classes to all actuators. Hence, there is one analysis table for each actuator. The analysis for one brake actuator of the FAR car is shown in Table 4. In the table the three different failure modes, *omission*, *commission*, and *stuck*, are applied to the actuator. The system effect is considered both if there is driver intent or not. As seen in Table 4, all single brake actuator failures are related to the dynamic stability of the car. When ranking the three different failures, *commission* has the highest severity effects and *omission* the lowest.

Table 4. Example of actuator based hazard analysis for the brake actuator on one wheel and a single fault

Failure	Description	System Effect		System severity (weight)	Distribution	Criticality	...
		Driver intent	No driver intent				
Omission	No brake power available	Car tends to drift to one side	N/A	Catastrophic (10)	20%	6.8	
				Critical (6)	80%		
				Marginal (2)	0%		
				Negligible (1)	0%		
Stuck	Constant brake power	Car tends to drift to one side when brakes are pressed	Car tends to drift to one side when brakes are released	Catastrophic (10)	40%	7.6	
				Critical (6)	60%		
				Marginal (2)	0%		
				Negligible (1)	0%		
Commis-sion	Full brake power	Car drifts to one side if not full brake request	Car drifts to one side	Catastrophic (10)	90%	9.6	
				Critical (6)	10%		
				Marginal (2)	0%		
				Negligible (1)	0%		

The next step in the analysis is the solvability analysis for ranking different design concepts. For the FAR car's braking system, three different control concepts for the computer nodes were analyzed. The computer nodes perform the calculations and are responsible for the signals to the actuators. Fig. 3 shows the three different concepts. *Concept 1* is a non-fault-tolerant direct coupling while *Concept 2* has monitoring node that can disable the actuator and the control signal. The most fault-tolerant and also most complex concept is *Concept 3* that has a monitoring node that can decide if the primary or secondary node should control the actuator.

In the solvability analysis shown in Table 5, the three design concepts are ranked against each other. The solvability parameters for Equation 1 are; $a=2$, $b=1$ and, $c=1$. Table 4 and Table 5 are two different parts of the same analysis that have been divided to be able to visualize the whole table content. The three different rows for each concept refer to the different failure modes of the actuator.

Table 5. The solvability analysis for the three different concepts in the evaluated case

Design 1			Solvability			
... Criticality	Fault handling	Complexity	Cost	Controllability	Priority
6.8	Redistribute force			1	3.4
7.6	Disable actuator	1	1	2	15.2
9.6	Disable actuator			2	19.2
					37.8

Design 2		Solvability			
Fault handling	Complexity	Cost	Controllability	Priority
Redistribute force			2	6.8
Disable actuator	2	2	3	17.1
Disable actuator			3	21.6
				45.5

Design 3		Solvability			
Fault handling	Complexity	Cost	Controllability	Priority
Redistribute force			4	21.8
Disable actuator	3	2	4	24.3
Disable actuator			4	30.7
				76.8

The data in Table 5 suggest that design *Concept 3* is the best for this actuator failure. Since *Controllability* was prioritized by setting $a=2$ it is a logical result from the analysis. The analysis is then repeated for all other actuators in the system.

4   Results

From the example in the previous section, several design requirements were taken. Primarily, it was shown that brake actuator failures could result in several catastrophic system effects unless handled in the system design by the design process.

The analysis also showed the preferred fail states for the different actuators. For instance, in case of single brake actuator failures, the preferred fail state is omission. If further analyses for the brake actuator in the design process do not contradict, the brake actuator should be designed such that it fails in an omission state. Hence, in case of a failure, for example a power loss or a control error, the brake actuator should be actively disabled.

Further, the solvability analysis showed that one design had a clear advantage over the two other design concepts. However, it is still required that the chosen design is verified to meet the dependability requirements of the system in the later design steps.

5 Discussion

The described analysis has proven valuable in the analysis of safety critical systems in an early design phase. Since the approach considers actuators and not implementations, it supports early design decisions before any unnecessary investments have been made in development activities.

From a hazard perspective, there is a clear advantage to focus on actuator failures instead of functional failures. This is expected sine it is only the actuators that affect the system environment. However, the functional failures are still relevant from a user perspective. One possibility is to use the actuator failure analysis as input to a functional failure analysis.

The use of three actuator fault classes allows for a sufficient analysis of system effects in case of actuator failures. These fault classes were chosen to represent possible actuator failures.

As for any analysis, one advantage is the requirement to document design choices and to reflect over the system before continuing with the next phase in the system design.

The presented analysis supports relative ranking between potential actuator failures to select the preferred fail state and also between different design concepts to select the most promising concept. There is no need for an absolute ranking that would require more efforts to perform. However, this qualitative analysis is followed by quantitative analyses in the later stages of the design process, for instance traditional FMEA and fault tree analysis.

The analysis is adaptable to different areas such as consumer or industrial products and products with different dependability requirements. This is achieved by setting the weights in the criticality and solvability rankings. Assigning weights is both complex and critical since it influences the analysis and design. However this is only done once per system or even discipline since the weights are reusable within the application area.

The limitations of the proposed analysis include lack of support for multiple failures and a relative high degree of inaccuracy in the analysis. Multiple failures is one area of further work. The inaccuracy of the analysis is a consequence of the limited information of the system that is available in an early design phase. Other hazard analysis approaches have the same limitation. To increase the level of accuracy by performing the analysis at a later stage results in higher risks of detecting design flaws that must the altered at high costs.

References

1. Eben, D., Saermisch, M.: System Safety Hazards Assessment in Conceptual Program Trade Studies. Proceedings of the 21st International System Safety Conference 2003, Ottawa (2003)
2. Leveson, N.: Safeware: System Safety and Computers, Addison-Wesley Publishing Company, Reading, MA (1995)
3. Storey, N.: Safety-Critical Computer Systems, Addison Wesley Longman, Essex (1996)
4. Johannessen, P.: Design Methods for Safety Critical Automotive Architectures. Department of Computer Engineering, Chalmers University of Technology (1999)
5. Society of Automotive Engineers: ARP-4761: Aerospace Recommended Practice: Guidelines and Methods for Conducting the Safety Assessment Process on Civil Airborne Systems and Equipment, 12th edition, SAE, Warrendale PA United Sates (1996)
6. Papadopoulos, Y., McDermid, J.: Hierarchically Performed Hazard Origin and Propagation Studies, Proceedings of SAFECOMP'99, 18th international Conference on Computer Safety, Reliability and Security, Toulouse (1999)
7. UK Ministry of Defence: HAZOP Studies on Systems Containing Programmable Electronics, UK Ministry of Defence, Glasgow (2000)
8. International Electro-technical Commission: IEC-61508: Functional safety of electrical/electronic/programmable electronic safety-related Systems, IEC (1998)
9. Backstrom et al.: Project FAR – Project report. Dept. of Machine Design, The Royal Institute of Technology (2003)

Performability Measures of the Public Mobile Network of a Tele Control System

Ester Ciancamerla and Michele Minichino

ENEA CR Casaccia, sp Anguillarese 301, 00100 Roma, Italy
{ciancamerlae,minichino}@casaccia.enea.it

Abstract. Performability measures of the Public Mobile Network (PMN) of a Tele Control System, under prototypal development inside the EU SAFETUN-NEL Project, are predicted by using stochastic models. The Tele Control System has the aim of reducing the number of accidents inside the alpine road tunnels, by implementing safety policies between Instrumented Vehicles and a Tunnel Control Centre, by means of a PMN. The use of the PMN, which supports both Global System Mobile (GSM), for voice connections, and the General Packet Radio Service (GPRS), for data connections, represents the most innovative and challenging research aspect of the system. To compute performability measures for voice and data services, we built modular sub models, hierarchically composed, by using Stochastic Activity Networks (SAN). At the first layer , we have built three sub models to compute pure unavailability and pure performance measures. Then, at the second layer, we have built two composed models. Each composed model joins the pure availability sub model and the related pure performance sub model, in order to compute performability measures, respectively for voice and data packet services.

1 Introduction

A Tele Control System is under prototypal development in the frame of the SAFE-TUNNEL EU Project [1]. The Tele Control System basically consists of a Tunnel Control Centre (TCC) interconnected to Instrumented Vehicles by a Public Mobile Network (PMN), that supports both Global System Mobile (GSM) connections and the General Packet Radio Service (GPRS) connections. The Tele Control System is designed to implement preventive safety actions in different tunnel scenarios (normal vehicular traffic, incidents, diffusion of emergency information) and the PMN is dimensioned for the expected throughput of voice and data, between the Instrumented Vehicles and the TCC, under such scenarios. The SAFETUNNEL Project designs the Tele Control System and implements a system Demonstrator, that is a prototypal subset of the Tele Control System. The validation of Tele Control System will be performed both by experimental tests and by modelling. A limited number of experimental tests are planned on the actual system Demonstrator; moreover a set of validation measures have to be predicted by system models, because the Demonstrator is not suitable for such measures. In fact the Demonstrator, that operates inside the tunnel, is not suitable for measures which would require long observation time inside the tunnel (that should be closed to the ordinary vehicular traffic, with loss of availability

M. Heisel et al. (Eds.): SAFECOMP 2004, LNCS 3219, pp. 142–154, 2004.
© Springer-Verlag Berlin Heidelberg 2004

and money) and measures which would require irreproducible tunnel scenarios (i.e occurrence of incidents and emergency scenarios). Less than ever, the System Demonstrator is suitable for performance and availability measures, which are typically predicted by modelling and simulation and rarely performed by using experimental data from long, inadequate and costly observations of the whole system (and not of a part of it, that is the System Demonstrator). Due to the complexity of the Tele Control System and according to the Validation Plan, the system validation by modelling will not be exhaustive but will be focused on system relevant properties, that could affect the Tele Control System safety and timeliness [2]. Validation by modelling will address relevant parts of the Tele Control System, including the PMN, which represents the most innovative and challenging research aspect of system. The present paper just deals with performability measures of the PMN [3], intended as performance measures explicitly tied to service degradation/recovery due to components failure and repair activities (availability measures). Performability measures are needed because performance measures, which ignore failures and recovery activities, but just consider resource contention, generally over estimate the system's ability to perform. On the other hand pure availability measures, where performance are not taken into account, tends to be too conservative. To compute performability measures (in terms of voice blocking probability and packet loss probability), we built modular sub models, hierarchically composed, by using Stochastic Activity Networks (SAN). At the first layer, we have built three sub models to compute pure unavailability and pure performance measures. Then, at the second layer, we have built two composed models , respectively for voice and data packet services. Each composed model joins the pure availability sub model and the related pure performance sub model, in order to compute the performability measure.

The paper is organized as follows. Section 2 and 3 describe the basic elements of the Tele Control system and of the GSM/GPRS architecture. Section 4 deals with the PMN modelling assumptions and introduces the performability measures. Section 5 describes the modelling formalism: the Stochastic Activity Networks. Sections 6, 7, 8 describe the PMN performability models and measures. Some numerical results are reported in section 9. In section 10 there are some discussions and conclusions.

2   Tele Control System

The Tele Control System implements its safety functions[1], transferring voice, commands and data between Instrumented Vehicles and the Tunnel Control Centre. TCC must be able to exchange information with more than one Vehicle at the same time in *bi-directional* way. Particularly, informative messages are transmitted in *uplink* (from Vehicles on-board system to TCC) for the purpose of diagnosis and prognostics of vehicles. Commands/messages are transmitted in *downlink* (from TCC to a single vehicle or to a set of vehicles) for notification of a dangerous conditions inside the tunnel, or for setting/updating vehicle parameters (such as vehicle speed, safety intra-vehicles distance). For each Vehicle entering the Safe Tunnel monitored area, the

---

[1]   The Tele Control System safety functions include: 1)Vehicle Prognostics, 2)Access & Vehicle Control, 3)Vehicle Speed and Intra-Vehicles Distances Control, 4)Dissemination of Emergency Information.

TCC sets up a dedicated GPRS connection. TCP transport protocol is used to guarantee the correctness of data by means of integrity checks in the receiver and foreseeing a retransmission mechanism for bad-received packets. Each Vehicle is characterized by a TCP address (IP address + TCP port) in order to be able to communicate to the TCC that is provided of an analogous address too. Moreover, bidirectional voice calls, supported by GSM connection, are also provided between Vehicles and TCC, in case GPRS data transfer are not sufficient to manage an emergency.

3   GSM/GPRS Architecture

GSM [4],[5] is a circuit-switched connection, with reserved bandwidth. At air interface, a complete traffic channel is allocated to a single Mobile Station (MS) for the entire call duration. A cell is formed by the radio area coverage of a Base Transceiver Station (BTS). One or more BTS are controlled by one Base Station Controller (BSC). Such a set of Stations form the Base Station Subsystem (BSS). A BSS can be viewed as a router connecting the wireless cellular network to the wired part of the network. GSM uses a mixed multiple access technique to the radio resources: Frequency Division Multiple Access/Time Division Multiple Access (FDMA/TDMA). Within each BSS, one or more carrier frequencies (FDMA) are activated, and over each carrier a TDMA frame is defined. TDMA allows the use of the same carrier to serve multiple MS. In the GSM system the frame is constituted by eight timeslots and so the same radio frequency can serve up to eight MS. A circuit (a channel) is defined by a slot position in the TDMA frame and by a carrier frequency. Typically one channel (time slot) is reserved to signaling and control. A MS can roam from a cell to a neighboring cell during active voice calls. Such a MS, that has established a voice call, and roams from a cell to another, must execute a handoff procedure, transferring the call from the channel in the old cell to a channel in the new cell entered by the MS.

GPRS is a packet switched connection with shared, unreserved bandwidth. For data services, which is a bursty traffic, the use of GSM results in a highly inefficient resources utilization. For bursty traffic, a packet switched bearer service, such as GPRS, results in a much better utilization of the traffic channels. A radio channel will only be allocated when needed and will be released immediately, after the transmission of packets. With this principle more than one MS can share one physical channel (statistical multiplexing). In order to integrate GPRS services into the existing GSM architecture, a new class of network nodes, called GPRS support nodes (GSN), are used. GSNs are responsible for the delivery and routing of data packets between the MS and the external packet data networks. A serving GPRS support node (SGSN) is responsible for the delivery of data packets from and to the MS [4].

GPRS exploits the same radio resources used by GSM. To cross the wireless link the data packets are fragmented in radio blocks, that are transmitted in 4 slots in identical position within consecutive GSM frames over the same carrier frequency [6]. Depending upon the length of the data packets, the number of radio blocks necessary for the transfer may vary. Mobile Stations execute packet sessions which are alternating sequences of packet calls and reading times. One time slot constitutes a channel of GPRS traffic, called Packet Data Traffic Channel (PDTCH) [4]. On each PDCH, different data packets can be allocated in the same TDMA frame or in different

TDMA frames. When a user needs to transmit, it has to send a channel request to the network through a Random Access Procedure, which may cause collisions among requests of different users. In this case a transmission is tried. The number of maximum retransmissions is one of the GPRS access control parameters. Typically, one of the channels, randomly selected out of the available channels, is dedicated to GSM and GPRS signalling and control.

4 PMN Modelling Assumptions and Measures

The dimensioning of the PMN accounts for several aspects including the length of the tunnel and the length of the tunnel monitored area, the recommended speed of vehicles and the safety distance between vehicles inside the tunnel, the number of carriage ways, the average and the worst demands of voice and data connections, the GPRS expected throughput per physical channel, the bit rate for the information exchange of each vehicle and the GSM expected connections. For GSM connection the same carrier frequency can serve up to eight vehicles. For GPRS connection, we assume that up to two vehicles are allocated in the same time slot, so the same carrier frequency can serve up to sixteen vehicles. One time slot (physical channel) is reserved as long as a voice call remains active, that is until the voice call is voluntarily released, then voice call generates an ON/OFF traffic on PMN. On the other hand, data transfer generates a bursty traffic (namely at vehicle registration/deregistration phases, in case of rare vehicle anomalies or incidents).

One of the channels, randomly selected out of the available channels, is dedicated to GSM and GPRS signalling and control. Then the total number of available physical channels of our PMN is obtained from the product of the number of carriers per the number of channels per each carriers minus one, which represents the control channel.

The PMN under analysis consists of one Base Station System (BSS), which contemporarily implements GSM and GPRS connections. Figure 1 shows the BSS with its essential components. GPRS connection is an updating service of the GSM architecture, which is born to deliver voice calls. We assume that GSM voice calls have higher priority than GPRS data transfer. That is, voice calls are set up as long as at least one physical channel is available in the BSS of interest; data packets can be transmitted only over the channels which are not used by voice connections. The handoff procedure [2], that allows roaming from a cell to a neighbouring cell is meaningful for GSM connections. Vice versa the handoff procedure is neglected for GPRS connections, since the duration of data transfer is typically much smaller than the time spent by a vehicle in a cell.

To sum up, for the sake of building manageable models of our PMN, the following assumptions have been made:

- we will focalize on a single Base Station System, constituted by one Base Station Controller and multiple Base Transceiver Stations
- data exploits the same physical channels used by voice
- channel allocation policy is priority of voice on data
- we account for handoff procedure for voice connection
- we neglect the possibility of the handoff procedure for data connection
- one Control Channel (CCH) is dedicated to GSM and GPRS signalling and control; CCH is randomly assigned to a BTS

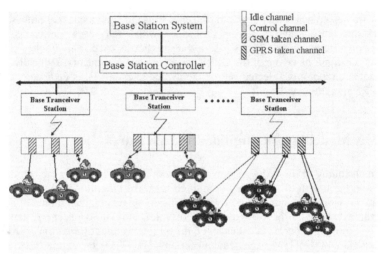

Fig. 1. PMN under analysis

- GPRS implements a point to point connection
- each Instrumented Vehicle embeds a Mobile Station, which allows the contemporarily use of GSM and GPRS connections.

4.1 Performability Measures

Considering the PMN under analysis limited to one BSS, as showed in figure 1, the GSM and the GPRS services can be denied, due to at least one of the following contributes: a) the BSS, as a whole, becomes unavailable or b) the BSS is available and all its channels are full or c) the BSS is not completely available and all the channels in it, which are available, are also full.

We named *TSB*, the Total Service Blocking Probability, as the performability measure of the denial of service both for GSM and GPRS connection due to the occurrence of at least one of the contributes a), b), or c).

Regarding the contribute a) the fact that the BSS and its channels are unavailable, depends upon the failure/repair activities of BSS physical components, which include the Mobile Stations, embedded inside the Instrumented Vehicles, the Base Transceiver Stations and the Base Station Controller. BSS components are assumed to fail and be repaired with their own and independent rates. Actually, the reliability figures of Mobile Stations are significantly better than those of the other network components, then we assume the MS as fault free. Each BTS can hosts eight traffic channels or, randomly, could hosts the Control Channel (CCH) plus seven traffic channels.

To sum up, the BSS Total Unavailability (*TU*) is approximately:

$$TU = BCF + CCF + ATF \qquad (1)$$

where:

- *BCF* is the unavailability of the Base Station Controller
- *CCF* is the unavailability of the Control Channel (CCF) which depends upon the unavailability of the BTS which randomly can host it.

In the third step, the criticalities are ranked and a preferred fail state can be determined. The criticality numbers are used to guide the continued design of the system. An example of a hazard analysis is shown in Table 4.

In the solvability analysis, different design concepts can be analyzed to determine the concept that is most suitable to handle the identified failure. The analysis is based on comparing different concepts to choose the most promising concept to continue with in the product design. An example of a solvability analysis is shown in Table 5.

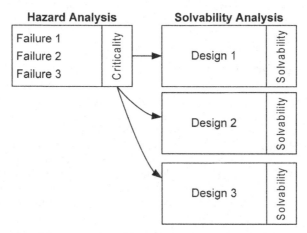

Fig. 1. The concept of the actuator based hazard analysis with a solvability analysis. The criticality numbers from the hazard analysis is used in the solvability analysis.

In most situations there are dependencies between failures and there are not only single faults occurring, an example is common cause faults. Therefore, a failure analysis that focuses on actuators should also consider multiple failures. In the work by Papadopoulos [6], one approach for considering multiple faults is presented. This approach uses tables with combinations of the different faults. There is one new table for each new dimension of faults that is introduced in the analysis. For few faults, this is a durable approach. However, for many faults this approach becomes complicated.

2.1 Fault Classes and Actuator Failures

The proposed hazard analysis method focuses on the system's actuators and the fault classes are chosen for this purpose. It was decided to use a reduced set of the fault classes Papadopoulos provided in [6]. The fault classes used are; *omission, commission*, and *stuck*. When using more fault classes, it is difficult to tell them apart in this early design stage, e.g. there is little difference between *late* and *omission*. Our experience also shows that using other fault classes at this stage do not add any value to the analysis.

The three chosen fault classes propagate to the worst case failures for any mechanical actuator. The class *omission* is interpreted as no force is available at the actuator, *commission* is interpreted as maximum force is applied to the actuator, and fined as the set of all markings that are reachable through any possible firing sequences of activities, starting from the initial marking. Other than the input and output *gates*, which allow to specifically control the net execution, SAN offers two more relevant high-level constructs for building hierarchical models: *REP* and *JOIN*. Particularly. such constructs allow to build composed models based on simpler sub-models, which can be developed independently and then replied and joined with others sub-models and then executed. The SAN model specification and elaboration is supported by Möbius tool [7] that allows to specify the graphical model, to define the performance measures through reward variables, to compute the measures by choosing a specific solver to generate the solution.

6   The Availability Sub Model

To compute *TU* (formula (1)), we have built the *availability* sub model of figure 2. The sub model includes the failure/repair behaviour of the Base Station Controller and the failure/repair behaviour of all the controlled Base Transceiver Stations, according to the terms of formula (1). A failed BTS hosts the Control Channel (CCH) with probability *c,* or complementary host the CCH, with probability *1 − c*. If the failed BTS hosts the CCH, the BTS failure implies the failure of the Control Channel, and in turn, the failure of the whole PMN. If the BTS, doesn't host the CCH, the BTS failure just implies the loss of the physical channels supported by it (eight channels/timeslots).

The marking of place *BTS_UP* represents the number of Base Transceiver Stations which are not failed. The firing of the activity *BTS_Fail* represents the failure of the BTS component. If the failed BTS hosts the CCH, it makes the whole BSS down (output gate *TU_CCH*, shown in table 1). If the failed BTS doesn't host the CCH, the channels which are currently up are decremented by the number of channels associated to the failed BTS (output gate *BTS_loss*). The marking of the place *BTS_DOWN* represents the number of failed BTS; one token in the place *CCH_DOWN* represents the CCH failure. The firing of the activities *BTS_Repair* and *CCH_Repair* represents the repair activities of the related BTS component.

One token in place *BCS_UP* represents that the BCS is not failed. One token in place *BCS_DOWN*, consequent to the firing of the activity *BCS_Fail*, represents the BCS failure. On the failure of the BCS, the whole BSS goes down and all the channels are lost (output gate *TU_BCS*) The marking of the place *working_channels* represents the number of available and idle channels. The marking of the place *channels_in_service* represents the number of available and connected channels. After the repair activities (*CCH_repair, BCS_repair, BTS_repair*) the channels are again up

Table 1. Definition of the output gate TU_CCH

Output Gate Attributes: TU_CCH	
Field Name	**Field Value**

Function	`total_unavailability->Mark()=1;`
	`working_channels->Mark()=0;`
	`channels_in_service->Mark()=0;`

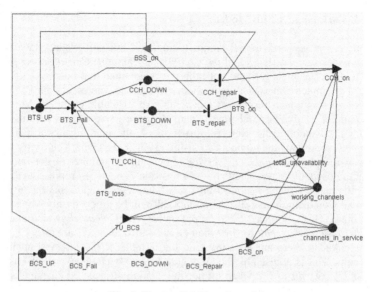

Fig. 2. The *availability* sub model

and ready to be taken in service (ouput gates *BTS_ON, BCS_ON, CCH_ON*). The firing time of the activities is assumed to follow a negative exponential distribution.

7   GSM Performability Composed Model

The *GSM performability* composed model computes the *Total Blocking Probability (TSB)* for voice service. To compute *TSB*, we consider our PMN as completely dedicated to the GSM services, due to the assumption of the priority of voice on data. The *GSM performability composed* model takes into account the contention of the radio channels from the voice calls (either new or continuous) modelled by a pure performance sub model, combined with the possible loss/recovery of the radio channels due to the failure/repair activity of the BSS components. Particularly, *GSM performability composed* model, figure 3, has been built joining the *availability* sub model of section 6, and the *GSM Performance* sub model, which models the pure performance aspects of the GSM service.

Fig. 3. *GSM performability* composed model

7.1 *GSM* Performance Sub Model

The *GSM performance* sub model, figure 4, computes two performance measures: the *New Call Blocking probability* and *the Continuous (handoff) Call Blocking probability*, due to all *N* channels full and not failed. It is assumed that blocked calls are lost and not re-attempted. The *GSM performance* sub model represents the PMN with a number of servers which represents the number of available channels. Moreover, a limited number of available channels, named *guard channels*, are exclusively reserved for the handoff calls. Referring to figure 4, the marking of the place *working_channels* represents the number of not-failed channels, that are currently idle. The marking of the place *channels_in_service* represents the number of not-failed channels, that are currently busy. The firing of transition *T_new_call* represents the arrival of new calls and the firing of transition *T_continuous_call* represents the arrival of a handoff call from neighbour cells. A handoff call will be dropped only when all channels are busy. This is realised by the input gate *I_Total_channels* which enables the transition *T_continuous_call* to fire when all not-failed channels are busy. A new call will be blocked if there are no more than the number of the reserved channels for handoff calls. This is realised by the *input gate Reserved_channels*, which enables the transition *T_new_call* to fire when all not-failed and not reserved channels are busy. The firing of the transitions *T__call_completation* and *T_handoff_out* respectively represent the completion of a call and the departure of an outgoing handoff call. All activities are assumed exponentially distributed.

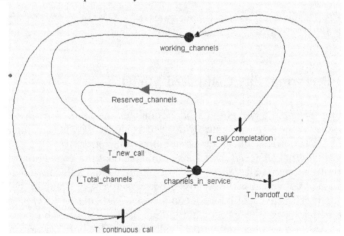

Fig. 4. The *GSM performance* sub model

8   GSM&GPRS Performability Composed Model

The *GSM&GPRS performability* composed model (figure 5) computes the *Total Blocking Probability (TSB)* on packet data service. The composed model joins the *GSM&GPRS performance* sub model, that represents the contention of the radio channels from the voice calls and data packets transfer request and the *availability* sub model that represents the possible loss/recovery of the radio channels due to the failure/repair activity of the BSS components. In case of GPRS, *TSB* does not directly measure the loss of information contained in data packets because they can be accumulated into a queue and retransmitted. Then, for GPRS connection, other than *TSB*, we also compute the probability of data packet loss for exceeding the buffer capacity and the probability of data packet loss for exceeding the maximum number of data packet sessions which can be simultaneously opened.

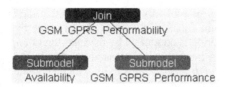

Fig. 5. The *GSM&GPRS performability* composed sub model

8.1 GSM&GPRS Performance Sub Model

The *GSM&GPRS performance* sub model computes the pure performance aspects of the GPRS service, which contends physical channels to the GSM service. Voice calls are set up as long as at least one channel is available in the PMN, while data packets can be transmitted only over the channels which are not used for voice service. A vehicle, which needs to communicate with Tunnel Control Centre or vice versa, tries to open a packet session. If the current number of open data packet sessions is less than the maximum number of data packet sessions which can remain simultaneously active, then a new data packet session can be opened. Into an active data packet session, the incoming data packets are queued in a buffer, as a sequence of radio blocks. Once in the buffer, the radio blocks can be transmitted with the proper GPRS transmission rate. The transfer of radio blocks over the radio link can be either successful, thus allowing the removal of the radio block from the buffer, or results in a failure; in the last case, the radio block is retransmitted.

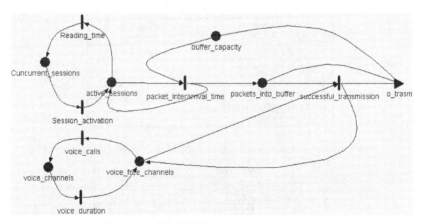

Fig. 6. The *GSM&GPRS performance* sub model

Referring to figure 6, if at least one token is in place *concurrent_section* a data packet session is opened, by the firing of *session_activation* activity. As a consequence one token is added in place *active_section*. Named *D,* the number of maximum simultaneously active data packet sessions and named *d*, the number of currently opened data packet sessions, a new session can be opened at the condition that $d < D$. Inside an open data packet session, data packets arrive with the rate of *packet_interarrival_time* activity and are queued into *packet_into_buffer* place. As a first step, we assume that one data packet has the length of one radio block, so each data packet increments the buffer by one unit (one radio block) at the condition that the buffer is not full (if $b < B$, where b is the current values of the radio blocks in the buffer and B is the buffer capacity). Such a condition is controlled by the marking of *buffer capacity* place. The radio blocks queued in the buffer are transmitted during the same set of 4 TDMA frames by the *successful_transmission* activity which keep into account that the radio block that can be served by the currently available channels (the ones not being occupied by voice).

9   Some Numerical Results

We conduct availability, performance and performability measures, executing the models described in the previous sections, by Mobius analytical solver [7]. The input parameters and their numerical values are summarized in Table 2, 3 and 4.

Some numerical results are shown in figure 7 and 8. Figure 7 shows the *Total Service Blocking Probability (TSB)* for voice service, versus time, computed by the *GSM performability* composed model. The computation of *TSB* is performed by using the *total_blocking* reward variable, which increments its value of 1 when the number of available channels, ready to serve, becomes equal to zero.

Table 2. Input parameters and values of the *availability* sub model

Parameter	Value
rate of BSC_fail	2,31 E-4 h^{-1}
rate of BSC_repair	1 h^{-1}
rate of CCF_fail	3.47 E-4 h^{-1}
rate of CCF_repair	0,5 h^{-1}
rate of BTS_fail	3.47 E-4 h^{-1}
rate of BTS_repair	0,5 h^{-1}
number of BSC	1
number of BTS	4
n. of channels of a BTS	8
number of CCH	1

Table 3. Input parameters and values of the *GSM performance* sub model

Parameter	value
arrival rate of new calls	0,27 s^{-1}
duration of the calls	180 s
arrival rate of handoff calls	0,027 s^{-1}
duration of outgoing handoff calls	80 s

7.1 *GSM* Performance Sub Model

The *GSM performance* sub model, figure 4, computes two performance measures: the *New Call Blocking probability* and *the Continuous (handoff) Call Blocking probability,* due to all *N* channels full and not failed. It is assumed that blocked calls are lost and not re-attempted. The *GSM performance* sub model represents the PMN with a number of servers which represents the number of available channels. Moreover, a limited number of available channels, named *guard channels*, are exclusively reserved for the handoff calls. Referring to figure 4, the marking of the place *working_channels* represents the number of not-failed channels, that are currently idle. The marking of the place *channels_in_service* represents the number of not-failed channels, that are currently busy. The firing of transition *T_new_call* represents the arrival of new calls and the firing of transition *T_continuous_call* represents the arrival of a handoff call from neighbour cells. A handoff call will be dropped only when all channels are busy. This is realised by the input gate *I_Total_channels* which enables the transition *T_continuous_call* to fire when all not-failed channels are busy. A new call will be blocked if there are no more than the number of the reserved channels for handoff calls. This is realised by the *input gate Reserved_channels,* which enables the transition *T_new_call* to fire when all not-failed and not reserved channels are busy. The firing of the transitions *T__call_completation* and *T_handoff_out* respectively represent the completion of a call and the departure of an outgoing handoff call. All activities are assumed exponentially distributed.

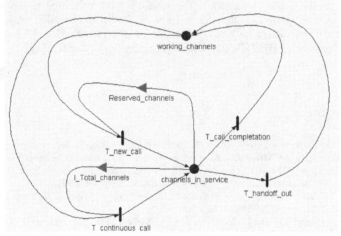

Fig. 4. The *GSM performance* sub model

8   GSM&GPRS Performability Composed Model

The *GSM&GPRS performability* composed model (figure 5) computes the *Total Blocking Probability (TSB)* on packet data service. The composed model joins the *GSM&GPRS performance* sub model, that represents the contention of the radio channels from the voice calls and data packets transfer request and the *availability* sub

10   Conclusions and Future Research

The work presented in this paper is in the framework of validation by modelling of a Tele Control system, based on a Public Mobile Network (PMN). We have computed performability measures of the denial of service for GSM and GPRS connections, such as the Total Service Blocking Probability (TSB), to better understand the effects of the degradation of the performance and of the availability of the PMN on the Tele Control system main functions. We have built modular sub models, hierarchically composed, by using Stochastic Activity Networks. Two different layers of modelling have been implemented. At the first layer, we built separate sub models to compute the pure unavailability and the pure performance for voice and data packet services. At the second layer of modelling, we have built two composed models joining the availability sub model and the performance sub models. The first numerical results have been presented. The research is still on going. At short term, we will refine the tuning of the models to the application. At longer term, we are going to join the performability models of the PMN with the performability models of the other parts of the Tele Control System in a whole model to evaluate if and how performability measures of the Tele Control System impact, in time and in value, the safety policies inside the tunnel.

Acknowledgements. The authors wish greatly acknowledge Andrea Bobbio for the fruitful discussions and suggestions. The research work presented in this paper has been partially supported by the IST – 1999-28099 SAFETUNNEL project and its consortium: Centro Ricerche Fiat (I), Renault VI (F), TILAB (I), SITAF (I), SFTRF (F), Fiat Engineering (I), TÜV (D), Un. Ben Gurion (Isr), Enea (I), TLC Tecnosistemi (CH)

References

1.   Project IST – 1999 – 28099, SAFETUNNEL - http://www.crfproject-eu.org
2.   E. Ciancamerla, M. Minichino, S. Serro, E. Tronci - Automatic Timeliness Verification of a Public Mobile Network – Safecomp 2003, 22nd International Conference on Computer Safety, Reliability and Security – Edinburgh, UK - September 23-26, 2003
3.   K. S. Trivedi, Xiaomin Ma – Performability Analysis of Wireless Cellular Networks – SPECTS2002 and SCSC2002 – July 2002
4.   ETSI – Digital Cellular Telecommunication System (Phase 2+) General Packet Radio Service (GPRS) - GSM 04.60 version 8.3.0
5.   C. Bettsletter, H. Vogel, J. Eberspacher GSM phase 2+ General packet radio service GPRS: architecture, protocols and air interface – IEEE Communications Survey vol. 2 , n.3 – 1999
6.   M. Meo, M. Ajmone Marsan, C. Batetta – Resource Management Policies in GPRS Wireless Internet Access System – 2002 IEEE
7.   W.H. Sanders, W.D. Obal, M.A.Qureshi, F.K. Widjanarko – The UltraSAN modelling Environment – Performance Evaluation J. special issue on performance modelling tools, vol. 24, pp 89 - 115, 1995

PLC-Based Safety Critical Software Development for Nuclear Power Plants

Junbeom Yoo[1], Sungdeok Cha[1],
Han Seong Son[2], Chang Hwoi Kim[2], and Jang-Soo Lee[2]

[1] Korea Advanced Institute of Science and Technology(KAIST) and AITrc/SPIC/IIRTRC
Department of Electrical Engineering and Computer Science,
373-1, Kusong-dong, Yusong-gu, Taejon, Korea,
{jbyoo,cha}@salmosa.kaist.ac.kr
[2] Korea Atomic Energy Research Institute(KAERI) MMIS team,
150, Deokjin-dong, Yusong-gu, Taejon, Korea,
{hsson,chkim2,jslee}@kaeri.re.kr

Abstract. This paper proposes a PLC(Programmable Logic Controller)-based safety critical software development technique for nuclear power plants' I&C software controllers. To improve software safety, we write the software requirements specification using a formal specification notation named NuSCR [1]. NuSCR specification is then mechanically transformed into semantically equivalent Function Block Diagram(FBD), a widely used PLC programming language. Finally, we manually refine the FBD programs so that redundant function blocks are identified and removed. As CASE tool supplied by PLC vendors automatically compiles the resulting FBD programs into PLC machine code, PLC software development is completed when the final FBD programs are essentially tested.

Proposed development technique offers several advantages. Requirement errors are reduced as we use the formal specification notation. Consistency and completeness checks are automated, and model checking can be performed on the NuSCR specification. Safety critical errors are less likely to be introduced to the synthesized FBD programming. As a consequence, cost of developing and validating the PLC-based software can be also reduced. The proposed approach is currently being applied in developing safety-critical control software for a Korean nuclear power plant, and experience to date has been positive.

1 Introduction

PLC [2] is widely used in industry to implement real-time safety critical software [3]. Such trend is especially true in the area of nuclear power plant's I&C(Instrumentation and Control) systems as aged RLL(Relay Ladder Logic)-based analog systems are being replaced by PLC-based digital systems [4].

Software development process for control software in nuclear power plants generally consists of analysis, design, and implementation phases. Software requirements are initially written in natural language, and a formal specification is developed on which various formal analysis techniques are applied. As embedded software controlling nuclear power plants usually run on PLCs, PLC programs, written in Ladder Diagram(LD)

M. Heisel et al. (Eds.): SAFECOMP 2004, LNCS 3219, pp. 155–165, 2004.

or Function Block Diagrams(FBDs) [2], are developed and documented in software design specification(SDS). In implementation phase, the hardware configuration for PLC, i.e. number of I/O cards, CPU speed, network communication, is decided, and then PLC programs are translated into machine code. This translation process is conducted automatically by an engineering tool, which is provided by PLC vendors. Therefore, the actual software development for PLC software is completed at the end of the design phase.

If software requirements specification is written in a natural language, much effort would be needed to certify its safety using inspection, simulation, and other safety analysis techniques. Likewise, manual programming of PLC programs is inefficient and a potentially error-prone task.

In this paper, we propose a PLC-based software development method. It consists of three phases: formal requirements specification, synthesis, and refinement phase. It uses the formal software requirements specification language, NuSCR [1], to express and analyze the software requirements. Formal software requirements specification allows developers to specify all requirements explicitly and completely while avoiding inconsistency in logic. Mechanical and formal verification methods, such as model checking [5] and mechanized theorem proving [6], can also be applied to NuSCR formal requirements.

In synthesis phase, we mechanically transform the NuSCR formal specification into FBD program using an intermediate notation called the *2C-Table*. Comparison of synthesized FBD against the manually developed FBDs revealed that experts could reduced the number of required FBD blocks by up to 50%. While the scan cycle of PLC is between 30 - 50ms, the total execution time of the manually programmed FBD program operating on PLC is usually at most 5 - 10ms. Therefore, the two times increase of the number of function blocks does not seriously affect timely execution of PLC code.

While FBD code can be automatically generated, domain engineers are still most likely to modify or manually optimize synthesized FBD code. In refinement phase, we are working on formal method support so that the semantic equivalence between the two FBD codes can be verified.

The remainder of the paper is organized as follows: Section 2 briefly introduces the PLC. In Section 3, we explain the proposed PLC based safety critical software development method. To aid the understanding we use the real case study, which is presently being developed in Korea. Conclusion and future work are in Section 4.

2 Programmable Logic Controller

Programmable Logic Controller(PLC), which is widely used in the real-time and safety-critical systems industry, has features as follows [7]:

Concise Hardware Architecture. PLC has a relatively simple hardware architecture that facilitate the input/output configurations. This architectural characteristics makes the exact analysis of the program execution time possible. Operating system for PLC is provided by PLC vendors, and the application programs operating on the real-time OS are programmed with SFC, LD, or FBD using CASE tool supplied by PLC vendors.

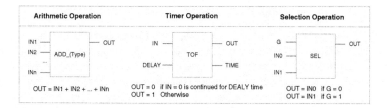

Fig. 1. IEC 61131-3 FBD samples

Program Execution Mechanism. PLC programs are executed in a permanent loop. In each iteration of loop, a scan cycle, inputs are read. The program computes a new internal state and output, and the outputs are updated. There exists an upper time bound for each cycle, which typically is in the order of milli-seconds.

Programming Languages. IEC 61131-3 standard include five PLC programming languages: ST(Structured Text), LD, IL(Instruction List), SFC, and FBD. In practice, FBD and LD are most widely used. FBD, similar to electrical circuit diagram in appearance, consists of a network of function blocks and regards the system as the flow of information expressed with primitive function blocks. (See ⟨Fig.1⟩ for samples of widely used basic function blocks.) Basic FBs can be classified into logical, arithmetic, selection, and timing operations, and it is known that the RPS(reactor protection system), which is presently being developed in Korea, can be programmed using 14 different types of FBD blocks belonging to the four groups mentioned above.

3 PLC-Based Software Development

An overview of the PLC-based software development process, starting with NuSCR formal specification and ending with validation of refined FBD code, is shown in ⟨Fig.2⟩.

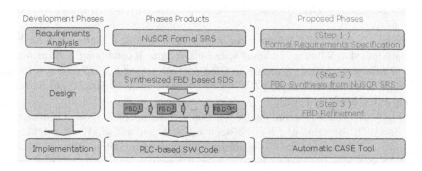

Fig. 2. Overview of formal method guided PLC based software development

3.1   Phase I: Formal Requirements Specification

NuSCR [1] was developed with active participation of and consultation by nuclear engineers who are familiar with software engineering knowledge in general and formal methods in particular. Readability of the specification to domain experts was a key concern when deciding which notation to use to capture various aspects of requirements.

It uses FOD(Function Overview Diagram) for the overview of data flows. In addition, it introduces three basic constructs, *function variable*, *history variable*, and *timed history variable*. These constructs are written in SDT(Structured Decision Table), FSM(Finite State Machine), and TTS(Timed Transition System) [8] notations respectively. *Function variables* specify mathematical functional behavior of system, and they are defined as SDT, which is a condtion/event table. *History variables* describe state-based behavior in finite state machine where transitions capture triggering events or conditions as well as generated actions. *Timed-history variables* express timing constraints in extended FSM notations.

⟨Fig.3⟩ describes the basic constructs of NuSCR. ⟨Fig.3 (a)⟩ is a FOD for *g_Fixed_Setpoint_Rising_Trip_with_OB* logic for fixed set-point rising trip in RPS(Reactor Protection System) BP(Bistable Logic), which is currently being developed at KNICS in Korea. *_g* means that it is a group of node in the FOD hierarchy and that details are further captured in a separate FOD diagram. It is composed of five internal nodes, and they are all defined individually. The prefixes *"f_"*, *"h_"*, and *"th_"* denote function variable nodes, history variable nodes, and timed history variable nodes, respectively. Arrows denote data-flow dependency relation.

⟨Fig.3 (b)⟩ is an TTS definition for timed history variable node *th_X_Trip* appearing in the FOD. TTS is a FSM extended with time duration constraint $[a, b]$ in transition conditions. TTS defines the time-related behavior of nuclear power plants control systems. The TTS definition for *th_X_Trip* is interpreted as follows: "If condition $f_X \geq k_X\_Trip\_Setpoint$ is satisfied in state *Normal*, it transits to *Waiting* state. In this state, if the condition is lasted for *k_Trip_Delay* then it fires the trip signal 0. If *f_X_Valid*, *f_Module_Error*, or *f_Channel_Error* occur, then trip signal is fired at once. In the state *Trip_By_Error* or *Trip_By_Logic*, if the trip conditions are canceled, then it comes back to the state *Normal* and the output is 1." The TTS expression in *Cond_b*, *[k_Trip_Delay,k_Trip_Delay]* means that the condition has to remain true for *k_Trip_Delay* time units.

⟨Fig.3 (c)⟩ is an FSM definition for history variable node *h_X_OB_Sta* in the FOD. It is interpreted as follows: " In initial state *No_OB_State*, if condition *f_X_Perm = 1 and f_X_OB_Ini = 1* is satisfied , it transits to *OB_State* with setting *h_X_OB_STA* is 1. In state *OB_State*, if condition *f_X_Perm = 0* is satisfied, then it transits back to *No_OB_State* with setting *h_X_OB_STA* is 0 again.

⟨Fig.3 (d)⟩ is an SDT definition for function variable node *f_X_Valid*. It is interpreted as follows: "If the value of *f_X* is between *k_X_MIN* and *k_X_MAX*, the output value *f_X_Valid* is 0, which means it is a normal case. Otherwise output value of *f_X_Valid* is 1." NuSCR recommends multiple correlated condition statements per row. In this way, NuSCR can resolve a large part of the table-size explosion problems, and also can increase the readability of SDTs [9].

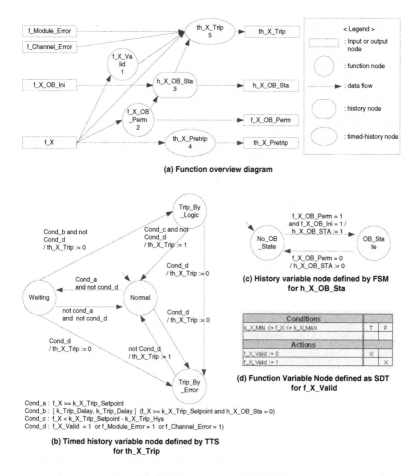

(a) Function overview diagram

(c) History variable node defined by FSM
for h_X_OB_Sta

Conditions			
k_X_MIN <= f_X <= k_X_MAX		T	F
Actions			
f_X_Valid := 0		X	
f_X_Valid := 1			X

(d) Function Variable Node defined as SDT
for f_X_Valid

Cond_a : f_X >= k_X_Trip_Setpoint
Cond_b : [k_Trip_Delay, k_Trip_Delay] (f_X >= k_X_Trip_Setpoint and h_X_OB_Sta = 0)
Cond_c : f_X < k_X_Trip_Setpoint - k_X_Trip_Hys
Cond_d : f_X_Valid = 1 or f_Module_Error = 1 or f_Channel_Error = 1)

(b) Timed history variable node defined by TTS
for th_X_Trip

Fig. 3. Basic constructs of NuSCR

3.2 Phase II: FBD Synthesis from NuSCR SRS

In this phase, we derive PLC-based FBD program from the requirements specification
written in NuSCR. See [10,11] for detailed discussion on the formal definitions of rules,
algorithms, and procedures. FBD generation process has 4 steps. First we perform consistency and completeness analysis of selected nodes, which are defined as SDT, FSM,
or TTS. After modifying all nodes to be complete and consistent, we produce 2C-Table
for corresponding FSM and TTS. 2C-Table is an intermediate notation that are used to
facilitate the FBD generation process for FSM and TTS. In the next step, FBDs are generated from SDTs of 2C-Tables. After generating the individual FBDs, we analyze the
dependency among nodes in FOD and decide appropriate execution orders for all nodes
in the FOD. As PLC executes its application programs sequentially, proper selection of
execution order is essential. Details of each step, along with an example, is explained
below:

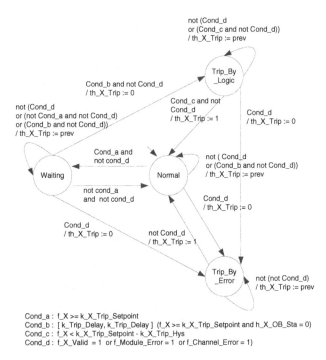

Cond_a : f_X >= k_X_Trip_Setpoint
Cond_b : [k_Trip_Delay, k_Trip_Delay] (f_X >= k_X_Trip_Setpoint and h_X_OB_Sta = 0)
Cond_c : f_X < k_X_Trip_Setpoint - k_X_Trip_Hys
Cond_d : f_X_Valid = 1 or f_Module_Error = 1 or f_Channel_Error = 1)

Fig. 4. Modified complete and consistent TTS for *th_X_Trip*

(Step 1) Completeness and Consistency Analysis. NuSCR allows inclusion of arbitrarily complex expressions and macros in SDT and automata such as FSM and TTS. When specifying state- and time-dependent behavior using (timed)automata notation, not all edges are drawn explicitly. In addition, SDT may contain nondeterminism if specific ordering of execution sequences does not matter. While such features reduce complexity of requirements, all the missing details and exceptional situations must be made explicit, complete and consistent. For example, ⟨Fig.4⟩ illustrates the results of performing consistency and completeness analysis applied on ⟨Fig.3 (b)⟩. FSM, which defines the history variable node, can be modified in the same way so that automata remains in the current state if no conditions initiating a transition to other states are satisfied. In this case, we need to specify the implicit transitions explicitly . If there is no action statement in the transition label in FSM and TTS, then NuSCR regards that the output is set to the same value in the previous scan cycle (i.e. *th_X_Trip := prev*).

(Step 2) 2C-Table Generation. While format is similar to that of SDT, 2C-Table has an additional action part capturing changes made to state variables. ⟨Fig.5⟩ is the 2C-Table obtained from modified automata shown in ⟨Fig.4⟩. *SV* is the state variable, and Output denotes the output of *th_X_Trip* node. For example, the second column of ⟨Fig.5⟩, shaded for the purpose of illustration, denotes that if condition "*Cond_a and not Cond_d*"

	1	2	3	4	5	6	7	8	9	10	11	12
SV = Normal	T	T	T									
Cond_a and not Cond_d	T	-	-									
cond_d	-	T	-									
Otherwise	-	-	T									
SV = Waiting				T	T	T	T					
not Cond_a and not Cond_d				T	-	-	-					
Cond_d				-	T	-	-					
Cond_b and not Cond_d				-	-	T	-					
Otherwise				-	-	-	T					
SV = Trip_By_Logic								T	T	T		
Cond_c and not Cond_d								T	-	-		
Cond_d								-	T	-		
Otherwise								-	-	T		
SV= Trip_By_Error											T	T
not Cond_d											T	-
Otherwise											-	T
Output := 0		X			X	X			X			
Output := 1								X		X		
Output := prev	X		X	X			X				X	X
SV := Normal(0)		X	X		X				X			
SV := Waiting(1)	X			X			X					
SV := Trip_By_Logic(2)						X		X		X		
SV := Trip_By_Error(3)											X	X

Fig. 5. 2C-Table for TTS of *th_X_Trip*

is satisfied in state *Normal*, the output value of *th_X_Trip* is the same as the previous one and the next state is *Waiting*.

(Step 3) Basic FBD Generation. The next step separately generates basic FBD from each SDT and 2C-Table. Reflecting the characteristics of PLC, where input values are first read before output values are computed, FBD generated from SDT and 2C-Table consists of two parts: (1) preprocessing routine in which conditions and macros used in the SDTs are first evaluated; and (2) computation routine where output and state values are determined. ⟨Fig.6⟩ is a generated from the SDT shown in ⟨Fig.3 (c)⟩. Complex conditions are internally decomposed into a collection of primitive predicates, and Boolean operators are replaced by the corresponding FBD blocks. [11] describes the details of the algorithm. The FBD is made from *Concept version 2.2 XL SR2*, a PLC programming assistant tool by *Schneider Automation GmbH* [12], and the numbers above the function blocks indicate the generation and execution orders. 2C-Table is also transformed, as shown in ⟨Fig.7 ⟩, into FBDs using the same procedure. SEL and MUX function block allows one of several inputs to be chosen as outputs and updated value of state variables.

⟨Fig. 7 (b)⟩ is the whole output processing part FBD for *th_X_Trip*. The selection among many condition statements and their corresponding action statements in 2C-Table or SDT are implemented in FBD with SEL function block. Each condition and output statements are preprocessed previously, and the results are used in the output calculation. The current state of automata node(FSM and TTS), *Status*, provides the basis of the

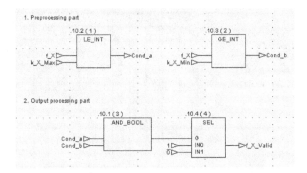

Fig. 6. FBD generated from SDT of *f_X_Valid*

decision about which one in SEL function blocks we have to select as an output, and this selection process is implemented using MUX function block with *status*. MUX function block generates a selected output according to *status*, and the variable *status* is implemented as ⟨Fig.7 (c)⟩ from the lower part of 2C-Table in ⟨Fig.5⟩. Variable *th_Prev_X_Trip*, which is the other output in the FBD, is the internal variable used in only the FBD. After these processes are finished, we get the individual FBDs for all nodes, s.t. function variable nodes, history variable nodes, and timed-history variable nodes, in FOD.

(Step 4) FBD Execution Order Decison. In the final step, the execution order for each FBDs in FOD is analyzed and then decided. The possible execution orders for the 5 nodes composed in FBD in ⟨Fig. 3 (a)⟩ is as follows: At first, there are two partial orders among the 5 nodes in FOD as their input/output relationships. As the node numbered 4 has no interaction with other nodes, it is considered independent of others.

Partial execution order 1: (1 ⟶ 5)
Partial execution order 2: (2 ⟶ 3 ⟶ 5)
Independent execution: (4)

   All possible combinations of execution orders are shown below, and one is picked nondeterministically as all are equivalent.

Execution order 1:
(Input) → 1 → 2 → 3 → 5 → (4) →(Output)
Execution order 2:
(Input) → 2 → 1 → 3 → 5 → (4) →(Output)
Execution order 3:
(Input) → 2 → 3 → 1 → 5 → (4) →(Output)

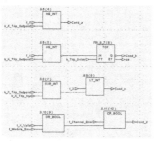

(a) Preprocessing part FBD

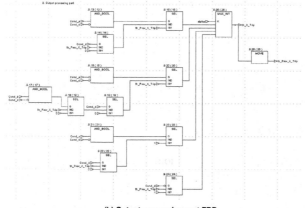

(b) Output processing part FBD

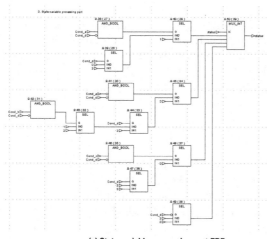

(c) State-variable processing part FBD

Fig. 7. FBD generated from TTS of *th_X_Trip*

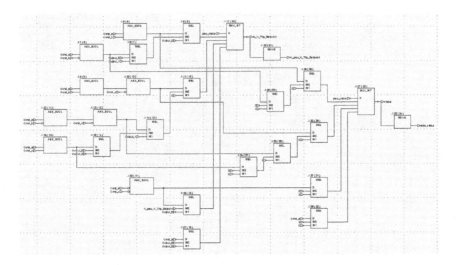

Fig. 8. An example of refined FBD from Fig.7(b) and (c)

3.3   Phase III: FBD Refinement

Finally in refinement phase, we allow domain experts to refine the generated FBD program. Our case study revealed that manually prepared FBD may contain fewer number of FBD blocks, and execution time takes less. Therefore, to increase chance that execution of PLC code satisfies the timing requirements, additional modification processes are provided to further reduce the size of generated FBD program. ⟨Fig.8⟩ is an example of refined FBD from the one in ⟨Fig.7 (b),(c)⟩.

However, the revised FBD code must be tested to demonstrate that it is still the same in its behavior. We are currently focusing on sequential equivalence [13] of two FBD programs to verify their behavioral equivalence. Some formal and automated techniques, such as VIS model checker [14] or COSPAN/FormalCheck [15], may be used to verify their behavioral equivalence.

4   Conclusion and Future Work

In this paper, we proposed a PLC based safety critical software development process in which formal methods played critical roles. It improves safety of embedded software and reduces time needed to develop safety-critical software.

We have been applying our proposed method successfully to develop the plant protection system to be deployed in a nuclear power plant in Korea. Experience by domain experts on the proposed approach has been positive, and we are currently working on development of analysis methods used to check the behavioral equivalence of subsequently modified FBDs. This analysis method is expected to accelerate the whole appliance of our proposed transformation-based PLC software development method.

Acknowledgements. This research was partially supported by Advanced Information Technology Research Center(AITrc), Software Process Improvement Center(SPIC), and Internet Intrusion Response Technology Research Center(IIRTRC) in Korea.

References

1. Yoo, J., Cha, S., Son, H.S., Kim, C.H., Lee, J.S.: A formal software requirements specification method for digital nuclear plants protection systems. Journal of Systems and Software to be published (2003)
2. Commission, I.E.: International standard for programmable controllers: Programming languages (1993) part 3.
3. Leveson, N.G.: SAFEWARE, System safety and Computers. Addison Wesley (1995)
4. NRC, U.: Digital Instrumentation and Control Systems in Nuclear Power Plants: safety and reliability issues. National Academy Press (1997)
5. Clarke, E.M., Emerson, E.A., Sistla, A.P.: Automatic verification of finite-state concurrent systems using temporal logic specifications. ACM Trans. Programming Languages and Sysems **8** (1986) 244–263
6. Dalen, D.V. In: Logic and Structure. 3 edn. Springer-Verlag (1994)
7. Mader, A.: A classification of plc models and applications. In: Discrete Event Systems-Analysis and Control: WODES 2000. (2000)
8. Henzinger, T.A., Manna, Z., Pnueli, A.: Timed transition systems. In: REX Workshop. (1991) 226–251
9. Yoo, J., Cha, S., Kim, C., Oh, Y.: Formal software requirements specification for digital reactor protection systems. Journal of KISS(Korea Information and Science Society) to be published (2004)
10. Yoo, J., Cha, S., Kim, C., Song, D.Y.: Synthesis of FBD-based PLC design from NuSCR formal specification. Reliability Engineering and System Safety to be published (2004)
11. Yoo, J., Bang, H., Cha, S.: Procedural transformation from formal software requirement to PLC-based design. Technical Report CS/TR 2004-198, Korea Advanced Institute of Science and Technology(KAIST), 373-1, Kusong-dong, Yusong-gu, Taejon, Korea (2004)
12. Electric, S.: (http://www.modicon.com/)
13. Huang, S.Y., Cheng, K.T.: 4. In: Fromal Equivalence Checking and Debugging. Kliwer Academic Publishers (1998)
14. Brayton, R.K., Hachtel, G.D., Sangiovanni-Vincentelli, A., Somenzi, F., Aziz, A., Cheng, S.T., Edwards, S., Khatri, S., Kukimoto, Y., Pardo, A., Qadeer, S., Ranjan, R.K., Sarwary, S., Shiple, T.R., Swamy, G., Villa, T.: ((vis)
15. Kurshan, R.P.: Computer Aided Vrification of Coordinating Processes: The Automata-Theoretic Approach. Princeton University Press (1994)

Compositional Hazard Analysis
of UML Component and Deployment Models*

Holger Giese, Matthias Tichy, and Daniela Schilling**

Software Engineering Group, University of Paderborn,
Warburger Str. 100, D-33098 Paderborn, Germany
{hg,mtt,das}@upb.de

Abstract. The general trend towards complex technical systems with embedded software results in an increasing demand for dependable high quality software. The UML as an advanced object-oriented technology provides in principle the essential concepts which are required to handle the increasing complexity of these safety-critical software systems. However, the current and forthcoming UML versions do not directly apply to the outlined problem. Available hazard analysis techniques on the other hand do not provide the required degree of integration with software design notations. To narrow the gap between safety-critical system development and UML techniques, the presented approach supports the compositional hazard analysis of UML models described by restricted component and deployment diagrams. The approach permits to systematically identify which hazards and failures are most serious, which components or set of components require a more detailed safety analysis, and which restrictions to the failure propagation are assumed in the UML design.

1 Introduction

Today, an increasing demand for dependable high quality software can be observed due to the fact that more ambitious and complex technical systems should be built. In [1], this trend is characterized by very complex, highly integrated systems with elements that must have a great autonomy and, thus, are very demanding w.r.t. safety analysis. Additionally, instead of single safety-critical systems today "systems of systems" have to be developed even though established techniques for their safety analysis are not in place (cf. [2]). The New Railway Technology (RailCab) project[1] used later in the paper as a motivating example is one very extreme example for such complex systems of systems with very demanding safety requirements.

The UML as an object-oriented technology is one candidate to handle these safety-critical systems with software and overwhelming complexity. However, the current and forthcoming UML versions do not directly support safety-critical system development.

---

* This work was developed in the course of the Special Research Initiative 614 – Self-optimizing Concepts and Structures in Mechanical Engineering - University of Paderborn, and was published on its behalf and funded by the Deutsche Forschungsgemeinschaft.
** Supported by the International Graduate School of Dynamic Intelligent Systems.
[1] http://www-nbp.upb.de

M. Heisel et al. (Eds.): SAFECOMP 2004, LNCS 3219, pp. 166–179, 2004.

Available hazard analysis techniques on the other hand have their origin in the hardware world and do not provide the required degree of integration with software design notations. They assume a very simple hardware-oriented notion of components and therefore do not directly support the identification of common mode faults. Some more advanced approaches [3,4,5,6,7] support a compositional treatment of failures and their propagation, but still a proper integration with concepts like deployment and the more complex software interface structure is missing.

The presented approach tries to narrow the described gap between safety-critical system development and available UML techniques by supporting the compositional hazard analysis of UML models. As there is little value in proposing extensions to UML if they are not accepted by the community and tool vendors (cf. [1]), we instead propose to use only a properly defined subset of the UML 2.0 [8] component and deployment diagrams. The approach builds on the foundation of failure propagation analysis [3] and component-based software engineering [9]. It provides a sound combination of these two techniques for compositional hazard analysis and permits automatic quantitative analysis at an early design stage. The failures can be modeled as detailed as required using a hierarchical failure classification where correct refinement steps ensure the complete coverage of all possible failures. The approach permits to systematically identify which hazards and failures are most serious, which components or set of components require a more detailed safety analysis, and which restrictions to the failure propagation are assumed. We can thus systematically derive all safety requirements, which correspond to required restrictions of the failure propagation of a single component or a set of composed components in the UML design.

The paper is organized as follows: We first review in Section 2 the current proposals for compositional hazard analysis and discuss their limitation when it comes to complex software systems. The foundations of our approach and the process integration are then outlined in Section 3. In Section 4, the application of the approach to some fragments of the mentioned New Railway Technology case study is presented. More advanced concepts of our approach which enable the systematic refinement of the safety analysis are presented in Section 5. We close the paper with a final conclusion and outlook on future work.

2   Related Work

Component-based hazard analysis is a hot topic in safety-critical systems research [1,4, 5,6,7]. The basic idea is to ease the hazard analysis by reusing already available information about failure behavior of the individual components rather than always start from scratch when performing a hazard analysis. The current approaches for component-based hazard analysis have in common that they describe the failure propagation of individual components (cf. failure propagation and transfer nets [3]). Outgoing failures are the result of the combination of internal errors and incoming failures from other components. The failure classification presented in [3,10] is widely employed (as in [4, 6]) to distinguish different failures.

Papadopoulos et al. [4] describe an approach for a component-based hazard analysis. The basic idea is a Failure Modes and Effects Analysis (FMEA) for each component based on its interfaces (called IF-FMEA). The outgoing failures are disjunctions of a combination of internal errors and a combination of incoming failures. They employ the notion of block diagrams [11] for their components. The results of IF-FMEA are combined to construct a fault tree for the complete system. A main advantage, besides reusing already available IF-FMEA results, is an improved consistency between the structure of the system design and the fault tree of the system. This approach has been integrated with component concepts of the ROOM [12] methodology in [6]. A major weakness of these approaches (as noted in [1]) is the usage of a fault tree for the combination of the individual IF-FMEA results, since fault trees do not inherently support common mode failures like a hardware crash failure which influences all software components executed on that node. Additionally, the authors impose an unnecessary restriction by the definition that the internal errors are always combined by an logical or with the incoming failures.

Kaiser et al. [5] present a component concept for fault tree analysis. They propose to divide a fault tree into fault tree components. A fault tree component has incoming and outgoing ports. These ports are used to connect the different components and create the complete fault tree. The main advantage of this approach is the possibility to reuse existing fault tree components. Thus, by building a repository of fault tree components for often used system components, the building of fault trees becomes easier. Unfortunately, the proposed fault tree components are not linked in any way to the system components, whose faults they are modelling. In [7] this approach has been integrated with ROOM [12]. The input and output actions are used to derive all failure ports. The failure ports which are used for the connection of the fault tree components are still not typed. In contrast, our approach additionally supports the flexible classification of failures at a greater level of detail. In contrast to all discussed approaches, we explicitly allow cycles in the failure propagation models.

3   The Approach

Following the ROOM [12] concepts in UML 2.0 [8], a well encapsulated software component has a number of ports. Each port is typed by provided and required interfaces. Two ports can be connected to each other by connecting a provided and a required interface. As additional elements, connectors are employed to describe these interconnections between ports. If we want to study the safety of systems described by UML components, we have to incorporate possible faults, errors, and failures as well as their effects into our component model. Due to the outlined restrictions of UML components, we can thus restrict our attention to the failure propagation taking place at specific ports. As we only want to study the higher level failure propagation during development and post-factum safety assessment, it is sufficient to consider the high level failure modes which are relevant at the more abstract software architecture level rather than considering the more detailed code level failure modes (cf. [2,10]). In addition, we will abstract from the component states and refer to Section 5 for our treatment of states.

All software ultimately relies on hardware for execution and all hardware can suffer from part failures, power outages, etc. Experience has shown, that random hardware faults can in contrast to systematic faults be appropriately modeled using probabilities (cf. [13]). Hardware failures have a direct influence on the executed software and therefore, due to hardware sharing, common mode failures can result. Thus, the deployment of the software components and connectors to hardware components must be an integral part of the safety analysis.

To describe software components and connectors as well as their deployment, we use a generalized model of components for software as well as the hardware components which are interconnected via ports. Special deployment ports are used to describe the possible effect of the hardware and the deployed components. We thus assume a set C of components $c \in C$ with software ports $sn \in \mathcal{P}$ and hardware ports $hn \in \mathcal{P}$ with $n \in \mathbb{N}$. A system S is characterized by such a set of components and two mappings $map_c : C \times \mathcal{P} \to C$ and $map_p : C \times \mathcal{P} \to \mathcal{P}$ which assigns connected ports to each other in a type correct manner.

The nature of faults, errors, and failures is that within a component a fault can manifest itself in form of an error which then may lead to a failure to provide the service offered by the component. Such a failure to provide a service results in faults for other components which depend on that component (cf. *chain of faults/failures* [14]). For our setting here we can restrict our attention to the failures of a component and their propagation and thus distinguish incoming and outgoing failures for each component port. We can further abstract from faults as long as they are dormant and can thus restrict our attentions to relevant errors only. Basic errors which are the direct results of local faults have to be included in form of events. Implied errors which result from incoming failures have in contrast to be omitted as they are not probabilistically independent and we require instead that their effects are directly propagated between incoming and outgoing failures. In addition, local probabilistic events such as the successful or not successful detection of two independent occurring value failures can be used to describe the required propagation more realistically.

To formally model the hazards and the failure propagation of the components we use Boolean logic with quantifiers (cf. [15]). We assume two disjoint Boolean variable sets V_F and V_E for failures and probabilistic independent local events, respectively. All elements can then be described by Boolean logic expressions where the basic propositions are built by occurrences of the failure variables ($f_j \in V_F$), event variables ($e_k \in V_E$), or one of the Boolean constants true and false. These basic propositions and Boolean formulas might be combined using the Boolean operators $\wedge, \vee, \neg, \Rightarrow, \Leftrightarrow$ and quantifiers $\forall$ and $\exists$.[2] For a formula ϕ we use $free(\phi)$ to denote the set of free variables.

To describe hazards and the combinations of faults that can cause them we employ standard fault tree analysis (FTA) [16]. In a fault tree the hazardous event is shown as top of a fault tree. This top node is caused by a combination (and, or) of its child nodes. This continues until the leaf nodes of the tree are reached. These leaf nodes describe the basic events which indirectly caused the hazardous event on the top. In our case, the basic events are failures of the system components. A hazard (top event) corresponds thus to a *hazard condition* γ in form of a Boolean formula which employs only the operators for $\vee$ and $\wedge$ and a subset of the outgoing failure variables of the system components. Note,

---

[2] The quantifiers can be mapped to standard Boolean operators using substitution ($[y/x]$; replace x by y) as follows: $\forall v : \phi$ equals $\phi[\text{true}/v] \wedge \phi[\text{false}/v]$ and $\exists v : \phi$ equals $\phi[\text{true}/v] \vee \phi[\text{false}/v]$.

that the hazard condition is thus never disabled by additionally present failures and thus monotonic increasing w.r.t. additional failures (cf. [15]).

Both failures, incoming and outgoing, have certain types, which are used to guide the connection of the component failure propagation models. Following [3,10], we distinguish the general failure classes: (1) for service provision we have omission (so), crash (scr), or commission (sco), (2) for service timing we have early (te) or late (tl) , and (3) for service value we have coarse incorrect (vc) or subtle incorrect (vs). In Figure 1 we use a UML class diagram and generalizations to specify this classification. Note that all generalization sets are complete ones and thus describe all possible subclassifications at once (cf. [8, p. 122]). If more specific or general failures are relevant for a specific port, they can be easily defined by extending the set of considered failures accordingly within the class diagram. In our case we define that protocol failures (p) are the union of possible omission and commission service and timing failures. We can therefore in the following restrict our considerations on the three failure types crash failure (scr), protocol failure (p), and value failure (v) which build a complete failure classification $\mathcal{F}$ (cf. Section 5). Failure and event variables are named according to the following schema: $f_{c,p,t}$ and $e_{c,t}$ for a component with $c \in \mathcal{C}$, port $p \in \mathcal{P}$, and failure type $t \in \mathcal{F}$. Note that in the case of events which do not relate to a specific failure type appropriate event types are simply added.

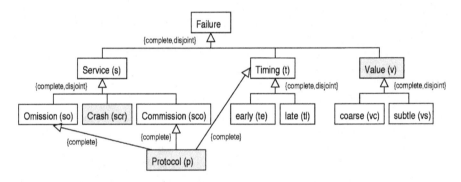

Fig. 1. Failure classification with a UML class diagram

To formally model the failure propagation of components as well as possible constraints, we can also use Boolean logic. For every component $c \in \mathcal{C}$ we employ a *failure propagation information* which consists of the following four elements: (1) A set of *outgoing failure variables* $O_F^c \subseteq V_F$, (2) a set of *incoming failure variables* $I_F^c \subseteq V_F$, (3) a set of possible internal *event variables* $V_E^c \subseteq V_E$, and (4) a failure dependency condition ψ_c which relates the variables for failures and errors to each other by a Boolean logic formula ($free(\psi_c) \subseteq O_F^c \cup I_F^c \cup V_E^c$). We require $O_F^c \cap I_F^c = \emptyset$.

If an incoming failure represented by the variable f_k can result in the outgoing failure represented by the variable f_l, the failure dependency ψ_c must include $f_l \Leftrightarrow f_k$. In general, the failure propagation for an outgoing failure $f_j \in O_F^c$ is described by the corresponding formula ϕ_j in the form $f_j \Leftrightarrow \phi_j$. We use fault trees which may additionally include negated elements for this purpose. For all outgoing failures $f_k \in O_F^c$ their failure propagation formulas ψ_k have to be AND-combined. Thus if a specific outgoing failure f_j is not possible we simply have to add $f_j \Leftrightarrow$ false to ψ_c.

The parallel composition of the failure information of a number of components is derived by simply renaming the failure and event variables appropriately and combining the failure dependencies. We require that the failures are identical ($f_{c,p,t} = f_{c',p',t}$) if and only if their component ports are matched to each other ($map_c(c, p) = c'$ and $map_p(c, p) = p'$). Additionally, the event variable sets for any two components $c \neq c'$ have to be disjoint ($V_E^c \cap V_E^{c'} = \emptyset$). Such a renaming of the failures and events requires that the failure variables used by two connected components for their connected ports must use compatible types. As ports with their protocols and interfaces are design entities of their own, this can be achieved by determining the relevant set of failure types when designing the port protocols and interfaces themselves.

For the AND-composition of the local failure propagation information of all component occurrences $c_1, \ldots, c_n$ with a hazard condition γ in form of the Boolean formula $\psi = \psi_{c_1} \wedge \ldots \wedge \psi_{c_n} \wedge \gamma$ satisfiability has to be checked to determine whether the hazard is possible. We can further abstract from the propagated failures $f_1, \ldots, f_m$ using existential quantification and check instead $\psi_\exists = \exists f_1, \ldots, f_m : \psi_{c_1} \wedge \ldots \wedge \psi_{c_n} \wedge \gamma$.

One option to compute these checks are binary decision diagrams (BDDs) [17] which have been successfully employed to analyze fault trees encoded as Boolean formulas [18]. The possible analysis includes the qualitative analysis (feasibility) and quantitative analysis (probability) of $\psi_\exists$. The related approaches for compositional hazard analysis discussed in Section 2 restrict the permitted propagation structures to acyclic ones to map their results to fault trees. However, for composed failure propagation information of multiple components cycles cannot be excluded. If such a cycle is present in the system, the above mentioned formula degenerates and the probability computation will return probability 1. Using the results of [15,19] and exploiting the fact that the hazard conditions are always monotonic increasing, we can check $\forall f_1, \ldots, f_m((\psi_{c_1} \wedge \ldots \wedge \psi_{c_n}) \Rightarrow \gamma)$ to derive a formula which includes all relevant minterms of $\psi_\exists$.[3] This formula can then also be used to compute the correct probability.

Our approach consists of the following steps, which are to some extent discussed in the following section by means of an application example:

It starts with a system-dependent part, where fault trees for all system hazards are derived. These fault trees only refer to outgoing component failures which can contribute to the hazard but do not look into the components and their interconnections (see Section 4.1).

In the next two steps, the propagation of component failures of each component (see Section 4.2) as well as the related behavior of the deployment nodes and hardware devices (see Section 4.3) have to be derived. If predefined components such as hardware devices, deployment nodes, or software components are used, we can simply reuse their failure propagation information. If, however, specific software has to be built, we have to derive its failure propagation information first.

---

[3] If instead of monotonic increasing conditions more general conditions have to be checked, no efficient standard Boolean encoding exists to derive the related formula. However, in [15] an efficient BDD operator to compute the related Boolean formula has been presented.

If a failure propagation information for each employed component is available, we can compose them as defined by the component and deployment diagrams and employ qualitative and quantitative analysis techniques to identify problems such as a single point of failure or very likely scenarios for hazards (see Section 4.4).

For identified problems often a more detailed safety analysis is required. We then have to refine the failure propagation information until all components are described at an appropriate level of abstraction. In Section 5 the systematic support for refinement and abstraction steps for our failure propagation models are presented.

When deriving a failure propagation model of appropriate level of abstraction, the designer can usually identify the relevant problems and systematically derive safety requirements of the software components and add them to the failure propagation information. Therefore, safety requirements such as the ability of a component to compensate or detect specific failures are systematically derived and documented.

Later in the design and implementation phase verification activities such as testing and formal verification have to be employed to ensure that more detailed design models and the final implementation still adhere to these identified safety requirements.

4   Application Example

The New Railway Technology project and its safety-critical software is used in the following as our application example. The project aims at using a passive track system with intelligent shuttles that operate autonomously and make independent and decentralized operational decisions. Shuttles either transport goods or up to approx. 10 passengers.

The track system, the shuttles are using, is divided into several disjoint sections each of which is controlled by a section control. To enter a section, a shuttle has to be registered at the corresponding section control. The shuttle sends its data, like position and speed, to the section control. The section control in turn sends the data of all other shuttles within the section. Thus, each shuttle knows which other shuttles are nearby. Shuttles can communicate with each other and decide whether it is useful to build a convoy (this reduces the air resistance and therefore saves energy) or not. If two shuttles approach at a switch, they can bargain who has right of way. Depending on the topology, the shuttles speed and its position an optimizer calculates the bid. A more detailed description of this scenario can be found in [20].

In our example, represented in Figure 2, two shuttle components, a switch and a section control interact with each other. A component is depicted as rectangle labelled with at least the component's type (string following the colon) and possibly labelled with the component's name (string preceding the colon). A component represents one instance of a given type. Consider for example the component on the left of Figure 2. This component is an instance of type Shuttle and is named sh1. The component has seven subcomponents and two ports. In our example there is also another shuttle component sh2. This component is of the same type as sh1, although its subcomponents are not shown in the diagram.

Component ports are shown as small squares at the component's border. These ports are used for interaction with other components. In Figure 2, one port of the shuttle component is connected with the SectionControl. In this case data is sent in both directions

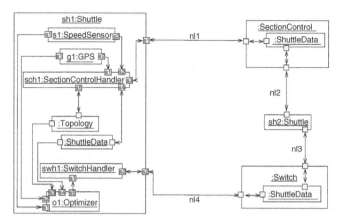

Fig. 2. Component structure with shuttles, switch, and section control

which is depicted by arrows at both ends of the connection. Some of the connectors are labelled with nl1..4, this indicates that a network is used for the communication of the corresponding components.

4.1 System Hazards

In a first step, those hazards are addressed that concern the system as a whole. The causes of these hazards are decomposed until we reach outgoing failures of the main system components.

Each shuttle exchanges periodically data with the section control and with the switch it is approaching. Thus for protocol and crash failures we have the following cases: no data is received (scr or so), not expected data is received (sco), or data is received too early or too late (te resp. tl). In each of these cases the corresponding component can switch to a fail-safe state or compensate those failures by pessimistic extrapolation of the old data. Only incorrect data can lead to a hazard.

In our example, one serious hazard that can occur is a sideway collision of two shuttles on a switch. Here we will mention only two of the possible failures that can lead to this hazard. First, one shuttle component has incorrect own data. Or second, one shuttle has incorrect data of the other shuttle. As the shuttle component's behavior is completely determined by its subcomponents, the main component itself cannot produce a failure but its contained ones. The incorrect own data can be caused by the SwitchHandler and the incorrect data of the other shuttle by the SectionControlHandler. As these failures

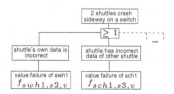

Fig. 3. Fault tree for sideway collisions of shuttles

are related to certain components of the system the analysis on this level is stopped. The resulting fault tree is depicted in Figure 3.

The corresponding hazard condition is: $\gamma = f_{sch1,s3,v} \lor f_{swh1,s2,v} \lor \ldots$. To keep the example simple we will in the following focus on the case that the Switch of sh1 delivers incorrect data. Thus, we only consider the hazard condition $\gamma' = f_{swh1,s2,v}$.

4.2   Components

In this section we will show the failure propagation models for the Optimizer, GPS and SpeedSensor components as well as the SwitchHandler component, which are contained within the shuttle component. These failure propagation models describe the relation between outgoing failures, incoming failures and internal events.

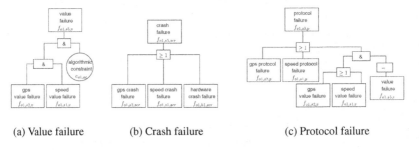

(a) Value failure   (b) Crash failure   (c) Protocol failure

Fig. 4. Optimizer failure propagation

Figures 4(a) and 4(b) show the failure propagation for value and crash failures of the Optimizer component. As is apparent from the component diagram of Figure 2, the Optimizer uses information provided by both the GPS and the SpeedSensor to compute the bids for the bargaining (to keep the example simple the used Topology and ShuttleData components are not considered). The Optimizer has the ability to detect value failures in the data, provided by the GPS and the SpeedSensor. Due to algorithmic constraints, the failure detection cannot detect simultaneous, similar value failures and therefore an internal event (event type ac) is added to model this algorithmic constraint.[4] The second failure propagation model specifies that the optimizer cannot tolerate a crash failure of one sensor or the execution hardware. A protocol failure of one of the sensors or detected value failures propagate to an outgoing protocol failure as specified in Figure 4(c). Thus, we get the following failure propagation: $\psi_{o1} = (f_{o1,s5,v} \Leftrightarrow ((f_{o1,s2,v} \land f_{o1,s1,v}) \land e_{o1,ac})) \land (f_{o1,s5,scr} \Leftrightarrow (f_{o1,s2,scr} \land f_{o1,s1,scr} \lor f_{o2,h1,scr})) \land (f_{o1,s5,p} \Leftrightarrow (f_{o1,s2,p} \lor f_{o1,s1,p} \lor ((f_{o1,s2,v} \lor f_{o1,s1,v}) \land (\neg f_{o1,s5,v}))))$.

Figures 5(a) and 5(b) show the failure propagation for value and crash failures of the SpeedSensor component. The SpeedSensor relies on a Speedometer hardware device

---

[4] We pessimistically abstract from the deployment of the Optimizer and SwitchHandler components w.r.t. value failures as already mentioned their crash errors simply result in a fail-safe state of the system.

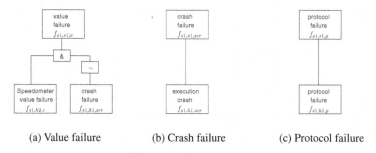

| (a) Value failure | (b) Crash failure | (c) Protocol failure |

Fig. 5. Speed failure propagation

to read its speed and it relies on a computer node for its execution.[5] Thus, both hardware devices influence the failure behavior of the SpeedSensor. The SpeedSensor has no internal events but its outgoing failures are influenced by incoming value resp. crash failures. A crash failure of the execution hardware will result in an outgoing crash failure; a value failure will result in an outgoing value failure unless the hardware has crashed. Incoming protocol failures simply propagate to outgoing protocol failures (cf. Figure 5(c)). Thus, we have the following failure propagation: $\psi_{s1} = (f_{s1,s1,scr} \Leftrightarrow f_{s1,h1,scr}) \wedge (f_{s1,s1,v} \Leftrightarrow (f_{s1,h2,v} \wedge \neg f_{s1,h1,scr})) \wedge (f_{s1,s1,p} \Leftrightarrow f_{s1,h1,p})$. We omit the fault tree and the failure propagation model of the GPS since the model is very similar to the SpeedSensor's model.

Concerning our example, the failure propagation of the SwitchHandler component is very simple as it just propagates all failures incoming from the optimizer to its outgoing port: $\psi_{swh1} = (f_{swh1,s1,v} \Leftrightarrow f_{swh1,s2,v}) \wedge (f_{swh1,s1,scr} \Leftrightarrow f_{swh1,s2,scr}) \wedge (f_{swh1,s1,p} \Leftrightarrow f_{swh1,s2,p})$.

4.3 Deployment

To describe the connection of hardware and the deployed software components we employ UML deployment diagrams. For presentation reasons, the UML deployment diagrams are visually slightly extended to include the additional hardware ports. These hardware ports are used to denote the propagation of hardware failures.

Figure 6(a) shows the deployment specification for the two software components s1 and g1. Both software components are deployed on the same node m1. As described in Section 3, nodes and software components are connected by special deployment connections and, thus, employ the same error and failure propagation concepts. Therefore, an internal crash error in the node m1 propagates indirectly to failures in both software components s1 and g1 as a common mode failure. In addition, both sensor software components use special hardware devices for the actual reading of the sensor data (a1 resp. p1). We omit the mapping of the network links nl1..4 of Figure 2 to a wireless network for the sake of clearer presentation.

---

[5] As the Speedometer hardware device is only used for simple data reads and does not have processing capabilities, only value errors have to be considered.

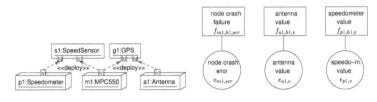

(a) Deployment specification   (b) Failure propagation model

Fig. 6. Deployment failure propagation

Finally, the failure propagation model of the hardware must be specified to map internal errors to outgoing hardware failures. For our example the simplified failure propagation model of the hardware node type MPC550 is shown in Figure 6(b). The figure shows that the crash error of the node manifests itself as outgoing crash failure. The same holds for the value failures of the other hardware devices which are used by s1 and g1.

Described in terms of the failure propagation model presented in Section 3 we have an event $e_{m1,scr}$ for the node type MPC550. This internal error manifests as failure $f_{m1,h1,scr}$ at the outgoing execution port of that node component. The same holds for the sensor hardware devices a1 and p1. Therefore we have: $\psi_{d1} = (f_{m1,h1,scr} \Leftrightarrow e_{m1,scr})$, $\psi_{d2} = (f_{a1,h1,v} \Leftrightarrow e_{a1,v})$, and $\psi_{d3} = (f_{p1,h1,v} \Leftrightarrow e_{p1,v})$.

4.4   Analysis

As presented in Section 3, all failure propagation models and the connections between the components are combined by and operators to get the failure propagation model for the hazard analysis of the complete system. In addition, the connections between incoming and outgoing ports specified by the mapping map (cf. Section 3) are used to combine their associated failures ($f_{m1,h1,scr} = f_{s1,h1,scr}, \dots$). After the combination of all failure propagation information ψ_c for $c \in \mathcal{C}$ with the hazard condition γ', we get the following Boolean formula for the representation of the system hazard by eliminating the failure variables via $\exists$-clauses:

$$\psi_\exists = e_{o1,ac} \wedge \neg e_{m1,scr} \wedge e_{a1,v} \wedge e_{p1,v}$$

This formula describes that the hazard γ' occurs, if (1) both hardware sensor devices (a1, p1) experience simultanoeus, similar value errors, (2) there is no crash error of the computing hardware m1, and (3) the value failures cannot be detected by the o1 component due to the similarity of the value errors. The formula can then be used to compute the likelihood of the system hazard. Assuming the probabilities $p(e_{o1,ac}) = 10^{-7}$, $p(e_{m1,scr}) = 10^{-6}$, $p(e_{a1,v}) = p(e_{p1,v}) = 10^{-8}$, the computed likelihood of the hazard is approximately: $p(\gamma') \approx 10^{-23}$. The likelihood of the hazard is mostly affected by the value errors of the sensors and the constraint of the value error detection algorithm. Therefore, these components are good targets for improvement to reduce the likelihood of the hazard (e.g. by a reliable GPS using additional integrity signals).

5 Advanced Concepts

System models like the proposed failure propagation model are always an abstraction which thus can fail to cover all relevant system properties. In our case, the model does not include the system state and the ordering of events. The failure propagation specified for each component is thus assumed to be a pessimistic abstraction such that if a sequence of system states or ordering of events exists, where a certain configuration of incoming failures and events can result in an outgoing failure, this case has to be covered. The considered abstraction can then only result in false negatives, but is maybe too coarse.

The outlined general failure classification (cf. Figure 1) as well as its extension by application specific failures results in refined directed acyclic graphs of failure types. We require that each applied set of failure types is a complete subclassification such that no failure type exists which is not covered by a combination of these types. Therefore, a correct selected subset of the failure classification such as crash failure, protocol failure, and value failure as highlighted in Figure 1 also preserves the coverage of all possible component failures.

If we want to abstract from a too detailed failure propagation information ψ_c of component $c \in \mathcal{C}$, we can simply replace a set of alternative failures $f_1, \ldots, f_n$ by their abstraction f by adding the condition $f \Leftrightarrow f_1 \vee \ldots \vee f_n$ and abstract from $f_1,$ $\ldots, f_n$ using existential qualification: $\psi_c' = \exists f_1, \ldots, f_n : \psi_c \wedge (f \Leftrightarrow f_1 \vee \ldots \vee f_n)$. For the analysis of complex systems, we can exploit the reduced complexity of such abstractions to check the absence of hazards using reduced models first and only employ the more detailed models when required. If we refine our behavior, the same condition can be employed to check whether our refinement does not contradict the more abstract specification.

Besides the failure classification also the hierarchical structuring of the components themselves can be subject to refinement. If the internal failures and errors are not relevant for the system hazards, appropriate abstractions can be derived using existential quantification as outlined above. If the system has been successfully analyzed using an abstract failure propagation information ψ_c of a composed component $c \in \mathcal{C}$, we can further decompose the safety analysis using ψ_c as a specification for the failure propagations ψ_{c_i} of the more detailed contained system of components c_i $(1 \leq i \leq n)$ which replace c in a more detailed view. Therefore, we have to check that for the internal failures $f_1,$ $\ldots, f_m$ holds: $(\exists f_1, \ldots, f_m : \psi_{c_1} \wedge \ldots \wedge \psi_{c_n}) \Rightarrow \psi_c$. Essentially, we have to ensure that the internal failure propagation does not exhibit any case that is not covered by the more abstract one.

However, it may also be the case that the system safety depends on non local properties which cannot be derived simply by composing the failure propagation information of its contained components. Therefore, we permit to add non local restrictions to the failure propagation. This concept can be employed to integrate non local knowledge about the system safety into our approach.

In our example, we informally argued in the beginning that protocol failures cannot result in a hazard. A more detailed analysis would have to distinguish between safe and unsafe protocol failures. In a safe protocol failure the receiver and sender remain in a state such that both employ correct pessimistic extrapolations about the possible positions of the other one. The ability of the protocol between two entities to exhibit no unsafe protocol state even in the presence of faults within the channel cannot simply be derived from the composed failure propagation model without states as presented. Therefore, the required additional non local property that a failure at one port cannot result in an unsafe failure at the connected port at the other side of the connector (channel) can be added but remains to be checked using other techniques.

In a similar problem of our application example, such a property has been checked using compositional model checking for an UML-RT model where the high level coordination properties which overlap multiple components have been modeled by means of coordination patterns[6] (cf. [22]). The checked non-local safety requirement for the component coordination ensured that the coordination between shuttles concerning the establishment of convoys cannot result in an unsafe protocol failure.

6   Conclusion and Future Work

The outlined compositional approach can be used to address the safety during the architectural design of complex software systems described by a restricted notion of UML component and deployment diagrams. As exemplified with the shuttle system example, the approach helps to identify safety concerns and addresses them by adding additional constraints on the failure propagation. Thus, the required safety requirements for the software components can be derived using the outlined concepts for refinement, abstraction, and non local cross-component properties. Additionally, the identified safety requirements have to be subject to verification in later phases of the process.

We are currently evaluating our approach using the RailCab project as well as an industry project to obtain statistical data about the feasibility of our approach. Therefore, we also started to realize some tool support for the outlined approach in the open source UML CASE tool Fujaba[7].

In the future, we plan to further integrate the approach with the already available state-based analysis techniques in Fujaba such as compositional model checking to ensure consistency between the component failure propagation behavior and the full UML model including statecharts.

References

1. McDermid, J.A.: Trends in Systems Safety: A European View? In Lindsay, P., ed.: Seventh Australian Workshop on Industrial Experience with Safety Critical Systems and Software. Volume 15 of Conferences in Research and Practice in Information Technology., Adelaide, Australia, ACS (2003) 3–8
2. McDermid, J., Pumfrey, D.: Software Safety: Why is there no Consensus? In: Proceedings of the 19th International System Safety Conference, Huntsville, AL, USA (2001) 17–25
3. Fenelon, P., McDermid, J.A., Nicolson, M., Pumfrey, D.J.: Towards integrated safety analysis and design. ACM SIGAPP Applied Computing Review 2 (1994) 21–32

---

[6] These pattern ensure required cross-component safety properties and can thus be seen as an extension notion of safety contracts as proposed in [21].

[7] www.fujaba.de

4. Papadopoulos, Y., McDermid, J., R. Sasse, b., Heiner, G.: Analysis and synthesis of the behaviour of complex programmable electronic systems in conditions of failure. Reliability Engineering & System Safety 71(2001) 229–247

5. Kaiser, B., Liggesmeyer, P., Maeckel, O.: A New Component Concept for Fault Trees. In: Proceedings of the 8th National Workshop on Safety Critical Systems and Software (SCS 2003), Canberra, Australia. 9-10th October 2003. Volume 33 of Research and Practice in Information Technology. (2003)

6. Grunske, L., Neumann, R.: Quality Improvement by Integrating Non-Functional Properties in Software Architecture Specification. In: Proc. of the Second Workshop on Evaluating and Architecting System dependabilitY (EASY), San Jose, California, USA (2002)

7. Grunske, L.: Annotation of Component Specifications with Modular Analysis Models for Safety Properties. In Overhage, S., Turowski, K., eds.: Proc. of the 1st Int. Workshop on Component Engineering Methodology, Erfurt, Germany. (2003)

8. Object Management Group: UML 2.0 Superstructure Specification. (2003) Document ptc/03-08-02.

9. Szyperski, C.: Component Software, Beyond Object-Oriented Programming. Addison-Wesley (1998)

10. McDermid, J., Pumfrey, D.: A Development of Hazard Analysis to aid Software Design. In: Proceedings of the Ninth Annual Conference on Computer Assurance (COMPASS94), Gaithersburg, MD, USA (1994) 17–25

11. Ogata, K.: Modern control engineering. Prentice Hall (1990)

12. Selic, B., Gullekson, G., Ward, P.: Real-Time Object-Oriented Modeling. John Wiley and Sons, Inc. (1994)

13. Birolini, A.: Reliability engineering : theory and practice. Springer Verlag, Berlin (1999) 3rd Edition.

14. Laprie, J.C., ed.: Dependability : basic concepts and terminology in English, French, German, Italian and Japanese [IFIP WG10.4, Dependable Computing and Fault Tolerance]. Volume 5 of Dependable computing and fault tolerant systems. Springer Verlag, Wien (1992)

15. Rauzy, A.: A new methodology to handle Boolean models with loops. IEEE Transactions on Reliability 52 (2003) 96–105

16. International Electrotechnical Commission Geneva, Switzerland: International Standard IEC 61025. Fault Tree Analysis (FTA). (1990)

17. Bryant, R.E.: Symbolic Boolean manipulation with ordered binary-decision diagrams. ACM Computing Surveys 24 (1992) 293–318

18. Coudert, O., Madre, J.: Fault tree analysis: 1020 prime implicants and beyond. In: Proceedings of the Annual Reliability and Maintainability Symposium, Atlanta, GA, USA, IEEE Press (1993) 240–245

19. Madre, J., Coudert, O., Fraisse, H., Bouissou, M.: Application of a new logically complete ATMS to digraph and network-connectivity analysis. In: Proceedings of the Annual Reliability and Maintainability Symposium, Anaheim, CA, USA, IEEE Press (1994) 118–123

20. Giese, H., Burmester, S., Klein, F., Schilling, D., Tichy, M.: Multi-Agent System Design for Safety-Critical Self-Optimizing Mechatronic Systems with UML. In Henderson-Sellers, B., Debenham, J., eds.: OOPSLA 2003 - Second International Workshop on Agent-Oriented Methodologies, Anaheim, CA, USA, Center for Object Technology Applications and Research (COTAR), University of Technology, Sydney, Australia (2003)

21. Hawkins, R.D., McDermid, J.A.: Performing Hazard and Safety Analysis of Object Oriented Systems. In: Proceedings of the 20th System Safety Conference (ISSC2002), Denver, USA (2002)

22. Giese, H., Tichy, M., Burmester, S., Schäfer, W., Flake, S.: Towards the Compositional Verification of Real-Time UML Designs. In: Proc. of the European Software Engineering Conference (ESEC), Helsinki, Finland, ACM Press (2003)

Automatic Test Data Generation from Embedded C Code

Eileen Dillon and Christophe Meudec

Institute of Technology, Carlow
Computing and Networking Department,
Kilkenny Road, Carlow, Ireland
Tel : +353 (0)59 9176266
Fax : +353 (0)59 9170517
{dillone,meudecc}@itcarlow.ie

Abstract. A fundamental area of software engineering that remains a challenge for software developers is the delivery of software with the minimum of remaining defects. While progress is constantly being made in the provision of static analysis tools to partly address this problem, the complementary dynamic testing approach, which remains an essential technique in the software industry for the verification and validation of software, has received less attention. Within the software testing activity, the actual generation of test data for the purpose of automated software testing is still mainly a manual task. We present CSET (C Symbolic Execution Tool) which automatically generates test data from C source code to fulfil code coverage criteria. CSET implements the symbolic execution technique with an intermediate path traversal conditions checker and a test data generation facility. We examine how the traditional problems associated with the symbolic execution technique have been overcome using Logic Programming and Constraint Logic Programming (CLP). The approach used to handle pointer manipulations is detailed. Interprocedural results on previously published sample code and industrial embedded C code with pointers are presented.

1   Introduction

Microprocessor based embedded systems are omnipresent in our everyday environment, from the telecommunication to the automotive industries. The thorough verification and validation of the software part of those embedded systems is critical for the overall success of the product. An automatic technique that has great potential in this phase of software development is symbolic execution. By abstracting the code under analysis using symbolic values rather than actual values, symbolic execution can be adapted via automatic test data generation to automatically support many of the tasks involved in the dynamic verification and validation of software [4], including: coverage testing (tests fulfilling adequacy criteria), security analysis (tests highlighting buffer overflows), reliability (tests exposing run-time errors) and validation (tests falsifying assertions).

M. Heisel et al. (Eds.): SAFECOMP 2004, LNCS 3219, pp. 180–194, 2004.

However, symbolic execution has not thus far fulfilled its full potential because of the many seemingly intractable difficulties that arise in its exploitation. While most of the difficulties encountered are common to the analysis of all application software, such as the automatic satisfiability checking of large and complex Path Traversal Conditions (PTCs) or the difficulty in implementing a test data generation step, the C programming language presents a unique challenge for the developers of tools based on symbolic execution that require a strong path feasibility checker: the pervasive use of pointers in C code. C is the dominant programming language for embedded systems [26]. This is largely due to its inherent flexibility, the extent of support, small code size, speed and the availability of compilers for a wide range of hardware.

MISRA C [24] is a well defined subset of C that forbids the use of C features that give concern in a safety-related context. For example, while pointers are allowed they can only reference statically declared data. MISRA C is used in the automotive industry for software up to, and including, SIL 3 [6]. Most safety-related automotive software are given a SIL of 1 or 2. As our work covers the MISRA C subset it has direct relevance for the safety aspects of today's automotive industry.

In this paper we present our automated tool CSET (C Symbolic Execution Tool), aimed at automatically generating test data to fulfil a code coverage criterion, that can be integrated in automatic verification and validation tools for embedded software written in C. This works builds on our previous results on SPARK-Ada [21,13] and Java Bytecode [9]. We extend our previous results [8] on C by tackling interprocedural test data generation, comparing our tool against a commercial equivalent [15] and also by presenting refined experimental results using our improved path feasibility checker. Our work is based on the use of the symbolic execution technique, Logic Programming and Constraint Logic Programming. For completeness we acknowledge that new test data generation techniques with as wide a range of applications as symbolic execution have been investigated [11,27,12,28]. Other techniques, with a smaller focus, have also been proposed [18,7].

The remainder of the paper is structured as follows. Section 2 introduces the symbolic execution technique. Section 3 presents our rationale for using Logic Programming and Constraint Logic Programming to overcome the problems inherent to symbolic execution in an automatic test data generation context. Section 4 introduces CSET, our tool for the symbolic execution of, and test data generation from, embedded C code. Its handling of C pointers is presented. In section 5 we discuss our experience so far of CSET on previously published sample code as well as on industrial code. The paper concludes with an overall assessment of our results.

2   Symbolic Execution

Symbolic execution [17] is primarily a static technique that follows the control structure of the code under analysis to generate symbolic information.

Table 1. PTC and symbolic values for path: 1, 2, 3, 4.

Line	Code	Path Traversal Condition	den	a
1	int map (int den, int a) {	true	Den	A
2	den = den*(a+a);	true	Den*(A+A)	A
3	if (den == 90)	Den*(A+A) = 90	Den*(A+A)	A
4	return -1/(den-90);	Den*(A+A) = 90	Den*(A+A)	A
5	else return -2;	-	-	-
6	}	-	-	-

2.1 The Symbolic Execution Technique

Symbolic execution does not execute a program. The notion of execution implies the traversal of a path through the program using a set of data values to represent the input variables [5]. A program that is executed in this way will result in a set of output values. In symbolic execution, on the other hand, information is extracted from the source code of a program by representing inputs as symbolic values rather than using actual values. A set of symbolic expressions, one for each variable, is produced. Each of these symbolic expressions is made up in terms of input variables and constants. The presence of a conditional statement such as an if ...else splits the execution of the program into different paths. Symbolic execution records for each potential path, a Path Traversal Condition (PTC). This is the logical combination of the Boolean logic conditions that were encountered along that path [21].

For example, consider the artificial code in Table 1. There are 2 potential paths through this program only one of which is analysed here. The PTC must be satisfiable in order for the path to be feasible i.e. if a set of values for the variables in the PTC exists that satisfies it (within the type and range of values allowed), then that path is a feasible path through the program. Infeasible paths are common; no set of values for the variables in the PTC exists which satisfy that expression. For accurate program analysis infeasible paths must be detected. This involves checking the PTC for satisfiability. Further, for test data generation purposes a solution to the PTC of feasible paths must be generated. For the path illustrated, our CSET tool correctly identifies the PTC as satifiable and therefore generates a suitable test, e.g. Den = -1, A = -45, which when executed, using a third party tool, generates a division by 0 run-time error. On this example, CSET generates just 2 tests to achieve full path coverage. On the other hand, the dynamic analysis part of C++Test [15], a popular testing tool, generates 64 tests but fails to cover the path illustrated thus only achieving 50% path coverage overall. The static analysis part of C++Test also fails to flag the division by 0.

2.2 Traditional Problems of Symbolic Execution

Despite the high promises that the introduction of the symbolic execution technique engendered, it has not, to date, been used to its full potential in industry at least for dynamic verification and validation purposes. This is due to a number of technical difficulties that have traditionally hampered its practical development.

Satisfiability Checking and Test Data Generation. The PTCs generated during symbolic execution are complex algebraic expressions and their satisfiability is in general undecidable [29]. Hence, automatic test data generators can never achieve completeness.

A PTC condition can contain many expressions involving integers, floating point numbers, pointer references and multi-dimensional input-dependent array references organised in arrays and structures combined by Boolean operators. Input dependent array references create ambiguities in PTCs.

In practice, determining the feasibility of such PTCs is very difficult. This implies that automatic test data generators based on symbolic execution are usually only applicable on restrictive subsets of programming languages, exhibit a high level of unsoundness and are not scalable.

Loops. Traditional symbolic execution cannot in general proceed beyond a loop unless the number of iterations is known. Difficulties arise when handling loops whose iterations are input-dependent. Analysing these accurately in the general case requires the use of recurrence relations [5].

Pointers. Pointers are problematic because all references to them are ambiguous until actual execution time (the aliasing problem). Further, pointer arithmetic, as allowed in C, is problematic since knowledge of the specific memory storage mechanism used is usually not included in symbolic execution tools.

Static analysis tools have efficiently tackled pointers on large industrial code. Lyle and Binkley [20] decompose C programs into program slices using a variation of symbolic execution to deal with pointer variables. Their approach is however not applicable to automatic test data generation. LCLint [10] is a static analysis tool used to detect errors in programs written in C. It requires the use of user annotations and the emphasis is on tractability rather than soundness (not all errors found are true errors—false positives) or completeness (all defects reported). PREfix [3] is a fully automated compile-time analyser, which detects errors, using symbolic execution, in large real-world examples in C and C++ code. It outputs the execution paths through the source code where these defects lie. It tries to avoid false positives but at the expense of completeness. The SLAM project [1] uses static analysis on C programs to determine whether they violate given usage rules. The programmer does not have to annotate the code and false error messages (noise) are kept to a minimum. It has been successfully applied to industrial code. The tool can analyse the feasibility of paths in the C program. SLAM is incomplete but sound within its context of application.

It thus emerges that static analysis tools have successfully handled pointers at the expense of soundness and completeness. They have nevertheless successfully demonstrated their usefulness on large industrial code. However, the approaches used, especially for pointer handling, cannot be used in the area of automated test data generation which requires stronger path satisfiability checking capabilities and an actual test data generation step.

Function calls. Interprocedural symbolic execution is problematic because of the complexity it engenders. In particular, the complex identifier scoping rules of high level programming languages are difficult to respect (including the pass-by-reference and pass-by-value mechanisms), the semantics of functions with side effects is intricate and finally, function calls substantially increase the complexity of the underlying control flow graph of the program under test.

2.3   Conclusion

Past symbolic executors that provide a test data generation facility only deal with subsets of programming languages that excludes pointers, do not incorporate a powerful PTC satisfiability checker, and do not integrate a subpath selection strategy. Further, the various techniques that have successfully been used in static analysis tools do not seem transferrable to dynamic tools.

Before detailing in section 4 how we have successfully tackled these issues, over a number of projects [21,13,9,8], we present the programming paradigm on which our work is based.

3   Logic Programming and Constraint Logic Programming

As seen, a symbolic executor needs to be implemented that is guided in its search by the feasibility of potentially large algebraic expressions. In particular, given an algebraic expression, along with the variables involved and their respective domains, it must be shown that there exists an instantiation of the variables which reduces the expression to true. In effect, an algebraic expression constrains its variables to a particular set of values from their respective domains. If any of the sets are empty, the PTC is unsatisfiable.

To implement the kind of solver required here, e.g. able to work with non-linear constraints over floating point numbers and integers, it is possible to implement heuristics by writing a specialized program in a procedural language (such as C, or using an existing solving routines library). Although the heuristics are readily available, this approach requires a substantial amount of effort and the resulting solver is likely to be hard to maintain, modify and extend. Further, because of the heterogeneity of the programming constructs that appear in PTCs, unsound simplifications need to made to make this approach tractable. We believe that this is the approach currently used in most static and dynamic state-of-the-art commercial tools that use the symbolic execution technique (although we have no means of verifying this) and that this is the source of their weak PTCs checking capabilities.

The advantages of using Logic Programming over procedural programming have long been recognized for testing tools [14] and in commercial static analysers (e.g. the SPARK Examiner [25]).

Prolog's in-built depth-first search procedure and its backtracking facilities make Prolog a strong candidate for implementing a symbolic executor that follows the control flow graph of the program under consideration according to a given testing criterion and backtracks whenever unsatisfiability of the current PTC is detected by a purpose built constraints solver.

Constraint Logic Programming (CLP) [16] improves the modelling capabilities of mathematical relationships between objects of Prolog by providing richer data structures on which constraints can be expressed and by using constraint resolution mechanisms (also known as decision procedures) to reduce the search space under consideration. When the decision procedure is incomplete—e.g. for non-linear arithmetic constraints—the problematic constraints are suspended, it is also said delayed, until they become linear. Non-linear arithmetic constraints can become linear whenever a variable becomes instantiated. This can happen when other constraints are added to the system of constraints already considered or during labelling.

The labelling mechanism further constrains the system of constraints according to some value choosing strategy. It can be viewed as a process to make assumptions about the system of constraints under consideration. This mechanism is used to awaken delayed constraints or generate a solution to an already known satisfiable system of constraints (as required for test data generation).

4   CSET

4.1   Overview

CSET (C Symbolic Execution Tool) is a symbolic execution tool for embedded C code which incorporates intermediate PTC checking and a test data generation stage. The main output from the tool are test data that can exercise the paths found feasible through a C source code. As schematised in Fig. 1, CSET is composed of the following:

Preprocessor. gcc is used to generate a C program free from macros.

Parser. The parser converts the preprocessed C code to a Prolog readable format for input into the symbolic executor adding scoping information for all variables. For example the Prolog terms obtained for the function given in Table 1 is represented in Fig. 2.

Symbolic Executor. The symbolic executor is implemented in ECLiPSe [19]. It takes as input the Prolog readable format of the C code under analysis and interacts with the solver to return test data.

Solver. The solver used is the PTC Solver [22] as introduced in Section 4.3.

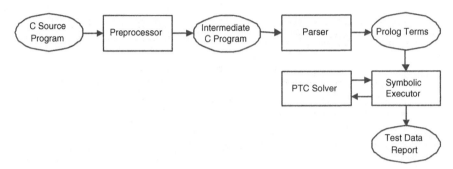

Fig. 1. CSET Architecture.

```
function_definition(map,[declaration(int,[Den]),declaration(int,[A])],
  [assignment(Den,multiply(Den,(A+A))),
   if_statement(8,expression(Den==90),[return(-1/(Den-90))],
                                        [return(-2)])
 ],int).
```

Fig. 2. Prolog Terms.

4.2   Algorithm Sketch

The main algorithm follows the design implemented in [21,9,13]. Details of the variables (such as their type, initial value and output value) in the Prolog readable format are added in a data structure that records changes to the variables during symbolic execution. The statements in the input file are processed sequentially. During an assignment the symbolic value of the assigned variable is updated to the assigned expression expressed in terms of input variables and constants only. Basic block statements proceed without creating choice points in the Prolog execution. Whenever a decision is encountered, it is symbolically executed i.e. expressed in terms of input variables and constants only, and a Prolog choice point is generated. The decision (or its negation) is then added to the current constraint store through the solver. If the solver fails to add a constraint then the PTC is unsatisfiable in which case, the symbolic executor will backtrack, undoing all actions up to the last choice point, and then proceeds forward again. This is achieved using the intrinsic backtracking facility of Prolog, which simplifies greatly the design of the symbolic executor and allows the intermediate checking of the PTCs. If successful, symbolic execution continues forward. On reaching a return statement all input variables involved in the current PTC are labelled by a call to the solver. This involves generating values for each input variables with respect to the PTC. If all the found feasible paths have been examined the symbolic executor terminates, otherwise backtracking occurs.

4.3   Addressing the Traditional Problems of Symbolic Execution

Here we detail how we have addressed the traditional problems of symbolic execution in CSET .

Satisfiability Checking and Test Data Generation. For the symbolic execution to be amenable, intermediate feasibility path checking is essential as otherwise many paths will be generated that are only discovered as infeasible at the end of the symbolic execution. In CSET, every time a decision in the code is encountered a choice point in the Prolog symbolic executor is created and the symbolically executed decision (or its negation) is immediately submitted to the PTC Solver. This allows many infeasible subpaths to be eliminated from the search space. This technique improves the scalability of CSET.

The PTC Solver [22], implemented in ECLiPSe [19], has been developed to check the satisfiability of PTCs as generated by a symbolic executor, and includes a labelling strategy. It has been used on a number of projects for a variety of target programming languages: Ada [21], Java Bytecode [9] and now C. It has a well defined Prolog interface and can be integrated in a Prolog or C++ [13] tool.

The solver is composed of the following components:

- fd, a constraint solver over integers (using domain propagation techniques) provided as a library by ECLiPSe;
- clpq, a constraint solver over infinite precision rational numbers (used to incorrectly model floating point variables) provided as a library by ECLiPSe;
- a bespoke bridge between fd and clpq to handle mixed constraints;
- custom extensions to handle C bitwise operators, constraints over arrays, records and enumeration literals. These make extensive use of the ECLiPSe delaying mechanism to handle constraints which cannot be resolved immediately (e.g. array access with unknown index).

Whenever a constraint is submitted to the solver it is added to its existing store of constraints and the solver can then:

- fail: the system of constraints was unsatisfiable, the system of constraint remains as it was before the addition of the latest constraint (i.e. the solver backtracks automatically);
- succeeds: the system of constraints may be satisfiable (e.g. if non-linear constraints are present the solver may fail to detect their unsatisfiability at this stage).

When the PTC is used to derive test cases the ambiguity can persist during symbolic execution and be resolved at the actual creation step of the test cases during labelling. This sampling is exhaustively attempted for variables over integers but of course only partially performed for the infinite precision rational numbers.

The PTC Solver can handle complex algebraic expression over integers, infinite precision rational numbers, enumeration literals, that are organised in arrays (including multi-dimensional arrays) and structures [21,9]. As the PTC solver properly models arrays and structures, these types can contain elements of any type including, of course, arrays and structures . . .

To understand how ECLiPSe's delaying mechanism can be used to handle unknown index reference, consider the following example:

```
1:      x = a[j];
2:      a[j-1] = x-1;
```

On line 1, the symbolic executor submits a constraint to the solver of the form $eq\_cast(X_1, element(A, [J]))$ where X_1 represents the new value of x in the symbolic executor. The solver delays the following constraint on the variable J: $element(A, [J], R_1)$ where R_1 will be the result of the element at position J in A whenever J becomes known. $eq\_cast(X_1, R_1)$, used to perform implicit casting, delays if necessary.

On line 2, the symbolic executor submits $A_1 = up\_arr(A, J - 1, X_1 - 1)$ where A_1 represents the new value of a in the symbolic executor. The solver delays $up\_arr(A, J - 1, eq\_cast(X_1 - 1), A_1)$ on J.

During labelling, as J will be instantiated, the delayed constraints are automatically resumed (in any order) and are eliminated. This implies that the symbolic values of a and x are now free from unknown index references.

While this is only an overview of how ambiguous array references are handled in the PTC solver (we have omitted the extra constraints placed by the PTC solver on the indices for example) it illustrates the general principles by which CSET can support all C array constructs.

Loops. As mentioned, traditional symbolic execution cannot proceed as usual in the presence of input-dependent iterative constructs. However, in the restricted case of trying to fulfil a given test coverage criterion, loops can accurately be dealt with according to the feasibility (or not) of the intermediate path followed in conjunction with a heuristics-based intermediate path selection strategy targeted at the chosen test data adequacy criterion. Integrating this approach in a symbolic executor that includes an intermediate PTCs checker, and for branch coverage at least, all loop constructs can be handled adequately as demonstrated in [21,9,13].

As currently the aim of CSET is to fulfil the path coverage criterion (because our ultimate aim is automatic Worst Case Execution Time estimation), which is harder to achieve than branch coverage for example, it does not include a path selection strategy. Thus CSET, will attempt to cover all the combinations of the Prolog choice points, as introduced by loops in the code, during the symbolic execution. Only the size of the definition domain of variables and the actual decisions in the iterative constructs limits CSET in its search.

Pointers. Previous symbolic executors, that include a test data generation phase, have avoided implementing pointers. Multi-level pointers indirection and static pointer arithmetic have been successfully incorporated into CSET. Similarly to [2] (which is not a dynamic analysis tool), CSET stores information about every variable in the source program in a memory map structure [8]. This structure is used to replicate the way that C pointers behave during execution.

& Operator. When a variable is declared all its details are stored into the memory map, this includes its name, type, initial value (if any) and an arbitrary memory address. When a pointer is assigned the address of a variable, that variable is located in the memory map and its memory address is retrieved. This is assigned to the output field of the pointer in the memory map. An array is stored as one variable in the memory map since arrays are stored in contiguous memory in C. Therefore assigning the address of an individual element to a pointer variable is more complex than just described. The name of the array has to be extracted and its position in the memory map is found. Next the memory address of the individual element is calculated. For example, if the array starts at memory address 1000 and is of type int, the third element is located at memory address 1008 since the type int is represented by 4 bytes in CSET. In a similar way the address of objects such as structures are handled.

* Operator. When a pointer is de-referenced, it is symbolically executed to see what memory address it holds. The memory map is searched to find the details of the variable stored at that address and if found the corresponding output value is returned. There are a number of reasons why the memory address may not be found in the memory map. If the pointer has not yet been assigned the address of any object the pointer is assigned a random value. If its value is not within the memory range allocated to the program the symbolic execution will halt. The pointer may refer to the memory address of an array element. As stated, arrays are stored as one variable in the memory map. In this instance, the memory address of the nearest variable is found and this variable is checked to see if it is an array. If so, the memory address is checked to see if it legitimately refers to an element of that array, and if so the value that that element contains is returned. Pointers to structures are handled in a comparable way.

Pointer Arithmetic. CSET only supports static pointer arithmetic within single array and structure objects. In other words, the symbolic executor must be able to identify the resulting element pointed to by a pointer arithmetic expression and it must be an array element or structure field value. For example, when a pointer to an array of integers is incremented, the type that the pointer is currently pointing to is first found and as the type int is represented as 4 bytes in CSET, the pointer now holds the memory address 4 bytes on from the one it initially held.

Dynamic Memory Allocation. The standard library functions `malloc` and `free` have been simulated in CSET. The allocation of memory is achieved by adding a variable of the type being allocated to the memory map. The pointer that points to this location is updated with the appropriate memory address. When memory is freed, the corresponding pointer and variable are removed from the memory map. This memory is then available for use by the program whenever other variables need to be allocated.

Function Calls. CSET handles interprocedural test data generation using an approach we previously described for SPARK-Ada code [21]. On encountering a function call, the symbolic executor matches the parameters with the arguments passed and processing proceeds as during actual execution. In addition, our memory map structure allows us to deal naturally with the pass-by-reference mechanism.

Furthermore, as during parsing of the source code identifiers are uniquely identified according to their scope our Prolog readable source code has a flat scoping level structure. Thus during symbolic execution scoping does not have to be taken into account.

4.4   Current Limitations

CSET does not check whether the input C code is beyond its limitations.

C Subset. While, the subset of C handled by CSET subsumes the MISRA subset [24], CSET cannot handle full ANSI C. The incompleteness of CSET is due to the following restrictions: only static pointer arithmetic within single array and structure objects is supported; and the following features are not handled: assignments within || and && expressions, pointers to functions, implicit modulo assignments, variables qualifiers such as extern, static and volatile. Finally only the `malloc` and `free` standard library functions are supported.

Large Integers. The PTC Solver can only handle 16 bit-encoded integers. This limitation can cause unsoundness in CSET.

Numerical Precision. Floating-point numbers in the code are incorrectly represented using infinite precision rational numbers within linear constraints but reverts to double precision floating-point numbers whenever non-linear constraints are posted to the solver. Again this can lead to unsoundness. Constraints solving over floating-point numbers is an area of on-going research [23].

PTCs Size. Symbolic execution can generate thousands of constraints involving thousands of variable occurrences. This is of course particularly true when analyzing code that contains loops that iterate a large number of times. Analyzing such code can therefore take several hours and in practice prevents the analysis of code containing large iterations.

Non-Linear Constraints. The analysis of PTCs that contain non-linear constraints can be hampered because the PTC Solver cannot always detect on submission their unsatisfiability. If such a path reaches the labelling stage its complete analysis is intractable in general using our approach.

5   Experience

CSET has been applied to a selection of functions from [28] and industrial C code made available to us by Pi Technology (Cambridge UK). All timings have been generated on a 2.5Ghz processor. Our results are compared against C++Test [15] which was also used to generate the path coverage measures quoted. For test objects containing loops (indicated by *) the path coverage quoted is an approximation.

5.1   Previously Published Samples

Table 2 illustrates the results obtained for test objects from [28] in where several thousands tests on each test objects are generated to achieve a high level of branch coverage. The number of iterations of both loops for `ComplexBranch` was reduced from 100 to 5 to make the code amenable to CSET. `Netflow` has proved too complex for CSET to handle.

Table 2. Published Samples Results.

Test Object			CSET Results			C++Test Results		
Name	Cyclomatic Complexity	Max. Nesting Level	No. Tests Generated	%Path Covered	Execution Time	No. Tests Generated	%Path Covered	Execution Time
Atof*	16	2	262	13	122secs	3	0	3secs
ClassifyFloat	14	2	26	25	94secs	1000	6	28secs
ClassifyInt	14	2	32	27	3.8hrs	1000	13	32secs
ComplexBranch*	13	2	304	51	24hrs	1000	29	26secs
IsElem	2	1	2	100	0.2sec	1000	100	26secs
LineCover*	8	4	12	16	9.2hrs	1000	16	25secs
Netflow*	14	2	0	0	failed	1000	0	58secs

For objectiveness we need to mention that C++Test is not explicitly targeted at path coverage and that it is a general purpose commercial tool with many functionalities that our tool does not provide. On the other hand, CSET is able to flag the subpaths that have been detected as infeasible.

The disappointingly long CSET running time of the some of these examples can be explained by the presence of non-linear constraints in infeasible paths in the code under analysis. To increase the soundness of CSET our timeout labelling strategy has been set to a generous value. Hence a high proportion of the total running time can be fruitlessly spent trying to generate tests for these paths. For `LineCover`, for example, this proportion amounts to 95%. We have no satisfactory solution to this problem.

While these results illustrate the limitations of our approach for handling complex algorithms, we are encouraged by the higher level of path coverage obtained by CSET, using a minimal number of tests, when compared to a popular dynamic analysis tool as it suggests a higher level of completeness for our path feasibility checking facility.

5.2   Industrial Code

Table 3 illustrates the complexity measures and the results obtained by CSET
for a selection of C functions from industrial code. The selection was chosen for
its wide variety of C features including arrays (single and multi-dimensional),
enumerations, loops, casting, function calls, pointers and pointer arithmetic.
Interprocedural test data generation was performed on the original code.

Table 3. Industrial C Code Samples Results.

Test Object			CSET Results			C++Test Results		
Name	Cyclomatic Complexity	Max. Nesting Level	No. Tests Generated	%Path Covered	Execution Time	No. Tests Generated	%Path Covered	Execution Time
Aip_med_filter	5	1	6	37	15secs	50	37	2secs
Byc_reset_boost*	3	2	1	16	51secs	50	16	3secs
Iti_engine_sync	6	2	10	55	18secs	1000	11	5secs
Oop_add_to_list*	7	3	123	59	59secs	50	7	18secs
Std_check-lrc*	2	1	1	33	4secs	50	33	2secs

Results reported in Table 3 are very promising as the running time is low
and the percentage of paths covered by our tests is always higher or equal to
what can be achieved using a common dynamic analysis tool. No limitations
were applied to the range of data inputs or to the number of iterations of any
loops encountered. It is worth noting that the industrial C code examples have
a lower cyclomatic complexity and nesting level than the test objects from [28]
that we examined.

6   Conclusions

CSET is the first automatic test data generator based on symbolic execution
able to handle pointers as found in embedded C code.

Thus, we believe that the many applications of the symbolic execution technique can finally be successfully implemented for the most popular programming
language in embedded systems. For example, although CSET is aimed at fufil-
ing the path coverage criterion, we have shown [21,9] how for our approach, the
easier, branch coverage criterion can be targeted. Further, CSET is able to handle a larger subset of C than the MISRA [24] subset that has specifically been
developed for the automotive industry.

Our use of Logic Programming and Constraint Logic Programming, to address the traditional problems associated with implementing a useful automatic
test data generator based on the symbolic execution technique, has been vindi-
cated in this work by the results obtained on industrial code.

Whilst CSET is not without its limitations, and much work remains to be
done to be able to tackle efficiently general C code, it seems sufficiently powerful
already to deal with industrial C code, the target language of this work.

Acknowledgements. Thanks to Mike Ellims (Pi Technology, Cambridge UK) for giving us the C source from an Engine Control Unit and to Joachim Wegener (Daimler-Chrysler, Berlin Germany) for making available his examples from [28].

References

1. T. Ball and S.K. Rajamani. The SLAM project: debugging system software via static analysis. *ACM SIGPLAN Notices*, 37(1):1–3, January 2002. URL http://research.microsoft.com/slam/.

2. J. Blieberger, B. Burgstaller, and B. Scholz. Interprocedural symbolic evaluation of Ada programs with aliases. In *In Ada-Europe'99 International Conference on Reliable Software Technologies*, pages 136–145, Stantander, Spain, June 1999.

3. W. Bush, J. Pincus, and D. Sielaff. A static analyzer for finding dynamic programming errors. *Software-Practice and Experience*, 30(7):775–802, 2000.

4. L.A. Clarke and D.J. Richardson. Application of symbolic evaluation. *Journal of Systems Software*, 5:15–35, January 1985.

5. P.D. Coward. Symbolic execution systems—a review. *Software Engineering Journal*, 3(6):229–239, November 1988.

6. B.J. Czerny, J.G. D'Ambrosio, P.O. Jacob, and B.T. Murray. Identifying and understanding relevant system safety standards for use in the automotive industry. In *Proceedings of the Society of Automotive Engineers World Congress*, Michigan, USA, March 2003.

7. R.A. DeMillo and A.J. Offutt. Constraint-based automatic test data generation. *IEEE Transactions on Software Engineering*, 17(9):900–910, September 1991.

8. E. Dillon and C. Meudec. CSET: Symbolic execution and automatic test data generation of embedded C code. In *Proceedings 16th IFIP International Conference on Testing of Communicating Systems*, Oxford, UK, March 2004. Position Paper.

9. J. Doyle and C. Meudec. Automatic structural coverage testing of Java bytecode. In *Proceedings of the Third Workshop on Automated Verification of Critical Systems*, April 2003.

10. D. Evans. Static detection of dynamic memory errors. In *Proceedings of the ACM SIGPLAN 96 Conference on Programming Language Design and Implementation*, 1996.

11. M.J. Gallagher and V.L. Narasimhan. ADTEST: A test data generation suite for Ada software systems. *IEEE Transactions on Software Engineering*, 23(8):473–484, 1997.

12. A. Gotlieb, B. Botella, and M. Rueher. Automatic test data generation using constraint solving techniques. In *Proceedings ISSTA'98*, pages 53–62, 1998.

13. M. Grogan. Visual symbolic execution. Master's thesis, Institute of Technology, Carlow, Ireland, 2002.

14. D. Hamlet. Implementing prototype testing tools. *Software-Practice and Experience*, 25(4):347–371, April 1995.

15. Parasoft Inc. *C++Test – version 2.2*, 2004. http://www.parasoft.com/.

16. J. Jaffar and J-L. Lassez. Constraint Logic Programming. In *Proceedings 14th ACM Symposium on Principles of Programming Languages*, pages 111–119, Munich, January 1987.

17. J.C. King. A new approach to program testing. In *Proceedings International Conference on reliable software*, pages 228–233, April 1975.

18. B. Korel. Automated test data generation for programs with procedures. In *Proceedings ISSTA '96*, pages 209–215, 1996.

19. Parc Technologies Ltd. *ECLiPSe Release 5.6*, 2003. http://www.icparc.ic.ac.uk/eclipse/.

20. J.R. Lyle and D.W. Binkley. Program slicing in the presence of pointers. In *Proceedings of the Foundations of Software Engineering*, pages 255–260, Orlando, FL, USA, November 1993.

21. C. Meudec. ATGen: automatic test data generation using constraint logic programming and symbolic execution. *Journal of Software Testing, Verification and Reliability*, 11(2):81–96, 2001.

22. C. Meudec. The PTC solver user manual – version 1.5.1. Technical report, Institute of Technology, Carlow, Ireland, May 2004.

23. C. Michel, R. Rueher, and Y. Lebbah. Constraints solving over floating-point numbers. In *Proceedings of the 7th International Conference on Principles and Practice of Constraint Programming*, pages 524–538, Paphos, Cyprus, November 2001.

24. MISRA. Guidelines for the use of the C language in vehicle based software. Technical report, Motor Industry Software Reliability Association, 1998.

25. Praxis Critical Systems Ltd, UK. *The Spark Examiner*, 2004. http://www.sparkada.com/.

26. V. Seppanen, A-M. Kahkonen, M. Oivo, H. Perunka, P. Isomursu, and P. Pulli. Strategic needs and future trends of embedded software. Technical Report 48/96, TEKES Development Center, Finland, October 1996.

27. N. Tracey, J. Clark, and K. Mander. Automated program flaw finding using simulated annealing. In *Proceedings ISSTA '98*, pages 73–81, 1998.

28. J. Wegener, A. Baresel, and H. Sthamer. Evolutionary test environment for automatic structural testing. *Information and Software Technology*, 43:841–854, 2001.

29. E.J. Weyuker. Translatability and decidability questions for restricted classes of program schemas. *SIAM Journal of Computers*, 8(4):587–589, 1979.

State-Event-Fault-Trees – A Safety Analysis Model for Software Controlled Systems

Bernhard Kaiser and Catharina Gramlich

Hasso-Plattner-Institute for Software Systems Engineering, Department of Software-Engineering and Quality Management, Prof.-Dr.-Helmert-Str. 2-3, Potsdam, Germany
{bernhard.kaiser,catharina.gramlich}@hpi.uni-potsdam.de

Abstract. Safety models for software-controlled systems should be intuitive, compositional and have the expressive power to model both software and hardware behaviour. Moreover, they should provide quantitative results for failure or hazard probabilities. Fault Trees are an accepted and intuitive model for safety analysis, but they are incapable of expressing state dependencies or temporal order of events. We propose to enrich Fault Trees with State/Event semantics. We use a graphical notation that is similar to Statecharts. Our model subsumes deterministic state machines that are suited to describe software behaviour and Markov Chains that model probabilistic failures. We allow exponentially distributed probabilistic events, deterministic delays and triggered events. The model is compositional and joins components by ports. Quantitative evaluation is achieved by translating the component models to Deterministic and Stochastic Petri Nets (DSPNs) and using an existing tool for analysis. We introduce the model and the analysis procedure and provide a small case study of a fire alarm system, completed by an outlook on our tool project ESSaRel.

1 Introduction

In technical systems, more and more mechanical and electrical components are replaced with software-controlled components. This includes safety critical domains such as avionics, automotive or industrial control. In these application fields safety and reliability analysis is a mandatory part of the development and must be supported by appropriate models and tools. Fault Tree Analysis (FTA) is one of the most widely used techniques in this context. Fault Trees (FTs) are intuitive for practitioners due to their hierarchical structure and the familiar logical symbols. They provide a set of qualitative and quantitative analyses. They have been used for several decades in the context of mechanical or electrical systems and are gaining importance in the context of software-controlled systems.

Nevertheless, some fundamental differences between Fault Trees and the models commonly used for embedded system design are obvious: Models for complex systems must be compositional. Modularisation of FTs, however, is only defined in a restricted way. Safety is principally a matter of behaviour and, in contrast to the state-space models used in systems design, FTs are not suitable for modelling behaviour. FTs are a combinatorial model that cannot capture sequences of actions and state history. The two-state abstraction (working or failed) of Fault Trees is not adequate for systems with complex state spaces.

M. Heisel et al. (Eds.): SAFECOMP 2004, LNCS 3219, pp. 195–209, 2004.

These differences not only hamper the application of FTA to software-controlled systems, but also obstruct the integration of state-based submodels into an FTA. This integration would be desirable for two reasons: first the reuse of state-based models from the design phase for safety analysis and second the integration of Markov Chains, which are an important state based safety and reliability model.

Existing approaches to overcome the semantic weaknesses of FTs often rely on formal methods that are not familiar to practitioners and do not offer visual integration for FTs and state based models.

We take a different approach by adding a notion of states and events to FTA: States describe conditions that last over a period of time whereas events are sudden phenomena, including state transitions. We call this extended model State-Event-Fault-Trees (SEFTs). States and events are depicted by different symbols. We propose typed FT gates for states and events (e.g. an OR gate with two event inputs and another OR gate with two states inputs). Regarding the AND gate that joins two events we distinguish a History-AND that remembers events that have occurred in the past and a Sequential-AND that remembers also if they have occurred in a given order (also known as Priority-AND gate). State-Event-Fault-Trees are partitioned into components which are interconnected by ports. Other kinds of state based models such as Markov Chains or state diagrams from CASE tools can be integrated.

SEFTs are well suited for industrial use since they unite familiar graphical notations; nevertheless, their semantics allows quantitative analysis. The analysis is performed by component-wise translation of the SEFT models into Deterministic and Stochastic Petri Nets (DSPNs) [6], a class of Petri Nets for which analysis tools exist (e.g. the tool TimeNET [19]). In the Petri Net domain the component models are merged to one flat model that is passed to an existing analysis tool.

In this paper we explain the application of SEFTs and the steps necessary for their translation to DSPNs. To illustrate the procedure we refer to a small case study of a fire alarm system. The rest of the paper is organised as follows: In Section 2 we give a short overview over FTA and previous adaptations to software-controlled systems. In Section 3 we introduce the modelling elements of SEFTs in summary and explain the analysis by translation to DSPNs. In Section 4 we introduce the case study and show how SEFT analysis is applied in practice. Section 5 concludes the paper and gives some pointers to ongoing and future research steps, in particular the implementation of the algorithm into our research tool ESSaRel (Embedded Systems Safety and Reliability Analyser [7], which is a successor of our current FTA tool UWG3.

2   Foundations and Previous Work

2.1   Introduction to Fault Tree Analysis

FTs [18] are a widely accepted model that graphically shows how influence factors (in general component failures) contribute to some given hazard or accident. They provide logical connectives (called gates) that allow decomposing the system-level hazard recursively. The AND gate indicates that all influence factors must apply together to cause the hazard and the OR gate indicates that any of the influences causes the hazard alone. The logical structure is usually depicted as an upside-down tree with the hazard to be examined (called top-event) at its root and the lowest-level influence factors (called basic events) as the leaves. Note that in the context of FTA the term "event" is applied in its probability theory meaning: an event is not necessarily some sudden phenomenon, but can be any proposition that is true with a certain probability.

The analyses to be performed on FTs can be qualitative or quantitative. Qualitative analyses list, for instance, all combinations of failures that must occur together to cause the top-level failure. Quantitative analysis calculates the probability of the top-event from the given probabilities of the basic events. Combinatorial formulas indicate for each type of gate how to calculate the output probability from the given input probabilities. These probabilities are either probabilities that an event occurs at all over a given mission time or they are understood with respect to a given point in time. The evolution of a system over time or any dependencies between the present system behaviour and the history cannot be modelled. An important assumption to obtain correct results is the stochastic independence of the basic events, which is hard to achieve in complex networked systems. Most current FTA tools use the efficient representation of Boolean terms as Binary Decision Diagrams (BDDs) to compute the quantitative results.

2.2 Fault Tree Analysis for Software-Controlled Systems

Like many safety and reliability analysis models, FTs were originally designed for non-programmable systems. When more and more technical systems became software-controlled, the need to adapt FTs to this application field grew.

There have been several attempts to adapt FTA to software or embedded systems, to derive FTs from software models and to enhance the expressive power of FTs. [16] integrate FTs with formal program specifications and use Interval Temporal Logic to give a formal semantics to Fault Trees. Formal methods are also used in [2] and [10]. Other approaches to model dynamic behaviour and multi-state components map FTs to Markov Chains [2] or different variants of Petri Nets [4][5][11][14]. Some researchers [10][2] proposed additional Fault Tree gates, for instance describing conditional probability, sequence enforcing or various spare usage situations (hot, cold and warm spare) in order to model special cases of dependencies.

For an efficient and sound development process different modelling techniques from system design and safety / reliability analysis should smoothly integrate with each other. Research projects aiming at the integration of different models can increasingly be observed during the last years [8][3]. Many of them consider FTs, but often they are applied in a rather informal or qualitative way.

2.3 Component Fault Trees

Models for complex technical systems must be compositional in order to be manageable. Traditional FTs have this property only in the sense that independent subtrees (called *modules*) can be cut off and handled separately. Technical components, however, are often influenced by other components and thus cannot be modelled by independent subtrees. To allow for a suitable modularisation in these cases, we recently proposed a more advanced component concept [15]. It allows cutting arbitrary parts out off a fault tree so that they can be modelled and stored independently. This allows a modularisation that reflects the actual technical components. The model is integrated and flattened during analysis. We call this enhanced model Component Fault Trees (CFTs). We introduced input and output ports that serve as interfaces to put the components together. Subcomponents are represented as black boxes with the ports visible at the edges.

From semantics point of view CFTs are ordinary FTs with the mentioned restrictions. However, apart from the better compositionality, the CFT concept prepared the ground for the use of ports to achieve integration of other models. We later refined our ports into State Ports and Event Ports, as will be explained in detail in the following. When we started to integrate components that are described by Markov Chains or Statecharts as subcomponents into CFTs, we found that the lack of semantic precision of FTs made it hard to connect states or events consistently to a FT. In response we took the approach of enhancing FTs by a State/Event distinction to allow the combination of different modelling elements techniques.

3   State-Event-Fault-Trees

3.1   Introduction to the SEFT Notation Elements

State-Event-Fault-Trees (SEFTs) are a model that combines elements from FTA and from Statecharts [13], ROOMcharts [17] or similar notations. We deal with a finite state space for each component, an abstraction that is sufficient for safety and reliability considerations. Each component is in exactly one state at each instant of time, called the active state (we leave out state hierarchy for now). We denote states by rounded rectangles, as in Statecharts. For safety analysis we consider *states* as conditions that remain valid for a non-empty interval of time. We call a propositional term over states a *state term* (e.g. "Component C1 is in state S1 *or* in state S2"). Note that more than one state term can be true at the same time. For each point of time we assign a value 0 or 1, representing the Boolean values false and true, to any state term. For probabilistic analysis the annotation domain is extended to a real value p with $0 \leq p \leq 1$ that represents the probability that the component is in this state at the given instant of time. In this case the meaning of AND and OR transfers from the propositional meaning to the meaning "probability, that state 1 AND / OR state 2 are active at the same time".

Event is the term we use for atomic phenomena that do not take time to occur (this is in contrast to the standard FT definition). In particular, state transitions are events, but there may be independent events as well, e.g. spontaneous actions that occur in the environment (e.g. "Tube breaks"). For quantitative analysis a probability density must be assigned to events. If an event is a transition from one state to another we call these states predecessor and successor state. We distinguish the *event* (denoting a class of similar phenomena that can happen at different times) from the *occurrence*, which is associated with an instant of time. Since we refer to a continuous time scale for our model we assume that any two independent events cannot occur at exactly the same time.

We mark events by solid bars. The resemblance to Petri Net transitions is not coincidental: we later translate events to Petri Net transitions for analysis. In our model events occur in one of three ways: either they are *triggered* by other events, or they occur after a deterministic delay t upon entry of their predecessor state, or they occur

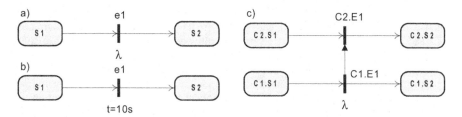

Fig. 1. a) Exponentially Distributed Transition b) Deterministic Delayed Transition c) Triggered Transition

after an exponentially distributed probabilistic delay. Thus, the expressive power of SEFTs subsumes both Statecharts that appropriately describe software behaviour and Markov Chains that are a customary state-based model for hardware failures. Fig. 1 shows all of these variants.

The example of the triggered transition is simplified for explanation purpose; it ignores the fact that the states and event belong to different components. Note that the two different kinds of directed edges: Those with light arrowheads mark the predecessor-successor relation between states and events (temporal edges) and those with bold arrowheads mark the triggering relation (causal edges). Causal edges between two events have the semantics that each time the source event occurs, the target event occurs as well, provided that it is enabled. Enabled means that the component the target event belongs to is in one of the predecessor states of the target event. If the source event happens at an instant t, then the target event occurs at t^+, so triggering does not encompass any delay. If, however, the modeller wants to introduce some explicit deterministic or probabilistic delay between source and target event, SEFTs offer a DELAY gate.

Causal edges can also have states as their source. States cannot trigger other states or events, but state terms can serve as guards for events, meaning that the event can only occur if the state term evaluates to true.

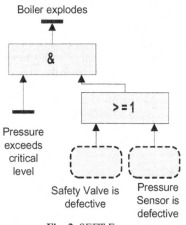

Fig. 2. SEFT Fragment

As in FTA, gates add logical connectors to the causal paths. Consequently the edges that connect gates are called causal edges as well. The most important gates are AND, OR and NOT in their different variants. SEFT gates are typed in the sense that they have different semantics depending on whether they are applied to state terms or to event triggering relations. For instance, the fragment in Fig. 2 has the semantics that the event "Pressure exceeds critical level" triggers the event "Boiler explodes" only if the state term "Safety Valve is defective" or the term "Pressure Sensor is defective" is true. In a complete example these unspecified state terms (drawn as dotted state symbols) could be states of two other components "Valve" and "Sensor".

SEFTs allow the extension of Fault Trees to Directed Acyclic Graphs (the same cause triggers multiple effects) and deal with repeated events or states correctly. Causal cycles without explicit delay are not allowed, because this would raise some semantic problems during analysis.

Just as Component Fault Trees, SEFTs are organized by components. *Components* are prototypes and must be instantiated. Components can be referenced as subcomponents of another component, forming a component hierarchy. The component on top of the hierarchy is the system to be examined. Each instance of a component defines a separate name space and all internal states and events are distinct from the state and events of other instances and hidden from the environment.

Ports achieve the connection of components across hierarchy levels. We distinguish input ports from output ports and state ports from event ports. Subcomponents appear as black boxes where only the ports are visible. Examples can be found in the case study in Section 4. Event ports allow triggering relations from one component to another: The information that some event occurs is transferred from the source component (the component where the output port belongs to) to the destination component (the component possessing the input port). There it can provoke some effect, provided that the destination component is ready to accept it. Otherwise, the event in the source component is neither blocked nor stored, but just discarded. The semantics of a state port is that the destination component has access to the information whether or not the state term in the source component is active, without having any means to influence that state.

3.2 Application of SEFTs

SEFTs are constructed like traditional FTs. Starting with some undesired system state (hazard) or event (accident), the analyst traces back its influences and finds out which system states or events play a role in initiating, propagating or inhibiting the fatal behaviour. The richer variety and semantic precision of gates allows better capturing chains of embedded systems behaviour. The basic events of standard FTA correspond to solitary exponentially distributed events in SEFTs. The project is structured hierarchically using the component concept.

Models that explain the relevant behaviour of subcomponents can be plugged in where necessary. For stochastic failures Markov Chains are appropriate. They have traditionally been used for hardware wear-and-tear, but there can also be stochastic models for software failures. To model software and control aspects of the system, Statecharts or similar models can be reused from the design phase, e.g. by importing them from a CASE tool. The visible difference is that the transitions, which are originally represented by labelled edges, now appear as explicit transition symbols. Software models can serve to check the reaction of the correct software on rare or unforeseen events from the environment or probabilistically model software failures.

3.3 Analysis by Translation to DSPNs

A model should not only be a graphical notation, but also provide analysis for relevant properties, supported by usable tools. Computer based analysis requires a formal semantics. Defining a formal semantics for a human-centred notation is a difficult task, as various attempts to formalise Statecharts or FTs show. A second issue is that being state-based models, SEFTs cannot be evaluated by the traditional combinatorial FTA algorithms. To tackle both issues at the same time we propose to translate SEFTs into an accepted formal notation where known analysis algorithms exist.

Petri Nets (PNs) are a model for discrete state systems that supports the concurrency we have to deal with in component based systems and provides stochastic variants. We chose Deterministic and Stochastic Petri Nets (DSPNs) [1] since they possess all kinds of transitions we need and provide analysis techniques for the properties we are interested in (in particular the probability of a place to be marked). They are an extension of Genaralized Stochastic Petri Nets (GSPNs) that lack deterministic delay that often has to be considered in software behaviour. Assuming some basic knowledge about Petri Nets we briefly point out the main features of DSPNs: DSPNs are a timed variant of Petri Nets, i.e. the (possibly probabilistic) time that a transition waits before it fires after becoming enabled is specified in the model. In particular, DSPN transitions fire in one of three ways: immediately on activation, after a constant delay (specified by an annotated time parameter) or after an exponentially distributed random delay (specified by an annotated rate parameter). Firing of transitions is atomic and takes no time. In the graphical representation, black bars depict immediate transitions, empty rectangles depict transitions with exponentially distributed firing time, and black filled rectangles depict transitions with constant delay unequal to zero. Transitions are joined to places by input arcs, output arcs or inhibitor arcs. The latter forbid firing as long as the corresponding place is marked. Priorities can be attached to immediate transitions to resolve conflicts. Places can have a capacity of more then one token and arcs can have a multiplicity of greater than one, but we currently do not exploit this property. The underlying time scale is continuous.

Analysis of DSPNs has been described in [6][9] and several tools are available. We are currently carrying out some experiments using TimeNET [19] that require manual translation, but we are working on an automated integration of both tools.

The translation of SEFT states and events to DSPN places and transitions is straightforward: each state is mapped to a place and each event to a transition. SEFT gates are translated as a whole by looking up the corresponding DSPN structure in a dictionary. A part of this dictionary, containing different kinds of AND, OR and NOT gates can be found in Fig. 3. The dashed places or transitions signify import places / transitions, which are references to other places / transitions (marked with "export") in other component DSPNs. During flattening (integration of the partial nets), the import elements will be merged with the corresponding export output. The semantics of the gates is best understood by playing the "token game". For instance, the export place P_{out} of the AND (State x State) gate net is marked if and only if someone puts tokens to both import Places P_{in1} and P_{in2}. The situation is different with the Sequential-AND (Event x Event) gate: here the left input transition must fire first and then the right input transition to make the output transition fire.

Our semantics that lies in the composition by state ports and event ports cannot be translated directly to a composition in the Petri Net domain, so special patterns are necessary when translating SEFT ports to DSPNs. The reasons are that ports must not introduce any backward influences and events are not stored as tokens are.

To translate an event port an additional place is added where the triggering transition puts a token when firing. Triggering only occurs if the triggered transition is feasible at the same instant of time and there is no storage of events. To capture this,

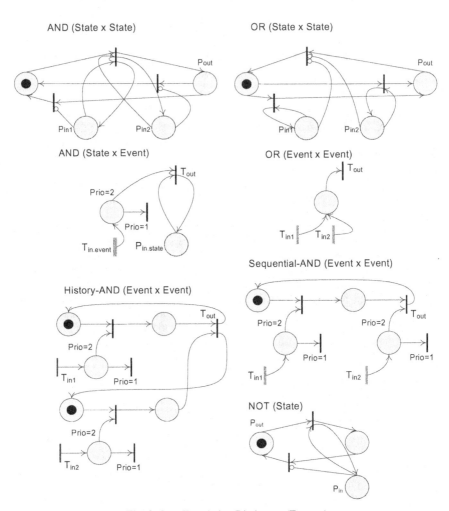

Fig. 3. Gate Translation Dictionary (Excerpt)

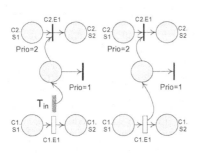

Fig. 4. Trigger / Event Port Pattern

we add an artificial immediate transition with lower priority than the triggered transition so that it consumes the token in those cases when it is not immediately used. The event port (or trigger) pattern can be seen in Fig. 4, before and after flattening. Note that n DSPNs priority 2 takes precedence over priority 1.

Regarding state ports, it is important that the target component must not backward modify the source component

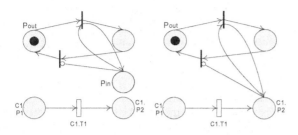

Fig. 5. State Port, exemplified by a NOT gate

state (and thus the DSPN marking). For this purpose we enrich the target component by a state machine with two states, reflecting whether or not the source component is in the relevant state. DSPN inhibitor arcs (depicted with a small circle at the end) are a useful means to sense that a place is *not* marked without reverse influence, because inhibitor arcs never consume a token. Unfortunately they have no positive counterpart that senses if a token *is* present without removing it. A way out is to accompany each arc that removes a token by a complementary arc that puts it back immediately after. As an example we show how in Fig. 5 a NOT-Gate (see dictionary) is merged to an export state (state connected to an output port) of some state machine. Notice how the inhibit edge and the pair of normal edges are connected in a way that excludes backward influences. We call this constellation the state port pattern.

3.4 The Translation Algorithm

The translation and preparation comprises the following steps:

Preconditions:
1. The component model to be analysed and all nested subcomponent models (recursively) are available at analysis time and are valid SEFT models
2. The component nesting hierarchy is free from cycles (a component must not refer directly or indirectly to itself as a subcomponent)
3. All component input ports are connected on the higher hierarchy level
4. All causal paths are free from cycles (this must be checked across component borders and hierarchy levels)

1st Step: Component-wise translation (creates a DSPN for each component)
For each component
-   Prefix the IDs of all modelling elements by the IDs of the component instance they belong to (to avoid name conflicts)
-   Represent each SEFT state by a DSPN place
    -   If the state is the initial state, mark it by a token
-   Represent each deterministic or exponential event by a deterministic or exponential DSPN transition and transfer the parameter
    -   If a transition is solitary (no predecessor and successor state modelled) then add one marked DSPN place which is both predecessor and successor place
-   Represent each triggered event or event with zero delay by an immediate transition
-   Transform each causal edge joining two events to the trigger pattern
-   Represent each temporal edge from SEFT by a DSPN edge

- Replace each Fault Tree Gate by the DSPN structure indicated by the dictionary
- For each port of the component and its subcomponents
  - Create for each connected causal edge an entry in the connection table (source and destination ID)
  - If a state / event is the source of the causal edge leading to a port, then label this state / transition as "*export*"
  - If a state / event is the target of the causal edge, then apply the state port / event port pattern and label the input state / transition of this pattern as "*import*"

2nd step: Flattening (creates one DSPN out of the component DSPNs)
- Resolve the connection table to remove any ports except output ports of the system
- Merge *import* with corresponding *export* places and transitions. The counterparts are found in the connection table

One exported place or transition can be merged with several counterparts. It is a failure if port references cannot be resolved or if import places or transitions have no export counterpart.

After the SEFT has been translated and flattened, the initial markings of the DSPN places must be applied where missing and the place or transition connected to the output port selected for analysis must be identified.

We intended to introduce a net simplification step before the flattening steps on each hierarchy level to reduce the state space.

3.5 Performing the Analysis

To do the analysis, the requested measure (e.g. average probability of a state term that is connected to an output port) must be translated into a measure that can be determined by the DSPN analysis tool (e.g. the marking probability for a place that corresponds to the system state of interest). Then a suitable analysis procedure must be started. The tool TimeNET that we are currently using offers both transient and steady-state analysis for DSPNs plus simulation. Analysis is faster but due to the used analysis algorithm it can only be applied in cases where at most one deterministic transition is enabled in any marking. If this condition is violated, simulation is still possible. At present state, we read back the results of the analysis manually. Our tool ESSaRel that is currently under development will start the analyser via API or command line call and later read the calculated values from the TimeNET result file to display them on its own GUI.

4 The Fire Alarm System

4.1 Description of the Example System

In this section we demonstrate the presented approach by the example of a fire alarm system. The system consists of two redundant fire alarm units which may fail stochas-

tically. The hazard to be analysed is the situation when both alarm units are simultaneously in the state "failed", since in this case a fire might break out without being
noticed. In order to restart a failed alarm unit a watchdog that periodically checks the
alarm units and restarts them if they are in failed state.

4.2 Constructing the SEFT

We start by modelling each of the units as independent components. The alarm units
are instances of the component "fire alarm unit" shown in Fig. 6a.

An alarm unit may be running properly or fail stochastically with a failure rate of
$\lambda=1/10$ hour^{-1}. In order to restart a unit an external trigger is needed. Before running
normally, some initialization steps taking a deterministic time of 0.1 hours have to be
performed. In order to notice when a unit is out of work, a state output port (depicted
by the filled S-triangle) that senses if the unit is running is used in the model. For
externally triggering the initialization routine an event input port (the empty E-
triangle) is needed. The watchdog, as shown in Fig. 6b, is simply depicted as a component with only one state. The triggering event is produced once every hour and can
be connected to other components via an event output port.

Now that the technical units are given, we combine the modelled units to form the
SEFT that describes the complete fire alarm system and explains the causal paths that
lead to the hazard situation. Figure 7 shows how the fire alarm system is modelled
using two instances of the "fire alarm unit" and an instance of the "watchdog" component. The inner structure of the instances is omitted in this view. The watchdog is
connected to the event input ports of both alarm units so that it can trigger a restart of
a failed unit when necessary. Since the fire hazard is present when both of the redundant alarm units are not working at the same time they are combined with a NOT gate
each, which in turn serve as inputs for a state AND gate. The output of the state AND
gate represents the hazard situation.

All preconditions for analyzing this model are fulfilled: There are no cycles in the
component hierarchy or in any causal relation and all state and event port have been
connected to their counterparts. The state output port of the AND gate does not need
to be connected since it represents the hazard situation to be analyzed.

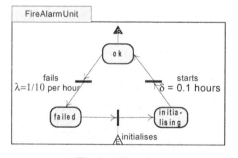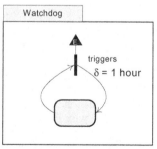

Fig. 6. a) Fire alarm component b) Watchdog component

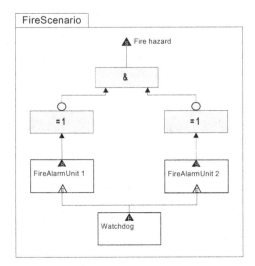

Fig. 7. The fire alarm system

4.3 Translation into DSPN

Before performing the analysis the model has to be translated into a DSPN. For the NOT and AND gates the corresponding DSPNs have already been shown in Fig. 3. The "alarm unit" and "watchdog" components can be translated step by step. Each state is mapped onto a DSPN place, the events that occur stochastically onto exponential transitions, the events occurring after a certain time onto deterministic transitions and externally triggered events onto immediate transitions respectively. The resulting parts have to be combined with the gate nets to form the complete flattened DSPN shown in Fig. 8. The dotted rectangles show the DSPN parts representing the components. The markings were set in a way so that the initial state of the alarm system is conceived: the alarm units are working properly and there is no fire hazard. Note the applied trigger pattern for combining the watchdog and the externally triggered events in the alarm units.

4.4 Analysis of the Flattened DSPN

The DSPN can now be examined using TimeNET. This step as well as the translation into DSPNs must currently be done manually but an export filter to the TimeNET file format will be integrated in our tool ESSaRel. The hazard situation is represented by the place marked with POut which was mapped on the output of the state AND gate. The probability that one token lies in place POut denotes the probability that both alarm units are out of work simultaneously. The corresponding expression in Time-NET is P{#POut=1}.

TimeNET cannot accomplish an analysis of the net, since more than one deterministic transition might be enabled at the same time. A steady-state simulation (continuous time) with the parameters given in Fig. 8 and a maximum relative error of 1% (a parameter TimeNET uses to specify the desired accuracy of the simulation) returns a resulting probability for the fire hazard as 0.003975. In about 0.4% of the time, both alarm units are not working so that a fire hazard persists.

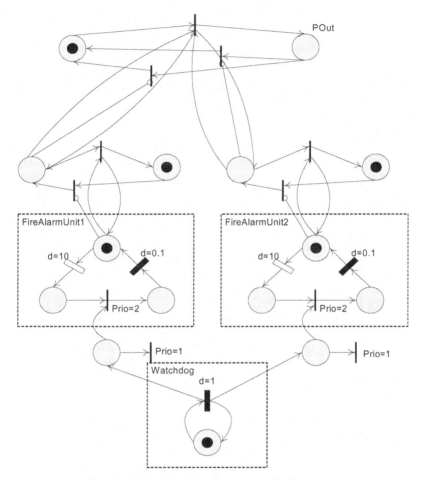

Fig. 8. DSPN of the fire alarm system after flattening

5 Conclusion and Further Research

We have proposed State-Event-Fault Trees as an extension to the FT concept that allows distinguishing states and events. This enables us to integrate finite state models with FTA. In particular we can integrate Statecharts and Markov Chains. This increases expressive power and allows the reuse of design models for safety analysis. We adapt the traditional set of FT gates by introducing typed gates for states and events. Phenomena like temporal order of events that were not expressible by FTs before can be expressed by SEFTs, because additional gates such as History-AND or Sequential-AND exist. The component concept allows partitioning SEFTs in accordance with the actual technical component structure and to handle complex projects. In summary, the established top-down analysis search for hazard causes provided by FTA can now be combined with powerful and reusable description of embedded system behaviour brought in by the integration of state-based models.

For quantitative probabilistic analysis of SEFTs we translate them component-wise into DSPNs, apply simplifications on component level and merge them to one flat net. Existing Petri Net analysis tools, for instance TimeNET, calculate the measures that correspond to the hazard probabilities in the original SEFT. We have shown the applicability of our method by the example of a fire alarm system. We carried out other small studies to validate the model; larger studies with industrial partners are under preparation.

SEFTs allow a more formal modelling of some gates that are part of standard FTA or later extensions, for instance inhibit, functional dependency, and different kinds of spare gates. We aim at developing new kinds of gates that match frequent structures of safety-critical systems, such as History-AND with a Reset input (for Repair / Restart situations) or History / Sequential-AND with a time parameter that indicates how close both events must occur to each other. We work towards a closer integration of state-based and combinatorial analysis approaches to obtain better analysis performance for subcomponents that can be described by a combinatorial model, similar to the approaches given in [12]. We also plan to do some simplification on component level before integration, exploiting the fact that only a few of the functional states of each component are relevant for safety or reliability considerations.

The ongoing integration of SEFTs into a usable tool is part of our research project ESSaRel. The platform for this integration is the existing CFT tool UWG3 which has been developed in cooperation with Siemens. We have defined the translation and flattening algorithm and are now implementing the export filter TimeNET and an import filter to read models from the CASE tool Rational RoseRT that are mainly based on ROOMcharts. In the end we are working towards an integrated tool chain for safety and reliability analysis of embedded systems.

References

1.   Ajmone Marsan, M., Chiola, G.: On Petri nets with deterministic and exponentially distributed firing times. European Workshop on Applications and Theory of Petri Nets 1986. Lecture Notes in Computer Science, volume 266, pages 132-145. Springer 1987
2.   Bechta Dugan J., Sullivan, K., Coppit, D.: Developing a low-cost high-quality software tool for dynamic fault tree analysis. Transactions on Reliability, December 1999, pages 49-59
3.   Bloomfield, E., Cheng, J.H., Górski, J.: Towards A Common Safety Description Model, Proceedings of the 10th International Conference on Computer Safety, Reliability and Security SAFECOMP'91 (Edited by J. F. Lindeberg), pp. 1-6, Pergamon Press, 1991
4.   Bobbio, A., Franceschinis, G., Gaeta, R., Portinale, L.: Exploiting Petri nets to support fault tree based dependability analysis. In: Proc. 8th Int. Workshop on Petri Net and Performance Models (PNPM'99), 8-10 October 1999, Zaragoza, Spain, pages 146-155. 1999

5. Buchacker, K.: Combining Fault Trees and Petri-Nets to Model Safety-critical Systems. In: A. Tentner (Ed.): High Performance Computing 1999. The Society for Computer Simulation International, 1999, pp. 439-444

6. Ciardo, G., Lindemann, C.: Analysis of deterministic and stochastic Petri nets. In Proc. of the Fifth Int. Workshop on Petri Nets and Performance Models (PNPM93), Toulouse, France, Oct. 1993

7. ESSaRel. Embedded Systems Safety and Reliability Analyser. http://www.essarel.de

8. Fenelon, P., McDermid, J.A.: An Integrated Toolset For Software Safety Analysis, Journal of Systems and Software, 21(3), 1993, pp. 279-290

9. German. R., and Mitzlaff, J.: Transient analysis of deterministic and stochastic Petri nets with TimeNET. in Proc. 8th Int. Conf. on Computer Performance Evaluation, Modelling Techniques and Tools and MMB (LNCS 977), Heidelberg, Germany, 1995, pp. 209-223

10. Górski, J.: Extending Safety Analysis Techniques with Formal Semantics, In Technology and Assessment of Safety Critical Systems (Edited by F.J. Redmill and T. Anderson), Springer Verlag, 1994

11. Górski, J., Wardzinski, A.: Timing Aspects of Safety Analysis, in F. Redmill and T. Anderson, Eds.: Safer Systems, Springer Verlag 1997, pp. 231-244

12. Gulati R., Bechta Dugan J.: A modular approach for analyzing static and dynamic fault trees. In Proceedings of the Reliability and Maintainability Symposium, January 1997.

13. Harel, D.: Statecharts: A visual formalism for complex systems. Science of Computer Programming, 8(3): 231--274, June 1987

14. Hura, G.S., Atwood, J.W.: The Use of Petri Nets to Analyze Coherent Fault Trees. In: IEEE Trans. Reliab. (USA), Vol. 37, No. 5, pages 469-474. 1988

15. Kaiser, B., Liggesmeyer, P., Mäckel, O.: A New Component Concept for Fault Trees. Proceedings of the 8th Australian Workshop on Safety Critical Systems and Software (SCS'03), P. Lindsay & T. Cant, Eds.

16. Schellhorn, G., Thums, A., Reif, W.: Formal Fault Tree Semantics. In: Proceedings of The Sixth World Conference on Integrated Design & Process Technology , Pasadena, CA, July 2002

17. Selic, B., Gullekson, G., Ward P.T:. Real-Time Object-Oriented Modeling, John Wiley & Sons, 1994

18. Vesely, W. E., Goldberg, F. F., Roberts, N. H., Haasl, D. F.: Fault Tree Handbook. U. S. Nuclear Regulatory Commission, NUREG-0492, Washington DC, 1981

19. Zimmermann, A., German, R., Freiheit, J., Hommel, G.: TimeNET 3.0 Tool Description. Int. Conf. on Petri Nets and Performance Models (PNPM'99), Zaragoza, Spain, 1999

Safety Requirements and Fault Trees Using Retrenchment

R. Banach and R. Cross

Computer Science Department, Manchester University, Manchester, M13 9PL, UK
{banach,r.cross}@cs.man.ac.uk

Abstract. In the formal modelling of safety critical systems, an initial abstract model captures the ideal, fault free, conception of the system. Subsequently, this model is enriched with the detail required to deal with envisaged faults that the system is designed to be robust against, resulting in a concrete extended system model. Normally, conventional refinement cannot provide a formal account of the relationship between the two models. Retrenchment, a liberalisation of refinement introduced to address such situations, allows model evolution, and is deployed to provide a formal account of the fault injection process that yields the extended system model. The simulation relationship of retrenchment is used to derive fault trees for the faults introduced during the injection process. A two bit adder example drawn from the FSAP/NuSMV-SA safety analysis platform is used to illustrate the technique.

1 Introduction

Safety-critical systems are required to behave in a predictable and acceptable way in the face of failures which have been forseen and designed for during their development. Generally speaking, the behaviour in both desired and undesired (degraded) situations must be fully documented to provide a comprehensive system description. The process of creating such a comprehensive description starts by writing down an ideal, fault free, abstract model of the system. In this model, only the desired behaviour of the system is expressed. Once this initial model has been created, the elicitation of safety requirements yields a fresh set of criteria that the system must meet. The incorporation of these into the ideal model yields an 'extended system model', which encompasses all system behaviour in both desired and undesired circumstances.

One framework for carrying out this task is the FSAP/NuSMV-SA safety analysis platform [11]. This is a toolkit that allows the creation of the ideal model, and then permits the automatic injection of possible faults into the ideal model from pre-defined libraries of generic faults. In this way the extended system model is obtained. Verification techniques such as Fault Tree Analysis can then be used to establish the root cause of a given failure, and relate it to the ideal model in an informal manner. Bozzano et al., the authors of the FSAP/NuSMV-SA platform, justify the use of such informal techniques in relating ideal and failure-sensitive models by pointing out the deficiencies of formal approaches,

M. Heisel et al. (Eds.): SAFECOMP 2004, LNCS 3219, pp. 210–223, 2004.

saying: "...even when formal methods are applied, the information linking the design and the safety assessment phases is often carried out informally".

The reason that this happens is not hard to see, and is due to the fact that the traditional formal relationship between an abstract and a more concrete model is refinement [27], [16], [15]. Unfortunately the formal proof obligations of refinement are quite stringent, and are parameterised only by the retrieve (or abstraction) relation between the state spaces of the two models. This restriction prevents the description via refinement of many of the kinds of modification or adaptation that arise naturally during system development, and often forces the abstract and concrete models to be much closer together than one might ideally like. The impact of this for using refinement in the case of safety critical development would entail committing, more or less at the outset, to an abstract model that already contains essentially all the desired fault tolerant behaviour, and this obviously flies in the face of the desire to create just the ideal model first, and only later to consider the incorporation of faults (and of the system's responses to them) via a separate safety requirements analysis phase.

In this paper, we show that retrenchment, a liberalisation of refinement which was introduced precisely to address the excessive stingency of the formal proof obligations of refinement in such situations, can fare better in the role of intermediary between the ideal and extended system models. Retrenchment achieves this by introducing extra data, the within, output and concedes relations, into the principal refinement proof obligation. These extra relations depend on the the two systems being discussed and introduce much greater parameterisation into the description of the relationship between them. So we gain much greater flexibility in capturing the desired relationship between models. We exploit this flexibility to give a credible formal account of the relationship between ideal and fault tolerant systems in the process of fault injection. Most importantly, such a formal account offers opportunities for formally tying together —via the bridge offered by retrenchment— other aspects of the safety critical development, hitherto done separately (even if formally) in the ideal and extended model worlds. We illustrate this potential for fault tree generation, and more briefly comment on model checking.

The rest of this paper is structured as follows: Section 2 describes the two-bit adder, the case study that will serve as a running example in this paper, and explains the way in which it will evolve to model implementation-level faults. Section 3 overviews refinement in a simple partial correctness formulation, and applies it to the two-bit adder to show the shortcomings of refinement in this context. Section 4 introduces retrenchment, and shows how it can be used to give a much improved account of fault injection for the two-bit adder scenario. Section 5 introduces the simulation relationship of retrenchment, and shows how it can be used to generate the fault tree for the two-bit adder via a resolution-like procedure. Section 6 comments briefly on a similar approach to model checking. Section 7 concludes, looking forward to more detailed expositions of the topics introduced briefly in this paper.

2   The Two-Bit Adder Example

In the rest of the paper, we will frame our discussions of relationships between models in terms of an abstract system Abs, and a concrete one Conc, which will be two adjacent systems in the development hierarchy. The abstract system Abs, will contain a number of operations Op_A, taken from its set of operations Ops_A. An abstract operation Op_A is a transition relation for which the individual transitions will be written:

$$Op_A(u, i, u', o)$$

or more evocatively:

$$u \text{ -}(i, Op_A, o)\text{-> } u'$$

where u, u' are elements of the state space U, and i and o are elements of the input space I_{Op} and the output space O_{Op} respectively. Below we will use the arrow format to fix the signature of an operation in terms of states and outputs, and will use the Op_A format when we simply wish to utilise the transition relation as a component of a more complex relational expression. It turns out that for the simple examples that appear in this paper, all variables are either read-only or write-only, so we will model them using input and output variables, finessing the absence of genuine updatable state by using one-element state spaces containing a single '*' value. Thus the typical abstract operation becomes $* \text{ -}(i, Op_A, o)\text{-> } *$. In addition to all this the system is started in an initial state u' satisfying the predicate $Init_A(u')$.

Corresponding concrete operations are defined in exactly the same way, except with operations Op_C taken from Ops_C, with state space $v \in V$, input $j \in J_{Op}$ and output $p \in P_{Op}$. Decoration is used to distinguish between before and after states of variables, with an operation Op being identified as abstract or concrete by use of a subscript A or C as necessary. The initialisation predicate is $Init_C(v')$.

The example that will be used to highlight the use of retrenchment is the two-bit adder adapted from [11]. From now on, unless stated otherwise, all I/O variables take values in $\{0, 1\}$ the usual one bit space. We follow the structure of [11] closely, and so the abstract two-bit adder $Adder_A$ is specified in terms of a subsidiary operation Bit_A. In fact Bit_A merely copies its input to its output, acting as a placeholder for subsequent injection of faulty behaviour. Note the use of pairing to turn two individual inputs i_1 and i_2 to $Adder_A$, into a single formal input (i_1, i_2).

$$* \text{ -}(i, Bit_A, o)\text{-> } * \quad = \quad (o = i)$$

$$* \text{ -}((i_1, i_2), Adder_A, o)\text{-> } * \quad = \quad (o = (i_1 + i_2 \bmod 2))$$

Following [11] again, these operations are wrapped up in an enclosing operation $Main_A$ which takes its input values, feeds them into the adder, and extracts the result.

$$* \text{ -}((r_1, r_2), Main_A, adder)\text{-> } * \quad =$$

$$(\exists\ b_1, b_2 \bullet Bit_A(*, r_1, *, b_1) \wedge Bit_A(*, r_2, *, b_2) \wedge$$
$$Adder_A(*, (b_1, b_2), *, adder))$$

The above abstract idealised model describes how the system should behave when it is functioning correctly. The next step is to specify how the system should behave in degraded situations (i.e. when a fault occurs in a part of the system). So safety requirements are added, through the process of fault injection, to create a concrete extended system model.

We will inject two types of fault into the above system: a corruption of the input bit of the *Bit* module, and a stuck-at-zero fault in the *Adder* module. These are incorporated into the two concrete module defnitions of Bit_C and $Adder_C$.

$$* \text{-}(j, Bit_C, p) \text{-}\!\!> * \ \ =$$
$$(ft = no\_failure \wedge p = j) \vee$$
$$(ft = inverted \wedge p = \neg j)$$

$$* \text{-}((j_1, j_2), Adder_C, p) \text{-}\!\!> * \ \ =$$
$$(ft_a = no\_failure \wedge p = (j_1 + j_2 \bmod 2)) \vee$$
$$(ft_a = stuck\_at\_zero \wedge p = 0)$$

Both the concrete *Bit* and *Adder* operations have an additional free variable, ft (fault_type), that indicates whether the fault in question is active. In the case of a faulty *Bit*, the input value is inverted, while in the case of a faulty *Adder*, the output is set to zero irrespective of the inputs. These definitions lead to a corresponding concrete extended *Main* operation, in which we relabel the (r_1, r_2) inputs and *adder* output as (s_1, s_2) and *sum* for later convenience.

$$* \text{-}((s_1, s_2), Main_C, sum) \text{-}\!\!> * \ \ =$$
$$(\exists\ c_1, c_2 \bullet Bit_C(*, s_1, *, c_1) \wedge Bit_C(*, s_2, *, c_2) \wedge$$
$$Adder_C(*, (c_1, c_2), *, sum))$$

Note that the choice of simply making the ft variables free in the definitions of Bit_C, $Adder_C$ and $Main_C$ is but one way of handling the relevant information. For us it was dictated by the desire for subsequent technical simplicity.

3   Refinement

In this section we outline a simple partial correctness formulation of model oriented refinement, and show that it will not describe the relationship between the abstract and concrete systems of the two bit adder. See [27], [15], [16] for treatments of model oriented refinement in general and [17], [23], [26], [28], for more details of the Z methodology, or [1], [24], [24] [25], for more details on B; both Z and B being particular incarnations of the model oriented approach.

For a concrete model of the kind we have been discussing to be a refinement of an abstract one, we need three things. Firstly that the sets of operation names at the two levels are identical, i.e. $\mathsf{Ops}_A = \mathsf{Ops}_C$. Secondly that the initilisation proof obligation (PO) holds:

$$Init_C(v') \;\Rightarrow\; (\exists\, u' \bullet Init_A(u') \wedge G(u', v'))$$

Thirdly for each corresponding pair Op_A and Op_C, the operation PO holds:

$$G(u, v) \wedge Op_C(v, j, v', p)$$
$$\Rightarrow\; (\exists\, u', i, o \bullet Op_A(u, i, u', o) \wedge G(u', v') \wedge (i = j) \wedge (o = p))$$

This shows that inputs and outputs are not permitted to change in the passage from abstract to concrete (in line with refinement's original objective of providing an implementaiton level model substitutable for all occurrences of the abstract one), and that the only scope for adjusting the relationship between the two models is via the retrieve relation G. Since G appears in both the antecedent and the consequent of the PO, there is often very little leeway indeed for the choice of G.

Let us examine the prospects for treating our running example via refinement. The initialisation PO is trivially satisfied because there is no state. On the other hand the operation PO for *Bit* obviously cannot be satisfied since equality of outputs does not always hold. Even if we are more permissive about I/O in the consequent of the PO, and supplant $(i = j) \wedge (o = p)$ by $In_{Op}(i, j) \wedge Out_{Op}(o, p)$ where $In_{Op}(i, j)$ and $Out_{Op}(o, p)$ are more general input and output relations as happens in eg. I/O refinement, [9], we are still in trouble since the only relation $Out_{Op}(o, p)$ that is independent of the fault_type parameter ft, and relates all instances of output pairs needed by the *Bit* operation, is the universal relation $\mathbf{true}$, since when ft $= no\_failure$ we want $Out_{Op}(o, p)$ to be equality, whereas if ft $= inverted$ we want $Out_{Op}(o, p)$ to be inequality. This makes $Out_{Op}(o, p)$ completely uninformative, and in the absence of state, leaves the relationship between abstract and concrete completely unconstrained. Entirely analogous remarks apply in the case of the *Adder* operation.

Thus although refinement does a good job of keeping development steps in check, to the extent that behaviour defined at the abstract level is preserved at the concrete level, it proves very inflexible in formally capturing many kinds of development step that do not fall within its rather exacting constraints, but that are entirely justifiable on engineering grounds. See [18], [10], [19], [4] for more discussion of this and related points.

4   Retrenchment

Retrenchment ([3], [4], [5], [6], [7], [8], [2]), was introduced to provide a formal vehicle which, while resembling refinement up to a point, provides greater flexibility to express relationships between the models that designers genuinely have in mind during development. Retrenchment achieves this by parameterising the relationship between abstract and concrete model in a development step more richly than by just a retrieve relation, having also within, output and concedes relations. These modifiy the shape of the operation PO as follows (the initialisation PO remains as for refinement):

$$G(u, v) \land P_{Op}(i, j, u, v) \land Op_C(v, j, v', p)$$
$$\Rightarrow (\exists \, u', o \bullet Op_A(u, i, u', o) \land ((G(u', v') \land O_{Op}(o, p; u', v', u, v, i, j))$$
$$\lor C_{Op}(u', v', o, p; u, v, i, j)))$$

In the preceding, $P_{Op}(i, j, u, v)$ is the within relation and serves to constrain the impact of the implicational relationship between abstract and concrete models where this is desirable; also it generalises the $(i = j)$ input relation of refinement and permits the mixing of input and before-state information where this is considered appropriate. Likewise the output relation $O_{Op}(o, p; u', v', u, v, i, j)$ generalises the $(o = p)$ of refinement, and the presence of the other variables u', v', u, v, i, j allows the inclusion of any other facts that designers wish to highlight concerning the case where the abstract and concrete steps re-establish the retrieve relation $G(u', v')$. The crucial feature of retrenchment though, is the presence of the disjunction between $(G' \land O_{Op})$ and C_{Op}, where C_{Op} is the concedes relation. C_{Op} features the same variables as O_{Op}, giving the same level of expressivity as O_{Op}, but this time in circumstances where the retrieve relation $G(u', v')$ need not be re-established. This *weakening* of the postcondition gives the much greater flexibility alluded to earlier, but of course comes at a price: the price of the reworking of the whole of refinement theory. Refinement starts with the general principle of substitutability of abstract by concrete and *derives* its operation PO; retrenchment starts with the above operation PO and *derives* whatever general principles might survive the modification. (See the cited references for indication of progress on general principles).

In practical terms what retrenchment does is to honestly but formally allow an abstract model to evolve to a more realistic one, acting as a more usable specification constructor than refinement alone.[1] In the case of safety critical design, it is the desire to separate initial design from safety analysis (and not the demands of refinement) that drives the order in which features and requirements are incorporated into the model, and retrenchment is better able to accomodate this agenda than refinement, as we see when we revisit our case-study.

Starting with the *Bit* operation, it is not hard to see that the abstract and concrete versions can be conveniently related by a retrenchment. Here is a reasonable choice for the various component relations needed for the *Bit* operation:

$$G_{Bit}(*, *) \; = \; \text{true}$$

---

[1] The usual assumption is that there is a process of gradually incorporating requirements via a collection of incomplete models (related to each other by retrenchment for example), until a final 'contracted model' is arrived at, which expresses all the needed requirements, and which can then be refined to an implementation. Such a picture is typically an oversimplification of a real development, but a nevertheless a useful one.

$$P_{Bit}(i, j, *, *) = (i = j)$$
$$O_{Bit}(o, p; *, *, *, *, i, j) = (\text{ft} = no\_failure \wedge o = p)$$
$$C_{Bit}(*, *, o, p; *, *, i, j) = (\text{ft} = inverted \wedge o = \neg p)$$

Note that a considerable element of choice has been exercised in designing the above relations. For instance, since there is no state to speak of, so that only inputs and outputs need to be kept under control, we could have chosen to put all the facts contained in the above O_{Bit} and C_{Bit} into either one of these relations, defaulting its counterpart to true or false as appropriate. The choice we actually made reflects our informal perception of which aspects of Bit's behaviour are viewed as refinement-like, and which are regarded as degraded. For the given G, P, O, C, when we substitute the various components into the generic PO we get:

$$\text{true} \wedge (i = j) \wedge ((\text{ft} = no\_failure \wedge p = j) \vee (\text{ft} = inverted \wedge p = \neg j))$$
$$\Rightarrow (\exists *, o \bullet (o = i) \wedge$$
$$((\text{true} \wedge \text{ft} = no\_failure \wedge o = p) \vee (\text{ft} = inverted \wedge o = \neg p)))$$

which is more or less selfevident.

Moving to the *Adder* operation, the relations for the retrenchment can be chosen as follows:

$$G_{Adder}(*, *) = \text{true}$$
$$P_{Adder}((i_1, i_2), (j_1, i_2), *, *) = \text{true}$$
$$O_{Adder}(o, p; *, *, *, *, (i_1, i_2), (j_1, j_2)) =$$
$$((\text{ft}_a = no\_failure \wedge (i_1 + j_1 + i_2 + j_2 = 0 \bmod 2) \wedge o = p) \vee$$
$$(\text{ft}_a = no\_failure \wedge (i_1 + j_1 + i_2 + j_2 = 1 \bmod 2) \wedge o = \neg p))$$
$$C_{Adder}(*, *, o, p; *, *, (i_1, i_2), (j_1, j_2)) =$$
$$(\text{ft}_a = stuck\_at\_zero \wedge o = (i_1 + i_2 \bmod 2) \wedge p = 0)$$

Note that the choice of within relation as true, is dictated by subsequent considerations. The reader can check that the operation PO now reduces to the easily verified:

$$\text{true} \wedge \text{true} \wedge ((\text{ft}_a = no\_failure \wedge p = (j_1 + j_2 \bmod 2)) \vee$$
$$(\text{ft}_a = stuck\_at\_zero \wedge p = 0))$$
$$\Rightarrow (\exists *, o \bullet (o = (i_1 + i_2 \bmod 2)) \wedge$$
$$((\text{true} \wedge$$
$$((\text{ft}_a = no\_failure \wedge (i_1 + j_1 + i_2 + j_2 = 0 \bmod 2) \wedge o = p) \vee$$
$$(\text{ft}_a = no\_failure \wedge (i_1 + j_1 + i_2 + j_2 = 1 \bmod 2) \wedge o = \neg p)))$$
$$\vee$$
$$(\text{ft}_a = stuck\_at\_zero \wedge o = (i_1 + i_2 \bmod 2) \wedge p = 0)))$$

Finally we can retrench the *Main* operation thus:

$$G_{Main}(*,*) = \text{true}$$
$$P_{Main}((r_1,r_2),(s_1,s_2),*,*) = (r_1 = s_1 \wedge r_2 = s_2)$$
$$O_{Main}(adder, sum; *,*,*,*,(r_1,r_2),(s_1,s_2)) =$$
$$(\text{ft}_1 = \text{ft}_2 = \text{ft}_a = no\_failure \wedge adder = sum)$$
$$C_{Main}(*,*, adder, sum; *,*,(r_1,r_2),(s_1,s_2)) =$$
$$(\text{ft}_a = stuck\_at\_zero \wedge sum = 0) \vee$$
$$(\text{ft}_a = no\_failure \wedge \text{ft}_1 \neq \text{ft}_2 \wedge adder = \neg sum) \vee$$
$$(\text{ft}_a = no\_failure \wedge \text{ft}_1 = inverted = \text{ft}_2 \wedge adder = sum)$$

Again, when we substitute these into the PO we get the messier but still easily verified:

$$\text{true} \wedge (r_1 = s_1 \wedge r_2 = s_2) \wedge$$
$$(\exists\, c_1, c_2 \bullet$$
$$((\text{ft}_1 = no\_failure \wedge c_1 = s_1) \vee (\text{ft}_1 = inverted \wedge c_1 = \neg s_1)) \wedge$$
$$((\text{ft}_2 = no\_failure \wedge c_2 = s_2) \vee (\text{ft}_2 = inverted \wedge c_2 = \neg s_2)) \wedge$$
$$((\text{ft}_a = no\_failure \wedge sum = (c_1 + c_2 \bmod 2)) \vee$$
$$(\text{ft}_a = stuck\_at\_zero \wedge sum = 0)))$$
$$\Rightarrow (\exists\, *, adder \bullet$$
$$(\exists\, b_1, b_2 \bullet r_1 = b_1 \wedge r_2 = b_2 \wedge (adder = (b_1 + b_2 \bmod 2))) \wedge$$
$$((\text{true} \wedge \text{ft}_1 = \text{ft}_2 = \text{ft}_a = no\_failure \wedge adder = sum)$$
$$\vee$$
$$((\text{ft}_a = stuck\_at\_zero \wedge sum = 0) \vee$$
$$(\text{ft}_a = no\_failure \wedge \text{ft}_1 \neq \text{ft}_2 \wedge adder = \neg sum) \vee$$
$$(\text{ft}_a = no\_failure \wedge \text{ft}_1 = inverted = \text{ft}_2 \wedge adder = sum))))$$

5 Fault Trees and Compositions

Associated with the retrenchment PO is the (one step) retrenchment simulation relationship, obtained from the PO by replacing the top level implication by a conjunction, and removing the existential quantification. It describes those pairs of steps of which the PO speaks, which make its antecedent valid:

$$G(u,v) \wedge P_{Op}(i,j,u,v) \wedge Op_C(v,j,v',p) \wedge Op_A(u,i,u',o) \wedge$$
$$((G(u',v') \wedge O_{Op}(o,p;u',v',u,v,i,j)) \vee C_{Op}(u',v',o,p;u,v,i,j))$$

and is written $(u\text{ -}(i, Op_A, o)\text{-> } u') \, \Sigma^1 \, (v\text{ -}(j, Op_C, p)\text{-> } v')$. We will now show that in the present context it can be used to extract fault trees for the *Bit* operation.

In a typical fault of Bit_C the input is 0 while the output is 1, in contrast to the ideal behaviour of Bit_A which has 0 for both. We know already that these abstract and concrete values validate the PO. Let Σ^1_{Bit} be the simulation relation for Bit (which is derived from the previous section's PO verification condition for Bit by applying the syntactic modifications mentioned). We conjoin expressions defining the values of i, j, o as 0 and p as 1, to Σ^1_{Bit}, and obtain:

$$i = 0 \wedge o = 0 \wedge j = 0 \wedge p = 1 \wedge \Sigma^1_{Bit}$$

Applying the substitutions and simplifying, we infer:

$$\text{true} \wedge \text{true} \wedge ((\text{ft} = no\_failure \wedge \text{false}) \vee (\text{ft} = inverted \wedge \text{true})) \wedge$$
$$\text{true} \wedge ((\text{true} \wedge \text{ft} = no\_failure \wedge \text{false}) \vee (\text{ft} = inverted \wedge \text{true}))$$

The only way that this can be true is if ft $= inverted$ holds. We have derived the cause of the fault from the definition of the fault's behaviour. A fault tree could now be constructed with the fault definition as top level event and its inferred cause, ft $= inverted$, as its child.

A similar technique could yield a fault tree for the $Adder$ operation, consisting of a single cause $\text{ft}_a = stuck\_at\_zero$, if the fault concerned concrete inputs $0, 1$ say and concrete output 0.

It will not have escaped the reader's notice that we are performing a kind of resolution to derive the fault tree. How then does it fare with compound operations such as $Main$? Operations such as $Main$ raise the question of how to understand $Main$'s retrenchment in the context of the retrenchments of its components. Preferably, we want to understand the former in terms of a parallel and sequential composition of the latter. Now, sequential composition of retrenchments has been explored in some depth in [22] but it turns out that a completely different notion of sequential composition is appropriate here.

We require a notion of composition that gathers any of the erroneous or degraded cases that arise during the information flow, into the concession of the composed retrenchment, leaving only the completely fault-free cases for the output relation. That there is some choice in the matter arises because, in this paper, the information flow is via the inputs and outputs rather than the state. Since O and C are in disjunction, a true fact about I/O can be accomodated in either O or C without changing the value of $O \vee C$. Several things conspire to make our goal an achievable one:

– Each operation is a total relation.
– In each operation the various correct and degraded cases are disjoint.
– The various output and concedes relations have been carefully structured.
– $Adder$'s within relation has deliberately been made unrestrictive.

Suppose we sequentially compose two retrenchments, each with trivial state $*$. Dropping the true retrieve relation and all mention of the state for economy's sake, the first retrenchment will give rise to a simulation relationship:

$$P^{\text{I}}_{Op}(i, j) \wedge Op^{\text{I}}_C(j, c) \wedge Op^{\text{I}}_A(i, b) \wedge (O^{\text{I}}_{Op}(b, c; i, j) \vee C^{\text{I}}_{Op}(b, c; i, j))$$

and the second one, a simulation relationship:

$$P^{\text{II}}_{Op}(b, c) \wedge Op^{\text{II}}_C(c, p) \wedge Op^{\text{II}}_A(b, o) \wedge (O^{\text{II}}_{Op}(o, p; b, c) \vee C^{\text{II}}_{Op}(o, p; b, c))$$

The distributive law applied to the conjunction of these yields a simulation:

$$P_{Op}^{I;II}(i,j) \wedge Op_C^{I;II}(j,p) \wedge Op_A^{I;II}(i,o) \wedge (O_{Op}^{I;II}(o,p;i,j) \vee C_{Op}^{I;II}(o,p;i,j))$$

where we define:

$$Op_A^{I;II} = Op_A^I; Op_A^{II} \qquad P_{Op}^{I;II} = P_{Op}^I$$
$$Op_C^{I;II} = Op_C^I; Op_C^{II} \qquad O_{Op}^{I;II} = O_{Op}^I; O_{Op}^{II}$$
$$C_{Op}^{I;II} = O_{Op}^I; C_{Op}^{II} \vee C_{Op}^I; O_{Op}^{II} \vee C_{Op}^I; C_{Op}^{II}$$

with ; denoting the usual composition of relations. Provided that $(O_{Op}^I \vee C_{Op}^I) \Rightarrow P_{Op}^{II}$ then all composable individual steps described by the individual retrenchments will survive to the composition. This simulation relationship can be understood as arising from a composed retrenchment with data $P_{Op}^{I;II}, O_{Op}^{I;II}, C_{Op}^{I;II}$ and trivial $G^{I;II}$. We re-emphasise that this is not the only viable definition of sequential composition for retrenchments, particularly in view of the special conditions that have to hold for it to be well defined.

Parallel composition is similar and easier. Again we have a conjunction, this time of simulation relationships acting on disjoint spaces. Denoting parallel composition by | (logically a conjunction), we get a simulation relationship corresponding to the data:

$$Op_A^{I|II} = Op_A^I | Op_A^{II} \qquad P_{Op}^{I|II} = P_{Op}^I | P_{Op}^{II}$$
$$Op_C^{I|II} = Op_C^I | Op_C^{II} \qquad O_{Op}^{I|II} = O_{Op}^I | O_{Op}^{II}$$
$$C_{Op}^{I|II} = O_{Op}^I | C_{Op}^{II} \vee C_{Op}^I | O_{Op}^{II} \vee C_{Op}^I | C_{Op}^{II}$$

It is not hard to see that doing the above for two *Bits* composed in parallel, with the outcome sequentially composed with an *Adder*, yields retrenchment data equivalent (in the variables' and other symbols' natural interpretations[2]) to that given for *Main*[3].

We note that if each of $O_{Op}^I, C_{Op}^I, O_{Op}^{II}, C_{Op}^{II}$, is a disjunction of cases, then all of $C_{Op}^{I;II}, C_{Op}^{I|II}$ proliferate the case analysis via the distributive law. With this observation, we can outline the construction of multilevel fault trees from a composed retrenchment as follows, using our *Main* operation with abstract inputs $r_1 \neq r_2$ and concrete output $sum = 0$ as a running example.

Our technique is to resolve the values defining the fault with the composed simulation relation Σ_{Main}^I, to yield any intermediate values needed, and apply these to the decomposition of the composed concedes relation whose structure

---

[2] Note that we are *not* claiming propositional equivalence here.

[3] We emphasise once more that this is a consequence of *design*, and the design of the retrenchment data for *Main* in particular. It is very easy to write down different retrenchment data for *Main*, which are equally adept at discharging the retrenchment operation PO for *Main*, but which do not arise as the composition of the retrenchment data for *Main*'s subcomponents.

will reveal the required fault tree. We need to work with both Σ^1_{Main} and C_{Main} as the latter need not contain all the data required during the decomposition.

The top level constructor of our system is a sequential composition, so the top level event of the fault tree corresponds to a collection of values that makes the composed simulation relation $(* \text{-}(i, Op^{I;II}_A, o)\text{->} *)\ \Sigma^1\ (* \text{-}(j, Op^{I;II}_C, p)\text{->} *)$, and specifically the concession $C^{I;II}_{Op}$, valid. Here II refers to *Adder* and I refers to two *Bits* in parallel. If $C^{I;II}_{Op}$ is a disjunction of cases, the ones that are true in the given valuation are the possible alternative causes of the fault, and lead to a disjunctive branching at the next level of the fault tree.

In our example we have two validated alternatives in C_{Main}, namely $(\text{ft}_a = stuck\_at\_zero \land sum = 0)$ and $(\text{ft}_a = no\_failure \land \text{ft}_1 \neq \text{ft}_2 \land adder = \neg sum)$. The first of these gives a bottom level explanation of the fault and needs no further analysis, closing off that branch of the fault tree. The second asserts $\text{ft}_a = no\_failure$ for the *Adder* component, and so does need further analysis.

We now decompose the composed simulation relation in a reversal of the process described above. This involves finding intermediate abstract and concrete values b_1, b_2, c_1, c_2, that can act as existential witnesses for both the (de)composed simulation relation, and for the decomposition of $C^I_{Bits}; O^{II}_{Adder}$, where C^I_{Bits} reduces to $O_{Bit_1}|C_{Bit_2} \lor C_{Bit_1}|O_{Bit_2}$. This gives a three way disjunctive structure at the top level of the fault tree.[4] (The third disjunct of C^I_{Bits} namely $C_{Bit_1}|C_{Bit_2}$ is excluded by $\text{ft}_1 \neq \text{ft}_2$ which we just derived.)

Summarising, either the *Adder* failed, or one but not the other of the two *Bits* failed. Aggregating the intermediate value cases which yield the same fault tree structure, each of the latter two options can now be seen as a conjunction of three facts:

1. $Bit_{(1+k)}$ failed.
2. $Bit_{(1+(1-k))}$ functioned correctly.
3. The *Adder* functioned correctly.

The first two conjuncts come from the parallel decomposition of C^I_{Bits} (which is a conjunction), while the third comes from the instantiation of the existential witness b_1, b_2, c_1, c_2, during the sequential decomposition of $C^I_{Bits}; O^{II}_{Adder}$ (this being $(\exists b_1, b_2, c_1, c_2 \bullet C^I_{Bits}((b_1, b_2), (c_1, c_2), \ldots) \land O^{II}_{Adder}((b_1, b_2), (c_1, c_2)))$).

With these three alternatives, we have derived the structure of the fault tree for this example as generated by the FSAP/NuSMV-SA toolkit [11]. See Fig. 1 (reproduced, with the authors' permission). It is not hard to see that the techniques described can be applied to more deeply nested compositions, to give derivations of fault trees for faults that occur deeper in the structure of a complex system. The derivation of the fault trees that we have outlined gives rise to fresh validation opportunities, by comparing this kind of derivation with more conventional routes.

---

[4] We have silently merged cases in which distinct data values lead to the same fault tree, for clarity of exposition.

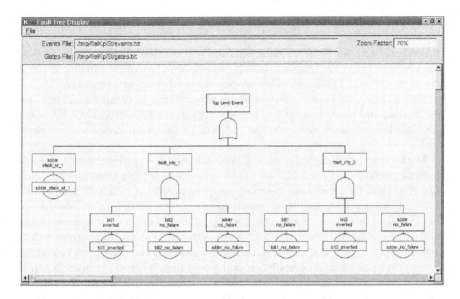

Fig. 1. The fault tree for the *Adder* example, from [11].

6 Model Checking

The fault tree analysis above was sensitive to the temporal order of the component transitions in a sequential composition, via the before/after ingredients of the retrenchment simulation relationship. A similar sensitivity is a feature of the model checking of temporal properties, so we can easily imagine that a retrenchment approach could also prove profitable in that sphere. Once more following [11], the ideal *Main* operation satisfies:

$$\mathbf{AG}(r_1 = 0 \wedge r_2 = 0 \; \rightarrow \; adder = 0)$$

while the degraded system satisfies:

$$\mathbf{AG}(s_1 = 0 \wedge s_2 = 0 \wedge sum \neq 0 \; \rightarrow \; (\mathrm{ft}_1 = inverted \vee \mathrm{ft}_2 = inverted))$$

and these are checkable via the model checker in the FSAP/NuSMV-SA safety analysis platform. Conventional formal techniques (i.e. refinement) cannot relate these two facts. However, in these two facts, it is not hard to recognise a very similar situation to the one analysed above, and so with retrenchment composition/decomposition techniques, we can expect a similar degree of success to that which we enjoyed for fault trees. To be sure there are technical issues to do with the integration of the retrenchment viewpoint and the temporal viewpoint, which will clutter the development somewhat, but these will not be onerous. The resulting analysis leads to fresh validation opportunities, as above.

7   Conclusions

In the preceding sections we have outlined a transition system model of fault injection similar to the one used in [11], and shown that while refinement struggles to describe the fault injection process, retrenchment accomplishes this in a natural manner. Of course the two faults we explored in detail are merely representative, and other typical faults dealt with in the FSAP/NuSMV-SA safety analysis platform, such as *random* or *glitch* could be accomodated without problems.

With fault injection under control, we indicated how retrenchment composition and decomposition could lead to the generation of fault trees for the simple *Adder* system. Retrenchment composition/decomposition is investigated in [20], [21], and the application of comparable ideas here is a gratifying endorsement of this family of techniques. Of course there is more left out than discussed, and a full treatment of the relationship between retrenchment and fault trees will be given elsewhere. (For instance the distinct results that can arise from monotonic versus non-monotonic analysis when faulty and non-faulty cases overlap can be brought out by finetuning the fault tree extraction algorithm.) Similar remarks apply to the promising interaction between retrenchment and model checking, which will also be pursued elsewhere.

Acknowledgements. The authors would like to express their thanks to Marco Bozzano and Adolfo Villafiorita for their feedback on an earlier version of this paper.

References

1. J R Abrial. *The B-Book: Assigning Programs to Meanings*. Cambridge University Press, 1996.
2. R Banach. Retrenchment and system properties. Submitted.
3. R Banach and C Jeske. Output retrenchments, defaults, stronger compositions, feature engineering. Submitted.
4. R Banach and M Poppleton. Engineering and theoretical underpinnings of retrenchment. Submitted.
5. R Banach and M Poppleton. Retrenchment: An engineering variation on refinement. *B'98: Recent Advances in the Development and Use of the B Method: Second International B Conference, Montpellier, France, LNCS*, 1393:129–147, 1998.
6. R Banach and M Poppleton. Retrenchment and punctured simulation. *Proc. IFM-99, Springer*, Araki, Gallway, Taguchi (eds.):457–476, 1999.
7. R Banach and M Poppleton. Sharp retrenchment, modulated refinement and punctured simulation. *Form. Asp. Comp.*, 11:498–540, 1999.
8. R Banach and M Poppleton. Retrenching partial requirements into system definitions: A simple feature interaction case study. *Requirements Engineering Journal*, 8:266–288, 2003.
9. E Boiten and J Derrick. Io-refinement in Z. In A Evans, D Duke, and T Clark, editors, *Electronic Workshops in Computing*. Springer-Verlag, September 1998. Proc. Third BCS-FACS Northern Formal Methods Workshop. Ilkley, U.K.

10. J P Bowen and S Stavridou. Formal methods and software safety. In H. H. Frey, editor, *Safety of Computer Control Systems (SAFECOMP)*, pages 93–98. Pergamon Press, October 1992. Proc. IFAC Symposium, Zurich, Switzerland.

11. M Bozzano and A Villafiorita. Improving system reliability via model checking: The FSAP/NuSMV-SA safety analysis platform. *Computer Safety, Reliability, and Security, LNCS*, 2788:49–62, 2003.

12. M Bozzano and A Villafiorita. Integrating fault tree analysis with event ordering information. *Proc. ESREL 2003*, pages 247–254, 2003.

13. M Bozzano, A Villafiorita, et al. ESACS: An integrated methodology for design and safety analysis of complex systems. *Proc. ESREL 2003*, pages 237–245, 2003.

14. M Bozzano, A Villafiorita, et al. Improving safety assessment of complex systems: An industrial case study. *International Symposium of Formal Methods Europe (FME 2003), Pisa, Italy, LNCS*, 2805:208–222, September 2003.

15. W P de Roever and K Engelhardt. *Data Refinement Model-Oriented Proof methods and their Comparison*. Cambridge University Press, 1998.

16. J Derrick and E Boiten. *Refinement in Z and Object-Z: Foundations and Advanced Applications*. Springer-Verlag UK, 2001.

17. J Jacky. *The Way of Z*. Cambridge University Press, 1997.

18. S Liu and R Adams. Limitations of formal methods and an approach to improvement. *Proc. 1995 Asia-Pacific Software Engineering Conference (APSEC'95), IEEE Computer Society Press, Brisbane, Australia*, pages 498–507, December 1995.

19. S Liu, V Stavridou, and B Duterte. The practice of formal methods in safety-critical systems. *The Journal of Systems and Software*, 28(1):77–87, January 1995.

20. M Poppleton and R Banach. Structuring retrenchments in B by decomposition. *International Symposium of Formal Methods Europe (FME 2003), Pisa, Italy, LNCS*, 2805:814–833, September 2003.

21. M Poppleton and R Banach. Requirements validation by lifting retrenchments in B. In *Proc. 9th IEEE International Conference on Engineering of Complex Computer Systems (ICECCS-04), Florence, Italy*. IEEE Computer Society Press, 2004. to appear.

22. M R Poppleton. *Formal methods for Continuous Systems: Liberalising Refinement in B*. PhD thesis, University of Manchester, Computer Science Dept., 2001.

23. B Potter, J Sinclair, and D Till. *An Introduction to Formal Specification and Z*. Prentice Hall, second edition, 1996.

24. S Schneider. *The B-Method: An Introduction*. PALGRAVE, 2001.

25. E Sekerinski and K Sere. *Program Development by Refinement: Case Studies Using the B-Method*. Springer, 1998.

26. J M Spivey. *The Z Notation: A Reference Manual*. Prentice-Hall, 1989.

27. J Woodcock and J Davies. *Using Z, Specification, Refinement and Proof*. Prentice Hall, 1996.

28. J C P Woodcock and C C Morgan. Refinement of state-based concurrent systems. *Formal Methods in Software Development, LNCS*, 428, 1990.

The Effects on Reliability of Integration of Aircraft Systems Based on Integrated Modular Avionics

Dominick Rehage[1], Udo B. Carl[1], Maximilian Merkel[1], and Andreas Vahl[2]

[1] Hamburg University of Technology,
Institute for Aircraft Systems Engineering, 21071 Hamburg, Germany
{rehage,carl,merkel}@tuhh.de
http://www.tuhh.de/fst
[2] Airbus Deutschland GmbH,
Kreetslag 10, 21129 Hamburg, Germany
andreas.vahl@airbus.com

Abstract. The integration of aircraft systems – based on INTEGRATED MODULAR AVIONICS (IMA) – has significant effects on reliability. This paper presents the state of development of a software–tool for interactive reliability analysis and evaluation of aircraft system configurations on the IMA platform. For this, a hybrid system model of each aircraft system, being composed of a reliability block diagram model and a model of hierarchical, concurrent finite state machines, is essential. Within the area of reliability, different aircraft system models can be analyzed after they have been logically combined. This novel functionality provides a platform for systems engineers, enabling the evaluation of the effects of system integration by reliability calculations as well as redundancy management in a fault–free state and in cases of component failures.

1 Introduction

The objective pursued with the concept of INTEGRATED MODULAR AVIONICS (IMA) is the integration of the application–specific control and monitoring functions of different air-craft systems on standardized electronic computing modules ("horizontal integration"). This leads to a more hardware–economic concept than the typical function specific LINE REPLACEABLE UNITS (LRU) used nowadays, arranged in single lane channels consisting of computing and peripheral systems (actuation, sensors etc.). This integration of differ-ent aircraft systems on modules consequently causes many common points, resulting in dependencies between those systems.

The design of aircraft systems based on IMA is a very complex and multidisciplinary process in the fields of avionic, communication and peripheral systems. System reliability is an essential part of aircraft system design and has to be considered from the very beginning of the design phase to reach an optimum for the product in costs and time. In this context, high reliability requirements drive the capabilities of aircraft systems to be fault tolerant and the invested degree of redundancy to fulfill these requirements is an indicator for the system complexity, which is concerning the IMA on a very high level.

During the design of aircrafts, systems engineers are confronted with the effects of system integration and they have to develop their system under questions like:

M. Heisel et al. (Eds.): SAFECOMP 2004, LNCS 3219, pp. 224–238, 2004.
© Springer-Verlag Berlin Heidelberg 2004

- *"What is the effect of a component failure on integrated aircraft systems assuming that the failure occurs on the IMA platform and induces the degradation of the system reliability or affects the failure propagation and reconfiguration?"*
- *"What effect has the integrated aircraft system on reliability of physically dependent systems?"*

Addressing these development challenges of aircraft systems this paper presents the state of development of the software–tool SYRELAN™ (SYTEM RELIABILITY ANALYSIS). This tool provides systems engineers with a computer aided development environment for reliability synthesis and analysis of aircraft systems based on IMA.

Basis for the aircraft system analysis and evaluation is a hybrid system model. The structural architecture of the fault tolerant aircraft systems are modelled in independent RELIABILITY BLOCK DIAGRAM (RBD) in *positive* logic. *Positive* logic means that the RBD–blocks are arranged to fulfill the system function and this leads to a mapping of the real system architecture. In order to represent the behavior of integrated systems under the event of component failures HIERARCHICAL, CONCURRENT FINITE STATE MACHINES (HCFSM) are operated in the background of each block within the RBD–model. This second modelling environment is used for visualization of failure propagation and reconfiguration processes within the redundancy management of a fault tolerant systems under the event of component failures.

During the system analysis various system states are to be analyzed in the hybrid system models (RBD, HCFSM) concurrently; starting from the nominal state without any component failure via several degraded system states caused by component failures until the state of system failure. For each of these states the failure probabilities are calculated in the RBD–models and the redundancy management is visualized by coloring the RBD–blocks with colors representing the current component states of the HCFSMs.

For IMA purposes the visualization of failure propagation and reconfiguration within the redundancy management is fulfilled integrative. This means, that failures of IMA components propagate across systems containing IMA components used in common. Furthermore, SYRELAN™ provides a novel functionality in this context making the logical combination of any aircraft systems possible. This functionality is essential for IMA systems, because it enables the evaluation of integration effects on reliability in a comfortable way. That means, that each of the aircraft systems based on IMA is modelled independently in RBD and HCFSMs. In order to analyze the reliability of whether physically dependent aircraft systems can be integrated on the same IMA module, SYRELAN™ provides the logical combination of RBD–models for any independent modelled aircraft systems, composed by the logical linking (**AND, OR**) of system blocks.

2   Models of Aircraft Systems Based on IMA

The software–tool SYRELAN™ provides system engineers with a RBD and an HCFSM environment for interactive system modelling of all aircraft systems of one aircraft type. This leads to a large number of hybrid system models where each of the models takes integration aspects of commonly used IMA resources into account. The logical combination of independently modelled hybrid system models is the basis for reliability analysis of integrated systems.

2.1 Hybrid System Model

In the first step a fault tolerant aircraft system architecture is modelled in the RBD–environment in the nominal state by linking RBD–blocks of components logically according to their functional dependency in the system architecture. In addition to this, the HCFSMs will be placed in the background of the RBD–model. The coupling of the two models occurs in both directions. From the RBD point of view the coupling exists in assignments of current component states of the HCFSMs to the RBD–blocks (Fig. 1). From the HCFSM point of view component failures are transferred from the RBD–blocks to the state machines that trigger the redundancy process.

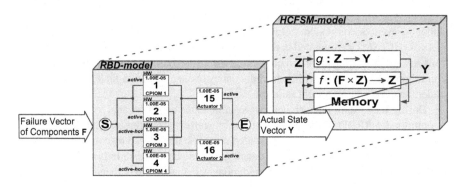

Fig. 1. Hybrid system model: RBD–model and HCFSM–model

RBD–Model

For fault tolerant aircraft system modelling in RBD it is necessary to determine a TOP EVENT depending on which the reliability modelling and analysis can be performed. This event specifies system states that are to be analyzed. BOOLEAN algebra describes the system model mathematically by using stochastically independent BOOLEAN indicator variables for each component [SCHNEE01]

$$K_i = 1 \qquad \text{component } K_i \text{ is up,} \tag{1}$$
$$K_i = 0 \qquad \text{component } K_i \text{ is down.} \tag{2}$$

The expected value of the indicator variable K_i is the *survivor function*

$$E[K_i] = 0 \cdot P[K_i = 0] + 1 \cdot P[K_i = 1] = P[K_i = 1]. \tag{3}$$

The reliability R_i of a component i is defined as the probability $P[K_i = 1]$ that component is in functional state. Using an *exponential* distribution by considering a constant component *failure rate* λ_i per hour [1/h], the reliability is [VAH98]

$$R_i(t) = e^{\lambda_i t}. \tag{4}$$

In general, the component failure rate λ_i is a function of time (BATHTUB CURVE [VAH98]), but in case of aircraft systems the component failure rate λ_i is sufficiently constant between two periodical component checks. Therefore failure of components are independent of age and stochastically distributed [VAH98]. Under the assumption of fulfilling monotony conditions and logical linking (**AND, OR, NOT**) of the variables K_i the system function ϕ is (see example in subsection 3.1) [VAH98]

$$\phi(\mathbf{K}) = 1 \qquad \text{system } \phi \text{ is up,} \tag{5}$$

$$\phi(\mathbf{K}) = 0 \qquad \text{system } \phi \text{ is down} \tag{6}$$

$$\text{with} \quad \mathbf{K} = \{K_1, \ldots, K_i, \ldots, K_m\}. \tag{7}$$

HCFSM–Model

The second modelling environment is the area of HCFSMs. This model can be built after the structural design of the system architecture is completed in the RBD–model. The complete HCFSM–model presentation is a 6–tuple and is composed of an input vector $\mathbf{F}$, an output vector $\mathbf{Y}$, a set of internal states in the elements of the state vector $\mathbf{Z}$, a set of initial states in the elements of the initial state vector $\hat{\mathbf{Z}}$, a next–state function f, and an output function g (Fig. 1) [GAJ94,TEI97]

$$\left(\mathbf{F}, \mathbf{Y}, \mathbf{Z}, \hat{\mathbf{Z}} \subseteq \mathbf{Z}, f : \mathbf{F} \times \mathbf{Z} \to \mathbf{Z}, g : \mathbf{Z} \to \mathbf{Y} \right). \tag{8}$$

The vector elements are MOORE–HCFSMs representatives for each component K_i (7) referring to a block in the RBD–model, which are described in detail in [REH03]. Vector $\mathbf{Z}$ contains in its rows $(i = 1, \cdots, m)$ the sets of internal states for each of the HCFSMs which are connected with component K_i. In this context it is important to assume that each component K_i is connected with at least one HCFSM and each of the applied HCFSMs has at least two ("*active*", "*isolated*") and up to five states (Fig. 2). These states can be reached by starting at the failure–free state $\hat{\mathbf{Z}}$ at initial operation time ($t_0 = 0$), via several degraded system states ($t_s \geq t_0$), up to system failure. Input vector $\mathbf{F}$ contains the injected failures of components K_i. This condition "**NOT** K_i" leads to the activation of the next–state function f of the HCFSMs of that component K_i and cause transitions from the current HCFSM states into states "*isolated*". The output vector $\mathbf{Y}$ of a system represents the current states of the MOORE–HCFSMs which are forwarded to the blocks above, by use of color assignments for each of the HCFSM states.

For the purpose of modelling the redundancy management, various HCFSMs of a fault tolerant system have to be coupled. The couplings exist by means of dependencies on the next state function as function of internal system states, as well as a function of component failures of multiple used components. It allows failure propagation and reconfiguration processes in the system model.

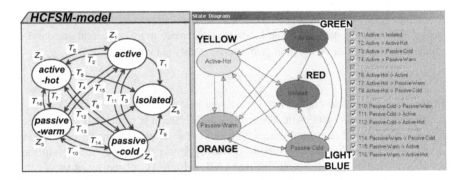

Fig. 2. States and transitions of an HCFSM and SyRelAn™ State Diagram

Each single HCFSM–model in the background of a RBD–block consists of up to five internal states $\{Z_1, \ldots, Z_5\}$ and up to 16 transitions $\{T_1, \ldots, T_{16}\}$ between the states, which define the next state functions using logical expressions as functions of states of HCFSMs neighbours (Fig. 2). In order to model the application specific HCFSM–model of an aircraft system, it is necessary to choose the transitions of each single HCFSM of the complete model in the State Diagram editor of SyRelAn™ in Fig. 2.

The variety of the internal states of the HCFSMs is motivated by stages of degradation from the reliability point of view. The next paragraph describes this context depending on the *failure rate* λ, which indicates the load of a stand–by component [VDI86]. It also contains the colors and *endings* representing the states of the HCFSMs. In case of current states of HCFSMs these states are transferred to the blocks above by assigning the corresponding colors in order to visualize the system states in the RBD–model.

"active" ← **GREEN**: From the start of the mission, the working component **a** is subjected to full stress. The failure rate is λ_a. The *ending* is "**a**".

"active–hot" ← **YELLOW**: From the beginning of the mission, reserve element **h** is subjected to the same stress as the actual working component **a**. For the failure rate, the following applies: $\lambda_h = \lambda_a$. The *ending* is "**h**".

"passive–warm" ← **ORANGE**: The reserve element **w** is subjected to less stress until failure of working component **a**, (or until **w** itself fails in advance). For the failure rate, the following applies: $0 < \lambda_w < \lambda_a$. The *ending* is "**w**".

"passive–cold" ← **LIGHT BLUE**: Until failure of working component **a**, reserve element **c** is not subjected to any stress. For the failure rate, the following applies: $\lambda_c = 0$. The *ending* is "**c**".

"isolated" ← **RED**: Failure state of component. The *ending* is "**i**".

The next–state function f, which contains the conditions for changing the actual state of an HCFSM to a succession state in the event of a component failure underlies a special syntax in SyRelAn™. In the corresponding transitions the equations, which combine states of several HCFSMs logically (**AND**: "&", **OR**: "|", **NOT**: "~") must be "**TRUE**" to fulfill the state transition.

To address the states of HCFSMs it is necessary to distinguish between blocks, which operate only one or multiple HCFSMs in the background. The following equations provide the syntax for addressing a state of a single HCFSM in the background of a block (9) and a state of one of several HCFSMs in the background of a block (10)

$$component : i, ending : \{a, h, w, c, i\} \quad \forall \quad K_i \in \mathbf{K}, \tag{9}$$

$$component : i, HCFSM : l, ending : \{a, h, w, c, i\} \tag{10}$$

$$\forall \quad K_i \in \mathbf{K} \quad \text{and} \quad l \in [1, d(i)] \quad \text{with} \quad d(i) \in I\!N.$$

Two examples are subsequently represented to clarify this syntax. $2, h$ addresses the state "*active–**h**ot*" of component K_2 related to a RBD–block with a single HCFSM in the background and $3, 7, c$ addresses the state "*passive–**c**old*" of HCFSM 7 of component K_3 in the background of its related RBD–block with several HCFSMs.

To model a fault tolerant aircraft system under the aspects of reliability and redundancy management various hardware and software components have to be represented. Therefore, SYRELAN™ provides three categories of blocks. Fig. 3 shows the modelling options for two hardware blocks and one software block.

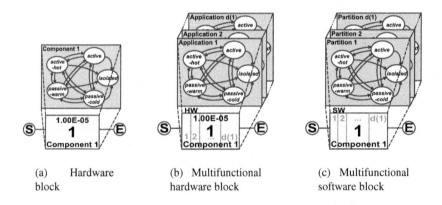

(a)   Hardware block

(b) Multifunctional hardware block

(c) Multifunctional software block

Fig. 3. Three RBD–block categories with its HCFSMs

The use of these blocks depends on the specific application of the component modelled by this block. The simple *hardware block* is used in aircraft system modelling for single used components (e.g. actuators, sensors etc.) and represents them with a constant *failure rate* λ (Fig. 3(a)). Within the redundancy management this block contains one HCFSM with its states and transitions in the complete system context.

A specific version of a *hardware block* is a *multifunctional hardware block*. This type of block incorporates the same reliability characteristics as a *hardware block* but has the advantage of components used in common (e.g. bus, ethernet switch etc.) to separate states of different applications by use of multiple HCFSMs. In case of a component failure all HCFSMs pass into the state *"isolated"* and the reliability reduces to zero.

The third category specifies the *multifunctional software block*. This block enables the modelling of different software applications within the RBD and further supports the characteristics of aircraft systems based on IMA. This is accomplished by separation of HCFSMs in the background of each *multifunctional software block*, which addresses the partitioning aspect of computing modules of the IMA systems. In the field of reliability the software blocks are failure–free ($R = 1$) or failed ($R = 0$) with respect to their HCFSMs. In contrast to the *multifunctional hardware block* an HCFSM of the *multifunctional software block* can be declared as failed independently. For this reason every HCFSM is associated with another RBD hardware block in an aircraft system model (e.g. Fig. 7: HCFSM 1 of K_7 is associated with K_{23}, see dashed arrow in system $\phi(\mathbf{K}_{aileron\ control})$). An HCFSM of a *multifunctional software block* in state *"isolated"* leads to a degraded system function (7) concerning the *minimal path* of associated RBD hardware block and, of course, the HCFSM of the *multifunctional software block*.

2.2 Superposition of Hybrid System Models

In order to take IMA specific characteristics of aircraft systems into account it is necessary to distinguish between components, which are used in a single aircraft system only, and those, which are used in various aircraft systems. Therefore SYRELAN™ offers different component lists. All components within an aircraft project, e.g. A380 or 7E7, are contained in the set of aircraft components

$$\mathbf{K_{AC}} = \{K_1, \dots, K_i, \dots, K_m\}. \tag{11}$$

All system models within an aircraft project access a subset of aircraft components (11), which is expressed by the transpose of system component vector

$$\mathbf{K_{SC}} = (\mathbf{K_{SC1}}, \dots, \mathbf{K_{SCj}}, \dots, \mathbf{K_{SCn}})^{\mathrm{T}} \tag{12}$$

$$\text{with} \quad \mathbf{K_{SCj}} \subseteq \mathbf{K_{AC}} \quad \forall \quad j = 1, \dots, n. \tag{13}$$

The corresponding transpose of the system vector with application of formula (5) is

$$\phi(\mathbf{K_{SC}}) = (\phi(\mathbf{K_{SC1}}), \dots, \phi(\mathbf{K_{SCj}}), \dots, \phi(\mathbf{K_{SCn}}))^{\mathrm{T}}. \tag{14}$$

An important property of various aircraft system models is that IMA based system models are able to access so-called *global blocks* (every *global block* is one of the three block types in figure 3). All of these *global blocks* are integral part of different system models. This means, that the *global blocks* represent characteristics of IMA components used common and thus have effects on the reliability of all RBD–models as well as all HCFSM–models of different systems using them (Fig. 4). Hence, current state variations of the *global block* HCFSMs lead to activation of the redundancy management of all systems using this blocks. If current state variations of the *global blocks* cause the activation of an HCFSM transition into the state *"isolated"*, the reliability of systems, which apply these, will be reduced. This is because the *global block* components are

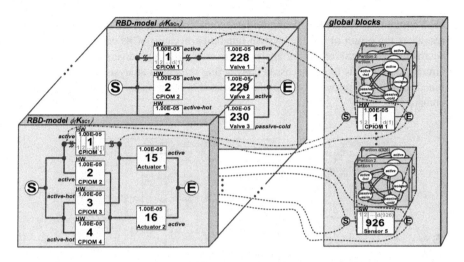

Fig. 4. Coupling of hybrid system models by using *global blocks*

treated as components, which are mapped in different systems (Fig. 4: K_1 of $\phi(\mathbf{K_{SC1}})$ and $\phi(\mathbf{K_{SCn}})$), but their existence in the context of all system models is unique according to their physically occurrence. The transpose of vector $\mathbf{K_{GC}}$ (15) consists of the *global block* components of each aircraft system within the aircraft project. The *global block* components are generated by building up the intersection of the sets of aircraft system components (16) with each other, because the condition of a *global block* component demands a component occurrence in more than one aircraft system.

$$\mathbf{K_{GC}} = (\mathbf{K_{GC1}}, \ldots, \mathbf{K_{GCj}}, \ldots, \mathbf{K_{GCn}})^{\mathrm{T}} \qquad (15)$$

$$\text{with} \quad \mathbf{K_{GCj}} = \{\mathbf{K_{SCj}} \cap \mathbf{K_{SCq}}\} \quad \forall \quad j,q = 1, \ldots, n \quad \text{and} \quad j \neq q. \qquad (16)$$

2.3 Logical Combination of Hybrid System Models

In order to analyze the effects on reliability of integration of aircraft systems based on IMA, it is necessary to combine integrated systems logically in the case of dependency of functional effects. Regarding aircraft systems with independent functional effects, integration has no significant effects on reliability, which is comparable to the reliability of an aircraft system operated on LRU computing resources – except for architectural differences of both avionic systems. The reliability becomes a crucial factor of system analysis in case of different aircraft systems are dependent on their functional behaviour. An example is the reliability analysis of an aircraft *rudder control* and *engine control* system. These two aircraft systems have to be analyzed independently from each other, as well as combined in a second analysis. The dependency between both systems leads to higher reliability requirements than the requirement of each single system, since a loss of both systems causes the loss of aircraft control ("*catastrophical*" failure event). In this context it is necessary to analyze whether both systems can be integrated on

IMA computing resources with appropriate redundancy level or are the IMA computing resources the origin of too low system reliability, because of its common point characteristic. Within the reliability analysis, the integration and diversification aspect of aircraft systems has to be discussed considering reliability analysis of logically combined aircraft systems with IMA components used in common used or on separated IMA components.

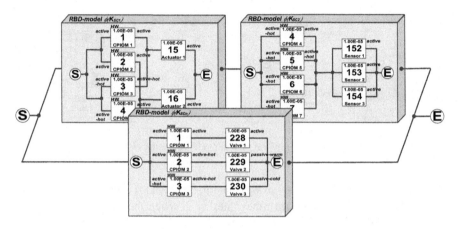

Fig. 5. Logical combinig of system models

Fig. 5 shows the possibilities to combine aircraft systems logically. In this case, three systems are combined on RBD system level, following the syntax of logic **AND** ($\wedge$) or **OR** ($\vee$) by depending on elements of the system vector (14). The set of components of logically combined aircraft systems $\mathbf{K_{LC}}$ is the union of the sets of system components $\mathbf{K_{SCj}}$ (13), which are involved in the combining process. Referring to Fig. 5 this is

$$\phi(\mathbf{K_{LC}}) = [\phi(\mathbf{K_{SC1}}) \wedge \phi(\mathbf{K_{SC2}})] \vee \phi(\mathbf{K_{SCn}}) \qquad (17)$$

$$\text{with} \quad \mathbf{K_{LC}} = \{\mathbf{K_{SC1}} \cup \mathbf{K_{SC2}} \cup \mathbf{K_{SCn}}\} . \qquad (18)$$

3   Analysis of Aircraft System Models Based on IMA

The analysis of RBD-models and HCFSM-models is performed separately for both model areas. However, the effects of component failures and state transitions of HCFSMs are interchanged.

3.1   Reliability Analysis

For reliability analysis of single and logically combined aircraft systems the CAOS (COMPUTER AIDED ORTHOGONALISATION SYSTEM) algorithm is applied for orthogonalisation processes of their BOOLEAN system functions $\phi(\mathbf{K_{SC}})$ (14) [VAH98]. Orthogonalisation means, in this case, that products of all disjunctive terms of a BOOLEAN system function (*minimal paths* M_r) are exclusive and thus zero [VAH98]. In case of system $\phi(\mathbf{K_{SC1}})$ in figure 5 the system function is

$$\phi(\mathbf{K_{SC1}}) = \phi(K_1, K_2, K_3, K_4, K_{15}, K_{16}), \tag{19}$$

$$\phi(\mathbf{K_{SC1}}) = K_1 K_{15} \vee K_2 K_{16} \vee K_3 K_{15} \vee K_4 K_{16} = M_1 \vee M_2 \vee M_3 \vee M_4. \tag{20}$$

After application of the CAOS orthogonalisation algorithm with its condition of orthogonalisation

$$M_r \cdot M_s = 0 \quad \text{with} \quad r, s = 1, 2, 3, 4 \quad \text{and} \quad r \neq s \tag{21}$$

the system function is in an unique linear form, which enables the application of real algebraic operators. By considering indicator variables as binary stochastical variables with the probability distribution (4), this leads to ($F_i = 1 - R_i$, see formula (4))

$$E[\phi(\mathbf{K_{SC1}})] = E[K_1 K_{15} + K_2 K_{16}\overline{K_1 K_{15}} + K_3 K_{15}\overline{K_1}\ \overline{K_2 K_{16}} + \cdots \tag{22}$$
$$\cdots + K_4 K_{16}\overline{K_2}\ \overline{K_{15}} + K_4 K_{15} K_{16}\overline{K_1}\ \overline{K_2}\ \overline{K_3}\ \overline{K_3}],$$

$$R_{SC1} = R_1 R_{15} + R_2 R_{16} F_1 + R_2 R_{16} F_{15} + R_3 R_{15} F_1 F_2 + \cdots \tag{23}$$
$$\cdots + R_3 R_{15} F_1 F_{16} + R_4 R_{16} F_2 F_{15} + R_4 R_{15} R_{16} F_1 F_2 F_3$$

A major advantage of the orthogonalisation process is, that multiple used blocks of the same component within a RBD–model are only considered as a single physical component in the reliability calculations.

Furthermore, SYRELAN^{TM} enables the analysis of *degraded* system states, which defines the minimal operational requirements as well as k–out of–n systems, where n components exist in "*active*" redundancy, of which k are necessary to perform the required function [VAH98]. To take k–out of–n into account in the reliability analysis there is a dialog in SYRELAN^{TM} in order to enter logical equations Γ, which represent operational conditions of components. Thus, these logically combined components must be available in *minimal path* of the system functions $\phi(\mathbf{K}_{SC})$ (14) [VAH98].

3.2 Redundancy Management

The redundancy management of integrated aircraft systems based on IMA is to be considered as an important task within the system analysis. In general the objective of the redundancy management is to support systems engineers with a software–tool environment to simulate different strategies of reconfiguration (e.g. *priorities*) in a fault tolerant system before applying them in the target system as well as special discussion of IMA related problems as failure propagation process in the integrated system. For this purpose, SYRELAN^{TM} enables separate RBD and HCFSM modelling of each IMA resource and each aircraft system operating on this resource (Fig. 9: "SYSTEM TREE"). This supports systems engineers in analyzing the effects of IMA component failures by visualizing the impact within the failure propagation and reconfiguration processes on aircraft system

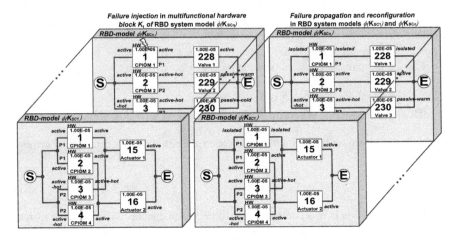

Fig. 6. *Redundancy management* on integrated aircraft systems

level. That means, that each state transition to a new current state of an HCFSM will be displayed in the RBD–model by a change of color of the corresponding RBD–block.

In this context Fig. 6 provides an example of the mode of operation of the *redundancy management*. As one can see, two systems ($\phi(\mathbf{K_{SC1}})$, $\phi(\mathbf{K_{SCn}})$) are modelled in their nominal system state on the left side. The use of IMA components $\{K_1, K_2, K_3\}$ (COMPUTING INPUT OUTPUT MODULE, CPIOM) leads to dependencies of both systems in the event of component failures of this entities used in common. This is demonstrated by *failure injection* in IMA component K_1 of system $\phi(\mathbf{K_{SCn}})$. It triggers the *redundancy management* process in system $\phi(\mathbf{K_{SCn}})$ in a first step, where both HCFSMs of K_1 pass over to current state "*isolated*" (Fig. 6: right side).

Afterwards, the *failure propagation* follows by state transition of the HCFSM of K_{228} to "*isolated*". The *reconfiguration* has to be fulfilled in consideration of *priority* P2 of CPIOM 2 to control the system. The transition T_1, from state "*active–hot*" to "*active*" of the second HCFSM of component K_2, describes this context in the following logical equation

$$\text{P2}: \quad T_1(K_2, \text{HCFSM 2}) = (1, 2, \text{i} \,\&\, 228, i) \,\&\, (2, 2, \text{h} \,\&\, 229, \text{w}). \tag{24}$$

This means equation (24) is "**TRUE**", because only the first control channel $\{K_1, K_{228}\}$ is "*isolated*" (condition of P2) and not the first and the second channel $\{K_2, K_{229}\}$ which is the condition of *priority* P3. After *reconfiguration* of system $\phi(\mathbf{K_{SCn}})$ the *redundancy management* propagates to system $\phi(\mathbf{K_{SC1}})$ in a second step, because HCFSM 1 of K_1 of this system is also in an "*isolated*" state. This leads to a *reconfiguration* process wherein redundant CPIOM 3 takes over control of actuator 1.

4   Application

The synthesis and analysis of fault tolerant aircraft systems based on IMA is related to nominal system state via degraded system states caused by component failures up to system failure. The example presented in this paper is the *roll control* system of a civil aircraft in the nominal state. The *roll control* consists of two systems: *aileron control* and *spoiler control*. The design question is whether both systems can be integrated on redundant CPIOMs of the IMA resource or is the implementation on separated redundant CPIOMs is necessary to fulfill the reliability requirement in the nominal system state of both systems.

The reliability requirement is related to the system classification of *roll control*. This is according to JAR 25 to be considered as *"catastrophic"* [JAA89]. The loss of this system in the low speed range can yield to fatal effects on the passengers and on fatal damage on aircraft and has a maximum failure probability of $F = 10^{-9}$ per flight hour. The TOP EVENT defines the system state, which is to be analysed in the RBD–model:

"Functionality of fault tolerant aircraft roll control system."

The RBD–model of an aileron control system is shown in Fig. 7. The HCFSM–model representation is shown by the block attributes, which describe the current states of the RBD–blocks. Usually, this is presented by colors of the RBD–blocks, which change in the event of component failures within the redundancy management process.

The system consists of two aileron hydraulic servo actuators on each wing. For pressurization, there are three hydraulic systems available (yellow, green, blue). As one can see there are two CPIOMs (CPIOM1: $\{K_1, K_7, K_{13}\}$ and CPIOM2: $\{K_2, K_8, K_{14}\}$) with their software blocks $\{K_7, K_8\}$ implemented. CPIOM1 controls the left and right outer aileron actuators (LO and RO) which are in an *"active"* mode in the nominal state. The first two of six partitions are occupied with the control applications represented by two HCFSMs (*multifunctional software block* of CPIOM1: K_7). CPIOM2 controls the

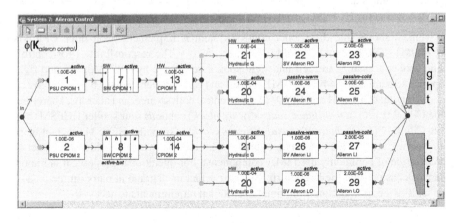

Fig. 7. *Aileron control*

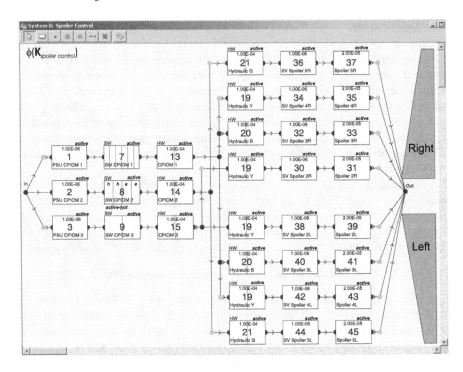

Fig. 8. *Spoiler control*

left and right inner aileron actuators (LI and RI), which are redundant in relation to the outer actuators. The controls of LI and RI actuators are located in the first two of four partitions of *multifunctional software block* K_8 of CPIOM2. These redundant actuator control channels are in the HCFSM current state *"active–hot"* from the software point of view and in the HCFSM current state *"passive–cold"* from the actuator point of view.

Fig. 8 shows that the spoiler control system is implemented on three CPIOMs (CPIOM1, CPIOM2 and CPIOM3: $\{K_3, K_9, K_{15}\}$). The responsibilities for controlling spoiler actuators are: left and right spoiler actuator 2 by CPIOM3, left and right spoiler actuator 3 and 4 by CPIOM1 and left and right spoiler actuator 5 by CPIOM2. It is obvious that CPIOM1 and CPIOM2 each control both spoilers and ailerons. Therefore, the CPIOM1 (K_7, a *multifunctional software block*) contains four spoiler HCFSMs and the CPIOM2 (K_8, a *multifunctional software block*) two spoiler HCFSMs each of them in *"active"* mode. This yields two hybrid system models, which consider the aspect of integration of commonly used IMA components. For operational purposes it is important to consider that the left and right spoiler actuators degrade in pairs. In the area of reliability the formulation of minimal operational requirements is necessary

$$\Gamma = [(K_{31} \wedge K_{39}) \vee (K_{33} \wedge K_{41}) \vee (K_{35} \wedge K_{43}) \vee (K_{37} \wedge K_{45})] . \tag{25}$$

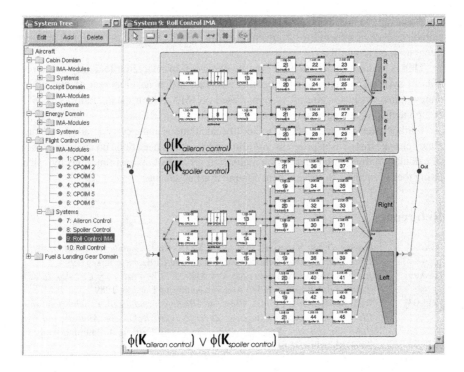

Fig. 9. Logical combining of *aileron control* and *spoiler control* in *roll control* system

In order to attain an answer whether the integration of *aileron control* and *spoiler control* on IMA resources fulfills the reliability requirements the systems must be logically combined (Fig. 9)

$$\phi(\mathbf{K_{LC}}) = \left[\phi(\mathbf{K}_{\text{aileron control}}) \vee \phi(\mathbf{K}_{\text{spoiler control}})\right] . \tag{26}$$

The reliability analysis of both logically combined systems based on the applied failure rates λ in Fig. 7 and 8 result in a failure probability of $F(t_s = 1\text{h}) = 3.47 \cdot 10^{-12}$. The conclusion of this failure probability is that the *aileron control* and *spoiler control* systems can be integrated on IMA resources used in common, because the reliability requirements are fulfilled. In this system the integration has no significant effect on reliability. The separation of these systems (e.g. *aileron control* on CPIOM 5 and 6) leads to less failure probability ($F(t_s = 1\text{h}) = 1.00 \cdot 10^{-12}$), but it is, nevertheless, not necessary to separate them.

5 Conclusion

This paper presents the approaches for a software–tool that can be applied for analysis and synthesis of fault tolerant aircraft systems based on IMA at a very early stage in system design. In this scope, SYRELAN™ provides with its hybrid system models a very suitable tool environment for system engineers to evaluate the effects of aircraft systems integration on reliability.

This is realised in SYRELAN™ by the extension of analyzing logically combined aircraft systems in the field of reliability and the further development of the redundancy management for aircraft systems based on IMA, which means failures of IMA components propagated throughout the relevant aircraft systems.

Further extension in the field of reliability calculations under consideration of redundancy characteristics is in progress. Additionally work has been done on an optimization of calculation time within the orthogonalisation process of system functions by calculating these functions in server client computer arrangements.

References

[Gaj94]   GAJSKI, D. D.; VAHID, F.; NARAYAN, S.; GONG, J.: *Specification and Design of Embedded Systems*. Prentice Hall, Englewood Cliffs, New Jersey, 1994.

[JAA89]   JOINT AVIATION AUTHORITIES: *1 to JAR 25.1309 – Advisory Circular Joint to Aviation Requirements*. Civil Aviation Authority, London, 1989.

[Reh03]   REHAGE, D., CARL, U. B., VAHL, A.: *Redundanzmanagement fehlertoleranter Flugzeug–Systemarchitekturen – Zuverlässigkeitstechnische Analyse und Synthese degradierter Systemzustände*. Deutscher Luft- und Raumfahrtkongress 2003, München, November 2003.

[Schnee01] SCHNEEWEISS, W. G.: *Reliability Modeling*. LiLoLe–Verlag, Hagen, 2001.

[Tei97]   TEICH, J.: *Digitale Hardware/Software–Systeme*. Springer Verlag, Berlin Heidelberg, 1997.

[Vah98]   VAHL, A.: *Interaktive Zuverlässigkeitsanalyse von Flugzeug–Systemarchitekturen*. Dissertation, Arbeitsbereich Flugzeug–Systemtechnik, Technische Unversität Hamburg–Harburg, Fortschritt–Berichte VDI, Reihe 10, Nr. 565, Düsseldorf, 1998.

[VDI86]   VEREIN DEUTSCHER INGENIEURE (HRSG.): *Mathematische Modelle für Redundanz*. VDI–Richtlinie 4008, VDI–Handbuch Technische Zuverlässigkeit, VDI–Verlag Düssledorf, 1986.

Automotive Telematics – Road Safety Versus IT Security?

Ralf G. Herrtwich

DaimlerChrysler AG, Research and Technology
Berlin, Germany

More and more vehicles are being equipped with communication devices. Whereas first phases of telematics deployment focussed on cellular telephone integration, future automotive communication channels will include broadband technologies such as Satellite Radio or Wireless LAN. Applications are manifold: they range from plain telephony or entertainment for vehicle drivers and passengers to more advanced vehicle-centric uses such as remote diagnosis, traffic-dependent navigation or electronic toll collection.

One particularly important goal for telematics is to increase road safety. Automated crash notification systems which call for help when a vehicle gets into an accident have been on the market for some time. A more recent development is to see a role for telematics not just in the aftermath of a crash, but in the stages before it. Vehicles getting involved in or exposed to hazardous situations (e.g., detecting some black ice on the road) may communicate the potential danger to approaching vehicles upstream and, thereby, prepare drivers to be alert.

With the opportunity of such applications rises the potential for misuse and malfunctioning. How can vehicle drivers trust the messages they receive? How can we prevent that malicious entities simulate road hazards and create traffic bottlenecks? How can it be avoided that drivers are being tracked and traced due to the messages sent by their vehicles? In the development of communication protocols for the applications mentioned before, these questions – so far – have received little attention. We will discuss methods and mechanisms that can help to prevent misuse and lack of confidentiality in these application scenarios.

Another completely different application domain in telematics is the downloading of data and code to the vehicle. With modern car functions increasingly being realized in software, modification of this software for error correction or function upgrading purposes becomes a common vehicle maintenance process. Through telematics, such operation could also be performed remotely – again, creating potential security and, in fact, road safety issues. We will discuss methods we believe to be appropriate for preventing loss of integrity and availability should such telematics applications be deployed.

M. Heisel et al. (Eds.): SAFECOMP 2004, LNCS 3219, p. 239, 2004.

Modular Formal Analysis of the Central Guardian in the Time-Triggered Architecture[*]

Holger Pfeifer and Friedrich W. von Henke

Fakultät für Informatik, Universität Ulm
D–89069 Ulm, Germany
{pfeifer|vhenke}@informatik.uni-ulm.de

Abstract. We present a modular formal analysis of the communication properties of the Time-Triggered Protocol TTP/C based on the guardian approach. The guardian is an independent component that employs static knowledge about the system to transform arbitrary node failures into failure modes that are covered by the rather optimistic fault hypothesis of TTP/C. Through a hierarchy of formal models, we give a precise description of the arguments that support the desired correctness properties of TTP/C. First, requirements for correct communication are expressed on an abstract level. By stepwise refinement we show that the abstract requirements are met under the optimistic fault hypothesis, and how the guardian model allows a broader class of failures be tolerated.

1 Introduction

The Time-Triggered Architecture (TTA) [1, 2, 3] is a distributed computer architecture for the implementation of highly dependable real-time systems. In particular, it targets on embedded control applications, such as *by-wire* systems in the automotive or aerospace industry [4]. For these safety-critical systems fault tolerance is of utmost importance. The Time-Triggered Protocol TTP/C constitutes the core of the communication level of the Time-Triggered Architecture. It furnishes a number of important services, such as atomic broadcast, consistent membership and protection against faulty nodes, that facilitate the development of these kinds of fault-tolerant real-time applications. However, these protocol mechanisms rely on a rather optimistic fault hypothesis and assume that a fault is either a reception fault or a consistent send fault of some node [5]. In order to extend the class of faults that can be tolerated a special hardware component, the so-called *guardian*, is introduced [6]. A guardian is an autonomous unit that protects the shared communication network against faulty behaviour of nodes by supervising their output. The original bus topology of the communication network employed local bus guardians, which were placed between the nodes and the bus. In the more recent star topology, central guardians are used in the hub of each star. The guardian makes use of static knowledge available in

---

[*] This research was supported by the European Commission under the IST project NEXT TTA (IST-2001-32111).

M. Heisel et al. (Eds.): SAFECOMP 2004, LNCS 3219, pp. 240–253, 2004.

a TTA-based system to transform arbitrary node failures into those that are covered by the optimistic fault hypothesis. For example, the time when a given node sends messages is statically determined in a TTA system and known *a priori*. The guardian can hence control the correct timing of messages by granting access to the network only during a node's pre-defined slot.

The goal of this work is to formally model TTP/C guardians and analyse their fault tolerance properties. In particular, we aim at describing the benefits of the guardians by giving a precise specification of the assumptions on which the derivation of the properties is based. Formal analysis can provide an additional source of confidence in correct behaviour of a system, which is particularly important in the context of safety-critical systems. Several aspects of TTP/C and related protocols have therefore been formally modelled and analysed, including clock synchronisation [7], group membership [8, 9, 10], and the startup procedure [11, 12]. A detailed overview of formal analysis work for the Time-Triggered Architecture is given by Rushby [13]. While so far the protocol algorithms of the time-triggered protocol have been the focus of the formal analyses cited above, we concentrate in this paper on the communication properties of TTP/C, thereby complementing and extending previous work.

To describe the behaviour and properties of the communication network and the guardians we develop various formal models, which are organised in a hierarchical fashion. We start by specifying the desired correctness properties of the communication in an abstract form. Subsequently, in a process of stepwise refinement, more detail is added to this initial abstract model. On the next level of the hierarchy, we consider a TTP/C system without guardians. We show that in this case the strong, optimistic fault hypothesis is necessary to guarantee correct communication. Another model then introduces guardians and specifies their behaviour. At this level we demonstrate that the optimistic assumptions can be relaxed, which leads to a fault hypothesis that covers a broader class of faults. The development of the models is in the spirit of, and builds on the work on modelling TTP-related aspects that has been carried out previously [7, 14, 9]. Specifically, it continues the use of the PVS specification and verification system [15] to both specify the model and the properties to be verified, and develop formal proofs that the model satisfies the stated properties. Previous work has demonstrated the suitability of PVS for this type of tasks.

The paper is organised as follows. In Sect. 2 we give a brief overview of the main aspects of the Time-Triggered Architecture. Section 3 describes the structure of the models and motivates their organisation. Details of the components of the formal models are elaborated in Sect. 4. Finally, we conclude in Sect. 5.

2   Brief Overview of the Time-Triggered Architecture

In this section we only briefly describe the main aspects of the Time-Triggered Architecture to the extent that is required for this paper. For more detailed presentations we refer to [3, 16, 17]. In a Time-Triggered Architecture system a set of *nodes* are interconnected by a real-time communication system. Nodes consist of the host computer, which runs the application software, and the communication controller, which accomplishes the time-triggered communication between different nodes. The nodes communicate via replicated shared media, the communication *channels*. There are two common physical interconnection topologies for TTA. Originally, the channels were replicated, passive buses, while in the more recent star topology the nodes are connected to replicated central star couplers, one for each of the two communication channels.

The distinguishing characteristic of time-triggered systems is that all system activities are initiated by the passage of time [18]. The autonomous TTA communication system periodically executes a time-division multiple access (TDMA) schedule. Thus, access to the network is divided into a series of intervals, called *slots*. Every node exclusively owns certain slots in which it is allowed to send messages. The times of the periodic sending actions are determined at design time of the system, and a static scheduling table, stored at each communication controller, contains the send and receive instants. It thus provides common knowledge about message timing to all nodes. A complete cycle during which every node has access to the network exactly once is called a *TDMA round*.

Messages are used as a life-sign of the respective sender, and whenever a node receives a correct frame on at least one of the channels it considers the sender correct. Correctness of a frame is determined by each receiving node according to a set of criteria. A node considers a frame correct, if it is well-timed, i. e. arrives within the boundaries of the TDMA slot, the physical signal obeys the line encoding rules, the frame passes a CRC check, and the sender and receiver agree on the distributed protocol state, the so-called *C-state*. One of the desired correctness properties of TTP/C is that all correct nodes always agree on whether or not a message is considered correct.

The Time-Triggered Protocol is designed to provide fault tolerance. In particular, the protocol has to ensure that non-faulty nodes receive consistent data despite the presence of possibly faulty nodes or a faulty communication channel. The provision of fault tolerance is based on a number of assumptions about the types, number, and frequency of faults. Altogether, these assumptions constitute the so-called *fault hypothesis*. The main assumption for the algorithms implemented in TTP/C is that a fault manifests itself as either a reception fault or a consistent send fault of some node [5]. In particular, the TTP/C services rely on transmission faults being consistent. That is, messages must be received correctly by either all non-faulty nodes or none. Moreover, nodes are assumed not to send messages outside their assigned slots. With respect to faults of the communication network, it is assumed that the channels cannot spontaneously create correct messages, and that messages are delivered either with some known bounded delay or never. With regard to the frequency and number of faults, TTP/C assumes that only one node becomes faulty during a TDMA round, and that there is at most one faulty node or one faulty channel at a time. However, the Time-Triggered Architecture can tolerate a broader class of faults by intensively using the static knowledge present in the TDMA schedule. This allows to transform arbitrary failure modes of nodes into either send or receive faults that can be tolerated by the protocol. The guardians monitor the temporal behaviour of the nodes and bar a faulty node from sending a message outside its designated slots. Thus, timing failures are effectively transformed into send faults.

Moreover, guardians also protect against so-called *slightly-off-specification* (SOS) faults, which are a particular class of *Byzantine* faults. A component is called SOS-faulty if it exhibits only marginally faulty behaviour that appears correct to some components, but faulty to others. A slightly-off-specification timing fault could occur if the transmission of a node terminates very close to the end of its scheduled transmission interval; thus, some receivers might accept the message while others might consider it mistimed. Because the duration of a particular transmission is known beforehand, the guardian can prevent such a cut-off scenario. A node must begin its transmission during a pre-defined period of time after the start of its slot, otherwise the guardian would terminate the right to access the communication network. Thus, the guardian can effectively prevent cut-off SOS faults if the transmission interval is chosen long enough to ensure that a transmission fits the interval whenever it is started in time. Specifically, TTP/C guardians protect against SOS faults in the line encoding of frames at the physical layer, SOS timing faults, transmission of data outside the designated sending slots, masquerading of nodes, and transmission of non-agreed critical state information [6].

3   Bird's Eye View of the Formal Models

The overall goal of modelling the communication network is to provide a concise description of the arguments that support the following three main correctness properties of the TTP/C communication:

- *Validity:* If a correct node transmits a correct frame, then all correct receivers accept the frame.
- *Agreement:* If any correct node accepts a frame, then all correct receivers do.
- *Authenticity:* A correct node accepts a frame only if it has been sent by the scheduled sending node of the given slot.

Once these properties are established, they can be exploited in subsequent analyses of protocol algorithms. This is preferable, since it is generally more feasible to base an analysis on properties of a supporting model or theory, rather than on the mere definitions of the model itself.

In order to facilitate the deduction, the formal proofs of these properties are decomposed into a series of smaller steps, and a hierarchy of corresponding models has been developed. Each of the single models focuses on a particular aspect of the communication. Altogether, we have identified the following four suitable model layers:

- General specification of the reception of frames.
- Channels without guardians, requiring a strong fault hypothesis.

- Channels with guardians, requiring only a weaker fault hypothesis.
- Different network topologies: local bus guardians and central guardians.

Each of the models contributes a small step towards proving the desired correctness properties. The steps themselves are each based on a set of assumptions or preconditions. Put in an abstract, and maybe also a slightly over-simplified way, on each model layer i one establishes a theorem of the form

$$assumptions_i \Rightarrow properties_i \; .$$

The idea is to design the different models in such a way that the properties on one level establish the assumptions on the next. Ultimately, the models are integrated and the reasoning is combined, yielding a chain of implications of roughly the following kind:

$$
\begin{aligned}
assumptions_0 \Rightarrow\; & properties_0 \\
=\;\; \text{or}\;\; \Rightarrow & \\
assumptions_1 \Rightarrow\; & properties_1 \\
=\;\; \text{or}\;\; \Rightarrow & \\
assumptions_2 \Rightarrow\; & \ldots \Rightarrow properties_f \; .
\end{aligned}
$$

The final properties, $properties_f$, correspond to the desired main correctness properties of the TTP/C communication as specified above, while the initial assumptions, $assumptions_0$, describe what constitutes the basic fault hypothesis.

We are going to briefly summarise the main aspects of the four model layers. At the bottom, the model describes the reception of frames by the nodes. Here, the various actions that nodes take in order to judge the correctness of the received frame are formalised. This amounts to considering the transmission time and the physical encoding rules of the frame, and the outcomes of the CRC check and the C-state agreement check, respectively [17]. The main correctness properties of the communication network are then expressed in terms of these notions. The assumptions of this model layer concern requirements about the functionality of the communication channels. In particular, they describe properties of the frames that a channel transmits, such as physical encoding or delivery times, and reflect the hypothesis about possible faults of the communication network. In essence, this model establishes a proposition that informally reads as follows:

$$general\_channel\_properties \Rightarrow Validity \wedge Agreement \wedge Authenticity \; . \tag{1}$$

On the next level, we model the transmission of frames through channels that are not equipped with guardians. The goal is then to derive the assumptions of the basic model, as covered by the expression $general\_channel\_properties$. However, in order to do so, a strong hypothesis on the types of possible faults of nodes is necessary. This strong fault hypothesis requires, for instance, that even a faulty node does not send data outside its sending slot, and nodes never send correct frames when they are not scheduled to do so. Using our informal notation, we can sketch the reasoning at this model layer as follows:

$$strong\_fault\_hypothesis \Rightarrow general\_channel\_properties \; . \tag{2}$$

Guardians are employed to transform arbitrary node faults into faults that are covered by the strong fault model. Thus, the strong fault hypothesis can be replaced with weaker assumptions on the correct behaviour of the guardians. The functionality and the properties of the guardians are formally specified in the third model of the hierarchy, where the following fact is established:

$$weaker\_fault\_hyp. \wedge generic\_guardian \Rightarrow general\_channel\_properties \ . \quad (3)$$

Ideally, we would have liked to demonstrate directly that – together with the guardian properties – the weak form of the fault hypothesis implies the strong one. However, it turned out to be rather challenging to accomplish a formal proof for this fact and hence we had to revert to reasoning according to (3).

The model of the guardians is generic, as it does not, for instance, stipulate the type of guardian to be used in the communication network. The final level of our hierarchy models each of the two typical topologies of a TTP/C network: the bus topology and the star topology. In the former, each node of the network is equipped with its own local bus guardian, one for each channel, while in the latter the guardians are placed into the central star-coupling device of the channels. On this model layer we show that the properties of the guardians are independent from the choice of a particular topology, given that both the local bus guardians and the central guardians implement the same algorithms. Hence, we establish the following facts:

$$local\_bus\_guardian \Rightarrow generic\_guardian \ . \quad (4)$$

$$central\_star\_guardian \Rightarrow generic\_guardian \ . \quad (5)$$

The hierarchic arrangement of the models for the communication network allows for a concise description of the dependencies of the three main correctness properties. On the basic level the fundamental prerequisites are described that are necessary for the desired correctness properties to hold, while the subsequent levels express what must be assumed from the nodes and guardians, respectively, to satisfy these prerequisites. In particular, the treatment precisely explains the benefits of introducing guardians into the communication network.

4   Formal Analysis of TTP/C Communication

In this section we present the main details of the formal models for the communication network according to the hierarchy that has been set out in the previous section. The presentation is in the style of a mathematical transcription of PVS modules that have been developed. However, due to space restrictions, only verbal explanations of proofs can be provided. For a comprehensive description we refer to an accompanying technical report [19].

4.1   General Model for the Reception of Frames

In our general formal model, we divide communication between nodes into three phases: the sending of frames by a sending node, the transmission of the frame on a channel, and the reception of the frame at the receiving nodes. To model the reception of frames we introduce a function $rcvd(n, c, r)$ to denote the frame a receiving node r receives in slot n on channel c. Similarly, $sent(n, c, p)$ denotes the frame that a node p has sent in slot n on channel c, while $transmit(n, c)$ models the frame that is transmitted on channel c in slot n. For a non-faulty node r we assume that it receives the frame that is transmitted on the channel, and that even faulty nodes cannot receive other messages than those transmitted – or nothing, in the case of a reception fault. As for the sending nodes, we assume that in their sending slots non-faulty nodes either send a correct frame on all channels, or do not send any frame on any channel; the latter is required for nodes that are not yet integrated.

In TTP/C, frames can be *null* frames, *valid* frames, or *correct* frames. The status of the frame received by node r on channel c in slot n will be denoted by $frame\_status(n, c, r)$. Frames are considered syntactically valid if the frame is transmitted during the receive window of the receiving node, no code violations are observed during the reception, and no other transmission was active within the receive window before the start of the frame. For a frame to be considered correct, it has to pass both the CRC check and the C-state agreement check [5].

Next, we formally state the desired correctness properties introduced in the previous section. The node scheduled to send in slot n is denoted $sender(n)$, while we use the (overloaded) notation $\mathcal{NF}^n$ to denote both the set of non-faulty nodes and the non-faulty channels in slot n; consequently, $r \in \mathcal{NF}^n$ and $c \in \mathcal{NF}^n$ indicate that node r and channel c are non-faulty in slot n.

Property 1 (Validity). *For all slots n, there exists a channel c such that if the sender of slot n sends a correct frame on c then all non-faulty nodes will receive this frame and assign the status* correct *to it:*

$$\exists c : sender(n) \in \mathcal{NF}^n \wedge sends\_correct(n, c, sender(n)) \Rightarrow$$
$$\forall r \in \mathcal{NF}^n : rcvd(n, c, r) = sent(n, c, sender(n)) \wedge$$
$$frame\_status(n, c, r) = correct$$

Here, the predicate $sends\_correct(n, c, sender(n))$ subsumes what is considered a correct sending action of a node: the sending node sends a non-null frame, does so at the specified time, the frame carries the correct C-state information and the physical signal obeys the line encoding rules.

Property 2 (Agreement). *All non-faulty nodes consistently assign the frame status* correct *to a frame received on a non-faulty channel c:*

$$p \in \mathcal{NF}^n \wedge q \in \mathcal{NF}^n \wedge c \in \mathcal{NF}^n \Rightarrow$$
$$frame\_status(n, c, p) = correct \Leftrightarrow frame\_status(n, c, q) = correct$$

Property 3 (Authenticity). *A non-faulty node r assigns the frame status* correct *to a frame received on a non-faulty channel c only if it was sent by the scheduled sender of the slot:*

$$r \in \mathcal{NF}^n \wedge c \in \mathcal{NF}^n \wedge frame\_status(n, c, r) = correct \Rightarrow$$
$$rcvd(n, c, r) = sent(n, c, sender(n))$$

In order to prove that these desired correctness properties hold for our model, several preconditions must be satisfied. We first list these general requirements and subsequently explain their respective purpose and why they are necessary.

General Requirements. The properties *Validity*, *Agreement*, and *Authenticity* can be proved if the following requirements are met:

1. A non-faulty channel either transmits the frame sent by some node, or nothing, or a corrupted frame.

$$c \in \mathcal{NF}^n \Rightarrow (\exists p : transmit(n, c) = sent(n, c, p))$$
$$\lor transmit(n, c) = null \lor corrupted(transmit(n, c))$$

2. If the scheduled sender exclusively accesses the channel and sends a correct frame, then this frame is transmitted by the channel.

$$c \in \mathcal{NF}^n \land single\_access(n, c) \land sends\_correct(n, c, p) \land p = sender(n) \Rightarrow$$
$$transmit(n, c) = sent(n, c, p)$$

3. Channels can only transmit what has been sent be some node.

$$transmit(n, c) \neq null \Rightarrow \exists p : sends(n, c, p)$$

4. In every slot, there is at least one non-faulty channel that is accessed only by a single node.

$$\exists c \in \mathcal{NF}^n : single\_access(n, c)$$

5. The transmission time of a correct frame on a non-faulty channel does not deviate from the sending time by more than some bounded delay d.

$$c \in \mathcal{NF}^n \land sends\_correct(n, c, p) \land single\_access(n, c) \Rightarrow$$
$$\exists d : d \leq max\_delay \land transmission\_time(f') = send\_time(f) + d$$
where $p = sender(n), f = sent(n, c, p), f' = transmit(n, c)$

6. If a non-faulty channel transmits a frame with a correct signal encoding, then the frame sent must provide a correct encoding of the sender's C-state.

$$c \in \mathcal{NF}^n \land transmit(n, c) = sent(n, c, p) \land sends(n, c, p) \land$$
$$signal\_encoding\_OK(transmit(n, c)) \Rightarrow$$
$$cstate\_encoding\_OK(n, sent(n, c, p), p)$$

7. A non-faulty channel transmits a correctly sent frame only if it originates from the scheduled sender of the given slot.

$$c \in \mathcal{NF}^n \land sends\_correct(n, c, p) \land transmit(n, c) = sent(n, c, p) \Rightarrow$$
$$p = sender(n)$$

Requirements 1, 2, and 3 constrain what is considered a correct behaviour of a channel. According to Req. 1, a channel either transmits a frame, or blocks the transmission completely, or invalidates the frame. The latter two cases particularly allow for the functionality of a guardian. On the other hand, Req. 2 enforces that a non-faulty channel does neither block nor invalidate a correct frame of the scheduled sender. Furthermore, Req. 3 accounts for the fact that channels are passive entities.

The remaining five requirements are necessary to establish formal proofs for the correctness properties. Consider the *Validity* property, which states two things: first, all non-faulty receivers must receive the frame sent by the sender, and, second, all of them must accept this frame. With respect to the first part, we know that all non-faulty nodes receive the frame that channel transmits. Furthermore, Req. 2 states that a non-faulty channel always transmits the frame sent by the sender, provided that there is no other node accessing the channel. To ensure this, Req. 4 is necessary. The expression *single_access* is an abstract parameter of the model, and its concrete interpretation will be defined only in the subsequent refining models layers. As for the second part of *Validity*, we need to demonstrate that all correct nodes receive a non-null, valid frame that passes both the CRC check the C-state agreement check. Non-emptiness of the frame can be proved from Req. 4 and Req. 2, and the fact that the original sender is non-faulty and sends a correct, i. e., non-null, frame. Requirements 5 and again 4 ensure that the received frame is valid, by constraining its timing and its uniqueness on the channel, respectively. C-state agreement is ensured by Req. 6. As for the CRC check, an incorrect CRC checksum is intended to signal a transmission fault. As the channel c under consideration is non-faulty, it is reasonable to assume that no transmission fault occurs on c and consequently that the frame received by a non-faulty receiver passes the CRC check.

The *Agreement* property can be derived in a similar way from the same set of requirements as *Validity*. Here, consistent reception is achieved by assuming that non-faultiness of two nodes comprises that they are synchronised to each other, which ensures that they will receive a frame within their respective receive window consistently. Finally, Req. 7 is necessary to prove *Authenticity*, which requires to show that if a frame is considered correct by a correct receiver r, then node r has in fact received the frame sent by the scheduled sender of the slot. The following two subsections describe under which fault hypotheses these requirements can be met, both for a scenario with and without guardians.

4.2   Strong TTP/C Fault Hypothesis

The general model expresses certain required properties in terms of $sent(n, c, p)$ and $transmit(n, c)$. In a technical sense, these entities are parameters of the model. We now give an interpretation to these parameters for a network without guardians and show that the general requirements are satisfied for these interpretations. In this model, $single\_access(n, c)$ is defined true if there are no two different nodes that send on channel c in slot n. The interpretation of $sent(n, c, p)$ and $transmit(n, c)$ is given in an axiomatic style, and the set of axioms essentially constitutes the fault hypothesis of the guardian-free setting.

Again, we first state all of the assumptions of the fault hypothesis and subsequently explain their respective purpose.

Hypotheses for a Network without Guardians. The requirements of the general model are satisfied for a communication network without guardians, if the following assumptions hold:

1. A non-faulty channel without a guardian will transmit a frame sent by a node p if no other node accesses the channel in the given slot n.

$$c \in \mathcal{NF}^n \wedge sends(n, c, p) \wedge \neg \exists q : q \neq p \Rightarrow sends(n, c, q) \Rightarrow$$
$$transmit(n, c) = sent(n, c, p)$$

2. If a channel broadcasts a non-null frame, then there is a corresponding node that has sent this frame.

$$transmit(n, c) \neq null \Rightarrow \exists p : sends(n, c, p)$$

3. The delivery time of a frame on a non-faulty channel does not deviate from the transmission time by more than some bounded delay d.

$$c \in \mathcal{NF}^n \wedge sends(n, c, p) \wedge f' \neq null \wedge \neg corrupted(f') \Rightarrow$$
$$\exists d : d \leq max\_delay \wedge transmission\_time(f') = sending\_time(f) + d$$
$$\text{where } f = sent(n, c, p), f' = transmit(n, c)$$

4. Frames sent must contain a correct encoding of the sender's C-state.

$$sends(n, c, p) \Rightarrow cstate\_encoding\_OK(n, sent(n, c, p), p)$$

5. Correct frames must only be sent by the scheduled sender of a given slot.

$$sends\_correct(n, c, p) \Rightarrow p = sender(n)$$

6. Nodes other than the sender of a slot, including faulty ones, will not send data on all non-faulty channels outside their assigned sending slots.

$$p \neq sender(n) \Rightarrow \neg \forall c \in \mathcal{NF}^n : sends(n, c, p)$$

7. In every slot, there is at least one non-faulty channel.

$$\exists c \in \mathcal{NF}^n$$

8. There is at most one faulty node in every slot.

$$p \notin \mathcal{NF}^n \wedge q \notin \mathcal{NF}^n \Rightarrow p = q$$

In the setting without guardians, all that can be assumed of the frame transmitted by a channel is that it depends on what is sent by the sending nodes. This is what Hyp. 1 does, and it is sufficient to prove Req. 2. To prove Req. 1 one additionally needs Hyp. 2, which, in fact, is actually also identical to Req. 3.

Because we cannot further constrain the behaviour of the channels, some of the requirements of the general model have to be restated as hypotheses at this level. This is also true to some extent for Hyp. 3, which is equivalent to Req. 5. Note, however, that this by no means just an inadmissible simplification of the matter. On the contrary, these hypotheses are direct formalisations of the strong fault hypothesis of the "raw" TTP/C protocol [6]. The other hypotheses are necessary to prove the other requirements of the general model. Specifically, Hyp. 4 and 5 justify Req. 6 and 7, respectively, while Hyp. 6 to 8 establish Req. 4.

What makes this set of hypotheses strong or optimistic is the fact that assumptions are not restricted to non-faulty nodes, but also encompass faulty ones, cf. Hyp. 4, 5, and 6. In the following subsection these hypotheses will be replaced with weaker ones about the behaviour of *non-faulty* guardians.

4.3   Guardians

In our guardian model, we use $g(c)$ to denote the guardian of channel c. We think of a guardian having incoming links from each of the nodes of the network, and corresponding outgoing links. The task of a guardian is to receive the frames sent by the nodes, analyse them, and relay them to the other nodes according to certain rules. Obviously, these rules would prescribe, among other things, that only the frame of the scheduled sender of a slot is relayed. Hence, to describe the functionality of a guardian we use a function $relay(n, g(c), p)$ that denotes the frame the guardian $g(c)$ relays from node p in slot n. Regarding the interpretation of $transmit(n, c)$, we say that a frame is transmitted on a channel c if there is a node p such that the guardian $g(c)$ of channel c relays that frame for p, and does not relay any frame for all nodes other than p. As the guardian prevents nodes from concurrently accessing a channel, we can define $single\_access(n, c)$ to yield true in the guardian model for all slots n. Furthermore, a channel is considered non-faulty if its corresponding guardian is. The following assumptions are made in the guardian model.

Hypotheses for Guardians. The requirements of the general model are satisfied for a network with guardians, if the following hypotheses hold:

1. If the scheduled sender of a slot sends a correct frame, then a correct guardian relays this frame.

$$p = sender(n) \wedge g(c) \in \mathcal{NF}^n \wedge sends\_correct(n, c, p) \Rightarrow$$
$$relay(n, g(c), p) = sent(n, c, p)$$

2. Frames of nodes other than the scheduled sender must not be relayed.

$$p \neq sender(n) \wedge g(c) \in \mathcal{NF}^n \Rightarrow relay(n, g(c), p) = null$$

3. If a sending node does not start to send its frame within the nominal sending window, the guardian closes the window with the effect that a null frame is relayed.

$$p = sender(n) \wedge g(c) \in \mathcal{NF}^n \wedge \neg \, sending\_time\_OK(n, sent(n, c, p), p) \Rightarrow$$
$$relay(n, g(c), p) = null$$

4. If the signal encoding of the frame sent by a node violates the coding rules the guardian terminates the transmission of the frame prematurely, thus corrupting the frame.

$$p = sender(n) \wedge g(c) \in \mathcal{NF}^n \wedge \neg signal\_encoding\_OK(sent(n, c, p)) \Rightarrow$$
$$corrupted(relay(n, g(c), p))$$

5. If the C-state encoded in a frame does not correspond to the guardians own C-state, then the guardian aborts the transmission of the frame, and the relayed frame will be corrupted.

$$p = sender(n) \wedge g(c) \in \mathcal{NF}^n \wedge \neg cstate\_encoding\_OK(n, sent(n, c, p), p)$$
$$\Rightarrow corrupted(relay(n, g(c), p))$$

6. Guardians are passive and can only relay frames that have actually been sent by some node.

$$relay(n, g(c), p) \neq null \Rightarrow sends(n, c, p)$$

7. A guardian transmits a relayed frame with a bounded delay.

$$g(c) \in \mathcal{NF}^n \wedge sends(n, c, p) \wedge f' \neq null \Rightarrow$$
$$\exists d : d \leq max\_delay \wedge transmission\_time(f') = sending\_time(f) + d$$
$$\text{where } f = sent(n, c, p), f' = relay(n, g(c), p)$$

8. For all slots, the guardian of at least one of the channels is non-faulty.

$$\exists c : g(c) \in \mathcal{NF}^n$$

9. A faulty guardian fails silently and does not relay any frame.

$$g(c) \notin \mathcal{NF}^n \Rightarrow relay(n, g(c), p) = null$$

Hypotheses 1 and 2 describe the basic functionality of a guardian, while the supervising functions are expressed by Hyp. 3, 4, and 5. Note that the only assumption that is made about a faulty guardian is that it fails silently, cf. Hyp. 9. These hypotheses ensure that a non-faulty guardian always transmits a correct frame sent by the scheduled sender of a given slot, cf. Req. 2, and corrupted or null-frames otherwise, see Req. 1. Combining these two facts establish Req. 7. Requirement 3 can be proved from Hyp. 6, while Req. 4 follows from Hyp. 8. Requirement 5 on the bounded delay of transmissions is established by Hyp. 7, and Hyp. 4 and Hyp. 5 are used to prove Req. 6.

4.4   Local Versus Central Guardians

The guardian model described above is generic in the sense that it does not determine the type of guardians used in the network. By refining the interpretation of the denotation $g(c)$, it can be applied to both an interconnection network with a star topology and one with a bus topology. In fact, the generic model can directly be matched to central guardians, while for an interconnection network that uses the bus topology one introduces a function *lbg* to denote particular guardian devices, such that $lbg(p, c)$ is the local bus guardian of node p for channel c. Then, the expression $g(c)$ would denote a function that yields for a given node its local bus guardian that controls channel c. For space reasons, however, we have to omit the details.

In essence we can state that, as long as the same algorithms and supervising functions are implemented in either guardian type, both the local bus guardians and the central guardians of a star coupler provide the functionality to satisfy the requirements stated in the basic model and thus ensure that the main correctness properties for the communication of TTP/C hold.

5   Conclusions

The goal of formally analysing aspects of the Time-Triggered Architecture is to provide mathematically substantiated arguments that architecture and algorithms provide certain services and satisfy certain critical properties.

In this regard we have presented a formal analysis of the guardian-based communication of TTP/C. We have developed a series of formal models of the interconnection network that are hierarchically structured and formalise different aspects of the communication of TTP/C nodes at various levels. The basic level provides a precise specification of the desired correctness properties of the TTP/C communication. It states several requirements on both the behaviour of the sending nodes and the channels that must be satisfied in order to guarantee that the correctness properties hold. These requirements serve as an interface of the model. In a process of stepwise refinement we have proved the validity of these properties for TTP/C by showing that the interface requirements hold for the refined model layers. The organisation of the model hierarchy not only facilitates the formal proof by dividing it into manageable steps. It also reflects the structure of what constitutes Time-Triggered Protocol, viz. the communication controllers of the nodes, and the guardians. The former provide the fault-tolerant protocol services on the basis of strong fault assumptions, which, in turn, are guaranteed by the guardians. Thus, one of the benefits of our formal analysis is that the formal models yield a concise formal description of the respective purposes and dependencies of these components, and precisely state the assumptions on a guardian, which previously have been stated only informally [6].

The analysis of the properties of the communication network of TTA supports the claim that the functionality of the guardians ensures that arbitrary node failures are converted into fault modes the TTP/C protocol algorithms can tolerate. Thus, the strong fault hypothesis of TTP/C can be replaced by a weaker, minimal fault hypothesis on the correct behaviour of the guardians, which has two direct advantages. First, applications of TTA can rely on the architecture to tolerate a broad class of faults, and, second, protocol algorithms of TTP/C can be designed for and analysed under the strong fault model, which allows for simpler algorithms and significantly facilitates formal analysis.

References

1. Kopetz, H.: The Time-Triggered Approach to Real-Time System Design. In: Predictably Dependable Computing Systems. Springer-Verlag (1995)
2. Kopetz, H.: The Time-Triggered Architecture. In: Proc. 1st Intl. Symp. on Object-Oriented Real-Time Distributed Computing. (1998) 22–31
3. Kopetz, H., Bauer, G.: The Time-Triggered Architecture. Proceedings of the IEEE **91** (2003) 112–126
4. Heiner, G., Thurner, T.: Time-Triggered Architecture for Safety-Related Distributed Real-Time Systems in Transportation Systems. In: Proc. 28th Intl. Symp. on Fault-Tolerant Computing, IEEE Computer Society (1998)
5. Bauer, G., Kopetz, H., Steiner, W.: Byzantine Fault Containment in TTP/C. In: Proc. Intl. Workshop on Real-Time LANs in the Internet Age. (2002) 13–16
6. Bauer, G., Kopetz, H., Steiner, W.: The Central Guardian Approach to Enforce Fault Isolation in the Time-Triggered Architecture. In: Proc. 6th Intl. Symp. on Autonomous Decentralized Systems. (2003) 37–44
7. Pfeifer, H., Schwier, D., von Henke, F.: Formal Verification for Time-Triggered Clock Synchronization. In: Proc. of Dependable Computing for Critical Applications 7, IEEE Computer Society (1999) 207–226
8. Katz, S., Lincoln, P., Rushby, J.: Low-Overhead Time-Triggered Group Membership. In: Proc. 11th Intl. Workshop on Distributed Algorithms. Volume 1320 of LNCS, Springer-Verlag (1997) 155–169
9. Pfeifer, H.: Formal Verification of the TTP Group Membership Algorithm. In: Proc. of FORTE XIII / PSTV XX, Kluwer Academic Publishers (2000) 3–18
10. Bouajjani, A., Merceron, A.: Parametric Verification of a Group Membership Algorithm. In: Proc. 7th Intl. Symp. on Formal Techniques in Real-Time and Fault-Tolerant Systems. Volume 2469 of LNCS, Springer-Verlag (2002) 311–330
11. Merceron, A., Müllerburg, M., Pinna, G.: Verifying a Time-Triggered Protocol in a Multi-Language Environment. In: Proc. 17th Intl. Conf. on Computer Safety, Security and Reliability. Volume 1516 of LNCS, Springer-Verlag (1998) 185–195
12. Steiner, W., Rushby, J., Sorea, M., Pfeifer, H.: Model Checking a Fault-Tolerant Startup Algorithm: From Design Exploration To Exhaustive Fault Simulation. In: Proc. Conf. on Dependable Systems and Networks, IEEE Computer Society (2004)
13. Rushby, J.: An Overview of Formal Verification for the Time-Triggered Architecture. In: Proc. 7th Intl. Symp. on Formal Techniques in Real-Time and Fault-Tolerant Systems. Volume 2469 of LNCS, Springer-Verlag (2002) 83–105
14. Rushby, J.: Systematic Formal Verification for Fault-Tolerant Time-Triggered Algorithms. IEEE Trans. on Software Engineering **25** (1999) 651–660
15. Owre, S., Rushby, J., Shankar, N., Stringer-Calvert, D.: PVS: An Experience Report. In: Applied Formal Methods. Volume 1641 of LNCS, Springer-Verlag (1998) 338–345
16. Bauer, G., Kopetz, H., Puschner, P.: Assumption Coverage under Different Failure Modes in the Time-Triggered Architecture. In: Proc. 8th IEEE Intl. Conf. on Emerging Technologies and Factory Automation. (2001) 333–341
17. TTTech: Time-Triggered Protocol TTP/C High-Level Specification Document. Available at **http://www.tttech.com/technology/specification.html** (2003)
18. Kopetz, H.: The Time-Triggered (TT) Model of Computation. In: Proc. 19th IEEE Real-Time Systems Symposium. (1998) 168–177
19. Pfeifer, H., von Henke, F.: Modular Formal Analysis of the Central Guardian in the Time-Triggered Architecture. Technical report, Fakultät für Informatik, Universität Ulm, Germany (2004)

Refinement of Fault Tolerant Control Systems in B

Linas Laibinis and Elena Troubitsyna

Åbo Akademi, Department of Computer Science,
Lemminkäisenkatu 14 A, FIN-20520 Turku, Finland
{Linas.Laibinis,Elena.Troubitsyna}@abo.fi

Abstract. Application of formal methods helps us to gain confidence in building correct software. On the other hand, to guarantee dependability of the overall system we need to build fault tolerant software, i.e., software which is not only fault-free but also is able to cope with faults of other system components. Obviously, this goal is attainable only if fault tolerance mechanisms constitute an intrinsic part of software behaviour. In this paper we propose a formal approach to model-driven development of fault tolerant control systems. We demonstrate how to integrate fault tolerance into the automated refinement process in the B method. The proposed approach is exemplified by a case study – a derivation of safe and fault tolerant controller of a heating system.

1 Introduction

In this paper we propose a formal approach to the model-driven development [14] of fault tolerant control systems. Our approach is based on stepwise refinement of formal system model in the B Method [1,15] – a formal framework with an automatic tool support. While developing a system by refinement, we start from an abstract specification and gradually incorporate implementation details into it until an executable code is obtained. This is an efficient way to cope with complexity of systems requirements. In this paper we demonstrate how to formally model fault tolerance mechanisms such as error detection, redundancy and error recovery and integrate them into the system specification.

While developing controlling software, called a *controller*, for dependable systems we aim at constructing software that 1) does not contribute to failure of the system by forcing it from a safe to an unsafe state and 2) prevents a critical system failure by forcing the system from an unsafe to a safe (but probably non-operational) state. The first goal essentially means that the controller should ensure safety of a fault-free system and not introduce failures into it. The second goal states that the controller should be able to detect failures of other components and cope with them by returning the system to a safe state. We assume that failures of components might bring the system into an unsafe state.

We argue that the development of systems by stepwise refinement [3] facilitates achieving these goals. Indeed, the stepwise refinement enables development of software correct by construction. The development starts at a high level of abstraction. The reasoning about safety at such an abstract level usually allows us to formulate safety properties in a clear and succinct way. The formal development by refinement

M. Heisel et al. (Eds.): SAFECOMP 2004, LNCS 3219, pp. 254–268, 2004.

ensures that the final implementation adheres to the initial abstract specification. This gives us means to guarantee that safety is also preserved at the implementation level.

Ensuring safety of a fault-free system is necessary yet insufficient for achieving dependability [11]. Indeed, due to various reasons, system's components are susceptible to different kinds of faults. A fault manifests itself as *error* – an incorrect system's state which potentially can lead to system's failure [2]. To prevent occurrence of system failure, fault tolerance should be employed. Since nowadays software plays an important role in implementing fault tolerance [12, 18], fault tolerance mechanisms should be an essential part of specification and refinement of the controller.

Although fault tolerance mechanisms usually constitute a significant part of software (sometimes up to 60% of program code), fault tolerance mechanisms are often introduced only at the implementation stage and in a rather ad-hoc fashion. However, fault tolerance usually imposes additional functional requirements on the system under construction and hence should be considered already at the abstract specification level.

In this paper we demonstrate how to specify a control system in such a way that fault tolerance mechanisms become an intrinsic part of the controller behaviour. We show that by refining a specification with fault tolerance mechanisms we can arrive at an executable code of a controller which is safe and fault tolerant by construction.

To overcome the traditional scepticism regarding scalability of formal refinement techniques, we use an automatic tool support available for the B Method to conduct our development. We exemplify the proposed approach by a case study – a derivation of a safe and fault tolerant controller of a heating system.

2   Safety Critical Control Systems and the B Method

Modelling with B. The B Method (further referred to as B) is an approach for the industrial development of highly dependable software. The method has been successfully used in the development of several complex real-life applications [5, 13]. The tool support available for B provides us with the assistance for the entire development process. For instance, Atelier B [17], one of the tools supporting the B Method, has facilities for automatic verification and code generation as well as documentation, project management and prototyping. The high degree of automation in verifying correctness improves scalability of B, speeds up development and, also, requires less mathematical training from the users.

The development methodology adopted by B is based on stepwise refinement. While developing a system by refinement we start from an abstract formal specification and transform it into an implementable program by a number of correctness preserving steps, called *refinements*. A formal specification is a mathematical model of the required behaviour of a (part of) system. In B a specification is represented by a set of modules, called Abstract Machines. The common pseudo-programming notation, called Abstract Machine Notation (AMN), is used in constructing and formally verifying them. An abstract machine encapsulates a state and operations of the specification and has the following general form:

MACHINE	
MachineName	**INITIALISATION**
SETS	parallel assignment of initial values to variables
Definition of local types	**OPERATIONS**
VARIABLES	OpName_1 = ...
list of variables	...
INVARIANT	OpName_N = ...
invariant properties of the machine	**END**

Each machine is uniquely identified by its name. The state variables of the machine are declared in the VARIABLES clause and initialized in the INITIALISATION clause. The variables in B are strongly typed by constraining predicates of the INVARIANT clause. The constraining predicates are conjoint by conjunction (denoted as &). All types in B are represented by non-empty sets and hence set membership (denoted as :) expresses typing constraint for a variable, e.g., x : TYPE. Local types can be introduced by enumerating the elements of the type, e.g., TYPE = {element1, element2, ...}.

The operations of the machine are defined in the OPERATIONS clause. The operations are atomic meaning that, once an operation is chosen, its execution will run until completion without interference.

There are two standard ways to describe an operation in B: either by the preconditioned operation PRE cond THEN body END or the guarded operation SELECT cond THEN body END. Here cond is a state predicate, and body is a B statement describing how state variables are affected by the operation. If cond is satisfied, the behaviour of both the precondition operation and the guarded operation corresponds to the execution of their bodies. However, these operations behave differently when an attempt to execute them from a state where cond is false is undertaken. In this case the precondition operation leads to a crash (i.e., unpredictable or even non-terminating behaviour) of the system, while the guarded operation blocks itself by waiting until cond is changed to true.

Preconditioned operations are used to describe operations that will be turned (implemented) into procedures that can be called by the user. On the other hand, guarded operations are useful when we have to specify so called event-based (reactive) systems. Then the SELECT operation describes the reaction of the system when particular event occurs.

B statements that we are using to describe a state change in operations have the following syntax:

$$S \quad == \quad x := e \quad | \quad \text{IF cond THEN S1 ELSE S2 END} \quad | \quad S1 ; S2 \quad |$$
$$x :: T \quad | \quad \text{ANY z WHERE cond THEN S END} \quad | \quad S1 \| S2 \quad | ...$$

The first three constructs - an assignment, a conditional statement and a sequential composition (used only in refinements) have the standard meaning. The remaining constructs allow us to model nondeterministic or parallel behaviour in a specification. Usually they are not implementable so they have to be refined (replaced) with executable constructs at some point of program development.

In our modelling of control systems we use two kinds of nondeterministic statements – nondeterministic assignment x :: T and nondeterministic block ANY z WHERE Q THEN S END. Nondeterministic assignment x :: T assigns variable x arbitrary value from given set (type) T. Nondeterministic block ANY z WHERE Q THEN S END introduces new local variable z which is initialised (possibly nondeterministically) according to predicate Q and then used in S.

Finally, S1 || S2 models parallel (simultaneous) execution of S1 and S2. The special case of a parallel composition is a multiple assignment which is denoted as x,y := e1,e2.

Event-based modelling of critical systems. The event-based modelling has proven its worth in the design of various complex parallel and reactive systems [13]. We will specify our control system as an event-based system which includes both a plant and a controller. As noted above, the event-based system consists of a set of SELECT-guarded operations. Any enabled operation – the operation with its condition being true – can be chosen for execution. Even while all operations are disabled the system is still considered to be running but in a "waiting" or "hibernating" mode.

For modelling safety-critical control systems [12,18] we need to model shutdown of a system – a situation when software ceases its functioning. In our previous work [16] we demonstrated that abort statement of Dijkstra's language of guarded commands [6] is an adequate specification statement to represent this. There is no explicit statement with abort semantics in B AMN. However, we can model such a construct as follows.

We specify abort as a separate operation which, once enabled, stays always enabled. Moreover, the condition of abortive operation is disjoint with the conditions of all non-abortive operations. This means that shutdown of the system is actually infinite execution of abort operation.

The body of abort operation is defined as chaotic (arbitrary) update of local variables, which can be coded in B as state :: STATE where state is a tuple of local variables and STATE is their corresponding types (sets). Such an approach to specifying abort operation is exemplified in machine AbortingSystem.

The "chaos" can be refined (and, finally, implemented) by any update of the local state. This allows us to implement any necessary actions that need to be undertaken before the actual shutdown of the system. At the very least, it can repeatedly remind the human operator that he/she needs to execute manual shutdown because the system is in a critical state.

```
MACHINE                               good_op =
   AbortingSystem                        SELECT failure = FALSE
SETS                                  THEN
   STATE = {state1, state2, state3}      IF <error is detected>
VARIABLES                             THEN
   failure, state                         failure := TRUE
INVARIANT                             ELSE
   failure : BOOL  & state : STATE        <execute routine control>
   ...                                 END
OPERATIONS                            END;

abort_op =
   SELECT failure = TRUE              END
THEN
   state :: STATE
END;
```

Next we demonstrate how to use event-based modelling in B to reason about safety and fault tolerance of control systems.

3 Specifying Fault Tolerant Control Systems in B

Specifying control systems. In general, a control system is a reactive system with two main entities: a plant and a controller. The plant behaviour evolves according to the involved physical processes and the control signals provided by the controller. The controller monitors the behaviour of the plant and adjusts it to provide intended functionality and maintain safety. In this paper we advocate the system approach to designing controllers for dependable systems, i.e., in our initial specification we model behaviour of the plant and the controller together.

The control systems are usually cyclic, i.e., at periodic intervals they get input from sensors, process it and output the new values to the actuators. In our abstract specification the sensors and actuators are represented by state variables shared by the plant and the controller. At each cycle the plant reads the variables modelling actuators and updates the variables modelling the sensors. In contrast, the controller reads the variables modelling sensors and updates the variables modelling the actuators. We assume that the reaction of the controller takes negligible amount of time so the controller can react properly on changes of the plant state.

In this paper we focus on safety and fault tolerance aspects of control systems. The requirements obtained from hazard analysis [12,18] are integrated into a specification as the safety invariant, i.e. they become a part of the invariant of the abstract machine specifying the system under construction. To integrate fault tolerance, we should specify its basic mechanisms, i.e., error detection and error recovery. The general structure of a control system that we propose is given in machine ControlSystem.

The overall behaviour of the system is an alternation between the events modelling plant evolution and controller reaction. As a result of the initialisation, the plant's operation becomes enabled. Once completed, the plant enables the controller. The behaviour of the controller follows the general pattern

Error detection; Shutdown or Routine control; Prediction

which is modelled by the corresponding assignments to variable flag.

```
MACHINE
   ControlSystem
VARIABLES
   flag, state_variables
INVARIANT
   flag : {pl,contr,pred,det} & safety_inv & fail : BOOL ...
INITIALISATION
   flag := pl || fail:=FALSE || ...
   ...
OPERATIONS
   Plant = SELECT flag=pl THEN evolution || flag:=det END;
   Detection = SELECT flag=det THEN
                     IF error is detected THEN fail := TRUE END || flag:=contr END ;
   Abort = SELECT flag= contr & (not safe ∨ fail=TRUE) THEN shutdown END;
   Control = SELECT flag= contr & safe & fail=FALSE THEN control_action || flag :=pred END;
   Prediction = SELECT flag = pred THEN prediction || flag := pl END
END
```

The common mechanism for error detection is to find a discrepancy between the expected state of the system and the state which is observed in the reality. Operation

Prediction specifies the calculations required to predict the expected state. Operation Detection models error detection by assigning value TRUE to variable fail.

In this paper we focus on *failsafe* [2] – one of the most common mechanisms for error recovery. Failsafe error recovery is performed by forcing the system permanently to a safe though non-operation state (obviously this strategy is only appropriate where shutdown of the system is possible). In the initial specification we shut down the system if an error is detected or safety is breached (as defined in the condition of operation Abort). The shutdown is modelled as described above. Routine control operations can be executed provided the system is safe and fault-free. The routine control is specified by operation Control.

We will decompose the overall system specification at the later refinement steps and eventually will arrive at the specification of the controller as such.

Example: the heater controller. To illustrate construction of specification of fault tolerant control system, we consider an example – a *heater controller* for a tank of toxic liquid. A computer controls the heater using a power switch on the basis of information obtained from a temperature sensor. The controller tries to maintain the temperature between certain limits. If the temperature exceeds the critical upper threshold, the toxic liquid can harm its environment in a certain way (we leave it unspecified). The abstract machine **Heater** specifies the system as proposed above.

The hazard analysis identifies the main hazard associated with the system – *overheating*. Therefore, in our safety invariant we postulate that, after the controller has reacted to the plant's state change (i.e., flag≠DET & flag≠CONT), the temperature temp should be below critical threshold t_crit. However, such an invariant can be guaranteed for an idealistic fault-free system but not for a real-life failure-prone application. Indeed, component's failures might exceed the limit of system's fault tolerance leading to a violation of safety invariant. The safety invariant of our abstract specification states that safety cannot be guaranteed in a faulty state, i.e., when fail=TRUE. This pessimistic view is taken because distinguishing between criticality of errors requires a more detailed level of reasoning and hence should be introduced at the consequent refinement steps.

Our initial specification of the plant is very abstract – it merely models nondeterministic changes of temperature. Such a specification allows us to guarantee the correct behaviour of the system even in the worst-case scenario. Operation Switch modelling the routine control is enabled when no error is detected and the system is safe. The operation body switches the heater on, if the temperature is low, and switches it off, if the temperature is high. However, if an error is detected or the safety is breached, the controller shuts down the system as modelled by abort_op. Since at the high level of abstraction the realistic mechanisms for error detection are often unknown, we model the outcome of the detection procedure as a non-deterministic assignment to variable fail. Finally, operation Prediction is essentially behaving like a skip statement because a more detailed level of reasoning is needed to specify the prediction.

Our initial specification entirely defines the intended functionality of a fault-free system but leaves the means for fault tolerance underspecified. This is explained by the lack of the implementation details, which is typical at the early stages of development. These details become available at the later stages of the development, e.g., when results of hazard analysis conducted at a lower level are supplied. Next we

```
MACHINE
  Heater
VARIABLES
  temp, heat, fail, flag
INVARIANT
  temp : NAT1 &
  heat : {ON, OFF} &
  fail : BOOL &
  flag : {PRED,ENV,DET,CONT} &
  (fail=FALSE & flag≠DET &
    flag≠CONT => temp<=t_crit)

INITIALISATION
  temp := start_temp ||
  heat := ON ||
  fail := FALSE ||
  flag := ENV

OPERATIONS
plant =
  SELECT flag = ENV
  THEN
    temp :: NAT1 || flag := DET
  END;

detection =
  SELECT flag = DET
  THEN
    flag := CONT || fail :: BOOL
  END

abort_op =
  SELECT flag = CONT & (fail = TRUE or temp > t_crit)
  THEN
    heat :: SWITCH
  END;

Switch =
  SELECT flag = CONT & fail= FALSE & temp <= t_crit
  THEN
    IF temp < t_low & heat = OFF
    THEN
      heat := ON
    ELSIF temp > t_high & heat = ON
    THEN
      heat := OFF
    ELSE
      skip
    END
    ||
    flag := PRED
  END;

prediction =
  SELECT flag = PRED
  THEN
    flag := ENV
  END;
END
```

demonstrate how the complete specification of fault tolerance mechanisms can be obtained in the refinement process.

4   Refining Fault Tolerance

The basic idea underlying formal stepwise development is to design the system implementation gradually by a number of correctness preserving steps, called refinements [3]. The refinement process starts from creating an abstract albeit implementable specification and finishes with generating an executable code. The intermediate stages yield the specifications containing a mixture of abstract mathematical constructs and executable programming artefacts. In general, refinement process can be seen as a way to reduce nondeterminism of the abstract specification, to replace abstract mathematical data structures by data structures implementable on a computer and to introduce underspecified design decisions. In the AMN, the results of the intermediate development stages – the refinement machines – have essentially the same structure as the more abstract specifications. In addition, they explicitly state which specifications they refine.

Refinement of error detection. We start refinement of control systems by replacing variable fail modelling error occurrence by the variables representing failures of system components. It is an example of data refinement. This data refinement expresses the fact that error occurs when one or several system's components fail. The refinement relation defines the connection between the newly introduced variables and the variables that they replace. While refining the specifications, we add the refinement relation to the invariant of the refined machine.

In addition to replacing variable fail, our next refinement step also introduces a more deterministic specification of plant's behaviour. In the abstract specification we modelled plant's behaviour as a nondeterministic update of sensor's values. Such an abstraction includes modelling of both fault-free and faulty behaviour. In the refined specification of the plant we separate them. The behaviour of fault-free plant evolves according to the certain physical laws which can be expressed as the corresponding mathematical functions. Moreover, these functions can be further adjusted to model deviations caused by imprecision of sensors measuring the physical values. We use these functions to model fault-free behaviour of the plant. On the other hand, faults make the plant to deviate from the dynamics defined by these functions. We specify occurrence of faults non-deterministically and locally to the plant. However, we model the effect of fault occurrence by assigning sensors values different from the ones which they would obtain in the absence of faults.

Refinement of plant's behaviour also allows us to refine error detection mechanism. Observe that the mathematical functions modelling the plant's behaviour as described above can be used to predict the next state of the system. Hence we can refine operation Prediction to include the calculation of the expected system states. Furthermore, we also can refine operation Detection to check whether the expected state matches the obtained sensor readings. The detected mismatch signals the presence of an error. The result of this refinement step is a specification of the following form:

```
REFINEMENT
      ControlSystemRefined
REFINES
      ControlSystem
VARIABLES
      state_variables of ControlSystem
      new variables for modelling failures of components
      variables modelling expected states
INVARIANT
      constraints of variables & data refinement relation
      ...
OPERATIONS
 Plant = SELECT flag=pl THEN simulation of evolution of the plant based on the
            corresponding physical laws and non-deterministic occurrence of failures END;

 Detection = SELECT flag=det THEN IF real state does not match expected state THEN
            failures of components are detected ... END;
 Abort = SELECT flag= contr & (not_refined_safe ∨ components failed) THEN abort END;
 Control = SELECT flag= contr & refined_safe & components are fault-free THEN
            controlling_action ... END;
 Prediction = SELECT flag = pred THEN calculate next expected state using
            the same physical laws as for simulating the plant ...END
END
```

To illustrate this refinement step, let us present the excerpt from the corresponding refinement of the heater system. In the refinement step variable fail is replaced by the variables modelling failures of the switch and the sensor, variables heater_fail and sensor_fail correspondingly. The refinement relation states that occurrence of error in the abstract specification is equivalent to failure of the sensor or the switch or both of them.

Operation Plant updates the value of the temperature sensor based on the dynamics of temperature changes defined by the functions min_incr, max_incr, min_decr, max_decr. We model the Byzantine behaviour of the switch, i.e., the switch might be stuck at both switched on and switched off states. The failure of the temperature sensor is modelled by assigning the corresponding variable a value lying outside of the scope defined by the dynamics of the fault-free system. Operation Prediction uses the same function as Plant to estimate the next expected state of the system. The prediction results in defining the upper and lower limits next_temp_max, next_temp_min within which the temperature of the fault-free system should stay. Operation Detection checks whether the sensor reading is indeed in the valid range.

Although at this refinement step we introduced the representations of sensor and switch failures we still cannot distinguish between them. Observe that, if a mismatch between the expected and real state is detected, Detection merely non-deterministically chooses to assign the failed status either to the switch or to the sensor or to the both. This is due to the fact that simplex systems, i.e., the systems without redundancy, are able to detect presence of errors but are unable to distinguish between faults causing them. An introduction of redundancy is the objective of our next refinement step (see p. 263).

5   Introducing Redundancy and System Decomposition

Let us note that in the specification obtained at the previous refinement step all errors are considered to be equally critical, i.e., leading to the shutdown. While introducing redundancy at our next refinement step, we obtain a possibility to distinguish between criticality of errors. The distinction is done with respect to safety as follows: an occurrence of a marginal error means that the system can continue its functioning without compromising safety; on the other hand, an occurrence of critical errors endangers system safety so the shutdown needs to be executed. In terms of the state space, we split the set of faulty system states into the subset of faulty but safe (and hence operational) states and the subset of faulty and unsafe states.

The introduction of redundancy into the specification allows us to transform the system from fault nonmasking to masking [9]. Fault masking is a mechanism that reconfigures the system upon error detection in such a way that the effect of the error is nullified. For instance, the simplest and the most common implementation of fault masking is triple modular redundancy (TMR) arrangement [11,18]. TMR uses majority voting to single out a failed component and reconfigures the outputs of redundant components in such a way that the erroneous output is disregarded. An occurrence of errors that can be masked leaves both functioning of the system and safety intact, so we call these errors marginal. On the other hand, occurrence of critical errors, i.e., the errors that cannot be masked, jeopardizes normal functioning and safety of the system. Hence the partitioning of faulty system states can also be thought of as the partitioning into a subset of masked and unmasked errors.

```
REFINEMENT                         plant =
  Heater2                            SELECT flag = ENV
                                     THEN
                                       ANY heater_fail_sim, sensor_fail_sim WHERE
REFINES                                  heater_fail_sim : H_FAIL &
  Heater                                 sensor_fail_sim : BOOL & ...
                                       THEN
INVARIANT                                IF sensor_fail_sim=FALSE
  ...                                    THEN
  sensor_fail : BOOL &                     IF (heat = ON & heater_fail_sim = OK) or
  heater_fail : H_FAIL &                      heater_fail_sim = ON_STUCK
  next_temp_max : NAT1 &                   THEN
  next_temp_min : NAT1 &                     temp :: min_incr(temp)..max_incr(temp)
  (fail=TRUE) <=>                          ELSE
     (sensor_fail=TRUE or heater_fail ≠ OK)   temp :: max_decr(temp)..min_decr(temp)
  ...                                      END
OPERATIONS                             ELSE
                                         temp :: {xx | xx:NAT1 & (xx<next_temp_min or
abort_op =                                                        xx>next_temp_max)}
  SELECT flag = CONT &                 END
    ((sensor_fail=TRUE or heater_fail ≠OK)  ||
       or temp>t_crit)                 flag := DET
  THEN                                 END
    abort                            END;
  END;
                                   detection =
prediction =                         SELECT flag = DET
  SELECT flag = PRED                  THEN
  THEN                                 IF temp > next_temp_max or temp < next_temp_min
    IF heat = ON THEN                  THEN
      next_temp_max,next_temp_min :=     ANY xx,yy WHERE xx:H_FAIL & yy:BOOL &
        max_incr(temp),min_incr(temp)        (xx ≠ OK or yy = TRUE)
    ELSE                                 THEN
      next_temp_max,next_temp_min :=       heater_fail,sensor_fail := xx,yy
        min_decr(temp),max_decr(temp)    END
    END                                ELSE
    ||                                   heater_fail,sensor_fail := OK,FALSE
    flag := ENV                        END
  END:                                 ||
                                       flag := CONT
                                     END
```

The introduction of redundancy as described above results in the refinement machine of the form ControlSystemRefinedRedundant. Observe that, although the guard of Abort operation is unchanged by this refinement step, the operation nevertheless becomes enabled less often. This is because Detection operation is now distinguishes between the critical and marginal errors so that the occurrence of the marginal failures does not enable Abort anymore.

Let us also note that the plant models not only failures of components but also possible recovery from failures resulting in marginal errors. However, error recovery has been "dormant" at the previous refinement steps since error occurrence has led to the immediate shutdown of the system. At the current refinement step the system continues to function in the presence of marginal errors. Therefore, assigning the fault-free status to a component corresponds to a possible error recovery.

```
REFINEMENT
    ControlSystemRefinedRedundant
REFINES
    ControlSystemRefined
VARIABLES
    state_variables of ControlSystem
    new variables for modelling redundancy
    variables modelling expected states
INVARIANT
    constraints of variables & data refinement relation...
OPERATIONS
Plant = SELECT flag=pl THEN simulation of the behaviour of the plant with
    redundant components and the occurrence of component's failures; ... END;

Detection = SELECT flag=det THEN
    IF mismatch between the states of redundant components is detected THEN
        IF the error cannot be masked THEN critical failure of redundant components is detected END
    ELSIF the real state does not match the expected state
        THEN critical failure of other components is detected
    ELSE ... END;
Abort = SELECT flag= contr & (not refined_safe ∨ components failed) THEN abort END;
Control = SELECT flag= contr & refined_safe &
    components are fault free or failures are masked THEN controlling_action; ...END;
Prediction = SELECT flag = pred THEN calculate next expected state using the
    same physical laws as for simulating the plant; ... END

END
```

To illustrate the introduction of redundancy by refinement, we demonstrate how to introduce TMR arrangement of temperature sensors into the specification of the heater.

We introduce new variables sen1, sen2, and sen3 to model redundant sensors. In general, the refinement relation defines how the measure of temperature used at the previous refinement step, i.e. variable temp, is connected with current temperature measure temp1 and sensor readings sen1, sen2, and sen3. Variable temp1 represents controller's approximation of temperature and is obtained as a result of voting in the TMR arrangement. The refinement relation describes the essence of TMR: the majority view is taken to produce measure of the temperature, failure of a single module is tolerated and, in case of multiple failures, a non-deterministic reading is produced. The plant operation is modified to accommodate redundant sensors: the physical functions from the previous refinement steps are inherited to simulate readings of redundant sensors. The failures of the sensors and their recovery are modelled non-deterministically.

In the plant operation definitions sensor_read and sensor_read2 model behaviour of sensors in the absence and the presence of faults correspondingly. The detection operation is modified to specify majority voting and distinguish between marginal and critical errors. The single sensor failure is masked, i.e., its occurrence is essentially ignored by disregarding the reading produced by the failed sensor. However, at the implementation level the messages reporting the failure are introduced to alert the operator. Multiple failures of sensors or failure of the switch are considered to be critical. We also observe that handling the switch failure can be more finely tuned if we take into account whether the switch failed at the safe temperature region or at the critical one. Such a tuning would result in the additional refinement steps to specify calculations required to implement this idea.

```
REFINEMENT
  Heater3
REFINES
  Heater2
INVARIANT
  sen1 : NAT1 & sen2 : NAT1 & sen3 : NAT1 & (temp1=temp or flag=DET or sensor_fail=TRUE) &
  (temp=sen1 or temp=sen2 or temp=sen3) & (sen1=sen2 => temp=sen1) & ...

OPERATIONS
plant =                                              detection =
SELECT flag = ENV                                    SELECT flag = DET
THEN                                                 THEN
  ANY heater_fail_sim,sensor_fail_sim WHERE            IF sen1 = sen2 THEN
    heater_fail_sim : H_FAIL &                           temp1,sensor_fail := sen1,FALSE
    sensor_fail_sim : BOOL &                           ELSIF sen2 = sen3 THEN
    (heat=ON => heater_fail_sim : {OK,OFF_STUCK}) &      temp1,sensor_fail := sen2,FALSE
    (heat=OFF => heater_fail_sim : {OK,ON_STUCK})      ELSIF sen3 = sen1 THEN
  THEN                                                    temp1,sensor_fail := sen3,FALSE
    IF sensor_fail_sim=FALSE                           ELSE
    THEN                                                 temp1 :: {sen1,sen2,sen3};
      IF (heat = ON & heater_fail_sim = OK) or           sensor_fail := TRUE
        heater_fail_sim = ON_STUCK                     END;
      THEN                                             IF sensor_fail = FALSE THEN
        sensor_read(min_incr(temp1),max_incr(temp1))    IF temp1 > next_temp_max THEN
      ELSE                                                heater_fail := ON_STUCK
        sensor_read(max_decr(temp1),min_decr(temp1))   ELSIF temp1 < next_temp_min
      END                                              THEN
    ELSE                                                 heater_fail := OFF_STUCK
      sensor_read2(next_temp_min,next_temp_max)        ELSE
    END                                                  heater_fail := OK
  ||                                                   END
    flag := DET                                       ELSE
  END                                                   heater_fail := OK
END;                                                  END || flag := CONT
                                                      END
```

Decomposition. The behaviour of our control systems is essentially a loop where both the plant and the controller take turns in executing their actions. However, the goal of our development is to arrive at an executable code of the controller as such. Therefore, at a certain point of the development we have to separate concerns and decompose our specification. We decompose it by moving controller's description to a new abstract machine which can be then developed and implemented separately.

The structuring mechanism of B often used for such a decomposition is the IN-CLUDES mechanism. If machine C "includes" machine D, it means that all variables and operations of D are visible in C. However, the only way to change the variables of D is via D operations. Also, the invariant properties of D are automatically included into C invariant. Therefore, machine C can be considered as the extension of machine D.

We decompose our control system by introducing a separate controller machine in the next refinement step. The structure of the decomposed system is as follows:

```
REFINEMENT                              MACHINE
DecomposedControlSystem                 Controller

REFINES ControlSystemRefinedRedundant
INCLUDES Controller
VARIABLES                               VARIABLES
 flag, variables of plant                variables of controller
INVARIANT                               INVARIANT
 invariant of plant & whole system       invariant of controller

OPERATIONS                              OPERATIONS
 Plant = SELECT fl=pl ....               Cont_Detection =
Detection =                              PRE ... <detection spec> END
 SELECT fl=det THEN Cont_Detection      Cont_Prediction =
Prediction =                             PRE ... <prediction spec> END
 SELECT fl=pred THEN Cont_Detection     Cont_Control = ...
Control = ...                           Cont_Abort = ...
Abort = ...
```

Note that DecomposedControlSystem retains all its operations. However, if an operation belongs to the controller, then its body just contains a call of the corresponding operation from newly introduced Controller machine. All operations of Controller machines are of the form PRE ... END which means that they can be implemented as ordinary procedures. The internal specifications of controller operations are taken from ControlSystemRefinedRedundant.

The program state is also decomposed – controller variables are separated from plant variables and now declared in Controller machine. Similarly, the system invariant is split into two parts. The controller machine can be now developed independently from the plant. We refine it into an implementation and generate executable code automatically by means of Atelier B. This is the final step of the refinement process. Due to the lack of space we omit its detailed representation.

6 Conclusions

In this paper we proposed a formal model-driven approach to the development of fault tolerant control systems. According to our approach the system model evolves as follows:

1. *Abstract specification of entire system*: the initial specification captures requirements for routine control, models failure occurrence and defines safety property as a part of its invariant

2. *Specification with refined error detection mechanism*: the abstract specification is augmented with the representation of failures of the components, more elaborated description of plant's dynamics and detailed description of error detection.

3. *Specification of the system supplemented with redundancy*: the specification is refined to describe behaviour of redundant components and control over them. The error detection mechanism is enhanced to distinguish between criticality of failures.

4. *Decomposition*: the specification of overall system is split into specifications of the controller and the plant.

5. *Implementation*: executable code of controller is produced.

Every evolution step of our development is a refinement of the initial formal specification in B. We validated all refinement steps by discharging proof obligations – the formal conditions which had to be verified to establish correctness of refinement. Atelier B tool generated the proof obligations and proved a significant part of them automatically. We argue that the system developed by an application of the proposed approach have a high degree of dependability because the complete formal verification within a logically sound framework was undertaken.

The idea of reasoning about fault tolerance in the refinement process has also been explored by Joseph and Liu [8]. They specified a fault intolerant system in a temporal logic framework and demonstrated how to transform it into a fault tolerant system by refinement. However, in their approach the specification of error detection mechanism is left aside, i.e., error detection is merely modelled by a non-deterministic assignment to a specific variable.

A successful attempt to use B for constructing a fault tolerant control system was undertaken in the development of the signalling system for the Paris Metro [5]. Within the project a procedural-based approach was adopted. The application of such an approach to the development of control systems usually involves manipulating complex data structures and creating rather complicated specification hierarchies to model the control loop. Event-based approach taken as a basis in our paper provides explicit specification facilities for modelling events and their interleaving. It significantly simplifies specifying and refining the system. Hence, our approach suits better for developing fault tolerant control systems.

Arora and Kulkarni [9] have done the extensive research on establishing correctness of adding fault tolerance mechanisms to fault intolerant systems. Correctness proof of such an extended system is based on soundness of their algorithm working with next-state (transition) relation. In our approach we start with an abstract specification of a system and develop a fault tolerant system by refinement, incorporating fault tolerance mechanisms on the way. Correctness of our transformation is guaranteed by soundness of the B method. Moreover, an automatic tool support available for our approach facilitates verification of correctness.

Reasoning about fault tolerance in B has also been explored by Lano et al. [10]. However, they focused on structuring B specifications to model a certain mechanism for damage confinement rather than general fault tolerance mechanisms.

In our paper we advocate the system approach to developing fault tolerant control systems. This approach has also been adopted by Hayes et al. [7] for specifying fault tolerant control systems within the duration calculus framework. The main idea of this work was to combine rely-guarantee approach and duration calculus to derive a specification of a fail-safe control system. However, the approach leaves aside the problems of refining the system towards its implementation and incorporating such mechanisms for error recovery as, e.g., fault masking or reconfiguration.

Formal reasoning about fault tolerance has been studied not only by the application of stepwise refinement but also by model checking (see, e.g., [4]). Model-checking approach is complementary to ours so we leave a discussion of it aside.

We believe that because of its generality and model-driven nature as well as availability of automatic tool support our approach has a potential to be integrated into the industrial practice. In the future we are planning to investigate reasoning about more sophisticated error recovery mechanisms and dynamic redundancy within our approach.

References

1. J.-R. Abrial. *The B-Book*. Cambridge University Press, 1996.
2. T.Anderson and P.A. Lee. *Fault Tolerance: Principles and Practice*. Dependable Computing and Fault Tolerant Systems, Vol 3. Springer Verlag, 1990
3. R.J.Back and J.von Wright.*Refinement Calculus: A Systematic Introduction*. Springer-Verlag, 1998.
4. T.Cichocki and J.Gorski. Formal Support for Fault Modelling and Analysis. In U.Voges (Ed.): *SAFECOMP 2001, LNCS 2187*, pp.190-199, September 2001.
5. D.Craigen, S.Gerhart, and T.Ralson. Case Study: Paris Metro Signaling System. *IEEE Software*, 11(1), pp.32 – 35, January 1994.
6. E. W. Dijkstra. *A Discipline of Programming*. Prentice Hall Int., Englewood Cliffs, N.J., 1976.
7. I.Hayes, M.Jackson, and C.Jones. Determining the Specification of a Control System from That of Its Environment. In K.Araki, S.Gnesi, and D.Mandrioli (Eds.): *FME 2003, LNCS 2805*, pp.154–169, Italy, 2003.
8. M.Joseph and Z.Liu. Verification of fault tolerance and real time. In *Proc. of 26th Annual Conference on Fault Tolerant Computing*, pp.220-229, IEEE Computer Society, Japan 1996.
9. S. Kulkarni and A. Arora. Automating the addition of fault-tolerance. *Formal Techniques in Real-time and Fault-tolerant Systems (FTRTFTS'2000)*, Pune, India. 2000.
10. K.Lano, D. Clark, K. Androutsopoulos, P. Kan. Invariant-Based Synthesis of Fault-tolerant Systems. In Proc. of *Formal Techniques in Real-Time and Fault-Tolerant Systems. FTRTFT 2000*, LNCS 1926, p. 46 -57. Pune, India, September 2000.
11. J.-C. Laprie. *Dependability: Basic Concepts and Terminology*. Springer-Verlag, Vienna, 1991.
12. N.G. Leveson. *Safeware: System Safety and Computers*, Addison-Wesley, 1995.
13. EU-project MATISSE: Methodologies and Technologies for Industrial Strength Systems Engineering, IST-1999-11345, 2003. *http://www.esil.univ-mrs.fr/~spc/matisse/Handbook/*
14. J. Miller and J. Mukerji. *Model driven architecture (MDA)*, via http://www.omg.org/mda
15. S.Schneider. *The B Method. An introduction*. Palgrave 2001.
16. K. Sere and E. Troubitsyna. Hazard Analysis in Formal Specification. In M.Felici, K.Kanoun, and A.Pasquini (Eds.). In *SAFECOMP'99, LNCS 1698*, pp. 350–360, France, September 1999.
17. Steria, Aix-en-Provence, France. *Atelier B, User and Reference Manuals*, 2001. Available at http://www.atelierb.societe.com/index uk.html.
18. Storey N. *Safety-critical computer systems*. Addison-Wesley, 1996.

Numerical Integration of PDEs for Safety Critical Applications Implemented by I&C Systems

Michael Vollmer

Lehrstuhl für Nachrichtentechnik, Ruhr-Universität Bochum,
Universitätsstr. 150, D-44780 Bochum, Germany,
Vollmer@nt.ruhr-uni-bochum.de

Abstract. In this paper, a method for numerical integration of partial differential equations (PDEs) in safety critical applications is suggested, based on multidimensional wave digital filters (MDWDFs). In comparison to other numerical integration methods the WD method has an outstanding robustness. WDFs have an excellent behavior against stability problems, like the prevention of overflow-errors and negative effects due to rounding errors, even in the case of limited wordlength. It seems that these outstanding properties make this method predestinated for the usage in safety critical applications. In our research project, we want not only to examine the theory but, the WD method is embedded in the commercial instrumentation & control (I&C)-system TELEPERM XS. In order to preserve all safety features, we verify the used C-language implementations by means of formal methods of software engineering.

1 Introduction

During the last decade, we have seen a change from hardwired to I&C-systems. The increasing computing power enables the possibility to process more complex tasks. Physical problems are often described by PDEs. Since analytic solutions cannot be obtained in general, numerical algorithms are used to find solutions by means of a computer. Naturally, the demand is growing for implementation of these algorithms in safety critical systems. One application in the field of nuclear power plants is the numerical integration of the neutron diffusion equation. The main aspect in this context is to ensure the safety. In this issue one has to deal with two key technologies, which are both discussed in this paper. At first, one is faced with the problem of finding an appropriate algorithm to solve the PDEs. The second goal deals with the software implementation of this algorithm. In particular with the verification of the used software against the specification.

Wave digital filters were invented by Fettweis in the early 1970s for the solution of many problems in the field of digital signal processing [1], [2]. Later on MDWDFs have been successfully used for multidimensional digital signal processing [3]. In [4] one can find the proposal how to use WDF for numerical integration of ordinary differential equations. This idea was extended for

M. Heisel et al. (Eds.): SAFECOMP 2004, LNCS 3219, pp. 269–282, 2004.

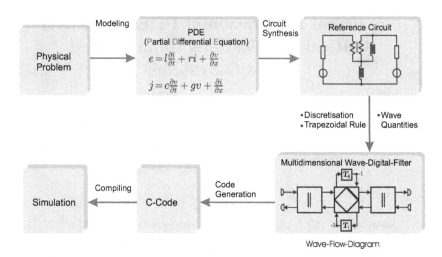

Fig. 1. Overview: Steps from the PDE to a wave digital filter.

integrating PDEs by means of MDWDF [5]. The basic idea of the numerical integration algorithm is the representation of the PDEs by an equivalent MD electrical circuit. This MD electrical circuit can be converted into a MDWDF using well established methods. The MDWDF can be simulated on a digital system. The whole developing process is illustrated in Fig.1.

The second key technology is the implementation of the algorithms. The theory of program verification was stimulated by McCarthy [6]. His intention was to verify the program by mathematical rigorous methods instead of testing the software. Hoare introduced in [7] the concept of using an axiomatic basis for computer programming, as it is used in other mathematical disciplines. Hoares work is the basis of the proof in this article.

2   Multidimensional Wave Digital Filters

First of all, we have to introduce the used independent variables. The physical problem is described in spatial cartesian coordinates x, y, z and the time t. These independent variables (t weighed by $v_4 > 0$) are summarized in

$$\boldsymbol{x} = [\, x \,,\, y \,,\, z \,,\, v_4 t \,]^{\mathrm{T}} \;=\; [\, x_1 \,,\, x_2 \,,\, x_3 \,,\, x_4 \,]^{\mathrm{T}} \;. \tag{1}$$

The physical system possesses the property of causality in the physical sense. This primary causality is only related to time. The system cannot be expected to be causal in a more general sense with respect to all coordinates of $\boldsymbol{x}$. In classical literature on MD-systems (e.g.[8]), the causality with respect to all coordinates of the newly introduced vector

$$\boldsymbol{t} = [\, t_1 \,,\, t_2 \,,\, \ldots \,,\, t_7 \,]^{\mathrm{T}}, \text{ with } \boldsymbol{x} = v_0 \, \boldsymbol{H} \, \boldsymbol{t} \;,\; v_0 > 0 \tag{2}$$

is used. The causality is an important property in order to determine the direction of computation and ensures the recursibility. In this paper, only the matrix

$$H = \begin{bmatrix} 1 & 0 & 0 & -1 & 0 & 0 & 0 \\ 0 & 1 & 0 & 0 & -1 & 0 & 0 \\ 0 & 0 & 1 & 0 & 0 & -1 & 0 \\ 1 & 1 & 1 & 1 & 1 & 1 & 1 \end{bmatrix} \quad (3)$$

is considered. For the discretization of the independent variables, we use the rectangular sampling in the newly introduced coordinates $t = T_0 \nu$. The discrete variables, which belong to x, are denoted by μ.

Wave digital filters are derived from electrical circuits. For this reason, we repeat some basics from electrical circuit theory. An electrical circuit consists of elements, which are described by differential and algebraic equations.[1] We will use only capacitances as elements described by differential equations. In the multidimensional case, the derivative of the voltage is not only defined with respect to time, but rather with respect to all variables t_1, t_2, ..., t_7. Furthermore, our electrical circuit consists of real electrical voltage sources. All other elements, which are described by algebraic equations, are called nonreactive elements.

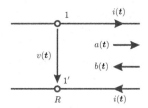

Fig. 2. An electrical port

Another important term in circuit theory is a port, which is characterized by a voltage $v(t)$ and a current $i(t)$, c.f. Fig.2. Please note that the current in the lower wire but is the same as in the upper wire in the opposite direction. $a(t)$ and $b(t)$ are the so-called wave quantities and will be explained later. We suppose that each electrical element is connected to the rest of the circuit by ports. The the topology of the electrical circuit is described by a graph with e edges. The number of edges of the tree is r and the number of co-tree edges is $m = e - r$, respectively. If we give each edge an orientation the graph is called an oriented graph. Applying the Kirchhoff laws on the oriented graph of a concrete circuit, we obtain an algebraic system of linear equations

$$Ai = 0 \quad , \quad Bv = 0 . \quad (4)$$

A is the node-incidence matrix and B the circuit matrix with $\dim A = r \times e$, $\dim B = m \times e$, $\operatorname{rank} A = r$, $\operatorname{rank} B = m$, $AB^\mathrm{T} = 0$. The vectors $v =$

---
[1] In this paper, we will restrict ourselves to linear time and space invariant elements.

$[v_1, v_2, \ldots, v_n]^T$ and $\boldsymbol{i} = [i_1, i_2, \ldots, i_n]^T$ contain the voltages and currents of all edges. A port can alternatively be described by the incident power wave $a = (v + Ri)/(2\sqrt{R})$ and the reflected power wave $b = (v - Ri)/(2\sqrt{R})$, where $R > 0$ is the so-called port resistance. Due to the one-to-one mapping of the wave quantities and Kirchhoff quantities, we have

$$v = \sqrt{R}[a + b] \; , \; i = [a - b]/\sqrt{R} \; . \tag{5}$$

In general, an circuit element has n ports. For such an n-port, we define vectors and a matrix, containing the wave-quantities and the port resistances, respectively,

$$\boldsymbol{a} = [a_1 \, , \, a_2, \ldots, a_n]^T \; , \; \boldsymbol{b} = [b_1 \, , \, b_2, \ldots, b_n]^T \; , \; \boldsymbol{R} = \mathbf{diag}\,(R_1 \, , \, R_2, \ldots, R_n) \; . \tag{6}$$

The scattering matrix $\boldsymbol{S}$ of linear, nonreactive elements with n ports obeys the equation $\boldsymbol{b}(t) = \boldsymbol{S}\boldsymbol{a}(t)$. Such an element is called passive, if the absorbed power

$$p = \sum_{\nu=1}^{n} v_\nu i_\nu = \boldsymbol{v}^T \boldsymbol{i} = \|\boldsymbol{b}\|^2 - \|\boldsymbol{a}\|^2 \tag{7}$$

is nonnegative for all times and arbitrary vectors $\boldsymbol{a}$.

After these preliminary explanations, we convert the descriptions of the electrical circuit with $\boldsymbol{v}$ and $\boldsymbol{i}$ into descriptions using the wave quantities $\boldsymbol{a}$ and $\boldsymbol{b}$. The resultant elements are called the WD elements. At first, we convert the connection network into WD elements. This can be performed by means of

$$\boldsymbol{S} = 2\boldsymbol{G}^{1/2}\boldsymbol{A}^T[\boldsymbol{A}\boldsymbol{G}\boldsymbol{A}^T]^{-1}\boldsymbol{A}\boldsymbol{G}^{1/2} - \mathbf{1}_n = \mathbf{1}_n - 2\boldsymbol{R}^{1/2}\boldsymbol{B}^T[\boldsymbol{B}\boldsymbol{R}\boldsymbol{B}^T]^{-1}\boldsymbol{B}\boldsymbol{R}^{1/2} \; , \tag{8}$$

c.f. [9]. Secondly, we convert the non reactive electrical elements into WD elements. In order to achieve a relation between the waves, we replace all currents and voltages by the wave quantities. The resultant equations have to be solved for $\boldsymbol{b}$. We would like to explain this procedure by means of a short example. Suppose, an ideal transformer, which is described in Kirchhoff quantities by $v_2 = nv_1$ and $i_1 = -ni_2$, where n is the transfer ratio. Expressing voltages and currents by the wave quantities, we have in matrix notation,

$$\begin{bmatrix} -n\sqrt{R_1/R_2} & 1 \\ \\ 1 & n\sqrt{R_1/R_2} \end{bmatrix} \begin{bmatrix} b_1 \\ b_2 \end{bmatrix} = \begin{bmatrix} n\sqrt{R_1/R_2} & -1 \\ \\ 1 & n\sqrt{R_1/R_2} \end{bmatrix} \begin{bmatrix} a_1 \\ a_2 \end{bmatrix} \; . \tag{9}$$

Multiplication from the left with the inverse of the left matrix yields

$$\boldsymbol{S} = \begin{bmatrix} \dfrac{R_2 - |n|^2 R_1}{R_2 + |n|^2 R_1} & \dfrac{2n\sqrt{R_1 R_2}}{R_2 + |n|^2 R_1} \\ \\ \dfrac{2n\sqrt{R_1 R_2}}{R_2 + |n|^2 R_1} & -\dfrac{R_2 - |n|^2 R_1}{R_2 + |n|^2 R_1} \end{bmatrix} \; . \tag{10}$$

In the next step, we convert the real sources into WD elements. We consider a real voltage source shown in Fig.3 a) with the resistance R_i, the voltage of the

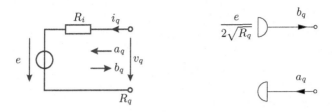

Fig. 3. Voltage source: a) Electrical element, b) Wave digital element

ideal source e and the voltage of the real source v_q. We replace in the mesh-equation $v_q = e + R_i i_q$ the occurring voltage and current by the wave quantities. We chose $R_q = R_i$ and yield $b_q = e/(2\sqrt{R_q})$, c.f. Fig.3 b). At last, we convert the reactive elements. An ideal capacitor with respect to the variable t_κ is given by

$$i(t) = C \frac{\partial}{\partial t_\kappa} v(t) \tag{11}$$

where C is constant. The conversion is performed in two steps. Firstly, the differential equation is approximated in the sense of the trapezoidal rule. Secondly, we express the voltages and currents by the wave quantities. Only both steps together ensures an explicit computation. Explicit in this context means that the voltage v depends only on past values of v and i. In order to assess a numerical integration method the consistency order is used in mathematics. Roughly spoken, the discretization error depends on the consistency order. The trapezoidal rule is the passive linear multistep method with the maximum consistency order and the lowest local error, (e.g. [10]). Integrating the current in equation (11) from point t to $t + T_0 \mathbf{e}_\kappa$, we have

$$v(t + T_0\mathbf{e}_\kappa) = v(t) + \frac{1}{C} \int_{t_\kappa}^{t_\kappa + T_0} i([t_1, \ldots, t_{\kappa-1}, \tau, t_{\kappa+1}, \ldots, t_{k'}]^T)\, \mathrm{d}\tau, \tag{12}$$

$$\text{where} \quad \mathbf{e}_\kappa^T = [\,\overset{1}{0}, \overset{2}{0}, \overset{\ldots}{\ldots}, \overset{\kappa}{0, 1, 0}, \overset{\ldots}{\ldots}, \overset{n}{0}\,]\,. \tag{13}$$

The integral is evaluated by the trapezoidal rule, c.f. Fig.4. Thus, we get an approximated value of the voltage at the sampling point $t + T_0\mathbf{e}_\kappa$

$$v(t + T_0\mathbf{e}_\kappa) \approx v(t) + \frac{1}{C} T_0 \frac{i(t + T_0\mathbf{e}_\kappa) + i(t)}{2}\,. \tag{14}$$

We define $R = T_0/(2C)$ as the port resistance. Henceforth, we describe the difference equations by discrete independent variables $\boldsymbol{\nu}$. Thus, we have

$$v(\boldsymbol{\nu}+\mathbf{e}_\kappa) = v(\boldsymbol{\nu})+R\left[i(\boldsymbol{\nu}+\mathbf{e}_\kappa)+i(\boldsymbol{\nu})\right] \iff v(\boldsymbol{\nu}+\mathbf{e}_\kappa)-Ri(\boldsymbol{\nu}+\mathbf{e}_\kappa) = v(\boldsymbol{\nu})+Ri(\boldsymbol{\nu}) \tag{15}$$

which results after division by $2\sqrt{R}$ in the notation of the wave quantities

$$b(\boldsymbol{\nu} + \mathbf{e}_\kappa) = a(\boldsymbol{\nu})\,. \tag{16}$$

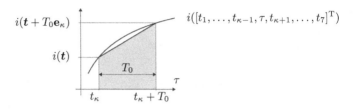

Fig. 4. Trapezoidal rule

Please note that the simplicity and the explicit form is important for the proof of correctness. Applying the trapezoidal rule to all reactive elements, the underlying partial differential equations descend into a difference equation system.

With these basics, we can now explain the WD concept for numerical integration. The classical analysis of electrical networks results in a set of ordinary differential equations, [11]. Since a MD circuit has also reactive elements with respect to more than one variable, a partial differential equation can be expected. The basic idea for numerical integration is to perform this procedure in the reverse order: Find an electrical circuit from a given system of PDEs. This electrical circuit can be simulated by means of MDWDFs. This is in essence similar to the conversion from an analogue system (PDEs) to a digital system (difference equation). However, the resultant algorithm has some extraordinary inherit properties.

In this work, we are only concern symmetric hyperbolic systems, that can be characterized by a system of partial differential equations of the form

$$\left[C^x D_x + C^y D_y + C^z D_z + C^t D_t + Y^k \right] v = j \ . \tag{17}$$

The matrices C^x, C^y, C^z, C^t are symmetric and the symmetric part of Y^k and the matrix C^t are positive definite. The components of the vector v and j are interpreted as voltages and ideal current sources, respectively. An automatic procedure for creation of the reference circuit from PDEs of the form in equation (17) was developed at the chair of communications engineering, [12]. Furthermore, the development on a computer-aided software engineering (CASE) tool for automatic C-Code-generation is under construction.

The next step towards a formal specification of the algorithm is the systematic description of the MDWDF by matrices. For this aim, we introduce the vectors b_q (a_q), b_v (a_v) and b_e (a_e), which contain the reflected (incident) waves of all sources, delay elements, and non reactive elements, respectively. Please note that we do not make a distinction between the WD description of the connection network and the WD description of the non dynamic elements in the wave domain. The reflected wave quantities b_e are determined by

$$b_e = S a_e. \tag{18}$$

The matrix S is the direct sum of all N_e scattering matrices of all non dynamic elements and the connection network, i. e.

$$S = \mathbf{diag}(S_1, S_2, \ldots, S_\nu, \ldots, S_{N_e}) . \tag{19}$$

The delay elements with respect to the variable t_κ are described by

$$b_v^\kappa(\nu + \mathbf{e}_\kappa) = a_v^\kappa(\nu) . \tag{20}$$

In order to characterize the complete MDWDF, it is useful to combine all vectors of the reflected and the incident waves into the two vectors

$$a = \begin{bmatrix} a_q^\mathrm{T} & a_v^\mathrm{T} & a_e^\mathrm{T} \end{bmatrix}^\mathrm{T} \text{ and } b = \begin{bmatrix} b_q^\mathrm{T} & b_v^\mathrm{T} & b_e^\mathrm{T} \end{bmatrix}^\mathrm{T} . \tag{21}$$

The connection of the elements in the wave domain is described by the permutation matrix P. The incident and the reflected power wave quantities are related to each other by

$$a = P b . \tag{22}$$

Permutation matrices possess the property to be orthogonal. Since we connect all elements in a piecewise manner, P is in addition a symmetric matrix, i. e. $P^\mathrm{T} P = 1$, $P^\mathrm{T} = P$. The MDWDF is based on a reference circuit. Thus every source, capacitance or non-reactive electrical element is connected by the connection network to another element. The connection network results in a non reactive element in the wave domain. This means that in the wave domain at least one element of two connected elements is non reactive, i. e. the matrix P has the structure

$$P = \begin{bmatrix} 0 & 0 & P_{qe} \\ 0 & 0 & P_{ve} \\ P_{eq} & P_{ev} & P_{ee} \end{bmatrix} = \begin{bmatrix} P_q \\ P_v \\ P_e \end{bmatrix} . \tag{23}$$

Now we are going to sort the equations in such a manner that we yield an algorithm. Due to the special choice of the matrix H, the reflected waves of the delay elements are known from the previous discrete sampling points of time. The wave quantities of the given vector $b_q(\nu)$ are also known. Our aim is to compute the missing vector b_e. This can be performed by inserting the last (vectorial) row of equation (22) into equation (18). Thus, we have

$$b_e = S \left[P_{eq} b_q + P_{ev} b_v + P_{ee} b_e \right]. \tag{24}$$

If we have a MDWDF, which contains no delay-free directed loop, a permutation matrix P_b always exists, which transforms the matrix $S P_{ee}$ by an orthogonal transform into a strict lower triangle matrix, i. e.

$$P_b S P_{ee} P_b^\mathrm{T} = \begin{bmatrix} 0 & \cdots & \cdots & 0 \\ \bullet & \ddots & & \vdots \\ \vdots & \ddots & \ddots & \vdots \\ \bullet & \cdots & \bullet & 0 \end{bmatrix} . \tag{25}$$

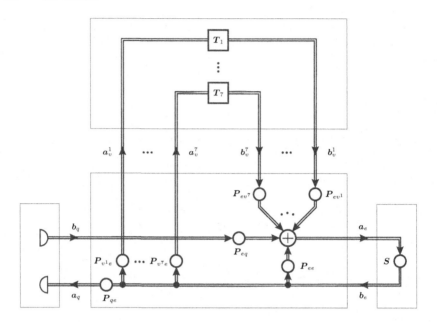

Fig. 5. Signal flow diagram

In that case the computation can be performed directly, without inverting a matrix. In the following, we suppose that the MDWDF has no delay-free directed loops. Furthermore, we suppose that we numbered the waves in such a way that $P_b = 1$. Thus, we can write equation (24) in the form

$$b_e = L_q\, b_q + L_v\, b_v + L_e\, b_e = Lb \quad , \quad L = S\,[\, P_{eq} \quad P_{ev} \quad P_{ee}\,] \qquad (26)$$

with a strict lower triangle matrix L_e. Fig.5 shows the signal-flow diagram.

3   Embedding MDWDFs in TELEPERM XS

In the following, we give a brief introduction to the I&C system TELEPERM XS. TELEPERM XS is a digital I&C-system for safety-critical automation and control tasks in nuclear power plants. The project planning of the digital I&C-system can be performed by means of the engineering system SPACE both for hardware and software. The software component can be developed by connecting given functional elements of a schematic diagram. The given elements are manually coded in ANSI-C language and manually verified. They are part of the SPACE library. After a successful consistency check, the automated code-generator of SPACE produces C-Code consisting of the generated project-dependent code. This C-code is compiled and linked with the project independent code of the function elements. Our aim is to embed MDWDF in the TELEPERM XS system. At first glance, one can think about implementing the WD elements as function elements of TELEPERM XS. Unfortunately, this idea fails, due to two reasons. Firstly, the consistency system detects delay-free directed loops, even if they do not occur. The reason is that a MDWDF needs and provides special elements. One port of such an element is free of reflection and disconnect the delay-free oriented directed loop. Secondly, the system is only for one-dimensional problems. To engage the first problem, we implement a complete MDWDF as a function element. Additionally, we extend the software interface of the function elements from scalars to arrays. Summarizing, we can state that one functional element implements the arithmetic unit of a MDWDF.

4   Used Methods for Software Proof

The Proof of correctness is based on [7]. However, we use some different notations as explained in the following. We use $x.v$ for the predicate logic variable of the program variable x and the simple x for the desired value, i.e. that value which is claimed by the algorithm. The length of a vector variable is denoted by $x.l$. The value -1 characterizes a scalar variable. A statement of the used program language is denoted by S. Statements which cannot be decomposed any more are called atomic statements. They are defined by axioms. The predicate logic formula (often more specific entitled as assertion or condition) which describes the properties of data before executing the statement S is called precondition. This predicate logic formula is denoted by V. The predicate logic formula which describes the properties of data after executing the statement S is called post-condition. This predicate logic formula is denoted by P. Of course, the chosen identifiers S, V and P can be exchanged by others. However, there must exist a wider consent for these terms and definitions. Due to Gödel's incompleteness theorem [13], there are propositions in any axiomatic mathematical system that can not be proved or disproved within the axioms of the system. These axioms are now introduced. In order to state the connection between the precondition V, the postcondition P, and the program statement S we use

$$\{V\}S\{P\} , \tag{27}$$

which is a predicate logic formula on its own. The trueness of this predicate logic formula is equivalent to:
"If the precondition V is true before initiation of a statement S, then the post-condition P will be true on its completion." In this case, the statement satisfies the specification and is called correct. Thus, showing that $\{V\}S\{P\}$ is true is necessary and sufficient to certificate the correctness of this statement.

Generally, a programs consist of a *sequence of axiomatic statements*. In order to combine pre- and postconditions of two consecutive statements, the *axiom of composition* is used. Suppose two consecutive statements S_1 and S_2 with $\{V\} S_1 \{R\}$ and $\{R\} S_2 \{P\}$, i.e. R is the postcondition of S_1 and the precondition of S_2. For the proof of the correctness of the sequence $S_1; S_2$, we infer from the formulae of S_1, S_2 to the predicate logic formula of the sequence

$$\{V\} S_1 \{R\} \wedge \{R\} S_2 \{P\} \Longrightarrow \{V\} S_1; S_2 \{P\} . \tag{28}$$

The consequence axiom is well-suitable for simplification of proofs. In order to explain this axiom, we suppose a precondition V_1 and a postcondition P_1 of the statement S. Firstly, the precondition V_1 may be exchanged by V, if the assertion V implies V_1. Furthermore a weaker postcondition P_1 may be exchanged by P, if the assertion P_1 implies P. Both rules can be formally expressed by

$$[(\{V_1\}\, S\, \{P_1\}) \wedge (V \Longrightarrow V_1) \wedge (P_1 \Longrightarrow P)] \Longrightarrow \{V\}\, S\, \{P\}. \tag{29}$$

A special category of statements are the atomic statements, which can not be built by combining other statements. As in every other mathematical theory, we have to define these atomic statements by axioms. Statements are built by means of statements and atomic statements. We defined the axioms in C-language from a practitioners point of view, using the ANSI-C-standard, since this standard is used by the engineering system SPACE. These statements are the declaration of scalar and vectorial variables, assignments, basic arithmetic operations (summation, subtraction, multiplication), logic operations (and, or, negation), the usage of brackets and for-loops. Only some of these axioms are imprinted in this contribution. The axiom of the for-loop is

$$\{V\}\, S_1\, \{I\} \wedge \{I \wedge (b.v \neq 0)\}\, S_4;\ S_3\, \{I\} \wedge b.typ = \texttt{int} \wedge b.l = -1$$
$$\tag{30}$$
$$\Rightarrow \{V\}\, \texttt{for}(S_1; b; S_3)\text{-}S_4''\, \{I \wedge (b.v = 0)\}.$$

The assertion axiom is

$$\{P\genfrac{[}{]}{0pt}{}{a.v}{b.v} \wedge \mathrm{Max}_{a.typ} \geq |b.v| \wedge a.l = b.l = -1 \wedge a.typ \in \mathcal{D} \wedge b.typ = a.typ\}\, \texttt{a = b;}\, \{P\}$$
$$\tag{31}$$

where $\mathrm{Max}_{a.typ}$ is the maximum number of the data type.

5   Specification of the Postcondition

As explained in section 3, the arithmetic unit of the MDWDF can be implemented as a function element of the engineering system SPACE. The task of this function element is to compute the MDWDF for a fixed point of time and for all spacial points of the computation area. The specification of the statement can be obtained from the MDWDF algorithm, as explained in section 2. The postcondition of the statement contains -among other things- the equality of the predicate logic variables of all delay elements b_v and their desired values. Formally, we have the predicate logic formula

$$\bigwedge_{\kappa=1}^{7} \bigwedge_{\mu_1=0}^{P_{x_1}-1} \bigwedge_{\mu_2=0}^{P_{x_2}-2} \bigwedge_{\mu_3=0}^{P_{x_3}-1} \bigwedge_{k=1}^{n_v^\kappa} b_{v\,k}^\kappa(\boldsymbol{\mu}) = b_{v\,k}^\kappa(\delta).v. \tag{32}$$

where P_{x_σ} is the number of sampling points in the direction σ and n_v^κ is the number of delay elements in the direction κ. Since the computation should be performed by the WD concept, the description of the MDWDF with equation

(20) and equation (26) is part of the pre- and the postcondition. This is the most important part of the assertions and is defined by

$$\boldsymbol{P}\boldsymbol{x} - \boldsymbol{o}$$
$$\bigwedge_{\mu'=0} b_e(\boldsymbol{\mu}) = \boldsymbol{L}_q b_q(\boldsymbol{\mu}) + \boldsymbol{L}_v b_v(\boldsymbol{\mu}) + \boldsymbol{L}_e b_e(\boldsymbol{\mu}) \ \wedge \ \boldsymbol{a}_{\mathrm{FB}}(\boldsymbol{\mu}) = \boldsymbol{A} b(\boldsymbol{\mu})$$

$$\bigwedge_{\kappa=1}^{3} \bigwedge_{\mu'=0}^{\boldsymbol{P}\boldsymbol{x}-\boldsymbol{o}-\boldsymbol{h}'_\kappa} \bigwedge_{k=1}^{n_v^\kappa} b_v^\kappa(\boldsymbol{\mu}+\boldsymbol{h}_\kappa) = \boldsymbol{P}_{v^\kappa e} b_e(\boldsymbol{\mu})$$

$$\bigwedge_{\kappa=4}^{7} \bigwedge_{\mu'=\boldsymbol{h}'_\kappa}^{\boldsymbol{P}\boldsymbol{x}-\boldsymbol{o}} \bigwedge_{k=1}^{n_v^\kappa} b_v^\kappa(\boldsymbol{\mu}+\boldsymbol{h}_\kappa) = \boldsymbol{P}_{v^\kappa e} b_e(\boldsymbol{\mu}) \wedge \bigwedge_{\mu=1}^{n_e} \bigwedge_{\nu=\mu}^{n_e} l_{e\mu\nu} = 0 \wedge \|\boldsymbol{x}\| \geq \|\boldsymbol{L}\boldsymbol{x}\| \ \forall \ \boldsymbol{x}$$

$$\bigwedge_{\kappa=1}^{3} [\mathrm{Max_i} \geq P_{x_\kappa} > 0 \wedge P_{x_\kappa} \in \mathbb{N}] \wedge P = P_{x_1} P_{x_2} P_{x_3} \wedge \mathrm{Max_i} \geq P$$

$$(33)$$

where $\boldsymbol{o}^\mathrm{T} = [\,1\ 1\ 1\,]$, $\boldsymbol{\mu}'^\mathrm{T} = [\,\mu_1\ \mu_2\ \mu_3\,]$ and $\boldsymbol{h}'^\mathrm{T}_\kappa = [\,h_{1\kappa}\ h_{2\kappa}\ h_{3\kappa}\,]$. As same as in section 2, the edge conditions are neglected here for reasons of space.

6   Implementation and Verification

This section deals with the implementation of the algorithm and the determination of the precondition. Since the MDWDF algorithm is in essence a package of equation systems and difference equations, each part of these equations can be processed sequentially. This consideration in advance yields to :

assertion statement comment		
$\{V\}$		
	S_{dekl}	declaration of the variables
$\{P_{\mathrm{dekl}}\}$		
	S_{be}	computation of the vector $\boldsymbol{b}_e$
$\{P_{\mathrm{be}}\}$		
	S_{aus}	computation of the output signals $\boldsymbol{a}_{\mathrm{FB}}$
$\{P_{\mathrm{aus}}\}$		
	S_{av}	computation of $\boldsymbol{a}_v$ at the edge
$\{P_{\mathrm{av}}\}$		
	S_{norm}	computation of $\boldsymbol{b}_v$ in the normal case
$\{P_{\mathrm{norm}}\}$		
	S_{rand}	computation of $\boldsymbol{b}_v$ at the edge
$\{P\}$		

The design of each of the statements result into for-loops, which cover all spacial sampling points and contain the equations to compute the wave quantities.

This simple structure enables a relatively elementary but extensive proof. Furthermore, the proofs of five of the six statements are quite similar. By using conventional algorithms, it is not an easy task to guarantee the limitation of all used variables. This problems does not occur by using the WD method.

We pass on imprinting the whole 70 pages long proof of the algorithm. Instead, we explain the proof procedure exemplary by means of the statement S_{be}. In order to simplify the statement, the three-dimensional spacial computation area is transformed into an one-dimensional area. The transformation from the spacial coordinates of $\boldsymbol{\mu}$ to δ is a one-to-one mapping. The computation of the vector $\boldsymbol{b}_e$ for all spacial samping points is performed within one for-loop with the loop variable `delta`. Within the loop, we have to evaluate the wave quantities $\boldsymbol{b}_e$ according to equation (26). In view of the consequence axiom equation (29), we suppose that each of the wave-quantities $\boldsymbol{b}_v$ and $\boldsymbol{b}_q$ are known (part of the precondition).

The postcondition P_{be} can be illustrated with respect to the precondition P_{dekl} by

$$\mathsf{P}_{\text{be}} \equiv \mathsf{P}_{\text{dekl}} \wedge \bigwedge_{\delta=0}^{P-1} \bigwedge_{k=1}^{n_e} [b_{ek}(\delta).v = b_{ek}(\boldsymbol{\mu}(\delta)) \wedge |b_{e\,k}(\delta).v|2\beta \leq \text{Max}_{\text{f}}] . \quad (34)$$

In order to match the assertions, we use the for-loop. We have the statement S_{be} in C-language

$$\{\mathsf{P}_{\text{dekl}}\}\texttt{for}(\texttt{delta} = 0; \texttt{delta} < P; \texttt{delta} = \texttt{delta} + 1) - S_{\text{be1}} \cdots S_{\text{ben}_e}"\{\mathsf{P}_{\text{be}}\}, \quad (35)$$

with the evaluation statements $S_{\text{be1}} \equiv$

$$
\begin{aligned}
\texttt{b\_e\_1[delta]} = & l_{11} \qquad * \texttt{b\_q\_1[delta]} \ + ... + l_{1n_q} \qquad * \texttt{b\_q\_n}_q\texttt{[delta]} \\
& + l_{1(n_q+1)} * \texttt{b\_v\_1\_1[delta]} + ... + l_{1(n_q+n_v)} * \texttt{b\_v\_6\_n}_v^6\texttt{[delta]};
\end{aligned}
$$
$$(36)$$

and for $k = 2 \ldots n_e$ we have $S_{\text{be}k} \equiv \texttt{b\_e\_k[delta]} =$

$$
\begin{aligned}
& l_{k1} \qquad\qquad * \texttt{b\_q\_1[delta]} \ + ... + l_{kn_q} \qquad\quad * \texttt{b\_q\_n}_q\texttt{[delta]} \\
& + l_{k(n_q+1)} \qquad * \texttt{b\_v\_1\_1[delta]} + ... + l_{k(n_q+n_v)} \qquad * \texttt{b\_v\_6\_n}_v^6\texttt{[delta]} \\
& + l_{k(n_q+n_v+1)} * \texttt{b\_e\_1[delta]} \ + ... + l_{k(n_q+n_v+k-1)} * \texttt{b\_e\_k\_1[delta]}; .
\end{aligned}
$$
$$(37)$$

The proof of $\{\mathsf{P}_{\text{dekl}}\} S_{\text{be}} \{\mathsf{P}_{\text{be}}\}$ uses the axiom equation (30) with the loop condition $b \equiv \delta.v < P \equiv \delta.v \leq P - 1$.

Theorem: The predicate logic formula

$$\mathsf{I} \equiv 0 \leq \delta.v \leq P \wedge \mathsf{P}_{\text{dekl}} \wedge \bigwedge_{\delta=0}^{\delta.v-1} \bigwedge_{k=1}^{n_e} [b_{ek}(\delta).v = b_{ek}(\boldsymbol{\mu}(\delta)) \wedge |b_{e\,k}(\delta).v|2\beta \leq \text{Max}_{\text{f}}]$$
$$(38)$$

is a valid invariance of the for-loop, where β is the maximum of all normalized port resistances and port conductances, i.e. $\beta = \max_{\mu} \{\max\{\sqrt{R_{N\mu}}, \sqrt{G_{N\mu}}\}\}$. According to equation (30), we can deduce the correctness from the correctness of the initialization $\{\mathsf{P}_{\text{dekl}}\}S_1\{\mathsf{I}\}$, the loop end $\mathsf{P}_{\text{be}} \equiv \mathsf{I} \wedge \neg b$, and the invariance $\{\mathsf{I} \wedge b\}S_4; S_3\{\mathsf{I}\}$.

Proof (in extracts): Application of equation (31) on `delta = 0` yields

$$0 \leq P \wedge \mathsf{P}_{\mathrm{dekl}} \wedge \bigwedge_{\delta=0}^{-1} \bigwedge_{k=1}^{n_e} [b_{ek}(\delta).v = b_{ek}(\boldsymbol{\mu}(\delta)) \wedge |b_{e\,k}(\delta).v|2\beta \leq \mathrm{Max_f}] \wedge \delta.l = -1.$$

(39)

This is the precondition $\mathsf{P}_{\mathrm{dekl}}$, since $\mathsf{P}_{\mathrm{dekl}}$ implies $0 \leq P$. The negated loop condition is $\neg b \equiv \delta.v \geq P$, so that we obtain the postcondition of the for-loop

$$\mathsf{I} \wedge \delta.v \geq P \equiv \delta.v = P \wedge \mathsf{P}_{\mathrm{dekl}} \wedge \bigwedge_{\delta=0}^{P-1} \bigwedge_{k=1}^{n_e} [b_{ek}(\delta).v = b_{ek}(\boldsymbol{\mu}(\delta)) \wedge |b_{e\,k}(\delta).v|2\beta \leq \mathrm{Max_f}].$$

(40)

This is after applying equation (29) in order to vanish $\delta.v = P$, the postcondition according to equation (34). The proof of the invariance $\{\mathsf{I} \wedge b\} S_4; S_3 \{\mathsf{I}\}$ is much longer and can not be explained here.

In this style all of the statements are proved. The proof of the complete statements, which implements the MDWDF algorithm, result in the precondition V. This precondition V implies in essence the equality of predicate logic variables and the desired values of all sources values b_q and delay elements b_v. Furthermore, the used (vectorial) variables of the sources and the delay elements must be declared and must have the correct length.

7   Summary

In this paper, we have shown some visions for the 4th generation of instrumentation and control (I&C) systems in nuclear power plants. We suggested a numerically approach to solve PDEs with I&C-systems. For this purpose we used the wave digital method.

The proposed development is not only for academic aim, but also for practical application in I&C-systems, which are already in service. For this purpose, we gave a brief introduction into the commercial I&C-system TELEPERM XS. We extended the software interface of TELEPERM XS in such a manner that MD-WDFs can be simulated with this I&C-system. In order to preserve all safety features of the I&C-system, we verified the used implementations in C-language by means of formal methods of software engineering. For reasons of space, the correctness proof was printed down in this contribution only in extracts. The proof of the implementation takes profit from the passivity property of the algorithm. This passivity property was also used to ensure the numerical stability, even for computer systems, which use the round to nearest point on the number lattice.

In conclusion, we can state on the one hand that we have a well-established theory in nuclear physics. This theory describes the nuclear physics with mathematical methods in the form of PDEs. On the other hand, we can observe an introduction of integrated hardware-software I&C-systems in the last decades. Additionally, we have powerful computer systems with steadily increasing floating point performance available, which will be introduced in the next generation I&C-systems. The questionable point in this context is whether this potential can be used for safety-critical applications. Key technologies are both the development of correct software and the implementation of the defence-in-depth concepts by I&C functions graded according to their safety significance (IEC 61226).

For this aim, we need correct algorithms as well as a correct implementations of the algorithms. As we have seen in this paper, we can provide both with the wave digital method and the following formal verification.

The solutions of the PDEs are processed in order to provide more detailed information of the reactor state. This increased amount of information can be used to gain the safety level of the nuclear power plant. Furthermore, the control closed-loop reactor can be optimized.

References

1. Fettweis, A.: Entwurf von Digitalfiltern in Anlehnung an Verfahren der klassischen Netzwerktheorie. NTZ-Fachtagung 15./16.10.1970 Stuttgart (1970)
2. Fettweis, A.: Wave digital filters: Theory and Practice. (invited paper) Proceedings of the IEEE (The Institute of Electrical and Electronics Engineers),vol. 74, no. 2, pp. 270-327 (1986) (Correction to "...", no. 75, vol. 5, p. 729.
3. Fettweis, A.: Multidimensional wave digital filters. In: 1976. Volume 2., Genoa, Italy (1976) 409–416
4. Fischer, H.D.: Wave digital filters for numerical integration. ntz-Archiv, Bd. 6, Nr. 2, S. 37-40 (1984)
5. Fettweis, A., Nitsche, G.: Massively parallel algorithms for numerical integration of partial differential equations. International Workshop on Algorithms and Parallel VLSI Architectures, Summaries of Contributions, S. 475-484, Pont-à-Mousson, France (1990)
6. McCarthy, J.: Towards a Mathematical Science of Computation. Proceedings of the IFIP Congress, S.21-28, North-Holland, Amsterdam (1962)
7. Hoare, C.: An Axiomatic Basis for Computer Programming. CACM, Bd. 12, Nr. 10, S. 576-580+583 (1969)
8. Bose, N.K.: Applied Multidimensional System Theory. Van Nordstrand Reinhold Company (1982)
9. Meerkötter, K.: Beiträge zur Theorie der Wellendigitalfilter. Doctoral dissertation, Ruhr-Universität Bochum (1979)
10. Ochs, K.: Passive Integration Methods : Fundamental Theory. Archiv für Elektronik und Übertragungstechnik, Bd. 55, Nr. 3, S. 153-163 (2001)
11. Seshu, S., Reed, M.B.: Linear Graphs and Electrical Networks. ADDISON-WESLEY (1961)
12. Vollmer, M.: An approach to automatic generation of wave digital structures from pdes. Proceedings of the IEEE International Symposium on Circuits and Systems (ISCAS '04), Vancouver, Canada, 23 May - 26 May (2004)
13. Gödel, K.: Über formal unentscheidbare Sätze der Principia Mathematica und verwandter Systeme I. Monatshefte für Mathematik und Physik, Vol. 38, P. 173-198 (1931)

An Integrated View of Security Analysis and Performance Evaluation: Trading QoS with Covert Channel Bandwidth

Alessandro Aldini and Marco Bernardo

Università di Urbino "Carlo Bo"
Istituto di Scienze e Tecnologie dell'Informazione
Piazza della Repubblica 13, 61029 Urbino, Italy
{aldini, bernardo}@sti.uniurb.it

Abstract. Security analysis and performance evaluation are two fundamental activities in the system design process, which are usually carried
out separately. Unfortunately, a purely qualitative analysis of the security requirements is not sufficient in the case of real systems, as they
suffer from unavoidable information leaks that need to be quantified. In
this paper we propose an integrated and tool-supported methodology en-
compassing both activities, thus providing insights about how to trade
the quality of service delivered by a system with the bandwidth of its
covert channels. The methodology is illustrated by assessing the effectiveness and the efficiency of the securing strategy implemented in the NRL
Pump, a trusted device proposed to secure the replication of information
from a low-security level enclave to a high-security level enclave.

1 Introduction

Multilevel secure computing enforces data access control in systems where sensitive information is classified into access levels, and users are assigned clearances,
such that users can only access information classified at or below their clearances. Such a controlled sharing of information is made harder by two aspects.
On the one hand, the recent trends to open and distributed computing increase
the vulnerability of network systems to attacks and of confidential data to information leaks[1]. On the other hand, the securing strategies used to improve the
degree of system security must minimize each unavoidable information leakage
without jeopardizing the quality of service (QoS) perceived by the users that
are allowed to access data. Therefore, trading QoS with information leaks is of
paramount importance in the system design process. This activity involves both
security analysis and performance evaluation, two tasks that – unfortunately –
are usually carried out separately.

In order to achieve a reasonable balance between QoS and security, in this paper we advocate the adoption of an integrated view of security and performance

---

[1] It is well known from real cases that it is not possible to eliminate in practice every
unwanted covert channel [MK94,R+01,AG02,ABG03].

M. Heisel et al. (Eds.): SAFECOMP 2004, LNCS 3219, pp. 283–296, 2004.

analyses. This is accomplished by proposing a tool-supported methodology that combines noninterference-based security analysis and performance evaluation on the same formal system description. Given a system, the integrated methodology we propose works as follows. The first step consists of providing a functional description of the system, on which a security check is applied in order to reveal all the potential nondeterministic covert channels from high-security level to low-security level. Such an analysis is based on a noninterference approach to information flow theory [GM82] and is essentially carried out through equivalence checking [FG95]. The unwanted covert channels that are captured by the security analysis are removed, if possible, by adequately changing the functional behavior of the system. Secondly, if some information leakage is revealed that cannot be removed, the bandwidth of each unavoidable covert channel is quantitatively estimated. This is carried out by enriching the functional description of the system with information about the temporal delays and the frequencies of the system activities. The second description considered in the methodology thus relies on a stochastic model that can be analyzed through standard numerical techniques or simulation [Ste94,Lav83]. The output of this performance analysis is given by the value of some relevant efficiency measures of the system together with the bandwidth of its covert channels, expressed as the amount of information leaked per unit of time. Such performance figures are then used as a feedback to properly tune the system configuration parameters in a way that lowers the covert channel bandwidth under a tolerable threshold without jeopardizing the QoS delivered by the system.

Although the proposed methodology is independent of the specific description language and companion tool – provided that the basic ingredients needed by the methodology itself are supplied – in this paper the application of the methodology is illustrated using the Æmilia description language [BDC02] and a suitably extended version of the related tool TwoTowers [AB04] that encompasses security analysis.

We exemplify the application of our methodology by means of a real case study: the Network NRL Pump [KMM98]. This is a trusted device used in multiple single-level security architectures to offer replication of information from low-security level systems (Low, for short) to high-security level systems (High, for short) with high-assurance security guarantees. Data replication is needed in this framework to minimize multilevel secure accesses to shared resources from processes at different security levels. Although at first sight illegal information leaks seem to be absent in a message passing from Low to High, some subtle behaviors must be paid attention to in order to prevent unauthorized users from obtaining access to confidential information. In fact, in order to offer reliable communications, an acknowledgement (ack) is usually required for each message that is successfully sent. The transmission of an ack from High to Low is more than enough to set up a covert communication channel if the timing of the ack is under the control of the High system. The NRL Pump, which basically acts as a delaying buffer between High and Low, makes it negligible such a timing covert channel (see, e.g., the security analysis conducted in [L+04]) with a minor impact on the QoS. However, some information can still be sent from High to Low through the NRL Pump. This is due to the feedback forwarded by the pump to notify Low that a connection is up/down. In fact, High can manipulate the notification procedure to set up a 1-bit covert channel. To mitigate the effect of such an unavoidable covert channel, the NRL Pump architecture is designed in such a way that a minimum delay is enforced between connection setup and connection closing/abort and between the connection reestablishment and the auditing of any connection that behaves in a suspicious way. Therefore, the question is no longer whether the NRL Pump is secure, but how much data per unit of time can be leaked by exploiting the backward information flow. By applying our methodology, we formally verify that such an information leakage is the unique functional covert channel suffered by the NRL Pump. Then we provide useful information about the relation between the bandwidth of such a covert channel and the NRL Pump configuration parameters. In particular, we emphasize the impact of the NRL Pump securing strategy on the QoS delivered by the system, expressed as the number of connection requests that are served per unit of time.

The rest of the paper is organized as follows. In Sect. 2 we describe the case study, i.e. the NRL Pump, which will be used throughout the paper to illustrate our methodology. Sect. 3 introduces the Æmilia specification language together with a sketch of the formal description of the NRL Pump. In Sect. 4 we apply our methodology to the analysis of the NRL Pump model. Some concluding remarks are reported in Sect. 5.

2 An Overview of the NRL Pump

The NRL Pump is configured as a single hardware device that interfaces a high-security level LAN with a low-security level LAN. In essence, the pump places a buffer between Low and High, pumps data from Low to High, and probabilistically modulates the timing of the ack from High to Low on the basis of the average transmission delay from High to the pump. The low-level and high-level enclaves communicate with the pump through special interfacing software called wrappers, which implement the pump protocol (see Fig. 1). Each wrapper is made of an application-dependent part, which supports the set of functionalities that satisfy application-specific requirements, and a pump-dependent part, which is a library of routines that implement the pump protocol. Each message that is received and forwarded by the wrappers includes 7 bytes of header field, containing information about the data length, some extra header, and the type of message (data or control).

The pump can be considered as a network router. For security reasons, each process that uses the pump must register its address with the pump administrator, which is responsible for maintaining a configuration file that contains a connection table with registration information. The pump provides both recov-

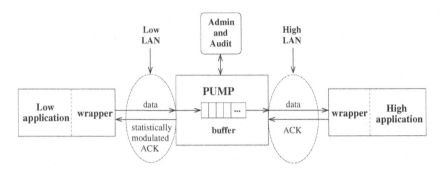

Fig. 1. Network NRL Pump architecture

erable and non-recoverable services[2]. Here, we concentrate on non-recoverable applications, like, e.g., FTP.

In brief, the procedure to establish a connection between Low and High through the pump is as follows. Initially, Low sends a connection request message to the main thread (MT) of the pump, which identifies the sending process and the address of the final destination. If both addresses are valid (i.e., they have been previously registered in the configuration file managed by the pump administrator), MT sends back a connection valid message, otherwise it sends a connection reject message. In the first case, the connection is managed by a trusted low thread (TLT) and a trusted high thread (THT), which are created during the connection setup phase to interact with Low and High, respectively. Registered High processes are always ready to accept a connection from the pump through the same handshake mechanism seen above. Once the new connection is established, the pump sends a connection grant message to both systems with initialization parameters for the communication. During the connection, TLT receives data messages from Low, then stores them in the connection buffer. Moreover, it sends back the acks (which are special data messages with zero data length) in the same order it receives the related data messages, by introducing an additional stochastic delay computed on the basis of the average rate at which THT consumes messages. On the other hand, THT delivers to High any data message contained in the connection buffer. The pump protocol also requires High to send back to THT the ack messages related to the received data messages. If High violates this protocol, THT aborts the connection. In such a case, as soon as TLT detects that THT is dead, it immediately sends all the remaining acks and a connection exit message to Low. Another special data message is connection close, which is sent at the end of a normal connection from Low to the pump.

In general, the pump is a reliable, secure, one-way communication device from Low to High, which minimizes the amount of (covert) communication in

---

[2] Recoverability safely assumes that any sent message will be delivered to the high system, even if connection failures occur.

the opposite direction. During the connection, only THT directly communicates with High and only TLT directly communicates with Low. Moreover, TLT and THT directly interact only through the connection buffer. However, even if the pump minimizes any timing covert channel from High to Low [L+04], it cannot avoid some data leak in that direction. This is because the pump notifies Low when a connection is down. Such a feedback is more than enough to set up a 1-bit covert channel from High to Low. In the following, we formally verify the existence of such a covert channel and we measure its bandwidth and its relation with QoS in terms of number of requests that are served per unit of time.

3   Architecting Systems with Æmilia/TwoTowers

In order to illustrate an application of our integrated methodology, we need a formal specification language through which it is possible to produce precise system descriptions whose security and performance properties can both be verified by some automated tool. For this purpose here we employ Æmilia [BDC02], an architectural description language that is recalled in this section by presenting a sketch of the NRL Pump specification, and the companion software tool TwoTowers 4.0 [AB04], which has recently been extended to deal with both security analysis and performance evaluation.

3.1   Formal Modeling with Æmilia

Æmilia is an architectural description language based on the stochastic process algebra $EMPA_{gr}$ [BB03]. A description in Æmilia represents an architectural type [BCD02], which is a family of systems sharing certain constraints on the component observable behavior as well as on the architectural topology. As shown in Table 1, the description of an architectural type starts with its name and its formal parameters, which can represent constants as well as exponential rates, priorities, and weights for $EMPA_{gr}$ actions. Each architectural type is defined through its architectural element types (AETs) and its architectural topology. An AET, whose description starts with its name and its formal parameters, is defined through its behavior, specified as a list of sequential $EMPA_{gr}$ defining equations, and its input and output interactions, specified as a set of $EMPA_{gr}$ action names occurring in the behavior that act as interfaces for the AET. The architectural topology is specified through the declaration of a set of architectural element instances (AEIs) representing the system components, a set of architectural interactions given by some interactions of the AEIs that act as interfaces for the whole architectural type, and a set of architectural attachments among the interactions of the AEIs that make the AEIs communicate with each other. Every attachment must go from an output interaction of an AEI to an input interaction of another AEI. Given that every interaction is declared to be a uni-interaction, an and-interaction, or an or-interaction, the only legal attachments are those between two uni-interactions, an and-interaction and a uni-interaction, and an or-interaction and a uni-interaction. An and-interaction and an or-interaction can be attached to several uni-interactions. In the case of execution of an and-interaction (resp. an or-interaction), it synchronizes with all (resp. only one of) the uni-interactions attached to it. The whole behavior of an Æmilia description is given by a family of $EMPA_{gr}$ defining equations obtained by composing in parallel the behaviors of the declared AEIs according to the specified attachments. From the overall behavior, integrated, functional and performance semantic models can automatically be derived in the form of labeled transition systems, which can undergo equivalence verification, symbolic model checking, security analysis, reward Markov chain solution, and discrete event simulation.

Table 1. Structure of an Æmilia description

ARCHI_TYPE	⟨name and formal parameters⟩
ARCHI_ELEM_TYPES	⟨architectural element types: behaviors and interactions⟩
ARCHI_TOPOLOGY	
ARCHI_ELEM_INSTANCES	⟨architectural element instances⟩
ARCHI_INTERACTIONS	⟨architectural interactions⟩
ARCHI_ATTACHMENTS	⟨architectural attachments⟩
END	

We illustrate Æmilia by presenting a sketch of the formal specification of the NRL Pump. Due to lack of space, we do not show the full Æmilia specification of the NRL Pump, which can be retrieved from:

    `http://www.sti.uniurb.it/bernardo/twotowers/`

The description starts with the name of the architectural type and its formal parameters with their initial values:

ARCHI_TYPE NRL_Pump_Type(const int buffer_capacity $:= n$,
              const rate conn_gen_rate $:= \gamma$,
              const rate conn_init_rate $:= \eta$,
              const rate data_trans_rate $:= \delta$,
              const rate ack_trans_rate $:= \kappa$,
              const rate ack_delay_rate $:= \theta$,
              const rate timeout_rate $:= \mu$,
              const weight valid_prob $:= p$)

The formal parameters represent the connection buffer capacity, the rates modeling some exponentially distributed delays, and the probability that a connection request is valid, respectively. In particular, **conn_gen_rate** is the Low connection request generation rate, **conn_init_rate** is the High connection initialization rate, **data_trans_rate** (resp. **ack_trans_rate**) is the data (resp. ack) message transmission rate, **ack_delay_rate** is the inverse of the stochastic delay added by the pump to the transmission of the acks to Low, and **timeout_rate** is the inverse of the maximum amount of time that the pump waits for an expected ack.

The Æmilia specification of the NRL Pump then proceeds with the definition of the AETs. Below we report only the definition of the main thread type:

```
ARCHI_ELEM_TYPES
  ELEM_TYPE MT_Type(const rate data_trans_rate, const weight valid_prob)
    BEHAVIOR MT_Beh(void; void) =
      <receive_conn_request, _>.
        choice {
          <conn_is_valid, inf(1, valid_prob)>.<wakeup_tht, inf>.
            <send_conn_valid, data_trans_rate>.MT_Beh(),
          <conn_not_valid, inf(1, 1 − valid_prob)>.
            <send_conn_reject, data_trans_rate>.MT_Beh()
        }
    INPUT_INTERACTIONS UNI receive_conn_request
    OUTPUT_INTERACTIONS UNI wakeup_tht;
                            send_conn_valid;
                            send_conn_reject
        :
```

The behavior of the main thread type is described through a single defining equation, which is built out of actions, action prefixes, choices, and behavior invocations, with every action being formed by an action name and an action rate expressing the inverse of the average duration of the action. The main thread monitors the port of the pump to which Low sends connection request messages, which is expressed through a passive action (rate _), then reacts to the reception of a connection request by verifying the validity of the received request. In order not to have to introduce a definition of the pump adminis-trator, the reaction is abstractedly modeled by means of a choice between two immediate actions (rate **inf**) and their associated weights based on **valid_prob**, which expresses the probability of receiving a valid request. More precisely, in response to a request, either the main thread activates the trusted high thread and sends back a connection valid message with probability **valid_prob**, or it sends back a connection reject message with probability $1 − $**valid_prob**. While the communication with the components outside the pump is assumed to take an exponentially distributed time, characterized by **data_trans_rate**, the com-munication delay within the pump is assumed to be negligible, hence the time to wake up the trusted high thread is approximated through an infinite rate. The definition of the main thread type is concluded with the declaration of some of the action names occurring in its behavior as being input or output interactions, which act as the interfaces of the main thread with the other components of the system.

Finally, the Æmilia specification of the NRL Pump contains the description of the system topology, in accordance with Fig. 1. Besides the declaration of all the instances of the AETs, below we show only the attachments involving the interactions of the main thread instance:

```
ARCHI_TOPOLOGY
    ARCHI_ELEM_INSTANCES
        LW : LW_Type(conn_gen_rate, data_trans_rate);
        MT : MT_Type(data_trans_rate, valid_prob);
        THT : THT_Type(conn_init_rate, timeout_rate);
        TLT : TLT_Type(data_trans_rate, ack_trans_rate, ack_delay_rate);
        B : Buffer_Type(buffer_capacity);
        HC : High_Channel_Type(data_trans_rate, ack_trans_rate);
        HW : HW_Type()
    ARCHI_INTERACTIONS
    ARCHI_ATTACHMENTS
        FROM LW.send_low_conn_request TO MT.receive_conn_request;
        FROM MT.wakeup_tht TO HW.receive_high_wakeup;
        FROM MT.send_conn_valid TO LW.receive_conn_valid;
        FROM MT.send_conn_reject TO LW.receive_conn_reject;
                    ⋮
END
```

4   Integrating Security and Performance Analyses

In this section we illustrate the use of our methodology by assessing the existence, the bandwidth, and the relation with QoS of an unavoidable covert channel in the NRL Pump. For the sake of simplicity, since the amount of data sent from Low to High does not alter the kind of communications between Low and High through the NRL Pump, we considered a system configuration where Low tries to establish a connection during which a single message is sent to High. After the transmission of the message either the connection is correctly closed or it is aborted by the pump. As a consequence, we assume that the pump buffer has capacity $n = 1$. The results we obtained are summarized as follows:

- The noninterference-based security analysis reveals the existence of a covert channel caused by a connect/disconnect strategy. Diagnostic information is also provided to detect the functional behavior of the NRL Pump that is responsible for the information leakage.
- Two metrics that are strictly related to the connect/disconnect strategy are evaluated. The result of this analysis is an estimation of the covert channel bandwidth and its relation with the NRL Pump configuration parameters.

In the following, we describe the noninterference property we checked and we formally show that the success/failure of a connection can be coded into a 1-bit value. Then, we specify some important assumptions that we made about the network scenario and the temporal behavior of the pump. Based on such assumptions and on the nature of the covert channel, we measured the information leakage through some suitable metrics.

4.1   Noninterference Analysis

The application of formal methods to the analysis of security properties (see, e.g., [Mea03] and the references therein) is a well-established approach accepted by the security community. In particular, we employ a technique based on the idea of nondeterministic noninterference [GM82]. Basically, supposing that low-security level users observe public operations only and high-security level users perform confidential operations only, an interference from High to Low occurs if what High can do is reflected in what Low can observe. The security check we apply verifies whether the Low view of the system behavior in the absence of High interferences is the same as that observed when High interacts with the system (see the Strong Nondeterministic Noninterference property of [FG95]). Formally, we divide actions into high-level and low-level actions, denoted *High* and *Low*, respectively, depending on the nature of the activities they represent. Then, from the functional model of a system P we derive two models that express the Low views specified above. On the one hand, the view of P without High operations, denoted $P \backslash High$, is obtained by preventing P from executing high-level actions. On the other hand, the low-level view of P with High interactions, denoted $P/High$, is obtained by turning all the high-level actions into invisible actions, since Low is not expected to observe them. Finally, the models we obtain are compared through equivalence checking. To this aim, the notion of equivalence relation we consider is the weak bisimulation equivalence [Mil89], which captures the ability of two processes to simulate each other behaviors up to invisible actions. If the equivalence check is satisfied, then Low cannot infer the behavior of High by observing the public view of the system, that means the system does not leak information from High to Low. The security analyzer of TwoTowers 4.0 allows the software architect to describe in an auxiliary specification file which actions belong to *High* and which belong to *Low*. All the other actions are simply disregarded by turning them into invisible actions.

As far as the NRL Pump is concerned, the low-level view of the system is represented by the communication interface between the Low wrapper and the pump, which interact through low-level actions. Analogously, all the actions modeling communications between the High wrapper and the pump are high-level actions. All the actions modeling communications among the internal components of the pump (like, e.g., the synchronizations between MT and THT, or between TLT and the buffer) are internal activities of the NRL Pump, which cannot be seen by an external observer. Therefore, as far as the security check is concerned, it is reasonable to assume that they are invisible.

Then, the security analyzer of TwoTowers 4.0 derives the models to be compared from the functional model of the Æmilia specification of the NRL Pump, which we call NRL_Pump_Type$\backslash High$ and NRL_Pump_Type$/High$, and performs the weak bisimulation equivalence check. The obtained result is that they cannot be weakly bisimulation equivalent. The distinguishing modal logic formula returned by TwoTowers 4.0 intuitively shows what follows: NRL_Pump_Type$\backslash High$ aborts all the connections (each connection terminates with the occurrence of the low-level action modeling the transmission of a connection exit message), while NRL_Pump_Type/*High* is able to close connections between Low and High (a connection may terminate with the occurrence of the low-level action modeling the transmission of a connection close message). The related covert channel is caused by the notification feedback from the pump to Low. Indeed, if we prevent Low from observing the result of each connection (by hiding the low-level actions modeling the connection close/exit message) we obtain that the system turns out to be secure. That means the covert channel described above is the unique nondeterministic information leakage that occurs in the NRL Pump.

4.2   Performance Analysis

By following the second step of our methodology, the bandwidth of an unavoidable covert channel revealed by the security analysis is measured by evaluating some relevant efficiency measures. For this purpose, action durations are taken into consideration. In particular, in the case of the Æmilia specification of the NRL Pump, in Sect. 3.1 we have shown that some delays, such as timeouts and transmission times, are modeled as stochastic random variables governed by exponential distributions. Thus, the stochastic model we obtain is a continuous-time Markov chain. To derive performance measures of interest, such Markov chain can be analyzed by the performance evaluator of TwoTowers 4.0 through standard numerical techniques. To this aim, the user describes in an auxiliary specification file the rewards to be attached to specific actions of the Æmilia description. These rewards are then exploited to compute reward-based metrics, such as throughput and utilization measures.

As far as the NRL Pump is concerned, the security check revealed that the unique information leakage from High to Low is given by the occurrence of a connection exit event (in case High is absent) with respect to the occurrence of either a connection exit event or a connection close event (in case High is present). Hence, the number of connections that can be closed/aborted because of the behavior of High represents an estimate of how many bits High can pass to Low in a certain period. Formally, such an estimate is obtained by measuring the throughput of the low-level actions modeling the transmission of the connection close and the connection exit messages that are observed by Low.

Before showing the analysis results, we explain some assumptions about the timing of the actions occurring in the Æmilia specification of the NRL Pump. All the delays are exponentially distributed with a certain rate expressed in $\sec^{-1}$. The data (resp. ack) transmission rate and the round-trip propagation rate experienced during the connection setup phase between the pump and High are δ (resp. κ) and η. We assume that the pump uses two 64 Kbps full-duplex lines and the (mean) length of data (resp. ack) messages is 512 (resp. 49) bits, so that $\delta = 125$ (resp. $\kappa = 1306.12$) and $\eta = 62.5$. The connection request generation rate γ varies in the range $[1, 1000]$, i.e. from one request per sec to one request per ms. The rate of the stochastic delay added by the pump before sending the ack to Low is θ. We assume such a delay to be equal to the

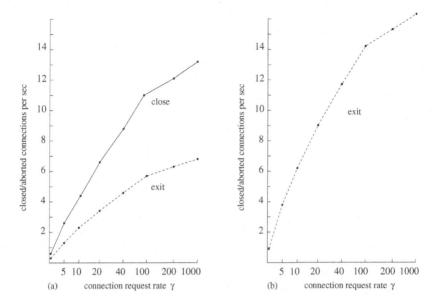

Fig. 2. Throughput of closed/aborted connections with and without High

transmission time of three ack messages[3], so that $\theta = 435.37$. The timeout delay used by the pump when waiting for the ack from High varies from 200 to 10 ms. Therefore, the corresponding rate, denoted μ, varies in the range $[5, 100]$. Finally, for each connection request we abstract from the configuration file look-up and we assume that each incoming request is valid with probability $p = 0.99$.

Fig. 2 reports the number of connection close/exit messages observed per sec in the case $\mu = 57.04$, corresponding to double the average time needed to send a data message and to receive the related ack (i.e., about 17 ms). Fig. 2(a) refers to the scenario in which High correctly executes the protocol. Therefore, most connections are normally closed, while aborted connections can occur because of the expiration of the timeout set by the pump. Fig. 2(b) refers to the scenario in which High is absent, i.e. all the connections abort. For both scenarios, we have that as the connection request rate γ increases, the number of closed/aborted connections increases as well. Note that abortions occur in both figures independently of the behavior of High. As a consequence, a connection exit message cannot reveal the presence/absence of High. Instead, Low deduces the presence of High if a connection is correctly closed, which is an event that occurs in Fig. 2(a) only. In particular, from Fig. 2(a) we derive that High succeeds in leaking its presence to Low up to 13 times per sec. Finally, note that the difference between the curve of Fig. 2(b) and the corresponding curve of Fig. 2(a) shows that the number of aborted connections observed per sec is appreciably altered by the

---

[3] This is long enough to hide the fluctuations of the transmission delays of the ack messages propagating from High to the pump.

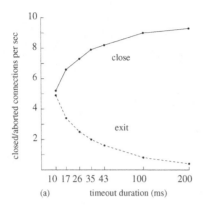 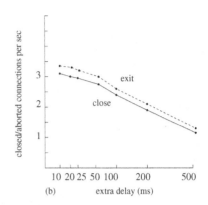

Fig. 3. Throughput of closed/aborted connections for different scenarios

absence of High. That means Low can deduce the presence of High by simply measuring the number of connection exit messages received per sec.

The number of connections that abort because of the timeout expiration can be limited by increasing the timeout duration. In Fig. 3(a) we show the tradeoff between the timeout duration and the pump throughput in terms of number of connections served per sec. In particular, we consider a scenario where both Low and High correctly execute the protocol, $\gamma = 20$ (corresponding to a connection request every 50 ms), and the timeout duration varies in the interval $[10, 200]$ ms (i.e., μ varies from 100 to 5). The curves show that as the timeout duration increases, the number of connection exit messages tends to zero, while the number of connection close messages rises up to 9 per sec. The most interesting result is that in the limiting scenario where the timeout expires after 200 ms, it is very likely that an ack sent by High arrives before the expiration of the timeout. In such a case, since an aborted connection does not occur because of the timeout expiration, High may exploit the connection exit message to leak a bit to Low. Indeed, the timeout is long enough to assure that its expiration is caused by a misbehavior of High. In other words, each connection really leaks a bit from High to Low (e.g., 0 if it succeeds and 1 if it fails). In order to measure the bandwidth of such a 1-bit covert channel, we consider a limiting scenario where $\gamma = 200$ (corresponding to a connection request every 5 ms), $\mu = 5$ (i.e., the timeout duration is 200 ms), and High alternatively completes and blocks (with equal probabilities) the connections in order to express a sequence of bits to be sent to Low. In this case, we obtain that about 3.14 connections are closed and 3.42 connections are aborted per sec, that means about 6 bits per sec are leaked from High to Low.

In general, the pump designer can quantitatively assess the relation between the amount of bits leaked from High to Low and the value of each configuration parameter that influences the QoS delivered by the pump. In particular, we have seen that covert channel bandwidth and pump throughput (in terms of number of connections served per sec) are directly proportional. A strategy to reduce the covert channel bandwidth consists of enforcing a minimum delay to elapse between subsequent connection establishments. Consider, e.g., the addition of an extra delay, exponentially distributed with rate λ, after the abortion of a connection and before its reestablishment. Then, let us evaluate the effect of this extra delay by considering the same limiting scenario as above (i.e., $\gamma = 200$, $\mu = 5$, and High tries to alternatively abort and complete a sequence of connections). The formal verification of the NRL Pump in such a scenario produces the results depicted in Fig. 3(b), which are obtained by varying the extra delay from 500 to 10 ms (i.e., $\lambda \in [2, 100]$). Note that as the artificial delay increases, the total number of closed/aborted connections per sec decreases from the upper bound of about 6 per sec to a lower bound of about 2 per sec. As a consequence, since each connection leaks a bit, we have that the covert channel bandwidth decreases, in spite of a reduction of the QoS in terms of requests served per sec. In practice, a tradeoff exists between the robustness against the 1-bit covert channel and the QoS delivered by the NRL Pump. To reduce the unfavorable impact of the proposed strategy on the QoS, which could be unacceptably burdensome, the pump should carefully activate the extra delay, e.g. only in the case of frequent abortions, which are an evidence of the misbehavior of High.

5   Conclusion

In this paper we have presented an integrated methodology – implemented through the Æmilia/TwoTowers technology – that combines noninterference analysis and performance evaluation in order to trade QoS with covert channel bandwidth.

On the one hand, the need for both qualitative and quantitative security assessment stems from the fact that real systems like the NRL Pump suffer from unavoidable information leaks, which have to be quantified in order to estimate the degree of system security. On the other hand, performance evaluation allows for a quantitative estimation of the efficiency (and the impact on the QoS) of the securing strategies implemented to reduce the covert channel bandwidth.

In general, the application of such a methodology can represent an effective support to validating the security guarantees of real systems while preserving the expected QoS. For instance, audio/video applications based on real-time channels require both critical QoS constraints and privacy guarantees. Such applications often offer customized security (choice of the authentication and privacy methods, tolerance to replay attacks, use of caching and prefetching strategies) to achieve a customized tradeoff between security and performance, which can be formally analyzed and supported by the use of our methodology.

As a future work, it would be interesting to extend the methodology to consider not only nondeterministic covert channels, but also interferences caused, e.g., by possible probabilistic aspects of the system behavior [ABG03].

References

[AB04]   A. Aldini and M. Bernardo. TwoTowers 4.0: Towards the Integration of Security Analysis and Performance Evaluation. *1st Int. Conf. on Quantitative Evaluation of Systems* (QEST'04), IEEE CS Press, to appear, 2004.

[ABG03]   A. Aldini, M. Bravetti, and R. Gorrieri. A Process-algebraic Approach for the Analysis of Probabilistic Noninterference. *Journal of Computer Security* 12(2), 2004.

[AG02]   A. Aldini and R. Gorrieri. Security Analysis of a Probabilistic Non-repudiation Protocol. *2nd Int. Work. on Process Algebra and Performance Modelling, Probabilistic Methods in Verification* (PAPM-ProbMiV'02), Springer LNCS 2399:17–36, 2002.

[BB03]   M. Bernardo and M. Bravetti, Performance Measure Sensitive Congruences for Markovian Process Algebras. *Theoretical Computer Science* 290:117-160, 2003.

[BCD02]   M. Bernardo, P. Ciancarini, and L. Donatiello. Architecting Families of Software Systems with Process Algebras. *ACM Trans. on Software Engineering and Methodology* 11:386-426, 2002.

[BDC02]   M. Bernardo, L. Donatiello, and P. Ciancarini. Stochastic Process Algebra: From an Algebraic Formalism to an Architectural Description Language. *Performance Evaluation of Complex Systems: Techniques and Tools*, LNCS 2459:236-260, 2002.

[CLS00]   W.R. Cleaveland, T. Li, and S. Sims. *The Concurrency Workbench of the New Century - Version 1.2 - User's Manual.* www.cs.sunysb.edu/~cwb/, 2000.

[FG95]   R. Focardi and R. Gorrieri. A Classification of Security Properties. *Journal of Computer Security* 3:5-33, 1995.

[GM82]   J.A. Goguen, J. Meseguer. Security Policy and Security Models. *Symposium on Security and Privacy* (SSP'82), IEEE CS Press, pp. 11-20, 1982.

[KMM98]   M.H. Kang, A.P. Moore, and I.S. Moskowitz. Design and Assurance Strategy for the NRL Pump. *NRL Memo* 5540-97-7991, Naval Research Laboratory, Washington, D.C., 1997, appeared in *IEEE Computer Magazine* 31:56–64, 1998.

[L+04]   R. Lanotte, A. Maggiolo-Schettini, S. Tini, A. Troina, and E. Tronci. Automatic Analysis of the NRL Pump. To appear in ENTCS, *Selected Papers from MEFISTO project "Formal Methods for Security"*, 2004.

[Lav83]   S.S. Lavenberg editor. *Computer Performance Modeling Handbook.* Academic Press, 1983.

[Mea03]   C. Meadows. What Makes a Cryptographic Protocol Secure? The Evolution of Requirements Specification in Formal Cryptographic Protocol Analysis. *12th Europ. Symp. on Programming Languages and Systems* (ESOP'03), Springer LNCS 2618:10–21, 2003.

[Mil89]   R. Milner. *Communication and Concurrency.* Prentice Hall, 1989.

[MK94]   I.S. Moskowitz and M.H. Kang. Covert Channels – Here to Stay? *9th Conf. on Computer Assurance* (Compass'94), National Institute of Standards and Technology, pp. 235–244, 1994.

[R+01]   P.Y.A. Ryan, J. McLean, J. Millen, and V. Gligor. Non-interference: Who Needs It? *14th Computer Security Foundations Workshop* (CSFW'01), pp. 237–238, IEEE CS Press, 2001.

[Ste94]   W.J. Stewart. *Introduction to the Numerical Solution of Markov Chains.* Princeton University Press, 1994.

Dependability Benchmarking of Web-Servers

João Durães[1], Marco Vieira[1], and Henrique Madeira[2]

[1] ISEC/CISUC - Polytechnic Institute of Coimbra
3030 Coimbra, Portugal
{jduraes,mvieira}@isec.pt
[2] DEI/CISUC - University of Coimbra
3030 Coimbra, Portugal
henrique@dei.uc.pt

Abstract. The assessment of the dependability properties of a system (dependability benchmarking) is a critical step when choosing among similar components/products. This paper presents a proposal for the benchmarking of the dependability properties of web-servers. Our benchmark is composed of the three key components: measures, workload, and faultload. We use the SPECWeb99 benchmark as starting point, adopting the workload and performance measures from this performance benchmark, and we added the faultload and new measures related to dependability. We illustrate the use of the proposed benchmark through a case-study involving two widely used web servers (Apache and Abyss) running on top of three different operating systems. The faultloads used encompass software faults, hardware faults and network faults. We show that by using the proposed dependability benchmark it is possible to observe clear differences regarding dependability properties of the web-servers.

1 Introduction

The term *dependability* translates to the quality by which a system can be relied on. This includes attributes such as availability, reliability, safety, integrity, etc. The relative importance of each attribute is dependent on the nature of the system considered. *Dependability benchmarking* is a process by which the dependability attributes of a system are assessed. The evaluation of the dependability properties of a computer system or component is a critical step when choosing among similar products. However, assessing system dependability is a very difficult problem as it is dependent on the fault probability, which in turn is dependent on many factors, either internal to the system (hardware and software) or external (environment or human made).

Dependability assessment has been addressed by using both model-based and measurement-based techniques. The former include analytical [1] and simulation [2] techniques. Measurement-based techniques include field measurement [3], fault injection [4] and robustness testing [5], just to mention a few examples.

Most of these dependability assessment techniques have been developed for mission-critical systems or for the business-critical area, and thus make assumptions about design or operating environment that affect their direct porting to more mainstream computing systems. The goal of dependability benchmarking is thus to provide

M. Heisel et al. (Eds.): SAFECOMP 2004, LNCS 3219, pp. 297–310, 2004.
© Springer-Verlag Berlin Heidelberg 2004

generic ways of characterizing the behavior of components and computer systems in the presence of faults, allowing for the quantification of dependability measures.

Following the well-established philosophy used in the performance benchmark world, the dependability benchmarking proposals are mainly inspired on measurement-based techniques. However, beyond existing techniques, such as fault injection and robustness testing, dependability benchmarking must provide a uniform, repeatable and cost-effective way of performing this evaluation, especially for comparative evaluation of competing or alternative systems and/or components.

A dependability benchmark can then be defined as a specification of a standard procedure to assess dependability related measures of a computer system or computer component. The main components of the dependability benchmark are [6]:

- **Workload**: represents the work the system must do during the benchmark run.
- **Faultload**: represents a set of faults and stressful conditions that emulate real faults experienced in the field.
- **Measures**: characterize the performance and dependability of the system under benchmark in the presence of the faultload when executing the workload.
- **Experimental setup and benchmark procedure**: describes the setup required to run the benchmark and the set of procedures and rules that must be followed during the benchmark execution.

This paper proposes a dependability benchmark for web-servers (the WEB-DB) with emphasis on the reliability, availability (readiness and service continuity) and integrity (non-occurrence of invalid information) attributes. To our knowledge, this is the first proposal of a dependability benchmark for this important class of systems.

The paper is organized as follows. Next section describes the related work. Section 3 presents the Web-DB dependability benchmark. Section 4 describes an example of the use of Web-DB to benchmark dependability aspects of the Apache and Abyss web servers. Section 5 concludes the paper.

2 Related Work

The idea of dependability benchmarking has become popular the last few years and is currently the subject of intense research, having already led to the proposal of several dependability benchmarks for several different application domains.

In [7] it is proposed a dependability benchmark for transactional systems - the DBench-OLTP dependability benchmark. This benchmark specifies the measures and all the steps required to evaluate both the performance and key dependability features of OLTP systems. A dependability benchmark for transactional systems considering a faultload based on hardware faults is proposed by [8].

A dependability benchmark for operating systems is proposed by [9]. The goal of this benchmark is to characterize qualitatively and quantitatively the OS behavior in the presence of faults and to evaluate performance-related measures in the presence of faults. The results of a research work on the practical characterization of operating systems (OS) behavior in the presence of software faults in OS components, such as faulty device drivers, is presented in [10].

Research work developed at Berkeley University has lead to the recent proposal of a dependability benchmark to assess human-assisted recovery processes [11].

The work carried out in the context of the Special Interest Group on Dependability Benchmarking (SIGDeB), created by the IFIP WG 10.4, has resulted in a set of standardized availability classes to benchmark database and transactional servers [12].

Recent work at Sun Microsystems defined a high-level framework [13] dedicated specifically to availability benchmarking. Within this framework, two specific benchmarks have been developed. One of them [14] addresses specific aspects of a system's robustness on handling maintenance events such as the replacement of a failed hardware component or the installation of software patch. The other benchmark is related to system recovery [15].

At IBM, the Autonomic Computing initiative (see http://www.ibm.com/autonomic) is also developing benchmarks to quantify a system's level of autonomic capability, addressing four main spaces of IBM's self-management: self-configuration, self-healing, self-optimization, and self-protection [16].

3 Measuring Dependability of Web-Servers: A Benchmark Proposal

A typical web environment consists on several clients performing their commands via a web-browser connected to the web-server through the Internet. In a simplified approach, the server is composed by three main components: the hardware platform, the operating system, and the web-server.

The WEB-DB dependability benchmark proposed in this paper uses the basic experimental setup, the workload, and the performance measures specified in the SPECWeb99 benchmark [17]. The following subsections present the WEB-DB dependability benchmark, with particular emphasis on the new components.

3.1 Experimental Setup and Benchmark Procedure

Figure 1 presents the key elements of the experimental setup required to run the WEB-DB dependability benchmark. The key elements are the **System Under Benchmarking (SUB)** and the **Benchmark Management System (BMS)**.

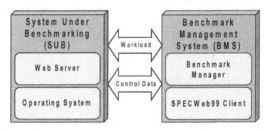

Fig. 1. Experimental setup overview

The SUB consists on a web-server installation, including all hardware and software necessary to run the web-server. From the benchmark point-of-view, the SUB is the set of processing units needed to run the workload. It is important to note that the

SUB is larger than (and includes) the component directly targeted by the benchmark (named **Benchmark Target - BT**), which is the web-server.

The BMS is a set of tools that control all aspects of the benchmark experiments. Its key functionalities are: submission of the workload, coordination and synchronization of the several components involved in the experiments, and collection of the raw data needed to produce the benchmark measures (measures are computed afterwards by analyzing the information collected during the benchmark run).

The execution of the WEB-DB benchmark includes two main phases:

– **Phase 1**: this phase corresponds to the execution of the SPECWeb99 performance benchmark (see [17]), and is used to determine the *baseline performance* of the SUB. The baseline performance corresponds to the performance attainable by the SUB in normal operation conditions (that is, without artificial faults) but with the BMS tools running. A key notion implied here is that the BMS is considered as part of the workload submitted to the SUB. A second result of this phase is a measure of the intrusiveness of the BMS which is directly given by the difference of the performance of the SUB with and without the BMS. Note that, the execution of the SPECWeb99 benchmark includes 3 runs and the results reported are the average of the results from those runs.

– **Phase 2**: in this phase the workload is run in the presence of the faultload to measure the impact of faults on the SUB to evaluate specific aspects of the target system dependability. As in phase 1, this phase includes 3 runs and the results reported represent the average of the results from those runs. During each run, all faults defined in the faultload are applied.

As shown in Figure 2, each run is made of several injection slots. An injection slot can be defined as a measurement interval during which the workload is run and some faults from the faultload are injected. The execution profile of each injection slot is closely related to the class of the faults to be injected.

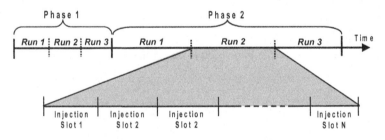

Fig. 2. Benchmark execution profile

3.2 Workload

The WEB-DB dependability benchmark adopts the workload of the well-established SPECWeb99 performance benchmark [17]. This workload represents typical requests submitted to real web-servers. Its definition was based on the analysis of web-based services in several real web-sites (see [17] for more details). The workload is composed of the typical operations allowed by the HTML (GET and POST operations, both static and dynamic). The workload also reproduces common actions such as on-line registration and advertisement serving.

3.3 Measures

The WEB-DB dependability benchmark measures are computed from the information collected during the benchmark run and follow the well-established measuring philosophy used in the performance benchmark world. In fact, the measures provided by existing performance benchmarks give relative measures of performance that can be used for system comparison or for system/component improvement and tuning. It is well known that performance benchmark results do not represent an absolute measure of performance and cannot be used for planning capacity or to predict the actual performance of the system in field. In a similar way, the measures proposed for this first dependability benchmark must be understood as benchmark results that can be useful to characterize system dependability in a relative fashion (e.g., to compare two alternative systems) or to improve/tune the system dependability.

The WEB-DB measures are grouped into three categories: baseline performance measures, performance measures in presence of faults, and dependability measures.

The **baseline performance measures**, inherited from the SPECWeb99 performance benchmark, are obtained during Phase 1 and include:

- **SPEC**: this is the main SPECWeb99 metric. It measures the number of simultaneous conforming connections. SPEC defines conforming connection as a connection with an average bit rate of at least 320 kbps and less than 1% of errors.
- **THR**: reports the number of operations per second (throughput).
- **RTM**: represents the average time in milliseconds that the operations requested by the client take to complete (medium response time).

The **performance measures in the presence of faults**, which represent the penalty in the performance of the web-server caused by the faults injected in Phase 2, include:

- **SPECf**: main SPEC measure in the presence of the faultload.
- **THRf**: throughput in the presence of the faultload.
- **RTMf**: response time in the presence of the faultload.

The **dependability measures** reported are also collected in Phase 2 and include:

- **Autonomy**: this metric gives an idea about the need of external administrative intervention to repair the web-server. Administration intervention is needed when the web-server dies or stops providing useful service. This measure is computed as: Autonomy = (100 – (No. administrative intervention / No. faults)*100).
- **Accuracy**: reports the error rate in the presence of faults. This measure is computed as: Accuracy = 100 – (No. request with errors / No. requests)*100. This measure relates to the dependability attribute of integrity.
- **Availability**: represents the time the system is available to execute the workload. It is worth noting that in the context of the WEB-DB dependability benchmark, availability is defined based on the service provided by the system. This way, the system is considered available when it is able to provide the service defined by the

workload. In other words, the system is not available if the clients get no answer or get an error. For each run in Phase 2, this measure is given as a ratio between the amount of time the system is available and the total duration of that run.

3.4   Faultload

The faultload represents a set of faults and exceptional events that emulate real faults experienced by web-servers in the field. A faultload can be based on three major classes of faults: operator faults, software faults, and hardware faults.

The WEB-DB benchmark use two different faultloads: one based on software faults that emulate realistic software defects (see [18, 19]) and another based on operational faults that emulate the effects of hardware and operator faults. Of course, a general faultload that combines these two is also possible (and is in fact the best option). The following subsections present and discuss the two faultloads.

3.4.1   Faultload Based on Software Faults

A representative faultload based on software faults is one that contains only faults that are representative of real program errors that elude traditional software testing techniques and are left undiscovered in software products after shipment. The results presented in [20, 18] identify a clear trend in the software faults that usually exist in available systems: a small set of well-defined fault types is responsible for a large part of the total software faults. Using this set of fault types as a starting point for a faultload definition, in [19] a generic faultload based on software faults for dependability benchmarking is proposed. WEB-DB follows the guidelines defined in [19] in the definition of the faultload based on software faults. Table 1 presents the fault types that compose this faultload and reproduces the statistical information regarding the representativeness of the fault types according to the field data analyzed in [18].

To emulate the software faults of Table 1, we use an implementation of the G-SWFIT technique [19]. This technique emulates the software faults by reproducing directly at low-level code the processor instruction sequences that represent programming errors. The instruction sequence inserted in the target code is equivalent to the code that would have been generated by a compiler if the emulated defect had been in fact presented in the high-level source code. A library of mutations guides the entire process. This technique has the important advantage that does not need source code of the target, and provides a good accuracy in the emulation of faults.

One important aspect is that the software faults must not be injected in the benchmark target (the web-server). As the injection of software faults implies the modification of the target code, any conclusion drawn afterwards might not apply to the original BT. We use the notion of Fault Injection Target (FIT) which is a component of the SUB other than the BT. The best option for FIT in the WEB-DB context is the operating system itself, as the OS is indispensable in a web-server installation, and its services are required for the execution of the workload. Because the OS is very large, specific portions of it were previously selected as prime candidates for fault injection. These portions correspond to the code of the API most used by typical web-servers when executing the SPECWeb99 workload (mostly network and file management API). The resulting faultloads are specific to a given OS and not of the web-server.

Table 1. Types of software faults considered in the faultload. The fault coverage is based on the field study presented in [18], which also agrees in general with another sudy from IBM presented in [20].

Fault Types	Fault Coverage
Missing variable initialization	2.25 %
Missing variable assignment using a value	2.25 %
Missing variable assignment using an expression	3.00 %
Missing "if (cond)" surrounding statement(s)	4.32 %
Missing "AND EXPR" in expression used as branch condition	7.89 %
Missing function call	8.64 %
Missing "If (cond) { statement(s) }"	9.96 %
Missing small and localized part of the algorithm	3.19 %
Wrong value assigned to a value	2.44 %
Wrong logical expression used as branch condition	3.00 %
Wrong arithmetic expression used in parameter of function call	2.25 %
Wrong variable used in parameter of function call	1.50 %
Total	**50.69%**

Because the implementation of a G-SWFIT injector is a complex task, the tools needed to inject software faults and the fault library for the different operating systems are provided with the benchmark specification. The idea is to simply download the tool and use it in the benchmark environment.

3.4.2 Faultload Based on Operational Faults
The faultload based on operational faults comprises hardware and operator faults. The types of faults considered have been chosen based on a estimation of the rate of occurrence, ability to emulate the effects of other types of faults, diversity of impact in the system, and portability. The faultload is composed by a set of faults from the types presented in Table 2 injected at different (and well-defined) instants.

The injection of the types of faults considered in this faultload is quite easy when compared to the injection of software faults. Simple applications can be developed to injected the hardware and operator fauls considered. The most right column of Table 2 presents some examples on how to introduce each type of fault in the SUB.

Table 2. Types of environment faults considered in the faultload.

Fault Types	Fault Injection
Network interface failure	Represents a failure in the server network card. This fault can be easily emulated by disabling the network interface at the operating system level.
Network connection failure	Represents a failure in a network connection and can be emulated by closing abruptly TCP sockets used to connect the web-server to the clients.
Abrupt web-server shutdown	Represents an operator/hardware fault that leads to the abrupt shutdown of the web-server. This fault can be emulated by killing the web-server processes at the operating system level.
Abrupt server reboot	Represents an operator fault that leads to the abrupt reboot of the server. This fault can be emulated by rebooting the operating system.

3.4.3 Injection Slots Execution Profile
After choosing the types of faults to inject and the technique to inject those faults, we have to define the profile for the injection of faults. As mentioned before, each execution of the WEB-DB benchmark is made of three runs and each run comprises several injection slots. Figure 3 shows the execution profile for each injection slot.

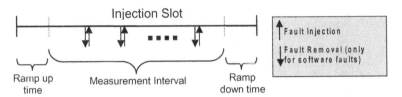

Fig. 3. Injection slot execution profile

In order to assure that each injection slot portraits a realistic scenario as much as possible, and at the same time assure that important properties such result repeatability and representativeness of results are met, the definition of the profile of the injection slot has to follow several rules. The following points summarize those rules:

– The SUB state must be explicitly restored at the beginning of each injection slot and the effects of the faults do not accumulate across different slots.
– The measurement interval starts when the system achieves the maximum processing throughput, which happens after a given time running the workload (ramp-up time). The ramp down time at the end of each injection slot represents the time the SPECWeb99 workload needs to end. Note that, no faults are injected during the SUB ramp-up and ramp-down. Ramp-up and ramp-down are 300 seconds long. These values are imposed by SPECWeb99 (see [17] for details).
– For the faultload based on software faults, faults are injected in intervals of 10 seconds and the measurement interval has a maximum duration of 20 minutes, which means that several slots may be needed to inject all the faults in the faultload, as the number of slots depends on the number of faults in the faultload. The 10 seconds injection intervals have been established based on the SPECWeb99 workload operations, which take less than one second, thus inserting each fault for a period of 10 seconds is enough time to activate the fault. Before injecting the next fault, the previous one is undone (i.e., the original code is restored). It is worth noting that as the fault target for software faults is the operating system code, different web servers are benchmarked with exactly the same faults, and the benchmark results compare the way the different web servers behave in the presence of an unstable/faulty operating system.
– For the faultload based on operational faults, four injection slots are needed (i.e., one slot for each type of fault). Several faults from a given type are injected in each slot. The duration of the measurement interval is 20 minutes. The time between injections depends on the type of the faults and is the following: 20 seconds for network connection failures, 40 seconds for network card failures, 10 seconds for abrupt web-server shutdowns, and 10 minutes for abrupt server reboots.
– After the injection of a fault an error diagnostic procedure has to be executed to evaluate the effects of the fault and to check if a recovery procedure is required (if an error is detected). This recovery procedure is controlled by the BMS and represents the external intervention needed to restore the service of the web server.

4 Apache Versus Abyss: An Example of Dependability Benchmarking

Our case-study is composed of the two web-servers: Apache (www.apache.com) and Abyss (www.aprelium.com/abyssws). Each web-server was installed over three different operating systems: Windows 2000 (SP4), Windows XP (SP1) and Windows 2003 Server. This resulted in a total of six different SUB configurations. It is worth noting that the benchmark proposal is in no way tied to a specific platform. The benchmark specification remains the same across different OSes and web-servers: all that is needed to use the benchmark on other platforms is to port the benchmark tools (we are currently working on a port for the Linux platform).

4.1 Experimental Setup

Each SUB configuration involves two computers connected via a 100 Mbps direct Ethernet connection. The SUB is entirely contained in one of the computers (the *server* computer). The BMS is composed of the following tools:

- The SPECWeb client, responsible for submitting the workload to the SUB and collecting measurements related to performance (placed in the client computer).
- The fault injector, responsible for all fault injection tasks. This tool is running in the server computer. The fault injector is also responsible for the assessment of the web-server process status. If the web-server process dies unexpectedly, or if it hangs or otherwise stops providing service, then it is restated by the fault injector. These events are useful to obtain the autonomy results.
- The availability evaluator, which continuously checks if the web-server is providing service by submitting a "GET" request and analyzing the result.

Fig 4 represents a client-server pair. All the computers used in our experiments have exactly the same configuration (1.6 GHz Pentium IV, 512 Mb RAM, 7200 rpm IDE hard disk, 100Mbit network interface). The software configuration of the client computers is the same for all SUBs (the SPECWeb client and the availability evaluator running on top of Windows XP). The server computers have six different configurations (i.e., six different SUBs: three OSes and two Web servers).

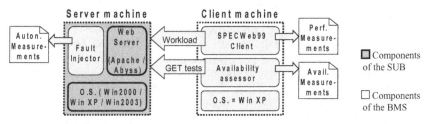

Fig. 4. Experimental setup.

Because some of the BMS tools are also running on the same machine as the web-server, there is a small performance penalty. To maintain our conclusions meaningful, we consider that the execution of the BMS tools is part of the workload subjected to the SUB, i.e., we want to observe the behavior variation induced by the presence of faults and not by presence of the BMS tools. This means that the normal behavior of the SUB must be assessed with the BMS running but with no fault being injected (we call this the *baseline performance*). To that effect, our fault injector has a profile-only mode that executes all the tasks related to fault injection except the injection itself. Later, the behavior of the web-servers in presence of faults will be compared to the baseline performance. The workload execution with and without the BMS tools have shown a performance intrusion less than 4%. We obtained the maximum performance attainable on our hardware configuration according to two guidelines:

- There was no specific effort towards custom performance optimization. Two factors contribute for *less than maximum* performance of our setups, when comparing to published results for similar hardware setups: the network interface has a maximum bandwidth of 100Mbits, and we used interpreted *perl* CGI-scripts instead of compiled scripts.
- The maximum workload subjected to each SUB was such that the *conformance* (as defined by SPECWeb99) is 100%, which means that every connection that was submitted to that SUB was fulfilled in a timely fashion (see SPECWeb99 specifications [17]). We also imposed that no errors are reported. The rationale behind the 100% conformance and 0% errors requirements is that we are interested in observing a 100% clean (no errors) SUB behavior. Any errors that occur during the benchmark experiments can then be assigned to the presence of the faultloads.

4.2 Benchmarking Results and Discussion

A complete benchmark experiment for a given SUB is composed of three complete executions for each faultload, following the SPECWeb99 style. The values for each benchmark measures are the average of the values obtained in each run for each measure. Table 3 presents results obtained for each faultload and the resulting average. To facilitate the comparison of the behavior of the SUB with and without faults, we also included in table 3 the baseline performance for each SUB (row "baseline").

Before analyzing the results, it is important to recall that the benchmark measures characterize the SUB. However, the SUB is the whole server (platform + operating system + web server), which is larger than the component the Web-DB is meant to characterize (called benchmark target - BT), which is the web server. The comparative analysis of different web servers is achieved by comparing the results obtained in more than one SUB, where the only difference between each SUB is the BT. For example, we can only compare the results obtained for Apache and Abyss when each web-server is running on the same platform and operating system.

Because the benchmark comprises six different measures, it is inevitable that some of the measures favor one of the BT, while the others measures favor others BT. Different benchmark-users may intend to deploy the web-servers in different environments. As such, the relative weight of each benchmark measure may have different relative weights across different benchmark users (e.g., user A may consider the availability more important than user B). In this case-study we assumed a general-purpose web-server scenario and assigned equal relevance to all six benchmark measures. To facilitate the identification of the SUB with the best dependability results, the values

Table 3. Benchmark measures results. The Autonomy (AUT%), Availability (AVL%) and Accuracy (ACR%) are given in percentage, the Throughput in the presence of fault (THRf) is given in operation per second, and the Response Time in the presence of fault (RTMf) is given in miliseconds. The SPECf measure has the same units as SPEC.

		Apache						Abyss				
	AUT%	AVL%	SPECf	THRf	RTMf	ACR%	AUT%	AVL%	SPECf	THRf	RTMf	ACR%
(Baseline)	(100)	(100)	(31)	(90)	345,9	(100)	(100)	(100)	(28)	(82.7)	(344.4)	(100)
Software	92,63	96,72	10,64	83,65	362,18	94,63	90,7	95,61	4,97	75,96	359,69	90,07
Operation.	95,32	93,84	17	74,83	402,23	99,79	98,02	97,09	15,67	75,96	367,75	99,48
Average	**93,98**	**95,28**	**13,82**	**79,24**	**382,2**	**97,21**	**94,36**	**96,35**	**10,32**	**75,96**	**363,7**	**94,78**
(Baseline)	(100)	(100)	(26)	(74.5)	(348.9)	(100)	(100)	(100)	(25)	(73.3)	(343.4)	(100)
Software (XP)	93,68	97,84	13,8	71,67	357,12	95,56	93,51	96,62	10,74	68,69	356,68	89,42
Operation.	97,28	98,04	22,33	71,59	362,33	99,63	98,43	98	16,67	67,74	367,4	99,57
Average	**95,48**	**97,94**	**18,07**	**71,63**	**359,7**	**97,6**	**95,97**	**97,31**	**13,71**	**68,22**	**362**	**94,5**
(Baseline)	(100)	(100)	(30)	(82.4)	(363.9)	(100)	(100)	(100)	(24)	(70)	(345.8)	(100)
Software (2003)	94,72	97,43	13,79	78,82	371,48	95,5	93,55	96,69	10,4	66,09	355,08	91,49
Operation.	98,81	97,81	8,75	79,59	374,77	99,07	98,94	98,37	15,42	66,26	362,27	99,6
Average	**96,77**	**97,62**	**11,27**	**79,21**	**373,1**	**97,29**	**96,25**	**97,53**	**12,91**	**66,18**	**358,7**	**95,55**

more favorable are presented with a gray background. The results presented in table 3 suggest that Apache presents better dependability properties that Abyss. Indeed, five out of six benchmark measures have their best values on the Apache side. For space reasons we cannot show the results in a form of charts, which would show the differences between Apache and Abyss much more clearly.

The benchmark is primarily intended for web-server comparison. However, accepting the faultloads as representative of real faults, the results can also be used to analyze and compare the properties of the OSes or the entire SUB (OS + Web-server). If we focus on one server, we can obtain information regarding which operating system provides better dependability properties for that server. According to our results and taking into account both faultloads and all six measures, Windows XP seems to provide the best platform for Apache and Windows 2003 the best for Abyss. The differences between XP and 2003 are smaller than the differences between 2000 and any of the other two OSes. On the other hand, if we focus on a given operating system we can obtain which of the two observed web-servers provides the most dependable behavior. We can also extract information regarding which of the six SUB presents the best dependability properties: the combination Apache/XP seems to be the one where the service degradation caused by faults is less noticeable.

Concerning software faults in the operating system, Apache shows a clear advantage when compared to Abyss. The only measure where Apache does not behaves better than Abyss is the response time in presence of faults (RTMf), in particular when the underlying OS is the 2003. However, all the other measures favor Apache.

When considering the faultload of operational faults, the differences between both servers are not as clear as when using the faultload of software faults. Apache presents a better overall behavior regarding Autonomy, SPECf and THRf, but Abyss is superior when considering Availability, Accuracy and RTMf. The benchmark user may weight each measure according to the operational environment where the web-server is to be deployed in order to better distinguish the behavior of the servers.

When considering both faultloads (global results), again it becomes clear the difference between Apache and Abyss. Although Abyss is better according to Availability and Response Time, Apache is superior regarding all other four measures.

The following remarks are worth noting:

- The faultload based of software faults is the one that causes the larger number of process hangs and aborts leading to lower Autonomy results. This agrees with the idea that correctness of OS is essential to the correct behavior of the applications.
- Abyss and Apache appear to have different internal strategies dealing with network mechanisms. Indeed, faults related to network (network connection failure, network interface failure) cause larger behavior differences than other fault types. The difference in network fault tolerance is also indirectly behind the differences between the Availability results: when Apache dies unexpectedly, its next instance has some trouble restoring the listening sockets; on the other hand, Abyss can restore its sockets more quickly in the same circumstances.

4.3 Benchmarking Execution Effort

The time involved in the execution of our benchmark for a given SUB is the sum of the time required for the setup procedures and the execution itself. The setup procedures are: OS and web-server installation, SPECWeb client, benchmark tools installation, and the faultload generation. The setup and configuration of the OS + web-server + tools took us less than one hour. It is not expected that other OSes and servers take significantly more than it took us to configure our setup. It is important to refer that we are interested in obtaining a basic, working web-server machine, not a customized specific-purpose portal; therefore the configuration procedures are relatively simple.

The only faultload that may require a specific preparation is the faultload based on software faults as it is specific to each OS (see [19]). The generation of this faultload using G-SWFIT [18] is an automated process that requires only simple parameter tuning. The entire process takes less than half an hour, provided that the tools for the generation are available. In our case we have an implementation of the G-SWFIT technique for the windows family which will be available for download on the web.

The execution of the benchmark is mainly dependent on the faultload size. Taking into account the three runs imposed by the SPECWeb99 rules and considering all slots needed to execute the complete faultload, the total benchmark execution time is 31 hours and 45 minutes (the worst-case scenarios are the SUBs involving Windows XP which has a faultload of software faults of nearly 3000 faults) Adding the setup timing, the total time required by the benchmark is a less than one and a half day.

5 Conclusions

In this paper we presented a proposal for the dependability benchmarking of web-servers. Given the central role that web-based services play today, the existence of a dependability benchmark aimed at the characterization of web-servers is a valuable tool when planning a web-based information system. The results of the benchmark are especially useful when comparing several web-servers to decide which one is best suited to include in a larger information system.

The benchmark components were specifically designed to be representative of the typical web-based services: the measurements address the both user and system-administrator perspectives and target all the key properties of the service expected from typical web-servers. The workload is composed of a standard widely accepted performance benchmark which represents the typical requests submitted to web-servers. The faultload addresses typical faults existing in the operational environment of web-servers including software, hardware, operator and network faults. A very important aspect of the benchmark is the fact that it was specifically designed to be independent from internal knowledge about the benchmark targets.

We illustrated the use of the benchmark through a case-study involving two web-servers running on top of three different operating systems. The results show clear differences between the two web-servers and confirm that the benchmark can be used to differentiate the dependability properties of web-servers. This is a valuable help whenever there is the need to choose between several web-servers. Given the current industry trend to used components-off-the shelf to build larger systems, a tool to evaluate the dependability properties of such components is indispensable.

References

[1]   K. S. Trivedi, B. Haverkort, A. Rindos and V. Mainkar, "Methods and Tools for Reliability and Performability: Problems and Perspectives", in Proc. 7th Int. Conf. on Techniques and Tools for Computer Perf. Eval., LNCS, 794, Springer-Verlag, Vienna, Austria, 1994.

[2]   E. Jenn, J. Arlat, M. Rimén, J. Ohlsson and J. Karlsson, "Fault Injection into VHDL Models: The MEFISTO Tool", in Predictably Dependable Computing Systems (B. Randell, J.-C. Laprie, H. Kopetz and B. Littlewood, Eds.), Springer, Berlin, Germany, 1995.

[3]   J. Gray, (Ed.), "The Benchmark Handbook for Database and Transaction Processing Systems", San Francisco, CA, USA, Morgan Kaufmann Publishers, 1993, 592 p.

[4]   J. Arlat, A. Costes, Y. Crouzet, J.-C. Laprie and D. Powell, "Fault Injection and Dependability Evaluation of Fault-Tolerant Systems", IEEE Trans. on Comp, vol.42, no.8, 1993.

[5]   P. Koopman and J. DeVale, "Comparing the Robustness of POSIX Operating Systems", in Proc. 29th Int. Symp. Fault-Tolerant Computing (FTCS-29), Madison, USA, 1999.

[6]   P. Koopman and H. Madeira, "Dependability Benchmarking & Prediction: A Grand Challenge Technology Problem", 1st IEEE Int. Workshop on Real-Time Mission-Critical Systems: Grand Challenge Problems; Phoenix, Arizona, USA, November 30, 1999.

[7]   M. Vieira and H. Madeira, "A Dependability Benchmark for OLTP Application Environments", 29th Int. Conf. on Very Large Data Bases (VLDB-03), Berlin, Germany, 2003.

[8]   K. Buchacker and O. Tschaeche, "TPC Benchmark-c version 5.2 Dependability Benchmark Extensions", http://www.faumachine.org/papers/tpcc-depend.pdf, 2003.

[9]   A. Kalakech, K. Kanoun, Y. Crouzet and A. Arlat. "Benchmarking the Dependability of Windows NT, 2000 and XP," in Proc. Int. Conf. on Dependable Systems and Networks (DSN 2004), Florence, Italy, IEEE CS Press, 2004.

[10] J. Durães and H. Madeira, "Characterization of Operating Systems Behaviour in the Presence of Faulty Drivers Through Software Fault Emulation", in Proc. 2002 Pacific Rim Int. Symp. on Dependable Computing (PRDC-2002), Tsukuba, Japan, 2002.

[11] A. Brown, L. Chung, W. Kakes, C. Ling, D. A. Patterson, "Dependability Benchmarking of Human-Assisted Recovery Processes", Dependable Computing and Communications, DSN 2004, Florence, Italy, June, 2004

[12] D. Wilson, B. Murphy and L. Spainhower. "Progress on Deining Standardized Classes of Computing the Dependability of Computer Systems," in Proc. DSN 2002 Workshop on Dependability Benchmarking, pp. F1-5, Washington, D.C., USA, 2002.

[13] J. Zhu, J. Mauro, I. Pramanick. "R3 - A Framwork for Availability Benchmarking," in Proc. Int. Conf. on Dependable Systems and Networks (DSN 2003), San Francisco,,2003.

[14] Ji J. Zhu, J. Mauro, and I. Pramanick, "Robustness Benchmarking for Hardware Maintenance Events", in Proc. Int. Conf. on Dependable Systems and Networks (DSN 2003), pp. 115-122, San Francisco, CA, USA, IEEE CS Press, 2003.

[15] J. Mauro, J. Zhu, I. Pramanick. "The System Recovery Benchmark," in Proc. 2004 Pacific Rim Int. Symp. on Dependable Computing, Papeete, Polynesia, IEEE CS Press, 2004.

[16] S. Lightstone, J. Hellerstein, W. Tetzlaff, P. Janson, E. Lassettre, C. Norton, B. Rajaraman, and L. Spainhower. "Towards Benchmarking Autonomic Computing Maturity", 1st IEEE Conf. on Industrial Automatics (INDIN-2003), Banff, Canada, August 2003.

[17] SPEC - Standard Performance Evaluation Corporation, "SPECweb99 Release 1.02 (Design Document)", http://www.spec.org/web99/, July 2000.

[18] J. Durães and H. Madeira, "Definition of Software Fault Emulation Operators: a Field Data Study", in Proc. of the International Conference on Dependable Systems and Networks, DSN2003, San Francisco, CA, June 22 - 25, 2003.

[19] J. Durães and H. Madeira, "Generic Faultloads Based on Software Faults for Dependability Benchmarking", accepted for publication at the Int. Conf. on Dependable Systems and Networks, Dependable Computing and Comm., DSN-04, Florence, Italy, June, 2004.

[20] J. Christmansson and R. Chillarege, "Generation of an Error Set that Emulates Software Faults", in Proc. of the 26th IEEE Fault Tolerant Computing Symposium, FTCS-26, Sendai, Japan, pp. 304-313, June 1996.

An Approach for Model-Based Risk Assessment

Bjørn Axel Gran, Rune Fredriksen, and Atoosa P.-J. Thunem

Institutt for energiteknikk, OECD Halden Reactor Project, NO-1751 Halden, Norway
{bjorn.axel.gran,rune.fredriksen,atoosa.p-j.thunem}@hrp.no

Abstract. Traditional risk analysis and assessment is based on failure-oriented models of the system. In contrast to this, model-based risk assessment (MBRA) utilizes success-oriented models describing all intended system aspects, including functional, operational and organisational aspects of the target. The target models are then used as input sources for complementary risk analysis and assessment techniques, as well as a basis for the documentation of the assessment results. The EU-funded CORAS project developed a tool-supported methodology for model-based risk analysis of security-critical systems. The methodology has been tried out within the telemedicine and e-commerce areas, and provided through a series of seven trials a sound basis for risk assessments. This paper gives an overview of the results with focus on how the approach can be applied for addressing security aspects in a safety critical application and discusses how the methodology can be applied as a part of a trust case development.

1 Introduction

It has been acknowledged that successful scientific results on dependability, such as availability, reliability, safety and security, of computerized systems are achieved by studying these systems from different yet interrelated perspectives. A major concern related to digital instrumentation and control (I&C) systems is how availability, safety and security are affected by potential new failure modes. This relates to the system aspects of digital I&C systems, which comprises issues such as architecture, communications, allocation of functions, real-time processing, and distributed computing. Of particular importance to dependability assessment is the communication and traceability of the requirements on service-oriented (functional) and quality-oriented (non-functional) system aspects and their interrelationships [1].

Quality assurance is of basic importance to all systems involving software. In general, a high quality product is characterized by conformance to clearly specified and well-understood requirements, including those defined by the customer. Therefore, activities on quality assurance should involve identifying the most effective techniques and approaches to achieve high quality for both the product (the system) and its development process. This is due to the belief that an improved quality of the process will contribute positively to an improved quality of the product.

Risk indicators for availability, reliability, safety and security factors are important when assessing the dependability degree of total systems involving digital I&C subsystems. In order to identify risk sources (e.g., errors, faults and failures), their roles with regard to intentional system aspects such as system functions, component behav-

M. Heisel et al. (Eds.): SAFECOMP 2004, LNCS 3219, pp. 311–324, 2004.

iours and intercommunications must be clarified. Hence, the paper's special focus on model-based risk analysis and assessment.

Traditional risk assessment is based on fault or risk models of the system. In contrast to this, model-based risk assessment (MBRA) utilizes success-oriented models describing all intended system aspects, including functional, operational and organisational aspects of the target. This is due to the observation that terms such as failures, faults and risks are meaningful only when related to the intended system aspects. The target models are then used as input sources for complementary risk analysis and assessment techniques, as well as a basis for the documentation of the assessment results [2-5].

2   The CORAS Project – Objectives and Results

The overall objectives of the CORAS project (IST-2000-25031) "A Platform for Risk Analysis of Security Critical systems" were [6]:

- to develop a practical framework for a precise, unambiguous and efficient risk analysis, by exploiting the synthesis of risk analysis methods with semiformal specification methods and computerized tools, in order to improve the risk analysis of security-critical systems;
- to assess the applicability, usability and efficiency of the framework by extensive experimentation in the fields of e-commerce and telemedicine; and
- to investigate the commercial viability of the CORAS framework and to pursue its exploitation within relevant market segments, while playing an influential role in standardisation organisations.

The CORAS project started in 2001 and was successfully completed in 2003. The CORAS project was managed based on an iterative process driven by seven field trials within the telemedicine and e-commerce areas. The field trials were all of industrial size, and the largest involved an effort of more than 500 working hours. This provided a sound basis for risk assessments [7].

The main deliverable of the CORAS project is the CORAS framework, which is structured into four main parts: terminology, library, methodology and computerized tool. The CORAS terminology integrates terminology for security and risk analysis with terminology for system documentation. There are two libraries implemented as computerized repositories within the CORAS tool. The CORAS experience repository supports the security analysis process by providing general reusable experience packages. By facilitating reuse, the repository helps the user avoid starting from scratch for every new analysis. Reusable experience packages contain UML-models, checklists, procedures and more. The assessment repository stores results from the actual security analysis. The start-up interface of the CORAS tool is shown in Fig. 1.

The CORAS methodology for security risk analysis integrates aspects from partly complementary risk analysis techniques and state-of-the-art modelling methodology. The methodology applies the risk analysis techniques: Hazard and operability study (HazOp) [8], Fault tree analysis (FTA) [9], Failure Mode Effect and Criticality Analysis (FMECA) [10], Markov analysis methods (Markov) [11] and Event tree analysis (ETA) [9]. In addition, the methodology is influenced by aspects from the CCTA Risk Analysis and Management methodology (CRAMM) [12]. The CORAS methodology employs the specification language UML [13] for three different purposes: (1) to describe the target of evaluation at the right level of abstraction; (2) to facilitate communication and interaction between different groups of stakeholders involved in a security analysis; and (3) to document security analysis results and the assumptions on which these results depend to support reuse and maintenance.

The project developed its own specialization of UML providing specialized support for security analysis. This specialization has been integrated in the "UML Profile for Modelling Quality of Service and Fault Tolerance Characteristics and Mechanisms" that was adopted as a recommended OMG standard in November 2003. [14,15]. The source-code for the CORAS tool [6] is available as open source on a GNU Lesser General Public License. The open source nature of the CORAS tool enables other developers and users to participate in its further development, by contributing bug reports, submitting new code and discussing its implementation and usage. Support is provided through mailing lists and discussion forums.

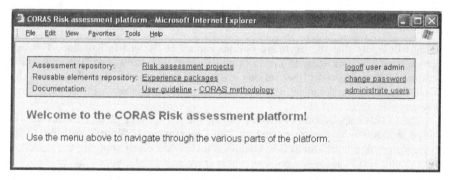

Fig. 1. The start-up interface of the CORAS tool

3   The CORAS Application of MBRA

The CORAS application of model-based risk assessment, applies the standardised modelling technique UML to form input models to risk analysis methods that are used in a risk management process. This process is based on the standard AS/NZS 4360:1999 "Risk Management" [16]. As indicated by Fig. 2, AS/NZS 4360 provides a sequential decomposition of the risk management process into sub-processes for context identification, risk identification, risk analysis, risk evaluation, and risk treatment. In addition, there are two implicit sub-processes targeting communication and consultation as well as monitoring and review running in parallel with the first five.

The CORAS risk management process is intended to run in parallel with other risk management activities, such as financial risk management, project risk management, etc. An organisation will also normally have more than one security critical system under assessment. Note in particular that the acceptance criteria applied in *Accept Risks* should be evolved by combining the security critical system's context with other on-going risk management activities and the available funding or other options available for mitigating unacceptable risks. Further, a balance should be struck between the risks the organisation faces in one system with respect to other systems.

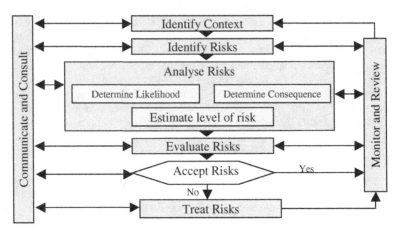

Fig. 2. The CORAS risk management process

This will imply that the treatment options cannot be viewed in isolation. The sub-processes *Communicate and Consult* and *Monitor and Review* will normally have common procedures for the various risk management activities. Also note that CORAS assumes risks to be negative. The focus is on unwanted incidents in terms reducing the value of an asset.

The CORAS application of MBRA can be utilized on three abstraction levels. The three abstraction levels are named as: "decision makers", "entry" and "full". The "decision maker layer" addresses a decision maker or a client applying the guideline. The "entry level" addresses projects where there is limited competence or resources with regard to performing risk analysis. The entry level could also be applied for smaller projects. The "full level" assumes the users to have a high competence and experience within the application of risk analysis and risk management methods. For each level, recommendations and guidelines are provided as well as templates, questionnaires and supportive descriptions.

The guideline is provided as web-based book, see Fig. 3. The left part contains the CORAS guideline on a selected level. The right part contains the supportive descriptions and links to templates, questionnaires and examples. One set of support is the tables to be filled in for documenting the results from a risk assessment, including the relationships between the tables. These relationships make it possible to check whether a result is consistent with other results from the same risk assessment. Another example of support is the additional guidewords for HazOp addressing security-aspects. The following list of guidewords is an extended version of that suggested by Winther et. al. [17], and is available in the repository for reusable elements of the CORAS tool: unintentional (as in unintentional fabrication of mail due to virus or improper handling of mail attachments), deliberate (as in deliberate disclosure of patient records due to social manipulation), disclosure, unavailability, delay, manipulation, distortion, destruction, fabrication (imitation of authorized action), replay (of repudiation (of any action) and allege (claim an action) message/request, intentional or unintentional),

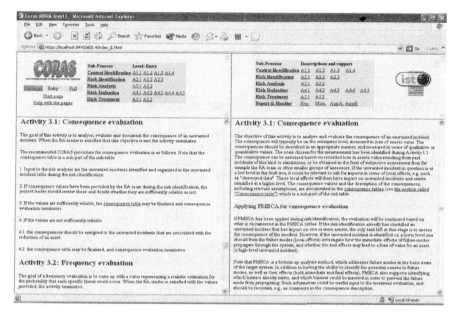

Fig. 3. A snapshot from the CORAS guideline for applying MBRA

4   Experiences from the CORAS Trials

In the following we summarize the experiences from these field trials structured in accordance with the five sub-processes of the CORAS risk management process, and in accordance with assessment criteria identified at the beginning of the project [6].

The CORAS application of MBRA has been applied in a trial on web-based collaboration service within telecardiology in Crete. The web-based infrastructure, "WebOnColl", was developed by FORTH. When a healthcare professional at a remote Primary Healthcare Centre has a patient with acute chest pains, the Tele-cardiology service can be used to send a medical request (containing a description of the patient and his condition, with all necessary information, such as digital ECG, blood pressure values, Xray images) to a cardiologist at the hospital. The service takes the necessary steps to alarm the cardiologist on duty. The information is stored in a central web-server, where the alarmed cardiologist can read the same information. The cardiologist provides his advice via the same web-server. The objective of the field trial was firstly to provide a security assessment of the service within the Cretan healthcare structure that consists of a number of geographically separated healthcare centres in a hierarchical organisation (HYGEIAnet), and secondly to offer a process of identification and assessment of potential solutions. The first risk assessment of this service was performed in the summer of 2002. Both technical and medical providers of the service took part in the risk assessment, and the assessment resulted in the identification of 97 unwanted incidents [18].

The CORAS application of MBRA has also been applied in a field trial to the electronic retail market subsystem of an e-commerce platform, developed in another IST project [19]. The security assessment focused on the user authentication mechanism, the secure payment mechanism and on the use of software agents for accomplishing specialized purchasing tasks, offering a process for identifying and assessing potential solutions.

4.1 Experiences Related to the Risk Management Process

Sub-process 1, Identify Context: The aim of the first sub-process is to describe the system and its environment. In the telemedicine trial an UML sequence diagram was used to model and assess a typical interaction scenario. The UML sequence diagram is an interaction diagram that emphasizes the time ordering of messages, as displayed in Fig. 4. The UML use-case diagram, as displayed in Fig. 5, proved useful in the process of describing the important scenarios. This process was performed in cooperation with both developers (technical team of FORTH) and users of the system (medical experts). The use of models proved useful in identifying the context of the system as they helped both risk assessment experts and other stakeholders to focus on the essential parts of the system. The identification of assets and stakeholders was performed in accordance with the recommendations in CRAMM [12].

In the e-commerce trial the same kind of modelling techniques were used as in the telemedicine trial. In addition a specific UML profile for risk assessment was used to describe more risk assessment specific documentation. For example, the results from a SWOT analysis (Strengths, Weaknesses, Opportunities, and Threats) analysis were documented by a SWOT diagram as illustrated by Fig. 6. UML component diagrams were employed to identify the platform environment, interfaces and architecture. The organisational context was described with a high level UML object diagram. A more detailed description of the e-commerce platform was provided using UML class diagrams, and UML sequence diagrams were employed to specify the dynamic behaviour.

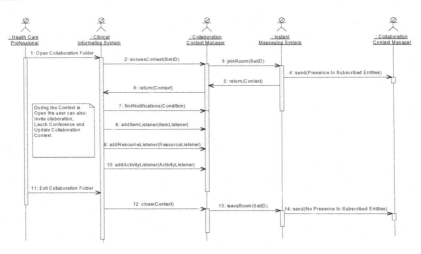

Fig. 4. An UML sequence diagram from the telemedicine trial

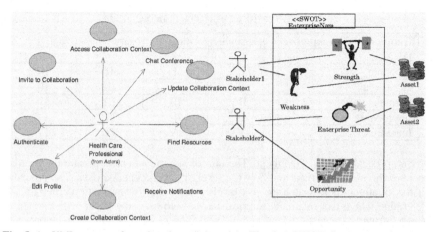

Fig. 5. An UML use-case from the telemedicine trial   **Fig. 6.** A SWOT diagram template

Sub-process 2, Identify Risks: The aim of the risk identification is to identify the potential threats to assets, the vulnerabilities of these assets and document the unwanted incidents. In both trials risk identification was performed using HazOp in order to identify possible threats for each of the identified assets and FTA to display the relationships between the threats. For the e-commerce trial also FMEA was employed for the identification of threats. The UML use case diagrams used in the context identification provided a suitable high-level abstraction regarding input to the risk identification. This supported the identification of threats that could have effects on assets. For the more low-level and detailed risk identification, both UML activity diagrams and UML sequence diagrams provided the right level of abstraction. Some new threats, compared to the preliminary assessment, were discovered during the process.

Sub-process 3, Analyse Risks: The aim of the risk analysis is to evaluate the frequencies and consequences of the unwanted incidents. In the telemedicine trial, FTA was applied in order to analyse the least understandable of the threats identified by the HazOp. One of the advantages of FTA, observed and remarked by all participants in the trial, stems from the way it in a structured manner helps the risk assessment experts to communicate and explain the threats to participants not familiar to risk assessment like doctors. Likewise FTA helped the doctors to understand and structure the causes of threats and the cause combinations that lead to the appearance of the threats. In order to conduct a more detailed analysis of some of the identified risks, FMEA was performed. This was very time-consuming, but gave the opportunity for uncovering many interesting details about the analysed threats. For these reasons FMEA was used only for the most security-critical parts of a system and it seems to require the participation of the experts on the specific aspect that is being analysed.

Sub-process 4, Risk Evaluation: The aim of risk evaluation is to identify the level of risk associated with the unwanted incidents, decide whether the level is acceptable, prioritise the identified risks and categorize risks into risk themes. In both trials a risk table was used to determine the level of risk. A risk table combines the values for consequence and likelihood into a description of the level of risk as suggested e.g. in IEC 61508 [21], as displayed in Table 1.

Table 1. The risk classification from IEC-61508

Frequency/ Consequence	Catastrophic	Critical	Marginal	Negligible
Frequent	I	I	I	II
Probable	I	I	II	III
Occasional	I	II	III	III
Remote	II	III	III	IV
Improbable	III	III	IV	IV
Incredible	IV	IV	IV	IV

Sub-process 5, Risk Treatment: The aim of risk treatment is to address the treatment of the identified risks and how to prevent the unacceptable risks. The procedure of risk treatment is to match the risk levels against the risk evaluation criteria and to determine which risk treatment to prioritise. In both trials the focus of risk treatment was to provide suggestions and communicate the possible solutions to improve the system according to the risk evaluation criteria. The UML models used previously in process for context identification and risk identification, was useful for communicating the necessary changes to the system to the stakeholders.

4.2   Experiences with Respect to a Set of Assessment Criteria

In this section, the CORAS framework (CORAS for short) is evaluated according to a set of criteria, grouped into four categories:
- *Applicability*: easiness for CORAS to address diverse types of applications
- *Effectiveness*: the precision and clarity with which the RA sessions proceed
- *Performance*: the effort and time required to understand and apply CORAS
- *Usability*: the readiness with which the CORAS risk analysis methods and results can be documented and understood by stakeholders

Applicability: CORAS has the ability to address the main security requirements for a system: availability, confidentiality, accountability and integrity. Specific security requirements were addressed by choosing the right guidewords for HazOp, so that the relevant threats could be identified. Moreover, for the telecardiology trial sessions the security requirements were classified into certain priority groups, which were used extensively for defining risk levels and priorities. In both the telemedicine and the e-commerce domains the risk analysis teams observed that all security requirements could be modelled and handled with the same easiness. CORAS seems to be capable of addressing security concerns of web-based systems in general, and there are no indications that CORAS lacks the ability to address security systems in general. The systems that were the targets of the risk assessments were handled successfully. CORAS includes a number of techniques and resulting models/tables, making the framework suitable for other cases as well. The last telemedicine trial session indicated the ability of the framework to handle unwanted incidents of different levels and large numbers of risks. With respect to the scalability of CORAS, however, more field experience is needed.

Effectiveness: During the initial steps negation of the four security properties (disclosure, manipulation, denial/delay, accountability) when identifying threats with HazOp and the use of security checklists were applied. This made it possible to address both manifest and latent threats to the target system. Nevertheless, it is obvious that not all latent threats can be identified. CORAS seems to handle different kinds of risks due to its strong business and asset orientation. The assessment starts by considering the enterprise level threats through SWOT and continues by exploring these enterprise level threats using FTA, HazOp and FMEA. CORAS covers also known vulnerability issues related to the target system. The experimental procedure showed that the models and the textual descriptions used to describe the target systems satisfy the purpose of the objective description of the system, being expressive and useful for both risk analysts and system developers with different levels of system knowledge. During a risk analysis session misconceptions can arise in many ways, e.g. through poor communication between the participants. The combination of graphical models, textual descriptions and guidelines for integrating risk analysis techniques ensured that misconceptions were avoided. The CORAS tool and the guidelines target both the issue of communication and the aspects of reducing possible misunderstanding related to how the different risk analysis methods should actually be carried out.

Performance: As a part of sub-process 1, context identification, CORAS includes an "approval" activity. The purpose of this activity is both to inform the participants, to agree on the descriptions provided and to make sure that everyone understands the models provided for the risk assessment. All the analysed systems were already in use, so the ability of CORAS to reduce system development costs is difficult to assess. As far as the e-commerce platform is concerned, certain treatments were proposed for the maintenance of the system. One approach for treatment of identified risks is to redesign or reprogram certain parts of a system. This will be used to enhance the systems maintainability.

Usability: CORAS is able to communicate all aspects related to the system and the results of the analysis. The usage of UML was suitable in expressing the system structure and behaviour. UML was also used to express patterns of undesirable behaviour as well as the relation between risks. During the telemedicine risk analysis sessions, the participation from medical professionals was intense and they could take part in the discussions related to the risk analysis of the system, either, for example, by stating specific threats that they knew about, or thinking about their causes and consequences. Some communication problems were experienced during the trials related to inconsistent usage of terminology, lack of expertise in the specific technology involved and lack of familiarity with risk analysis techniques by some participants. This is further discussed in the next chapter. The CORAS UML Profile for model-based risk assessment to document results from the trial has been considered so that further improvement of the ability of CORAS for communicating results to the different stakeholders is obtained. Based on the experimental trials conducted, a conclusion is that CORAS contains a comprehensive documentation set and most of the parts of CORAS are easy to use even by a non-expert user.

Some points that need refinement for making application of the CORAS framework easier, clearer and more efficient have been observed and are already receiving attention through the establishment of a CORAS user group [6] and projects applying the CORAS framework, among others, the SECURIS project [20].

5 Applying the Framework for Security in Safety Applications

The increased use of I&C systems, combined with the tendency to apply distributed networks to control or monitor safety related applications, has put focus on how to address the security aspects in a safety critical application. An important question is therefore whether the CORAS framework, targeted on security and based on AS/NZS 4360 [16], also can be applied for addressing security aspects in a safety critical application as defined by IEC 61508 [21]. AS/NZS 4360 provides a generic guide for the establishment and implementation of the risk management process through establishment of the context and through identification, analysis, evaluation, treatment, communication and monitoring of risks. The primary purpose of IEC 61508 is to provide a "unified approach" for all safety lifecycle activities that is "rational and consistent". As such, the standard covers all lifecycle phases for system components, from concept through decommissioning. According to Herrmann [22], the standard promotes a broad range of principles, techniques and measures to achieve and assess functional safety: a fundamental premise being the risk-based determination of safety integrity levels (SILs).

A high-level comparison of the two standards is that they provide different, but to a certain degree, complementary view on risk assessment. The major differences lies in that AS/NZS 4360 provides an "asset-driven" approach while IEC 61508 focuses on "functional safety". Another fact is that IEC 61508 covers the entire system lifecycle, while AS/NSZ 4360 focuses on risk assessment during what would be considered to be the first "phases" of IEC 61508, e.g. concept, overall scope definition, hazard and risk analysis, overall safety requirements, and safety requirements allocation. The CORAS ontology presented in Fig. 7 illustrates the importance of assets during the risk assessment, as both threat and vulnerability are related to asset value and the asset itself [23].

In Fig. 7 the concepts are drawn as classes in a simplified class diagram. The guiding words give some extra explanation about the specified relations. Starting from the bottom right corner one sees that the context influences the target of evaluation (TOE) that contains assets and has its security requirements. Security requirements lead to security policies which protect assets by reducing their vulnerabilities. Continuing, a threat may exploit the vulnerability of an asset, thereby reducing the value of the asset. A risk contains an unwanted incident having a certain consequence and frequency of occurring.

In Fig. 8 we propose a safety-related ontology to reflect the fact that when using IEC 61508 for risk assessment, the "asset" we are focusing on safety. At a high level this approach seems to be valuable, however at this point the revised approach is not tested in practice. How the different risk assessment methods are applied may also differ when used in a safety assessment instead of a security assessment (as in CORAS).

6 Applying MBRA for Trust Case Development

The concept of a trust case refers to the need of providing a complete and explicit argument justifying trust in the computer system being used in a given application

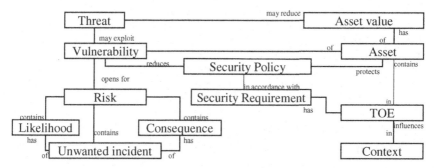

Fig. 7. The CORAS high level ontology for security

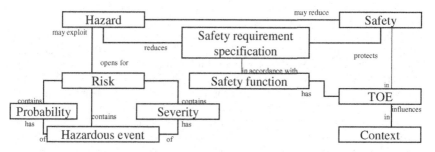

Fig. 8. A safety-related ontology

context, addressing both safety and security aspects [24]. The evidence used to support an argument about trust can be:

- facts, e.g. demonstrating adherence to established principles, documented design decisions, results of performed analyses;
- assumptions, which are used by the argument and do not require explicit justification (nevertheless, they can be later converted into claims and supported by further argumentation);
- and sub-claims, that are developed further down by giving arguments that support them.

For both safety and security it is recommended to provide the facts in parallel with the specification and design of the system, e.g. through risk analysis and assessment of the system. This is one of the characteristics of model-based risk assessment approaches, such as the CORAS framework, as they facilitate success-failure links. The success-failure links are explicit in the CORAS framework by using models both as basis for the assessment and by using updated models for communicating risk assessment results. Examples are the use of UML use-cases for assessment and the use of "misuse-cases" for documenting the risk assessment and integrating the results into the models in use [25,26]. It also fits well with the approach to trust case development proposed by Gorski et.al. [24], as they apply UML to represent claim models and related context models of the trust case.

The CORAS framework is based on an assumption that different types of interconnections between models are taken care of by the modelling language itself, in this case UML. However, all the different UML diagrams do not have the power to describe all inter-model structures, reflecting the resemblances, discrepancies, interrelationships and interconnections among the system's functional, operational and structural properties. Therefore, the inter-model structure can be viewed as an area where the framework has a potential for further development [27].

7 Conclusions

The systems and applications targeted by the field trials were all analysed successfully, and it was concluded that the CORAS framework is capable of addressing security concerns of similar systems. Moreover, the CORAS framework was also found to be general since it gives the analyst freedom to select analysis methods and modelling techniques depending on the target and the security issues to be analysed. By focusing on systems modelling prior to the assessment and by complying with standards, the CORAS application of MBRA is a promising approach for risk assessment of security-critical systems. Furthermore, the focus on the practical experiences and hence the applicability of the results through the trials has added a valuable quality to the application. The CORAS project in general and the CORAS application of MBRA in particular have contributed positively to the visibility of model-based risk assessment and thus to the disclosure of several potentials for further exploitation of various aspects within this important research field. In that connection, the CORAS methodology's possibilities for further improvement towards utilization in more complex architectures, and also in other application domains, is a topic for further research. Finally, this paper has also discussed how the CORAS application of MBRA can be applied as a part of a trust case development.

Acknowledgement. CORAS was a European R&D project funded by the 5th framework program on Information Society Technologies (IST-2000-25031). The CORAS consortium consisted of eleven partners from industry, research and academia in four European countries: Solinet GmbH (DE), CLRC Rutherford Appleton Labs (GB), Queen Mary & Westfield College, University of London (GB), Computer Technology Institute (GR), FORTH (GR), Intracom (GR), Norwegian Centre of Telemedicine (NO), Norwegian Computing Centre (NO), SINTEF ICT (NO), Telenor Communication II (NO) and Institutt for energiteknikk (NO). The results reported in the paper have benefited from joint efforts of the whole consortium.

References

1.   Thunem, A. P-J: "Modelling of Knowledge Intensive Computerised Systems Based on Capability-Oriented Agent Theory (COAT)", In Proc. *International IEEE Conference on Integration of Knowledge Intensive Multi-Agent Systems, IEEE-KIMAS'03*, pp 58-63, Cambridge (MA), USA, 2003.

2. Garrett, C.J., Guarro, S.B., Apostolakis, G.E: "The dynamic flow graph methodology for assessing the dependability of embedded software systems". *IEEE Trans. on Systems, Man, and Cybernetics*, Vol. 25, No. 5, pp 824-840, 1985.
3. Jalashgar, A. (Thunem, A. P-J): "A Cognitive and Formal Terminology for Descriptive Parameters in Concurrent Real-Time Distributed Software Systems", Ch. 2, Part 3, pp 229-248, in *"Soft Computing for Risk Evaluation and Management"*, Physica Verlag Publisher, 2001.
4. Jalashgar, A. (Thunem, A. P-J): "Identification of Hidden Failures in Process Control Systems Based on the HMG Method", *International Journal of Intelligent Systems*, Vol. 13, pp 159-179, 1998.
5. Kim, I.S., Modarres, M.: "Application of Goal Tree-Success Tree Model as the Knowledge-Base of Operator Advisory System", *Nuclear Engineering & Design J.*, 104, pp 67-81, 1987.
6. CORAS: A Platform for Risk Analysis of Security Critical systems, IST-2000-25031, (2000). (http://coras.sourceforge.net/)
7. Fredriksen, R., Gran, B.A., Stølen, K., Djordjevic, I.: "Experiences from application of model-based risk assessment". In. Proc. *European Conference on Safety and Reliability* (ESREL'2003), vol. 1, pp 643-648, Swets & Zeitlinger, 2003.
8. Redmill, F., Chudleigh, M., Catmur, J.: *Hazop and Software Hazop,* Wiley & sons, 1999.
9. Andrews, J.D., Moss, T.R.: *Reliability and Risk Assessment*, 1st Ed. Longman Group UK, 1993.
10. Bouti, A., Kadi, A.D.: "A state-of-the-art review of FMEA/FMECA", *International Journal of Reliability, Quality and Safety Engineering*, vol. 1, no. 4, pp 515-543, 1994.
11. Littlewood, B.: "A Reliability Model for Systems with Markov Structure", *Applied Statistics*, 24(2), pp 172-177, 1975.
12. Barber, B., Davey, J.: "Use of the CRAMM in Health Information Systems", *MEDINFO* 92, ed Lun K.C., Degoulet P., Piemme T.E. and Rienhoff O., North Holland Publishing Co, Amsterdam, pp 1589 –1593, 1992.
13. OMG. *Unified Modeling Language specification*. Version 1.4, 2001.
14. Houmb, S-H., den Braber, F., Lund, M. S., Stølen, K.: Towards a UML profile for model-based risk assessment. In Proc. *UML'2002 Satellite Workshop on Critical Systems Development with UML*, pp 79-91, Munich University of Technology, 2002.
15. Contribution in response to request for proposals for *UML Profile for Modelling Quality of Service and Fault Tolerance Characteristics and Mechanisms* issued by the Object Management Group. Submitted by SINTEF in collaboration with OpenIT, September 9, 2002. Resubmitted in revised form, May and August, 2003.
16. Australian Standard: *Risk Management*. AS/NZS 4360:1999. Strathfield: Standards Australia, 1999.
17. Winther, R., Johnsen, O.A., Gran, B.A.: "Security Assessments of Safety Critical Systems Using HAZOPs". Paper presented at Safecomp 2001, Budapest. *Computer Safety, Reliability and Security* (LNCS 2187), Voges, U. (Ed.), Springer, pp. 14-24
18. Stamatiou, Y. et. al.: "The CORAS approach for model-based risk management applied to a telemedicine service". In Proc. *Medical Informatics Europe* (MIE'2003), pp 206-211, IOS Press, 2003.
19. Raptis, D., Dimitrakos, T., Gran, B. A., Stølen, K.: "The CORAS Approach for Model-based Risk Management applied to e-Commerce Domain", In Proc. *Communication and Multimedia Security* (CMS-2002), Kluwer, pp 169-181, 2002.
20. SECURIS, *Model-driven development and analysis of secure information systems*, Research Council of Norway 152839/220.
21. IEC 61508: *Functional Safety of Electrical/Electronic/Programmable Electronic Safety-Related (E/E/PE) Systems*, 1998-2000.
22. Herrmann, D.S.: *Software Safety and Reliability*. IEEE Computer Society, 1999.

23. den Braber, F., Dimitrakos, T., Gran, B.A., Soldal Lund, M., Stølen, K., Aagedal, J.Ø.: "The CORAS methodology: Model-based risk assessment using UML and UP". Chapter in the book *UML and the Unified Process*. Liliana Favre (ed), pp 332-357, IRM Press, 2003.
24. Górski, J. et al.: "An approach to trust case development." Paper presented at Safecomp, Edinburgh. *Computer Safety, Reliability and Security* (LNCS2788), Anderson, S., Felici, M., Littlewood, B. (Eds.), Springer, pp. 193-206, 2003.
25. Sindre, G., Opdahl, A.L.: "Eliciting security requirements by misuse cases". In Proc. *TOOLS_PACIFIC 2000*. IEEE Computer Society Press, pp 120-131, 2000.
26. Stølen, K., den Braber, F., Fredriksen, R., Gran, B.A., Houmb, S.H., Soldal Lund, M., Stamatiou, Y.C., Aagedal, J.Ø.: "Model-based risk assessment - the CORAS approach". In Proc. *Norsk Informatikkkonferanse* (NIK'2002), pp 239-249, Tapir, 2002.
27. Thunem, A. P-J, Fredriksen, R., Gran, B.A.: "An Information Retrieval Terminology for Model-Based Risk Assessment". Paper to appear in proceedings from ESREL/PSAM7, Berlin, 2004.

How Explicit Are the Barriers to Failure in Safety Arguments?

Shamus P. Smith*, Michael D. Harrison**, and Bastiaan A. Schupp

Dependability Interdisciplinary Research Collaboration,
Department of Computer Science,
University of York, York YO10 5DD,
United Kingdom.
{Shamus.Smith, Michael.Harrison, Bastiaan.Schupp}@cs.york.ac.uk

Abstract. Safety cases embody arguments that demonstrate how safety properties of a system are upheld. Such cases implicitly document the barriers that must exist between hazards and vulnerable components of a system. For safety certification, it is the analysis of these barriers that provide confidence in the safety of the system.

The explicit representation of hazard barriers can provide additional insight for the design and evaluation of system safety. They can be identified in a hazard analysis to allow analysts to reflect on particular design choices. Barrier existence in a live system can be mapped to abstract barrier representations to provide both verification of barrier existence and a basis for quantitative measures between the predicted barrier behaviour and performance of the actual barrier. This paper explores the first stage of this process, the binding between explicit mitigation arguments in hazard analysis and the barrier concept. Examples from the domains of computer-assisted detection in mammography and free route airspace feasibility are examined and the implications for system certification are considered.

1 Introduction

Barriers are often complex socio-technical systems: a combination of technical, human and organisational measures that prevent or protect against an adverse effect. Barriers for safety critical systems include physical representations, for example a mechanical guard on an electronic throttle [1], as well as beliefs, such as confidence in system safety based on conformance to applied standards. A no smoking sign is a typical example of a barrier as a complex system. Although the sign aims to prevent fire from cigarettes, it is not just the sign. The barrier includes awareness of how smoking may cause fires, awareness of the significance

---

* Now at the Department of Computer Science, University of Durham, Durham DH1 3LE, shamus.smith@durham.ac.uk
** Now at the Informatics Research Institute, University of Newcastle Upon Tyne, Newcastle Upon Tyne, NE1 7RU, michael.harrison@ncl.ac.uk

M. Heisel et al. (Eds.): SAFECOMP 2004, LNCS 3219, pp. 325–337, 2004.

of the sign, the sign's visibility, training of the smokers, and its relation to other barrier systems such as an installed smoke alarm and sprinkler system [19].

Barriers embody both abstract and concrete representations of properties commonly argued in a safety case. Kelly et al. [11] defines a safety case as the document, or set of documents, presenting the argument that a system is acceptably safe to operate in a given context. Such cases implicitly document the barriers that must exist between hazards and hazardous states and vulnerable components of a system. For certification it is the verification of these barriers that provide confidence in the safety of the system. However, explicit representations of such barriers are commonly absent from safety case documentation and the associated arguments for compliance to particular standards.

Explicit barrier description in hazard analysis can provide insight throughout the development of safety critical systems and in addition aid safety certification by documenting barrier development through design to implementation in a live system. For example if there is a hazard mitigation that an interlock[1] inhibits some type of behaviour, this may feature as evidence in a safety case. It should be possible to prove that it is in place in the live system and that its performance can be accessed and compared to predicted performance in the initial hazard analysis.

This paper investigates the binding of explicit mitigation arguments in hazard analysis to the barrier concept. Identifying explicit barriers early in system development can allow informed decision making through design and implementation phases of a system's development. The remainder of this paper is as follows. Section 2 describes barriers in relation to risk reduction in design and implementation. Section 3 presents an overview of barriers in the context of hazard analysis. The use of explicit barriers to highlight hazard and barrier properties are exemplified in two case studies in Sections 4 and 5. Section 6 overviews the use of explicit barriers for certification. Section 7 presents conclusions.

2   Risk Reduction and Barriers

Risk reduction is a key factor in the design of safety critical systems and in assessment of their operational safety. It is achieved either by preventing hazards or by protecting against hazards. Prevention typically involves design modifications of the total system, including for example operating procedures. Protection involves the design of additional systems, which embody barriers that fend against adverse events, damage or harm [19]. Barriers represent the diverse physical and organisational measures that are taken to prevent a target from being affected by a potential hazard [10, pg 359]. A barrier is an obstacle, an obstruction, or a hindrance that may either (i) prevent an action from being carried out or an event from taking place, or (ii) prevent or lessen the impact of the consequences, limiting the reach of the consequences or weakening them in some way [9].

---

[1] An interlock is a mechanism which ensures that potentially hazardous actions are only performed at times when they are safe [22].

The concepts and terminology related to barriers or safety features vary considerably [7], for example Hollnagel [9] presents a classification of barrier systems based on four main categories:

1. *Material barriers* physically prevent an action from being carried out or the consequences of a hazard from spreading. For example a fence or wall.
2. *Functional barriers* impede an action from being carried out, for instance the use of an interlock.
3. *Symbolic barriers* require an act of interpretation in order to achieve their purpose. For example a give way sign indicates a driver should give way but does not actively enforce/stop non-compliance.
4. *Immaterial barriers* are not physically present or represented in the situation, but depend on the knowledge of the user to achieve their purpose. For example the use of standards.

This paper makes no commitment to the terminology of barriers and instead focuses on the presence of barriers, in whatever form, in the context of a hazardous event or action. The pre- and post-condition states of a hazard are represented by preventive and protective barriers respectively. Therefore the use of barriers, either for the prevention of hazards or the protection from hazardous effect, is considered to be part of the process of hazard analysis.

3   Hazard Analysis and Barriers

Hazard analysis is at the heart of any safety programme [13, pg 287]. It is a necessary first step before hazards can be eliminated or controlled through design or operational procedures. Within hazard analysis, descriptive arguments[2] are implicitly used to justify prevention arguments of identified hazards.

Previous work has demonstrated that explicit mitigation arguments allow an analyst to reflect on the mitigations present and constitute an initial step to processes such as argument reuse in hazard analysis [20,21]. In addition, explicit arguments document the reasoning being applied in an analysis session. If such decisions are lost, evaluation of the analysis and certification can be problematic.

Mitigation arguments to hazards are implicitly described in terms of barriers. Barriers against hazards may take a variety of forms for example procedures, training, human action, as well as, systems and components that prevent accidents or provide mitigation of consequences and constitute barriers against injury [14, pg A-1].

Although a range of methods have been developed to support systematic hazard analysis, for example, HAZOP (Hazard and Operability Studies) [12], FMEA (Failure Modes and Effect Analysis) [3] and THEA (Technique for Human Error Assessment) [15], such methods stop short of explicitly defining barriers. The explicit representation of barriers is a step towards defining a semantics of

---

[2] Descriptive arguments can be considered as informal arguments in contrast to more quantitative, numeric arguments.

safety arguments and allows analysts to reflect on the hazards being mitigated and the associated implications for design and implementation of safe systems so that risk reduction techniques can be more effectively implemented.

In Sections 4 and 5, two existing hazard analyses will be examined and the explicit barriers inherent in the analysis identified. Barrier implications are drawn out and areas of concern for both the hazard analysis and any associated design are highlighted. The case studies are the proposed design of a computer-aided detection tool (CADT) for mammography and the feasibility of eight-state free route airspace.

4   Computer-Aided Mammography Example

The UK Breast Screening Programme is a national service that involves a number of screening clinics, each with two or more radiologists. Initial screening tests are by mammography, where one or more X-ray films (mammograms) are taken by a radiographer. Each mammogram is then examined for evidence of abnormality by two experienced radiologists [8]. A decision is then made as to whether to recall a patient for further tests because there is suspicion of cancer [23]. Within the screening process it is desirable to achieve the minimum number of false positives (FPs), so that fewer women are recalled for further tests unnecessarily, and the maximum true positive (TP) rate, so that few cancers will be missed [8]. Unfortunately the radiologists' task is a difficult one because the small number of cancers is hidden among a large number of normal cases. Also the use of two experienced radiologists, for *double readings*, makes this process labour intensive.

Computer-based image analysis techniques are being explored to enable a single radiologist to achieve performance that is equivalent or similar to that achieved by double readings [2,8]. Computer-aided detection systems can provide radiologists with a useful "second opinion" [24]. The case study in this section involves the introduction of a CADT as an aid in screening mammograms. When a CADT is used, the radiologist initially views the mammogram and records a recall decision. The CADT marks a digitised version of the X-ray film with "prompts" that the radiologist should examine. The proposed procedure is that the radiologist records a decision before looking at the CADT prompted x-ray film. A final decision on a patient's recall is then taken by the human radiologist based on the original decision and the examination of the marked-up X-ray. A summary of this process can be seen in Figure 1 (from [23]).

A system based on the model shown in Figure 1 has been investigated to identify the undesirable consequences that may arise. An incorrect recall decision resulting from a misdiagnosis of cancer is an example of such an consequence. The general argument for safe use involves a number of argument legs covering three main activities namely (i) human analysis of the X-ray, (ii) CADT analysis of the X-ray and (iii) the recall decision by the human, based on a review of their original analysis and the CADT analysis. A HAZOP [12] style analysis for the system was completed by a team including the authors [21]. HAZOP is described as a technique of *imaginative anticipation* of hazards and operation problems [16,

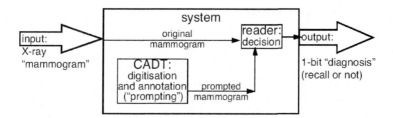

Fig. 1. Model for person using computerised aid for reading mammograms in breast screening.

pg43]. It is a systematic technique that attempts to consider events in a system or process exhaustively. The output from this process was a HAZOP table summarising cause, consequence and protection relations to hazards identified in the proposed system (see Table 3 in Appendix A for four example HAZOP rows).

The CADT HAZOP contained 105 HAZOP rows and 61 hazards that required mitigation. In total 99 barriers were identified in the mitigation arguments of the 61 identified hazards. Typical implied barriers included human oriented barriers such as "staff training", environmental conditions, for example "room layout", and system components, for example "bar codes on x-rays". The barriers were identified through the examination of the mitigation arguments present in the HAZOP. Each barrier was considered independent as validating true independence between the associated mitigation arguments is non-trivial and outside the scope of this paper. By examining these barriers further insight into the implications of the hazard mitigation can be derived in the context of the proposed system. The following sections present several views on the nature of barriers identified in post HAZOP analysis. However, it should be noted that these are not necessarily an exhaustive set of the barrier properties or implications for safety.

4.1   Preventive Versus Protective Barriers

It is common for hazard mitigations to be considered in terms of independence and diversity. The belief that a hazard has been mitigated may be given a higher level of confidence if multiple diverse arguments are present. Also the nature of the associated barrier in the context of the initiating hazard event is also of relevance. Classifying preventive and protective barriers highlights this consideration. For example if a hazard has only preventive barriers there is no fault tolerance in the system, as provided by protective barriers.

In the mammography analysis there are 7 examples of protective barriers and 92 examples of preventive barriers. Two of the protective barriers and 15 of the preventive barriers are unique. Therefore the majority of the barrier protection in this system is based on preventive barriers. This has implications for the fault tolerance of the system as the failure of preventive barriers may lead to a potentially hazardous system state not anticipated by the designers.

4.2   Barrier Frequency and Type

Commonly there is not a one-to-one relation between hazards and barriers. One hazard may be protected against by several barriers (see Section 4.3) and one barrier may feature in the mitigation arguments of several hazards. A barrier mitigation with a number of high consequence hazards will require greater reliability as more of the system safety will be dependent on it. This is particularly the case if a single barrier is the only defence to a hazard (see Section 4.3). In addition there may be cost-benefit tradeoffs between barriers. Expensive barriers, in terms of physical cost, time to implement and/or ongoing maintenance, that provide protection against a single hazard may be less desirable than alternative barrier solutions that provide protection from multiple hazards. Such knowledge can provide justification for particular design decisions.

Table 1. Eight most common barriers in the mammography analysis

Barrier	Frequency	Barrier	Frequency
Staff training	23	Good practice following	19
CADT reliability	12	Timetable enforcement	7
Safety culture	6	Bar codes on x-rays	6
User experience	6	CADT testing	5

Table 1 shows the eight most common barriers in the mammography analysis. The top two most common barriers are human oriented and together contribute 42% of the barriers for this example. This may seem surprising considering this system is a technology based solution to a labour intensive process. Even in this computer-based system there is reliance on appropriate training in the mitigation of hazards. Also these human oriented barriers operate when the system is live and are therefore prone to performance variation and other human-error issues (see [17]). Technology based barriers, e.g. "CADT reliability", "bar codes on x-rays" and "CADT testing", contribute 23% of the barriers. From a total of 17 unique barriers identified in the hazard analysis, barriers in the top eight represent 85% of the total barriers. Identifying the barriers that have the most impact can allow developers to focus their efforts.

In addition to the occurrence of particular barriers in this case study, the frequency of demand of barriers significantly modifies the predicted risk. Expectations on how often a barrier will be expected to be active, and not fail, will determine how critical it is to the system it is protecting. However, the analysis material discussed in this paper does not provide details of such expectations and will therefore not be discussed here further.

4.3   Barriers per Hazard

Accidents happen because barriers fail and hazards are present. Hollnagel [9] observes that accidents are frequently characterised in terms of the events and conditions that led to the final outcome or in terms of the barriers that have failed. As a consequence, redundancy is a common feature in the safety aspects of dependable systems. In particular, redundancy is used to prevent the failure of a single component causing the failure of a complete system - a so-called *single-point failure* [22, pg 132]. Identifying potential single-point failures is essential for determining problem areas in a system's reliability. Hazards with only single barriers, and in particular single preventive barriers, represent a significant threat to system safety. In addition, identifying multiple barriers does not necessarily imply greater prevention or tolerance properties. Barrier interdependence will compromise any diversity based arguments if combined dependability between barriers results in single-point failure situations. A common preventive barrier pair in the mammography example is the use of "staff training" and "good procedure following" which are clearly interrelated.

In the mammography analysis 33 hazards are protected against by single barriers, 14 hazards by double barriers, 12 hazards by triple barriers and 2 hazards by quadruple barriers. Therefore 54% of the barriers in this analysis suffer from potential single-point failures. Of the single-point failure barriers 5 are protective barriers and 29 are preventive barriers. This reinforces the barrier bias demonstrated in Section 4.1. In this case the additional 2 protective barriers examples are double barriers with, the same, one protective ("bar codes on x-ray") and one preventive ("good procedure following") barrier each. In this case independence can be observed informally between a technology based barrier and a human oriented barrier. There is a need to determine such independence if accurate predictions of barrier performance are to be generated.

5   Airspace Route Feasibility Example

Eurocontrol's European Air Traffic Management Programme requires a safety assessment to be performed for "all new systems and changes to existing systems." [5]. Therefore a safety assessment was commissioned for the eight-states[3] free route airspace concept. The overriding aim of the concept was to obtain benefits in terms of safety, capacity, flexibility and flight efficiency by removing the constraints imposed by the fixed route structure and by optimising the use of more airspace [6, pg xiii]. The principal safety objective was to ensure that free route airspace operations are at least as safe as the current fixed route operations. A functional hazard assessment was completed to determine how safe the various functions of the system need to be in order to satisfy the safety policy requirements. This assessment investigated each function of the proposed system and identified ways in which it could fail (i.e. the hazards) [6, pg 10].

This hazard assessment has been examined in a similar manner to that described in Section 4 (see Table 4 in Appendix A for three example hazard assessment rows). Although the two cases are not directly comparable, examining

---

[3] Belgium, Denmark, Finland, Germany, Luxembourg, The Netherlands, Norway and Sweden.

the explicit barriers present in the airspace route provides insight into the identification of barriers as both a design tool and possible analysis metric. Analysis is based on the mitigations associated with the new hazards introduced by the implementation of free route operations and ignores existing mitigations in the previous system.

The functional hazard assessment contains 105 rows of which 69 contained new hazards that required mitigation. Newly identified hazards are not mitigated by existing mitigating factors in the system. The output of the hazard assessment was a set of safety requirements for the proposed free route environment. In total 128 barriers can be identified in the safety requirements. For example assessment 210 in Table 4 of Appendix A contains four existing mitigating factors and four proposed barriers described as safety requirements. Other implied barriers in this case study include human oriented barriers such as "controller training", environmental conditions, for example "airspace design", and system components, for example "MTCD[4] system usage". The following sections are indicative of the set of barrier properties and of their implications for safety.

5.1   Preventive Versus Protective Barriers

No protective barriers and 128 preventive barriers were identified in the free route airspace example. The majority consist of the enforcement or review of different operating procedures. Other barriers include controller and pilot training and monitoring system technology. Twenty two different preventive barriers can be identified as unique barrier forms. All of the barrier protection is based on preventive barriers here, which has implications for the fault tolerance of the system.

5.2   Barrier Frequency and Type

Table 2 shows the eight most common barriers in the airspace analysis. The two barriers that appear most common in the hazard analysis are technological systems and together contribute 39% of the barriers. In Table 2 technological systems represent 48% of the total barriers and the human oriented barriers represent 24%. From a total of 22 unique barriers identified in the analysis, those in Table 2 represent 84% of all the barriers in this hazard analysis.

Table 2. Eight most common barriers in the airspace analysis

Barrier	Frequency	Barrier	Frequency
MONA (MONitoring Aid) system	32	MTCD system	18
Controller training	18	Free Route Airspace contingency procedures	15
Airspace design	8	Review procedures	8
Transfer procedure	5	Area Proximity Warning (APW) system	4

---

[4] Medium Term Conflict Detection.

5.3 Barriers per Hazard

In this analysis 28 hazards are protected against by single barriers, 31 hazards by double barriers, 10 hazards by triple barriers and 3 hazards by quadruple barriers. Therefore 22% of the barriers in this analysis suffer from potential single-point failures. Although this is less than in the CADT for mammography example it represents a considerably percentage of the barriers proposed in this assessment. As with the CADT analysis (see Section 4), each barrier was considered independent and determining independence between barriers is outside the scope of this paper.

6 Explicit Barriers for Certification

Storey [22] notes three typical aspects to the certification of safety-critical systems:

1. A demonstration that all important hazards have been identified and dealt with, and that the integrity of the system is appropriate for the application.
2. Evidence of compliance with some particular standard.
3. A rigorous argument to support the claim that the system is sufficiently safe and will remain so throughout its life.

Explicit barrier definition through the development phases of a safety-critical system form a traceable hazard mitigation link in the associated documentation. Barriers identified via hazard analysis will require representation in any design rationale and associated safety case used to assure system safety. In addition whether hazard mitigations, as represented by abstract barriers in a design, are in fact present and functioning in a live system can be determined. Therefore the explicit representation of barriers highlights the hazard mitigations that are in place and their continuing performance.

There is little information on final implementation and performance of the case studies described in this paper. However, they can be examined in the context of the proposed designs. This allows designers to reflect on the identified barriers and their influence on any future certification.

User training as a preventive barrier has played a considerable part in the mitigation of hazards in both the CADT for mammography and the free route airspace examples. Verification that appropriately qualified staff are part of the human-machine system would therefore be required. This may require the introduction of additional barriers, such as qualification checking, confirmation of accreditation of training schemes and continuous assessment of actual performance.

The majority of barriers in the free route airspace example were based on the development and implementation of future products, for example, the review and definition of good operating procedures in particularly hazardous situations and the deployment of proposed traffic monitoring technology. It is likely that these barriers would feature predominantly in any safety case based in part on this hazard assessment. Verification of the existence of these procedures and their acceptance in the organisational structure of the domain would be required. Also the barriers indicating the use of the new traffic monitoring technology (MONA) provides a minimum level of functionality for the deployed system. Therefore the performance between any predicted barrier behaviour, commonly presented as evidence as part of a safety case, and the actual barrier behaviour in the live system can provide a quantitative measure of barrier reliability for certification purposes.

7   Conclusions

Barriers are important for the understanding and prevention of accidents and are an intrinsic part of safety-critical systems. They feature implicitly throughout a system's development life-cycle. In additional to having physical presense in a live system, they provide a representation for safety concerns in hazard analysis, design decisions, safety case construction and certification.

In this paper several views on the explicit representation of barriers have been presented. These aid the understanding of hazards as represented in the analysis of safety-critical systems. Reflecting on the choice and nature of barriers is an essential part of constructing more dependable systems. Two case studies have been examined and the implication of barriers in the context of a hazard analysis have been defined. The process of hazard mitigation in a design can be documented by considering barriers explicitly. In addition, this process provides a framework for a quantitative measure of barriers as part of the certification process.

Analysing and defining barrier descriptions is a time consuming process which would be aided considerably by a barrier notation and tool support. The authors are currently investigating the use of the Hazard-Barrier-Target model [18] and the Safety Modelling Language [19] as the next step to incorporating explicit barriers in safety-critical system development. This is ongoing work.

Acknowledgements. This work was supported in part by the UK EPSRC DIRC project [4], GR/N13999 and by the ADVISES research training network, GR/N 006R02527.

References

1. Stephen Barker, Ian Kendall, and Anthony Darlison. Safety cases for software-intensive systems: an industrial experience report. In Peter Daniel, editor, *16th International Conference on Computer Safety, Reliability and Security (SAFE-COMP 97)*, pages 332–342. Springer, 1997.
2. Caroline R. M. Boggis and Susan M. Astley. Computer-assisted mammographic imaging. *Breast Cancer Research*, 2(6):392–395, 2000.
3. B. S. Dhillon. Failure modes and effects analysis - bibliography. *Microelectronics and Reliability*, 32(5):719–731, 1992.

4. DIRC - Interdisciplinary Research Collaboration on Dependability of Computer-Based Systems, http://www.dirc.org.uk [last access 6/06/2003], 2003.
5. European air traffic management programme safety policy, November 1995. SAF.ET1.ST01.1000-POL-01-00, Edition 1.0.
6. Eurocontrol. Safety assessment of the free route airspace concept: Feasibility phase. Working Draft 0.3, European Organisation for the Safety of Air Navigation, October 2001. 8-States Free Route Airspace Project.
7. Lars Harms-Ringdahl. Investigation of barriers and safety functions related to accidents. In *Proceedings of the European Safety and Reliability Conference ESREL 2003*, Maastricht, The Netherlands, 2003.
8. Mark Hartswood and Rob Proctor. Computer-aided mammography: A case study of error management in a skilled decision-making task. In Chris Johnson, editor, *Proceedings of the first workshop on Human Error and Clinical Systems (HECS'99)*. University of Glasgow, April 1999. Glasgow Accident Analysis Group Technical Report G99-1.
9. Erik Hollnagel. Accidents and barriers. In J-M Hoc, P Millot, E Hollnagel, and P. C. Cacciabue, editors, *Proceedings of Lex Valenciennes*, volume 28, pages 175–182. Presses Universitaires de Valenciennes, 1999.
10. C. W. Johnson. *Failure in Safety-Critical Systems: A Handbook of Accident and Incient Reporting.* University of Glasgow Press: Glasgow, Scotland, October 2003. ISBN 0-85261-784-4.
11. T. P. Kelly, I. J. Bate, J. A. McDermid, and A. Burns. Building a preliminary safety case: An example from aerospace. In *1997 Australian Workshop of Industrial Experience with Safety Critical Systems*, Sydney, Australia, 1997. ACS.
12. Trevor Kletz. *Hazop and Hazan: Identifying and Assessing Process Industrial Hazards.* Institution of Chemical Engineers, third edition, 1992. ISBN 0-85295-285-6.
13. Nancy G. Leveson. *Safeware: System Safety and Computers.* Addison Wesley, 1995.
14. P. Neogy, A. L. Hanson, P. R. Davis, and T. E. Fenstermacher. Hazard and barrier analysis guidance document. Technical Report EH-33, Department of Engery, Office of Operating Experience Analysis and Feedback, USA, November 1996. Rev 0.
15. Steven Pocock, Michael Harrison, Peter Wright, and Paul Johnson. THEA - a technique for human error assessment early in design. In Michitaka Hirose, editor, *Human-Computer Interaction: INTERACT'01*, pages 247–254. IOS Press, 2001.
16. David. J. Pumfrey. *The Principled Design of Computer System Safety Analysis.* PhD thesis, Department of Computer Science, The University of York, 2000.
17. James Reason. *Human Error.* Cambridge University Press, Cambridge, 1990.
18. Bastiaan A. Schupp, Saul M. Lemkowitz, and Hans J. Pasman. Application of the Hazard-Barrier-Target (HBT) model for more effective design for safety in a computer-based technology management environment. In *CCPS ICW: Making Process Safety Pay: The Business Case*, pages 287–316. AIChE/CCPS, 2001.
19. Bastiaan A. Schupp, Shamus P. Smith, Peter C. Wright, and Louis H. J. Goossens. Integrating human factors in the design of safety critical systems: A barrier based approach. In *Proceedings of IFIP 13.5 Working Conference on Human Error, Safety and Systems Development (HESSD 2004)*. Forthcoming, 2004.
20. Shamus P. Smith and Michael D. Harrison. Improving hazard classification through the reuse of descriptive arguments. In Cristina Gacek, editor, *Software Reuse: Methods, Techniques, and Tools (ICSR-7)*, volume 2319 of *Lecture Notes in Computer Science (LNCS)*, pages 255–268, Berlin, 2002. Springer.

21. Shamus P. Smith and Michael D. Harrison. Reuse in hazard analysis: Identification and support. In Stuart Anderson, Massimo Felici, and Bev Littlewood, editors, *Computer Safety, Reliability and Security (SAFECOMP 2003)*, volume 2788 of *Lecture Notes in Computer Science (LNCS)*, pages 382–395, Berlin, 2003. Springer.
22. Neil Storey. *Safety-Critical Computer Systems*. Addison-Wesley, 1996.
23. L. Strigini, A. Povyakalo, and E. Alberdi. Human-machine diversity in the use of computerised advisory systems: a case study. In *IEEE International Conference on Dependable Systems and Networks (DSN 2003)*, pages 249–258. IEEE, 2003. San Francisco, U.S.A.
24. Bin Zheng, Ratan Shah, Luisa Wallance, Christiane Hakim, Marie A. Ganott, and David Gur. Computer-aided detection in mammography: An assessment of performance on current and prior images. *Academic Radiology*, 9(11):1245–1250, November 2002. AUR.

A   Raw Hazard Analysis Fragments

Table 3. Fragment of HAZOP for the CADT for mammography design

Ref	Item	Guideword	Cause	Consequence/Implication	Indication/Protection
1.1.1a	Make initial decision	Wrong	Radiologist inexperience	Wrong detection result	Training
...					
1.1.1.1g	Examine x-ray	Repeat	X-rays out of order	Mixed up detection and patient record	Barcoding on x-ray and patient record. Srict procedure
...					
1.2a	Process digital x-ray	Omit	System failure	No CADT image. Reliance on human decision	CADT reliability
...					
1.3.3a	Record decision	Omit	Operator lapse	Loss of records	Interlock to force form completion

Table 4. Fragment of safety assessment for the free route airspace concept

Task	Function	ID	Failure Condition	Operational Consequences	Existing mitigating factors	Proposed Free Route safety requirement
Handling aircraft	Conflict identification	210	Controller fails to identify conflict	Potential collision risk	Controller training. Pilot awareness of other traffic. STCA[b], TCAS[c]	MTCD[a].
Handling aircraft	Conflict identification	211	Controller unable to make timely identification of conflict	Potential collision risk	Controller training. Pilot awareness of other traffic STCA, TCAS.	MTCD. Airspace design. Controller training. Transfer procedures
Handling aircraft	Conflict identification	212	Controller mistakenly identifies conflict when none existed	Extra workload	Controller training. Traffic monitoring	MTCD. Controller training.

[a] Medium Term Conflict Detection system.
[b] Short Term Conflict Alert system.
[c] Traffic Alert Collision Avoidance System.

Author Index

Lecture Notes in Computer Science

For information about Vols. 1–3137

please contact your bookseller or Springer

Vol. 3193: P. Samarati, P. Ryan, D. Gollmann, R. Molva (Eds.), Computer Security – ESORICS 2004. X, 457 pages. 2004.

Vol. 3192: C. Bussler, D. Fensel (Eds.), Artificial Intelligence: Methodology, Systems, and Applications. XIII, 522 pages. 2004. (Subseries LNAI).

Vol. 3191: M. Klusch, S. Ossowski, V. Kashyap, R. Unland (Eds.), Cooperative Information Agents VIII. XI, 303 pages. 2004. (Subseries LNAI).

Vol. 3190: Y. Luo (Ed.), Cooperative Design, Visualization, and Engineering. IX, 248 pages. 2004.

Vol. 3189: P.-C. Yew, J. Xue (Eds.), Advances in Computer Systems Architecture. XVII, 598 pages. 2004.

Vol. 3187: G. Lindemann, J. Denzinger, I.J. Timm, R. Unland (Eds.), Multiagent System Technologies. XIII, 341 pages. 2004. (Subseries LNAI).

Vol. 3186: Z. Bellahsène, T. Milo, M. Rys, D. Suciu, R. Unland (Eds.), Database and XML Technologies. X, 235 pages. 2004.

Vol. 3185: M. Bernardo, F. Corradini (Eds.), Formal Methods for the Design of Real-Time Systems. VII, 295 pages. 2004.

Vol. 3184: S. Katsikas, J. Lopez, G. Pernul (Eds.), Trust and Privacy in Digital Business. XI, 299 pages. 2004.

Vol. 3183: R. Traunmüller (Ed.), Electronic Government. XIX, 583 pages. 2004.

Vol. 3182: K. Bauknecht, M. Bichler, B. Pröll (Eds.), E-Commerce and Web Technologies. XI, 370 pages. 2004.

Vol. 3181: Y. Kambayashi, M. Mohania, W. Wöß (Eds.), Data Warehousing and Knowledge Discovery. XIV, 412 pages. 2004.

Vol. 3180: F. Galindo, M. Takizawa, R. Traunmüller (Eds.), Database and Expert Systems Applications. XXI, 972 pages. 2004.

Vol. 3179: F.J. Perales, B.A. Draper (Eds.), Articulated Motion and Deformable Objects. XI, 270 pages. 2004.

Vol. 3178: W. Jonker, M. Petkovic (Eds.), Secure Data Management. VIII, 219 pages. 2004.

Vol. 3177: Z.R. Yang, H. Yin, R. Everson (Eds.), Intelligent Data Engineering and Automated Learning – IDEAL 2004. XVIII, 852 pages. 2004.

Vol. 3176: O. Bousquet, U. von Luxburg, G. Rätsch (Eds.), Advanced Lectures on Machine Learning. IX, 241 pages. 2004. (Subseries LNAI).

Vol. 3175: C.E. Rasmussen, H.H. Bülthoff, B. Schölkopf, M.A. Giese (Eds.), Pattern Recognition. XVIII, 581 pages. 2004.

Vol. 3174: F. Yin, J. Wang, C. Guo (Eds.), Advances in Neural Networks - ISNN 2004. XXXV, 1021 pages. 2004.

Vol. 3173: F. Yin, J. Wang, C. Guo (Eds.), Advances in Neural Networks – ISNN 2004. XXXV, 1041 pages. 2004.

Vol. 3172: M. Dorigo, M. Birattari, C. Blum, L. M. Gambardella, F. Mondada, T. Stützle (Eds.), Ant Colony, Optimization and Swarm Intelligence. XII, 434 pages. 2004.

Vol. 3170: P. Gardner, N. Yoshida (Eds.), CONCUR 2004 - Concurrency Theory. XIII, 529 pages. 2004.

Vol. 3166: M. Rauterberg (Ed.), Entertainment Computing – ICEC 2004. XXIII, 617 pages. 2004.

Vol. 3163: S. Marinai, A. Dengel (Eds.), Document Analysis Systems VI. XI, 564 pages. 2004.

Vol. 3162: R. Downey, M. Fellows, F. Dehne (Eds.), Parameterized and Exact Computation. X, 293 pages. 2004.

Vol. 3160: S. Brewster, M. Dunlop (Eds.), Mobile Human-Computer Interaction – MobileHCI 2004. XVII, 541 pages. 2004..

Vol. 3159: U. Visser, Intelligent Information Integration for the Semantic Web. XIV, 150 pages. 2004. (Subseries LNAI).

Vol. 3158: I. Nikolaidis, M. Barbeau, E. Kranakis (Eds.), Ad-Hoc, Mobile, and Wireless Networks. IX, 344 pages. 2004.

Vol. 3157: C. Zhang, H. W. Guesgen, W.K. Yeap (Eds.), PRICAI 2004: Trends in Artificial Intelligence. XX, 1023 pages. 2004. (Subseries LNAI).

Vol. 3156: M. Joye, J.-J. Quisquater (Eds.), Cryptographic Hardware and Embedded Systems - CHES 2004. XIII, 455 pages. 2004.

Vol. 3155: P. Funk, P.A. González Calero (Eds.), Advances in Case-Based Reasoning. XIII, 822 pages. 2004. (Subseries LNAI).

Vol. 3154: R.L. Nord (Ed.), Software Product Lines. XIV, 334 pages. 2004.

Vol. 3153: J. Fiala, V. Koubek, J. Kratochvíl (Eds.), Mathematical Foundations of Computer Science 2004. XIV, 902 pages. 2004.

Vol. 3152: M. Franklin (Ed.), Advances in Cryptology – CRYPTO 2004. XI, 579 pages. 2004.

Vol. 3150: G.-Z. Yang, T. Jiang (Eds.), Medical Imaging and Augmented Reality. XII, 378 pages. 2004.

Vol. 3149: M. Danelutto, M. Vanneschi, D. Laforenza (Eds.), Euro-Par 2004 Parallel Processing. XXXIV, 1081 pages. 2004.

Vol. 3148: R. Giacobazzi (Ed.), Static Analysis. XI, 393 pages. 2004.

Vol. 3147: H. Ehrig, W. Damm, J. Desel, M. Große-Rhode, W. Reif, E. Schnieder, E. Westkämper (Eds.), Integration of Software Specification Techniques for Applications in Engineering. X, 628 pages. 2004.

Vol. 3146: P. Érdi, A. Esposito, M. Marinaro, S. Scarpetta (Eds.), Computational Neuroscience: Cortical Dynamics. XI, 161 pages. 2004.

Vol. 3144: M. Papatriantafilou, P. Hunel (Eds.), Principles of Distributed Systems. XI, 246 pages. 2004.

Vol. 3143: W. Liu, Y. Shi, Q. Li (Eds.), Advances in Web-Based Learning – ICWL 2004. XIV, 459 pages. 2004.

Vol. 3142: J. Diaz, J. Karhumäki, A. Lepistö, D. Sannella (Eds.), Automata, Languages and Programming. XIX, 1253 pages. 2004.

Vol. 3140: N. Koch, P. Fraternali, M. Wirsing (Eds.), Web Engineering. XXI, 623 pages. 2004.

Vol. 3139: F. Iida, R. Pfeifer, L. Steels, Y. Kuniyoshi (Eds.), Embodied Artificial Intelligence. IX, 331 pages. 2004. (Subseries LNAI).

Vol. 3138: A. Fred, T. Caelli, R.P.W. Duin, A. Campilho, D.d. Ridder (Eds.), Structural, Syntactic, and Statistical Pattern Recognition. XXII, 1168 pages. 2004.